SANFORD BALLARD DOLE

and His Hawaii

Portrait by Sandona
Original at Punahau School

...ard Dole

and His Hawaii

By ETHEL M. DAMON

With an Analysis of
Justice Dole's Legal Opinions
by SAMUEL B. KEMP

Published for the
HAWAIIAN HISTORICAL SOCIETY
by Pacific Books

PACIFIC BOOKS

Palo Alto, California

To THE YOUTH OF MANY RACES,
WHO, CLEAR-EYED, WILL MEET HAWAII'S CHALLENGE
TODAY, TOMORROW AND BEYOND

PREFACE

IN PIECING together the story of *Sanford Ballard Dole and His Hawaii* I have had the definite advantage of his personal memories dictated near the end of his life. Those written ten years earlier at the urging of his friend and colleague, Lorrin A. Thurston, to cover the political changes in Hawaii which had come under his own observation, were intended to be used with those of Mr. Thurston as a newspaper series about 1913. This plan was not fulfilled. Twenty-three years later, and ten years after Judge Dole's death, this projected newspaper series was withdrawn from the collaboration and became a companion volume to Mr. Thurston's *Memoirs of the Hawaiian Revolution,* well edited by the late Andrew Farrell and published by the *Honolulu Advertiser.*

Family letters have added their quota of fact and feeling to the present story.

Everything Mr. Dole wrote or said was essentially modest. It was toward his friends and fellow citizens working loyally with him that his commendation was directed. In his account of the Courthouse Riot following Kalakaua's election, Mr. Dole makes only brief mention of his own attempt to stem the tide of the infuriated mob of Queen Emma partisans when they attacked the legislators of their own race who had voted for Colonel David Kalakaua, though the calm figure with restraining outstretched arms remained long in the memory of those who witnessed the wanton destruction of property before the intervention of United States and British troops.

As a review of vital political events, Sanford Dole's contemporary *Thirty Days of Hawaiian History* has been used as a complete chapter. This was first published serially in the *Pacific Commercial Advertiser* of 1874, and in 1915 it was republished as a

vii

paper of the Hawaiian Historical Society. It was also the leading chapter in the published Thurston-Dole *Memoirs* of 1936. As explained by Mr. Dole, "It exhibits some partisan enthusiasm, which I trust will not be found in the papers especially written for this series (those of 1874). It was intended to be more than a mere narrative, and does not hesitate to indulge in some comment on events rather than merely on persons." President Dole's letter of December 23, 1893, to United States Minister Wills likewise appears here in full, for its revelation of both the unflinching character of the writer and the high order of his statesmanship. In reference to his outstanding State Paper of January 11, 1894, the *Philadelphia Press* of February 17, 1894, characterized the Hawaiian president as "adroit, self-poised, dexterous in fence and unerring in logic. He thoroughly knows his ground in law and in reason and he holds it with a coolness, courage and confidence which are altogether admirable. In comparison with his deft art both Gresham and Willis appear like woodchoppers in diplomacy."

A definitive biography of Sanford Dole has yet to be written. This present account was undertaken only at his express wish. Throughout the writing I have felt something of his own restraint, yet have tried to reproduce the spirit of the man himself, the man who, in earliest infancy dependent for his very life on the breast of his Hawaiian nurse, became doubly a native son.

If the frequent absence of quotation marks seems confusing, let me say that, while I have often paraphrased his review of events, it is chiefly Sanford Dole who tells the story; and where another is quoted the source has been identified whenever possible.

Characters and incidents which to some may seem extraneous are offered without apology, as part of Sanford Dole's time and experience, and possibly new to later generations.

With elements of greatness, of which modesty is one, Sanford Dole was moved by a deep compassion and a sense of justice which set from the flower of his Island boyhood. The Territory of Hawaii under the Stars and Stripes, with self-governing individuality, is to a large extent their fruit.

Without the help of friends this story could not have been told. Their name is legion.

From the beginning Dr. Ralph S. Kuykendall of the University of Hawaii has encouraged and suggested, and has given the manuscript a critical reading. Miss Emily V. Warinner has assisted throughout with enthusiasm and skill. The Hawaiian Historical Society, the Hawaiian Mission Children's Society, the University of Hawaii Library, the Archives of Hawaii, the Library of Congress, and Columbia University Library have put us deeply in their debt. For permission to quote copyrighted material I am also grateful. With loyal interest Dole friends and relatives, as well as my own, have cooperated in putting together the story of one during whose life span the focus of Hawaiian history shifted from one race to another.

The Hawaiian Historical Society has met very generous response for costs of publication from these local trusts: McInerny Foundation, Frear Eleemosynary Trust, S. N. and Mary Castle Foundation, Juliette M. Atherton Trust, Charles M. and Anna C. Cooke Trust, G. N. Wilcox Trust, and Elsie H. Wilcox Foundation.

Special acknowledgment is due Judge Samuel B. Kemp, who, as a justice of the Supreme Court of Hawaii, was familiar with Judge Dole's judicial work. Dole it was, more than any other, Judge Kemp feels, who hewed to the line in interpreting the Constitution of 1887, particularly those portions designed to limit the authority of the sovereign. He concludes that, if Justice Dole's dissents had been majority opinions, there might never have been a revolution.

ETHEL M. DAMON

CONTENTS

CHAPTER   PAGE

I. Decision, 1867 1

II. Punahou, 1841–1855 3

III. Koloa, 1855–1866 32

IV. New England, 1866–1868 53

V. Honolulu, 1869–1873 78

VI. Thirty Historic Days, 1872–1873 105

VII. Honolulu, 1874–1879 125

VIII. Town Meetings, 1880–1883 153

IX. In the House, 1884–1886 174

X. Revolt and Counter-Revolt, 1887–1889 196

XI. Lull Before the Storm, 1890–1892 221

XII. Revolution, 1893 244

XIII. Mr. Dole to Mr. Willis 274

XIV. Provisional Government and Republic, 1893–1897 289

XV. Annexation and Governorship, 1898–1903 313

XVI. At Ease, 1903–1926 354

Justice Sanford B. Dole's Legal Opinions, 1887–1893. By Samuel B. Kemp 379

Index 389

ILLUSTRATIONS

FACING
PAGE

Sanford Ballard Dole .... *Frontispiece*   iii
Ewa Church above the home of the Reverend and Mrs.
  Artemas Bishop 18
Daniel and Charlotte Dole 19
Sanford and George Dole about 1854 19
Wedding of Kamehamcha IV and Emma Rooke 31
"Old Sixty-Seven" at Williams College 50
Sanford Dole on his return from college in 1867 50
Sanford Dole about 1875 51
Bernice Pauahi and Charles R. Bishop about the time of their
  marriage 82
Old Royal Palace 83
Kawaiahao Church in the late 1880's 83
Sanford B. Dole and Anna C. Dole about 1886 114
Entrance to the Emma Street home and interior view 115
Queen Liliuokalani wearing the Order of Kalakaua 146
King Kalakaua in full-dress uniform 146
Princess Kaiulani for whom Sanford wished a regency
  established 147
Original letter from President Dole and his Advisory
  Council requesting the raising of the Stars and Stripes
  over Hawaii 178, 179
Executive Council of the Provisional Government 210
Cabinet and Executive Council of the Republic of Hawaii 210
The Constitutional Convention of 1894 211
A mainland version of President Cleveland's dilemma 274
Flag raising over Iolani Palace, 1898 275
Mr. and Mrs. George H. Dole and family at Riverside in 1906 306

FACING
PAGE

President and Mrs. Dole at Oakland Mole on their return
from Washington 306

Manning the yards for President Dole in Honolulu harbor 307

Judge Dole, Captain Henri Berger, the ex-Queen, and
Governor Pinkham, 1914 338

Punahou "boys" playing *aipuni* at the school's 75th anni-
versary 339

Harbor of Honolulu with troops drilling in Government
Square 370

Sanford B. Dole on his eightieth birthday 371

Portrait bust of Sanford B. Dole by Allen Hutchinson 379

Chapter I

DECISION
1867

NEAR the end of his one year at Williams College, where he had entered as a Senior, Sanford Dole debated with himself which turning he should take on the road of life. Before leaving home he had known of his parents' wish that he should follow his father as a Christian minister among Hawaiians. Under wise guidance the future of these island people held much of promise. Many Hawaiians he counted as his personal friends, and to one of them on his home island of Kauai had been entrusted the job of *luna* or overseer on the plantation fields which Sanford himself had plowed in the hope that the proceeds might cover the expense of a year at college.

In some ways Christian work in his homeland seemed an obligation. But was it clearly destiny? Would his life as a preacher reach its highest usefulness? Just how much hung in the balance of this decision not even he could dream. In honest doubt he discussed it all by letter with his father and mother on Kauai:

By what life I can do the most good is yet to be decided. I envy those who have settled the question and have but to follow it out. I must do it soon, the end of the term must see this indecision ended. I need your prayers.

Four months later he had found his solution. Painful as was the necessity, he wrote home:

You shall no longer be in suspense as to my plans. I have deferred writing in regard to this, not wishing to say anything till I could write with certainty. I have decided to study law, with reference to practicing at Honolulu. I have given the subject much thought for months past,

1

have prayed over it, and, if I know my own heart, worthy motives have actuated me in the choice.

Circumstances too, as near as I can read them, point this way. The general bankruptcy at the Islands discourages me from returning at present with plans for business, unless it should be to buy a plantation cheap. But I do not feel inclined to speculate with borrowed money. I do not feel called to the ministry as I do to law; and the three years of confinement and study, with such food as I have had the past year, would leave me a confirmed dyspeptic. Besides, the want of funds seems to forbid this.

Medicine is not exactly my style. Will Brigham's father offers me a desk in his office and the use of his library. I have talked with President Mark Hopkins on the subject, and he favors the idea. I believe, whether I may be talented or not, I can be thoroughly honest. I look upon law as a possible stepping stone to influence and power in the Government, where they need good men and where a good man could, I think, do more for the nation, for morality and justice, than preaching to the natives.

After the next letter from home he reaffirmed this stand:

Your speaking of my coming back to preach to the natives is very pleasant to me; but it is too late to change my plans. I waited till the last minute, so to speak, of my time at college, so as to give myself the greatest possible chance of being influenced in my choice; and then, when further indecision would have been a weakness, I decided by the light which I then had, according to the best of my ability.

The fact that my profession is chosen, and that I have a definite plan at which to aim my efforts, helps to make me contented and hopeful. Law is I trust only to be the channel of my life's work, God and humanity the ends toward which I work, and self last. The office of a true lawyer as a peacemaker is second only to the office of a minister.

This was the Dole of 1867: modest, slow to act without weighing every pro and con, yet resolute once a stand was taken; frank in stating his case, while showing every consideration for those from whom he differed.

It remained for time to fit into historical perspective the life of this loyal son of Hawaii, who with his Islands stood on the threshold of destiny.

PUNAHOU
1841–1855

A S INDIGENOUS as a Hawaiian tree, Sanford Ballard Dole had grown, roots thrusting deep into native soil. Like many of his contemporaries a son of the American Protestant Mission, he was, also like them, *kama aina* (child of the land).

Dedication to the cause and the people they had come to serve bound these Mission workers into one family; to each other they became Brother and Sister, later Father and Mother, their descendants naturally calling each other Cousin. And while this sense of the family bond was strengthened, both parents and children wove their lives into the very texture of Hawaiian life. To Sanford Dole, Hawaii was always to be home, though the tie with New England, whence his parents had come, would always be strong, and on visits there he felt a warmth of welcome and response.

He was born into a century which in the mid-Pacific had already begun to adjust to the impact of Western ways of life. Past was the time of sandalwood shiploads to the Orient; gone were the older high chiefs of Hawaii; gone too, in the first of the fatal epidemics, were many of the people who had built the early *heiaus* and laid up the first great stone churches. At hand was the era of traders and New England whaling ships to winter at Honolulu or Lahaina; just beginning was the movement among king and chiefs toward representative law-making. During more than a score of years eight companies of American Protestant Mission workers had brought the best they knew of this life and the next to their Polynesian neighbors, to meet of course active opposition on all sides.

3

Gradually the little hamlet of Hanaroora (Honolulu) was losing its grass huts; dusty tracks were widening out into rough roads; and when a vessel was towed into port Hawaiian women were beginning to ask for *patena hou* (new dress goods and patterns). Foreign families were increasing, both on Oahu and at other island stations among Mission workers whose hearts were cut to the quick by the cruel necessity of sending little children "round the Horn," often in the care of strange sea captains, because no schooling could be had for "foreign" children in the Islands.

The very sharpness of this suffering shaped its own remedy. Work started on an adobe building for a Mission boarding school at Punahou, across the dusty plain to the east of Honolulu village. And when at General Meeting time in May of 1841 four new Mission couples arrived after a voyage of more than six months from Boston, each of the couples in turn was asked to superintend this new boarding school. Setting aside long cherished plans for direct Christian work among Hawaiians, the Reverend Daniel Dole and his wife accepted what seemed manifest duty. And after a few happy weeks as guests of Brother and Sister Knapp, teachers in the Mission schools for Hawaiian children near Honolulu, the Doles moved out to Punahou to superintend construction of the combined dwelling and schoolhouse.

Emily Ballard, who was to touch so vitally the earliest years of Punahou School, had grown up on the banks of the blue Kennebec, the Long-Land-Water of Maine. Born in Hallowell, she lived later in Gardiner. She was tall and fair, her eyes a dark hazel, her manner one of ease and dignity, altogether so lovely and lovable that friends more than once named their little daughters for her. An eager student she was, who loved her work and her pupils in the Young Ladies' Academy of Norridgewock, where she is still known as its first preceptress. Stricken by the sudden death of her father, a sea captain, in far New Orleans, she had turned desperately and at last with complete confidence, to the help of her Heavenly Father. Before long she could do no less than follow His summons to labor in the field of foreign missions.

Of like mind and zeal, not far up the river at Skowhegan (Bloomfield), Maine, was young Daniel Dole, a graduate of Bowdoin College and Bangor Theological Seminary. When he came one day to ask Miss Emily Ballard to go to some mission field as his wife, a sudden light shone over her and her heart cried, This then is the awaited call!

Three years passed before they could be married and sent by the American Board of Commissioners for Foreign Missions to the Sandwich Islands. In 1840 they were both thirty-two years of age. While as bride and groom they awaited the sailing of the ship *Gloucester,* a young artist in their lodging house was so moved by Emily's loveliness that he asked the privilege of painting her miniature. To the lifelong regret of her son, Sanford Ballard Dole, this portrait was left in Boston and disappeared without a trace.

Punahou was a romantic retreat, Emily Dole wrote from Honolulu to her family in Maine, so relieving to the eye after the dusty village and lying as it did just below the entrancing valley of Manoa. Some of the Honolulu ladies had clumsy wagons, or little four-wheeled coaches drawn by natives, to post about town in, but the two miles out to Punahou were most pleasantly covered on horseback. Quite a cavalcade of Mission Sisters rode out one day in August with Dr. Judd and Brother Knapp to see the cellar and plan for doors and clothes closets.

To Emily's eyes, Punahou covered about thirty acres of sugar plantation and broad taro patches, separated by walks and banana trees bending beneath their fruit; all surrounded by a six-foot wall built at the order of Kaahumanu, the late Queen Regent, and commanding an extensive view of the ocean and neighboring country. So clear was the air that Diamond Hill five miles away appeared barely two. Beyond the taro fields a clear new spring, *Puna hou,* for which the district was named, issued out of the rocks, its fresh abundance giving fertility and beauty in delightful contrast to the arid plain extending to the ocean a mile distant. The spring itself divided into many streams after forming quite a pond—as large as the whole Ballard garden on the Kennebec River! The water, after serving for bathing and washing in this pool, was frugally carried along in ditches to fill taro patches; to water the garden near the house; in another channel to run through the pantry to cool it; and in still another to meet a little vineyard back of the house where some fine grapes were ripening in the sun.

Not many rods to the northeast opened out the exceeding

beauty of the green valley, the depth and delicacy of its coloring eluding all efforts of pen or pencil to delineate.

Amid all this beauty Saturday preparations were duly made for the New England Sabbath: Daniel Dole, writing his sound, solemn sermon for delivery as supply pastor at the Seamen's Bethel in the village; and Emily baking bread, veal pie, and pies of dried apples, making over a calico dress, wondering whether her bonnet would serve, for Honolulu ladies perforce saw much company and were particular in their dressing. As to Daniel Dole, Miss Marcia Smith, Emily's efficient assistant, writing to her sister on Hawaii, found him "an admirable preacher. Brother S. thinks he doesn't thunder out quite enough against certain sins. He is very convincing and pointed, but it is all with a gentleness of manner peculiar to himself. He is, I should think, a man of a most lovely spirit."

To Emily Dole's dear Mission Sister Mary Rice, shipmate during six months on the *Gloucester,* consuming homesickness at times slipped into her letters to Hana on Maui where the Rices were already at work. "Yesterday," Emily wrote in June, 1841, "I had the honor of translating from French to English a letter from the French Consul to the Governor of Oahu, that Dr. Judd might put it into native language." She became increasingly attached to Sister Knapp, a scholar in Hebrew, Greek and Latin, yet a person of true modesty; also to Sister Conde, waiting to return to work at Hana, who often came in and sometimes rode out with her.

At Honolulu, Emily continued, the squadron of the United States Exploring Expedition had been in to port and gone again. Such excitement! Foreign company and Navy officers were all that could be attended to for a while, even the Mission ladies having a good many new dresses.

Meanwhile old roofing thatch on the Punahou cottage had begun to leak and even threatened to collapse when November rains set in. Daniel and Emily therefore moved back to Honolulu to board for six months with Brother Dimond, the Mission bookbinder. To their joy this change freed them for teaching Mission children in a little day school in thatched rooms near the oldest of the Mission houses. As the winter days passed, Emily's thoughts flew back to her mother and sisters, especially to her dear brother, trying what the sunshine of the West Indies might do for him. But at last came the dreaded word that his life had been cut short. This grief and the separation from them all seemed more than Emily's heart could bear, yet the burden of her closely written letters carried home as always the abiding hope that all her loved ones might come to follow in the Master's footsteps.

Christmas Day Emily spent the morning at the Mission depository with Sister Chamberlain, whose little daughter, one of Emily's pupils, gladdened her by the gift of their first rose from a bush tended for years, and this called up fragrant memories of Emily's own childhood. New Year's Day brought a combined Thanksgiving dinner at Dr. Judd's across the street, every family contributing something to the feast for twenty-five grown-ups and as many children, in an arbor in the garden.

In March, 1842, on a week's vacation from the little Mission school, Daniel, Emily, and two of the Gulick boys rode horseback over the narrow and often precipitous trails westward toward Waialua. Rough going it seemed to Emily, often up or down such a steep *pali* that she preferred to dismount and walk; fording streams often too rapid to allow of bridges, through groves of coconut and breadfruit or deserts of mammoth cactus; at the end of five miles coming out upon the rim of the king's salt lake, several miles in circumference, where salt formed and was gathered for market. Unable to proceed far or rapidly, Emily was grateful to stay the week at the Ewa station, while Daniel and the two boys rode on to Waialua. From afar they had seen the great thatched church crowning the hill to the west of the Bishops' homestead in a valley near Pearl River, a romantic stream, Emily thought, which wound in and out, to fall into the sea a mile or two below. Artemas and Delia Bishop made Emily very welcome in a home which was balm to her soul, a truly missionary home, imbued with religion, kind and restful after the noise and dust and hurry of Honolulu.

By May 1, 1842, the work at Punahou was so far advanced that Daniel and Emily were able to move out again in time to accommodate themselves to the new house before their first son was born on June 6. The lives of both mother and child were at first in grave danger. Dr. Judd brought out Sister Lowell Smith and Sister Andrews. Next day came also Sisters Chamberlain and

Marcia Smith to help in the emergency. Gradually health returned and the baby was named George for a dear friend of his father, though often called George Sandford by his mother. Later she tucked a lock of the baby's fair hair into her home letter, describing him as blue-eyed, fat and healthy, in his little white frock and red stockings; a pair of pink shoes had been given him, but his little feet were too active to tolerate such encumbrances. His eyes would glisten with delight whenever his father appeared or Miss Smith came to frolic with him, his fingers fascinated by the play of her curls.

On July 11 the new school opened with fifteen children, nine boarders, and the others, mostly girls, came out from town in the Chamberlain wagon behind Old Gray. Thus began the daily duty of morning and afternoon journeys to the school, Brother Chamberlain wishing it might have been six years earlier, when with heavy heart he had put his oldest sons, Warren aged seven and Evarts only five years old, aboard a vessel bound for New England under a captain who might find scant time or interest for small boys.

Marcia Smith was indeed a tower of strength, Emily Dole realizing that the new Punahou could not have flourished without her. And Marcia in her turn discovered that everything proceeded more harmoniously than she had anticipated, though even Mission children seemed a little slow to learn the meaning of industry and obedience. Her stern code of punishment often worked hardship, even among the boys; and seven-year-old Mary Parker began to cherish for her whole lifetime bright, contrasting memories of beautiful Mrs. Dole's gentleness, particularly with the little girls, who shyly adored her.

The first nine boarders were all boys: five Gulicks, two Alexanders, two Emersons. And in Marcia's eyes Daniel Dole seemed a pleasant man, conscientious and spiritually minded, a thorough scholar and a good teacher; no "hen-huzzy," but more than ready to set his hand to any chore, from laying up stones for the kitchen oven and chimney to yoking Brother Chamberlain's two gaunt oxen and toiling after them to guide a plowshare across the garden field.

In the daily routine of the new school Sister Marcia Smith saw to the cooking and cleaning, while the boys helped her and worked in the garden to raise corn, beans, melons, sweet potatoes, bananas, and grapes. Beside nearly all the teaching, Daniel did the plowing and supervised the boys. As Emily's health improved, she kept the boys' clothes mended, taught two hours a day in school, and also helped at the butter churning, as well as serving at the long dinner table. Before the end of the year there were twenty-five pupils, with twelve boarders, and Emily wrote her sisters that Daniel had now never a moment for letter writing, after six hours of teaching every day and endless other demands, even at times taking little George to the schoolroom where he was the happiest of the group.

By the time George was fifteen months old he was beginning to toddle about after his mother or Miss Smith from one courtyard to the other; his mother wrote her sisters Sarah and Lucy:

Tell little Louisa that we cannot box up this baby to send the long way to her. He is too precious. He sends sweet kisses to you all. He is eating sugar cane by my side, one of his enjoyments.

I have been teaching arithmetic and writing. Amid so many things that cannot be omitted, do you ever expect to get a drawing of our house? But I will just scratch out a plan of it here at the end of my letter for you. The small divisions are closets. You see we have a large house as well as a large family. I hope sometime to send you a tolerable view of it.

Will Sarah send me a drawing of our house? I do long for anything from home, perhaps an engraving of the church.

How exiled Emily did yearn for letters, though every one sent overland by way of Mazatlan in Mexico cost a dollar, by ship of course only a trifle. After receiving word of her mother's death, she often dreamed of being at home again. Naturally her pen slipped into tales of little George,

a happy boy, twenty months old, with fair complexion. He loves pictures and will not leave one until I explain it to him. Should I have another son, I shall call him Sandford Ballard; if a daughter, Lucy Elizabeth. Miss Smith sends love to you. She loves George and he shares her caresses or whippings, as he deserves, this year.

Daniel has gone this eve to a missionary party at the English Admiral's. The latter expects to leave soon, he has been here six months. He is an affable, lovable old gentleman. We shall be sorry when he is gone.

This British commander was of course Rear Admiral Richard Thomas, who had won the affection of all Hawaii by restoring native sovereignty after provisional cession five months before to a British commission under Lord George Paulet. On July 31, 1843, in the open plain east of the town, at the spot since known as Thomas Square, it was made clear that this cession of the Hawaiian Islands had been only provisional.

Among Mission brethren paying an official call aboard the Admiral's flagship, the frigate *Dublin,* shortly after her arrival was Levi Chamberlain. He noted in his journal that the *Dublin,* which in Hawaiian waters seemed an immense man-of-war, was actually a razee, a former line-of-battle ship mounting seventy-four guns, but now cut down by one deck to carry fifty guns and a complement of five hundred men.

A new Hawaiian flag, made aboard the *Dublin* at the Admiral's express command to replace earlier flags destroyed by order of Captain Lord George Paulet, was unfurled to the breeze at Thomas Square with poignant significance on that last day of July. This became a national holiday. Following the brilliant official cere-mony, crowds gathered for a Hawaiian service of thanksgiving in the new Stone Church at Kawaiahao. Levi Chamberlain re-corded the king's short address of exhortation to chiefs and people to deal justly and to give devout thanks that, according to his hope, the life, the very breath, of his land had been forever restored in righteousness. These Hawaiian words, passing for more than a century from mouth to mouth and from island to island, have shaped the national watchword: *Ua mau ke ea o ka aina i ka pono.*

After the formal transfer of sovereignty Admiral Thomas sent his battleships to sea and settled ashore for the winter, devoting himself, Sister Judd noted, to advancing the best interests of the people, as well as establishing rules of court etiquette. For with the arrival of an American commissioner and an English consul-general, the French and other foreign representatives already in residence began to form quite a diplomatic corps in the life of the little Sandwich Islands capital at this crossroads of the Pacific. More than once Admiral Thomas took tea with the Mission families or dined with court officials, and on February 26 all were bidden to a brilliant assembly to take leave of him at Dr. Judd's official residence adjoining the palace, where in both house and garden flaring torches and lanterns lent unwonted gaiety.

Honolulu was growing, Emily remarked in her letters, though

it was still a wicked place, especially for sailors who stepped ashore into rows of grog shops down every lane where vice walked abroad in open day. Brought up as she had been in pleasant New England towns, she confessed that the very soul of her was wearied by streets thronging with naked men and half-clad women, often singing and shouting in their uncouth tongue. To give home people glimpses of Honolulu, Emily several times added to her letters copies of *The Friend of Temperance and Seamen,* a little periodical recently started by the Reverend S. C. Damon, the new seamen's chaplain, who went offshore to meet every incoming vessel with a genial welcome to the chapel and reading room. His little sheet soon added foreign and local news especially of the American Mission, with arrivals and departures of vessels and passengers, and in this year, 1844, was headed by a woodcut of the village from the harbor. It was beginning to be a cosmopolitan little town with over fifteen nationalities represented in the 1,000 of foreign birth among its total population of 9,000.

The previous year had seen at Honolulu eleven ships of war: British, American and French, as well as thirty merchant vessels and a hundred whaleships, one of the trading vessels known to be carrying to Canton forty tons' measurement of Connecticut clocks! Distance never dimmed the intensity of love for their homeland among these Mission crusaders. Vivid items of news from the Atlantic seaboard and points west, eagerly scanned in the columns of the Honolulu *Polynesian,* told of Boston harbor being frozen over to a point ten miles below the city where fifteen hundred men were hacking open a passage for English mail steamers; of American and English negotiations proceeding as to "the Oregon," with an increase of English naval and military forces on Atlantic and Pacific stations; the Territory of Iowa, filled as it still was with Indian tribes, had actually applied for statehood. And when in this same year of 1844 the rumor spread that the wilds of Texas had been received into the Union, Brother Chamberlain confided to his journal that, if true, this would probably act as an entering wedge toward the dissolution of the Union!

These early Mission colonists formed, indeed, a family group close knit by affection, with Punahou speedily becoming another shelter for those in need, or a missionary hotel, as Sister Rice once termed it. In March of 1843 Sister Smith and Brother Dole accompanied some of the Punahou children on vacation to Maui and Hawaii. In June, Emily Dole and also Sisters Parker and Conde watched constantly with Sister Chamberlain, whose baby daughter did not survive. In October Brother Locke died suddenly at Punahou and the Chamberlains took little Mary Locke home with them. In November, Emily Dole came to town in the Chamberlain wagon to take Lucy Locke to the doctor. In December word arrived from Sister Knapp on Kauai that her husband was critically ill, a blow to Emily and Daniel who had come to love Charlotte and Horton Knapp as their own.

On April 23, 1844, appeared at Punahou the second child to be born there, Sanford Ballard Dole. But all Emily's strength was spent, and on the fourth day she yielded up her life for his. Remembering the loss of their own babe the year before, the Chamberlains took baby Sanford home with them, Brother Chamberlain recording most of these facts in his invaluable journal. On the 28th of April Emily was laid in the little Mission cemetery at Kawaiahao, the young seamen's chaplain preaching at a memorial service later in the native meeting house nearby. Young Sister Castle, looking across from Emily's grave to that of her own first-born son, made six months before near a lengthening row of small, unmarked mounds, grieved that God did not take Emily's poor infant with its mother; but in after years Mother Castle often wondered what Hawaii would have done without this Mission son, had God answered the prayer of a half-century before.

For the first three weeks of Sanford's life Sister Chamberlain cared for him with a Hawaiian nurse, Mailou's wife, at whose breast he began to take his intimate Hawaiian heritage. When he was eight days old the baby weighed eight pounds. On May 22, at four weeks, his father took him on horseback to the Mission station at Ewa to leave him with Brother and Sister Bishop in the home which a scant two years before had brought such consolation to Emily's heart. It was a home too where father and mother yearned for a child in the house after their only daughter Jane and son Sereno had been sent to New England because there was then no school at Punahou.

Emily's sudden death left her husband desolate. Little George would at times cry for his mother, although Marcia Smith loved him dearly and gladly cared for him. The baby Sanford knew, of course, only the loving care of Mother Chamberlain, of his Hawaiian nurse, and later of Mother Bishop. But to their father, even with constant demands of school and farm, nothing seemed as empty as the pleasant corner rooms which Emily had made into their own particular and delightful home. During the day the shared life of the school occupied his hands and thoughts mechanically; at night the strangely familiar rooms were no longer home.

Desperately his mind, thus turned inward upon itself, became even more intensely preoccupied than before with the vital interests which had absorbed him for years in long talks with Emily. Bit by bit plans evolved for an attempt to fill an acute need in the isolated island life. Often both parents and children, waiting months for a ship to bring new books and papers, would be overwhelmed by the abrupt arrival of a whole year's numbers of, for example, *The Youths' Companion*. To relieve this mental indigestion, Daniel began to assemble articles, maxims, anecdotes and verse, trusting that friends would send in similar contributions with a view to printing a small sheet to circulate monthly among parents and children. It was work which might fill lonely hours after prayers were said and all the children asleep.

For just the twelvemonth of 1845 *The Monitor* was issued, an earnest, well-named little sheet of four large quarto pages printed at the Mission press. Daniel planned to have its usefulness tell among children, yet in all its forty-eight pages there occurred only one picture, a delightful woodcut to head a story of squirrels crossing a lake on pieces of bark, waving their bushy tails as sails. Occasionally lines of verse from Emily's pen appeared, sad and serious. With the passing of Brothers Dibble, Knapp and Whitney, all in this one year of 1845, it is perhaps no wonder that the last page of *The Monitor* opened with the question, "Have you ever seen a man die?" and that Editor Daniel felt in duty bound to admonish old and young to be ready for the last summons. But as a children's paper the little monthly could hardly survive, even a century ago.

At General Meeting in 1844, by Daniel Dole's urgent request,

Brother and Sister Rice had been transferred from Maui to help the growing school at Punahou. Mary Rice had named her second baby Emily Dole, in loving memory, but now her heart misgave her at the prospect of trying to take up even part of Emily's work. Marcia Smith, however, found little Sister Rice a rare woman; Punahou boys soon learned to love and admire her.

Punahou summer vacation in those days began in May, when this extended Mission home, like all those in the village, must air out spare beds and bedding in preparation for guests during the two months of General Meeting. With Sister Rice's help Marcia was able to take little George for a week's rest at the Kaneohe Mission station. Marcia wrote with evident relief that Sister Rice took hold with energy and systematic efficiency. Brother Rice also fitted in admirably, taking charge of the boys in the farm work, and especially with getting in stone and necessary materials to rebuild the north corner of the long adobe building to afford four more rooms for boarders and living quarters for the Rice family.

When Charlotte and Horton Knapp came out early in 1845 for rest and change, Horton sketched the building showing this two-story addition at the north corner. Although an epidemic of influenza delayed the workmen, Brother Rice succeeded in getting this stone addition ready by November.

After Horton Knapp's death in March of 1845, Charlotte came out to Punahou for a fortnight's visit. After this visit, Marcia and little George returned to Honolulu village with her for several weeks. One of the closest ties formed in the isolation of mission work was among friendships begun on the long voyage around Cape Horn. Marcia and her sister had been shipmates of Charlotte and Horton Knapp aboard the bark *Mary Frazier* in 1836. In May of 1845 Charlotte wrote to Horton's mother that Marcia seemed like a sister and had been with her most of the time since Horton's death. Riding out to Waialua a few days later, Charlotte was accompanied by both Marcia and Daniel, for one object of the visit was to have a glimpse of Sanford at Ewa. Here they were delighted to find him a big healthy boy, thriving on milk from Brother Bishop's flock of goats. Writing to her sister, Lucia Lyons, Marcia told with pleasure that Sanford's eyes were dark hazel, much like his mother's, also that his pleasant disposition fortunately seemed to be thoroughly grounded upon a good degree of resoluteness.

More than a year later, on June 22, 1846, one of the Punahou boys chronicled briefly as a General Meeting event out of the ordinary "the long expected marriage of Mr. Dole and Mrs. Knapp." The ceremony was performed by Brother Armstrong at eleven in the morning, with all the Mission as invited guests. Again, a few days after the wedding, the three friends, Marcia, Charlotte and Daniel rode out to Ewa station, this time to bring Sanford home. He was a serious little fellow of two. When asked his name, he would reply solemnly, "Sanfa Balla Dole Bishop." Ewa had given him a quiet, gentle home among elderly people. His father had come out a number of times, once accompanied by Sister Chamberlain. But this time it was different, and all his life Sanford kept a vivid recollection of the three riding into the yard and taking him away on horseback next day. That was something that had never happened before.

Even more indelible was the memory of riding on the front of his father's saddle into the Punahou yard which seemed to be filled with strange boys, one of the younger ones in a state of excitement, squealing, jumping up and down, and clapping his hands. Such behavior was foreign to Sanford's sedate life. In fact, it seemed, he used to tell, a most undignified and inappropriate display of levity. Strange to have a brother, stranger still to find him agitated by such undue hilarity.

Presently, however, George and Sanford were playing together, often too with little Maria and Emily Rice who were of almost the same ages as the Dole boys. The girls had too a baby brother Willie, born a month after Sanford had come home. The boys went in to see him as often as they were allowed, and Sister Rice felt quite as if they were a part of her own family.

His new Mother Charlotte, who had had some misgivings as to taking on family duties, especially in such a school as Punahou, found that Sanford quickly became attached to all. He proved very biddable too, she wrote, seemed very eager to do right; and George, although so long in Marcia Smith's care and still with her some of the time, often seemed inclined to follow his new mother about. And both boys were so affectionate that she felt fully rewarded for all she did for them.

Some of Sanford's earliest Punahou memories were of wandering about the courts, quite at home among the older boys, who often ejected him from their rooms when studying was interrupted. But Orramel and Charles Gulick, two of the oldest boys, welcomed him to their room when he strayed in, showing him a friendliness that he loved to recall. Nor could he forget the tearing down of the adobe corner rooms when he was about four years old, for Father Rice was again ready with native workmen and stone from Rocky Hill to rebuild the Doles' rooms into a more permanent two-story addition to correspond to that on the north corner. Both the Dole boys had whooping cough, as did others in the school, and perhaps for this reason Sanford remembered their moving into rooms adjoining the south corner and watching the men bringing up stones and laying them up one by one. Bits of wood left by the carpenter he often picked up and kept in a big wooden box to use in the serious construction of his own houses and bridges. One night he dreamed that Arabs in huge turbans were attacking with volleys of shots fired into the side of the house. The dream was so vivid that on waking he ran at once to his big box, to find one whole end of it riddled with birdshot, an amazing corroboration of his dream.

When George was five, Charlotte began to teach him to read. Family prayers were said with all the boarders every morning and evening, many of them reading or reciting verses from the Bible. When little Willie Rice was two years old, Sanford was profoundly impressed to hear his own father say, "This child is old enough to love God."

One day when Sanford had learned to read and had advanced from books with sentences to short stories, his mother instructed him to go upstairs to the study. He did so obediently and found his father waiting for his small son. Without saying a word, he handed Sanford a large volume bound in calfskin. It seemed so formidable and held promise of so much work in study that the child burst into tears upon receiving it. It was the Bible, and he remembered beginning at once to read it, starting with Genesis and proceeding right through to the end of Revelation. Even reading every day, this required several years. After the completion of this task, he heard that if one should read three chapters a day, two in the Old and one in the New Testament, the great book would be finished in exactly a year. Later he followed this course and found it to work successfully. He never recalled any impression made by this diligence, yet even as a boy he developed precision and care in the use of language, a characteristic which grew with the years.

Was it perhaps this early reading of the Scriptures, so steadily pursued by dutiful children, which gave rise to boyhood nicknames at Punahou? Joseph Emerson, one of Sanford's contemporaries, was long known as Joe Hemolele, the Hawaiian equivalent of Holy Joe. And Sanford Ballard was inevitably called Sanballat, the name of the Samaritan overlord who vigorously opposed the rebuilding of Jerusalem's fortifications by returned Babylonian captives under Nehemiah.

Daniel Dole was indeed a man of conviction and one who made it a point never to spare the rod, this often taking the shape of his formidable red ruler. Yet even he was known to break into a grin and lay aside his Hebrew studies to hold off his small sons, towering above them as they made a rush at him. Little Anna Charlotte Rice would often cry for Papa Dole; once when Emily Rice suddenly appeared at his study door, hauling in small sister Mollie rolled up in a blanket to ask him if he would buy a pig, Papa Dole replied, Yes, he would take a pound; whereupon Emily, nothing daunted, shoved her bundle into the hall out of sight as she shouted, "Oh dear, the pig has run away!" And certainly no early Punahou boy ever forgot Father Dole's broad, but instantly suppressed smile one Sabbath morning in the Seamen's Bethel, when tall Chaplain Damon walked up the pulpit steps wearing the halo of a neatly folded handkerchief from the moment he had removed his high silk hat on entering the sanctuary. At the other end of the Punahou pew Miss Marcia Smith, meeting this emergency with frowns and agitations of her fan, at once quelled what seemed to young Henry Lyman an imminent outbreak of impiety.

Severe and conscientious as was Dole, the first principal of Punahou School, by nature and by training as well, his endowment included too a very human quality and often what his Brother Bond called sanctified common sense. Not content with exclusively academic and spiritual instruction, he interested himself practically and theoretically in physical education long before it became customary in schools, using athletic apparatus when it was available and advocating a certain number of hours daily in farm labor. When George was quite small, his father fenced off a little play yard for him, even adding a swing which brought great joy later to both of his boys. With quiet pleasure he wrote to Emily's sister, Lucy Ballard, that for the gratification of Marcia Smith an artist from Michigan had painted a portrait of five-year-old George which was a very fine resemblance, adding that Brother Bishop was talking of having Sanford's done as well.

With character and intelligence, Charlotte Dole took hold of her new life, writing in 1847 to Emily's sister, Lucy Ballard, as if to her own sister, and telling of sewing to prepare her family of four for a visit to the island of Kauai; of George standing beside her asking when his Aunt Lucy was coming to visit at Punahou and insisting that he was going to see his uncle Nathan Dole, and of how he loved Miss Marcia. Also, added Charlotte, both children were quick to leave their play whenever their mother could read them a story. Like other boys of his age, George had learned to make his own bed every day, and was piecing a patchwork quilt, sewing for his own amusement. New Year's Day of 1848 brought out a joyous exchange of wishes and little gifts among Punahou children and teachers; Christmas Day the week before had been celebrated by a picnic with almost a hundred Mission friends from town, lonely Miss Ogden so happy that she felt like crying for joy all day.

Before the end of 1848, however, the school was broken up for weeks, first by influenza and measles, and then by whooping cough. From Hilo, Sister Lyman, who had not yet sent her children down to school, wrote of the pleasure it afforded her to have them with her while the measles were prevalent. Among Hawaiians, utterly unused as they were to coping with such manifestations, measles and whooping cough often proved fatal. In Honolulu there followed not only mumps but Panama fever which complicated life there still further. By 1850 the number of boarders at Punahou had increased to twenty-one. George and Sanford were also now in regular attendance on classes. One of the oldest boys, Curtis Lyons from Hawaii, began a life-long friendship with Sanford about this time, and Charlotte wrote of their fears that Curtis, among others of the older ones, might soon be sent away to the United States to school.

Ewa Church above the home of the Reverend and Mrs. Artemas Bishop. This was the center of community life when Mrs. Emily Dole visited the Bishops soon after her arrival in Honolulu in 1841. Original drawing, never before published, in possession of the family of the late A. C. Alexander.

Left: Daniel and Char-
lotte Dole

Right: Sanford and
George Dole about
1854

Courtesy Clara and Emily Dole

Not only were older children growing up, but more and more children were appearing on the Mission scene, giving their parents many an anxious thought for the future. In New England scarcity of funds was felt, and early in 1849 came a long letter from the American Board of Missions to the effect that the Sandwich Islands Mission, having reached its majority, must learn to consider itself a home mission, no longer a foreign one. To this end the brethren were urged to settle permanently in the Islands and counseled to find gradually their own means of support. Dismay spread among members of the Mission.

Wise Brother Chamberlain however, who had watched over its secular welfare until his strength was exhausted, concluded that, although this decision of the Board seemed sudden and at first premature, it was an inevitable move. He rejoiced therefore, shortly before his death in July 1849, to learn that among certain new measures under way the Mission would no longer oppose Hawaiian citizenship for any of their number going into business or government office. Brother Hall soon left the Mission to become editor of *The Polynesian* for the government. And it was unanimously voted that Brother Cooke should take his place with Brother Castle in the Mission depository, looking forward in time to making it an independent trading house of their own. Ultimately, in 1851, this became the firm of Castle & Cooke, a natural outgrowth in the process of Mission colonization.

Changes were to be expected, but by some of the sisters and brethren this broadening and apparent secularization of their work was deeply deplored. Charlotte Dole, shipmate of both the Castles and the Cookes in 1836, grieved especially that Brother Cooke's interests had become worldly. As a matter of fact, however, he was only obeying the Board's injunction to support his wife and six young children. The Chiefs' Children's School, which he and his wife had conducted with devotion for ten years, had come to its natural close as the young chiefs grew up. Never in all their after life did Brother and Sister Cooke lose their interest in the welfare of their royal pupils or of the people at large. This was emphatically true too of Brother and Sister Castle, as well as of others who made permanent homes in the Islands.

With the readjustment, the missionaries were given their homes, as fee simple titles became available. This granted **Mother**

Chamberlain her house and lot on King and Kawaiahao streets and enabled her to take in boarders, as many another Mission Sister did to eke out a living for a large family. Mindful always of Mother Chamberlain's kindness to their own mother, George and Sanford Dole, as soon as they were old enough, took alternate weeks walking down from Punahou to spend the night at the Chamberlains' and milk their cows before walking back to school next day. Those were simple, direct days of friendly exchange. The Punahou farm had given these boys healthy bodies and trained hands, as well as readiness to *kokua,* to help in time of need.

George was a light-hearted, merry boy and the two brothers were close companions in their play on the rambling slopes of Punahou's campus. Kite-flying often absorbed their interest, George proving adept and enterprising in building large kites. At times a favorite one would break loose, and away the two would go after it, far down the rough track today called Punahou Street. Other playmates were fun too, but Sanford never forgot the special joy of sharing griefs or delights with an own brother. They soon learned to swim in the pond and to swim well, though ignorant of present-day strokes. This led once to unusually severe whippings from their father when the boys had not only disobeyed during their parents' absence, but on the return of the family carriage denied having been in the pond. Comparing notes later, the two conspirators agreed that, had they realized the dire consequences of lying, they would have told the truth.

Into valleys near home George and Sanford sometimes went on foot with their father, who helped them to find land shells on the trunks and branches of trees, the boys then climbing up to get them. Once on Tantalus Father Daniel discovered a new variety of tree shell called *Decora,* but later renamed. In July or August when mountain apples were ripe, the boys would saddle their horses and be off, to come home laden with bags of luscious red *ohias.* Willy Rice, two years younger than Sanford, recalled with a little envy the horseback hurdle races frequently run off by the Dole boys, along the narrow lane later broadened out as Beretania Street, races ending with the plains at the first sign of the town, a trim little house of adobe bricks near Thomas Square.

Secrets were shared too, like the one betrayed by covert smiles exchanged between the two boys one Sunday afternoon, when a swear-word occurred in their catechism drill with their mother. Interrogation followed. No, it was not a word well known to them, in fact they had heard it for the first time the day before from an angry Hawaiian who had used it with emphasis as he pounded violently on the bottom of an empty Hingham bucket. The boys had then not done wrong, concluded their mother, but they must learn that levity was bad form during a discussion of the Shorter Catechism.

In June of 1852 the event in the Dole family was a week's horseback ride around the north and east coast of Oahu. The first day covered the twelve or thirteen miles to Sanford's old home, as he called it, at Ewa, where they spent the night at the home of the Bishops. After riding next day the eighteen miles farther to the Emersons' at Waialua, Charlotte, whose letters tell most of the story, found herself grateful indeed for a cup of tea and a good *lomilomi* (old-fashioned massage) from a native woman. This was the first time the family had gone so far without a native helper to carry a child or the clothing, and none of them had ever been around Oahu before, although Charlotte had been in the Islands sixteen years and Daniel eleven, George ten, and Sanford eight.

Sanford long remembered that for George and himself the occasion called for new straw hats, ever afterward designated as their "round-island" hats. The two boys rode the same horse, one on a cushion behind the saddle, positions which were supposed to be exchanged frequently. Sanford, however, recalled most of the journey from the viewpoint of the rear seat. Short of going afoot, horseback was the only transportation to be had. The days spent at Waialua were sheer joy to the boys at least, as they tramped in the hills looking for tree shells, or swam at the beach or for hours in the river. With the Emerson boys, they would swim the quarter of a mile upstream to the home of the Gulicks, where some of the Gulick boys joined them for a great time diving and jumping into the river from a high bank near the house.

On Monday morning, after a quiet Sabbath, the Doles rode on ten miles to a native pastor's house, only to discover that he had left for Honolulu to embark as one of the first Hawaiian missionaries to Micronesia. So the travelers ate some crackers and rode on ten miles farther to Punaluu where they made halt for the night. Daniel and the boys had brought extra clothes in their saddlebags, but no one seems to have carried any food except Mother Charlotte, who from the capacious folds of her riding habit could in emergency be counted on to produce a cracker or a bit of bread.

At Punaluu they again found that Brother Emerson's parishioners had departed for Honolulu, but they managed to discover an old kettle to make tea. This, with some roasted taro and Charlotte's bit of bread, sufficed for supper, the travelers being far too weary to wait until a kind native neighbor roasted a chicken for them. All four in fact were ready to turn in for the night in the one big bed, where Charlotte observed that the children did not lose the power of locomotion by going to sleep. Sanford however recalled that he and George slept very comfortably at the bottom of the huge four-poster, a type of bed very popular among the chiefs and many other Hawaiians.

Breakfast of coffee, with the postponed chicken and taro, was most welcome and soon eaten from odd bowls and spoons, Charlotte especially taking pleasure in sitting down and talking with the natives. After morning prayers they set off on the next twenty miles toward Brother Parker's station at Kaneohe. At Kualoa Dr. Judd's man gave them a fine melon which was supplemented by the bit of bread from Charlotte's ever-ready pocket.

Rounding a deep bay, they met Brother Parker holding meeting four or five miles from home, his family being in Honolulu. He gave Daniel the key to his house where they would find an old native woman to start a fire for coffee. Charlotte made griddle cakes and had all ready when their host returned. After a good night's rest and breakfast of chicken, taro, sweet potato, and coffee, as well as bread and butter, the travelers did not hurry, but set out for home about ten after a lunch of watermelon. An hour's gallop brought them to the half-hour's steep pull up the rough *pali* trail. Daniel warned them that at the top they must expect to meet a violent wind which would whirl away everything not made fast. Riding down slowly from the summit, it took them two hours and a half to reach Punahou, making a total distance of more than eighty miles since they had set out. Another week would have made the jaunt of more benefit to them all, but pupils were due for the opening of the new year and the school must go on.

And this year Punahou must for the first time go on, somehow, without the household superintendence of Sister Marcia Smith. Her blind and aged mother needed her care; and she was accordingly released by the General Meeting of the Mission in 1852 with heartfelt expressions of appreciation for her self-denying care of Mission children since her arrival in 1837; it was further specified that her share of the proceeds from the division of the Punahou herd be placed at her disposal, as also part of the division realized at the merging of the Honolulu and Waialua herds. Stowed carefully in her luggage went also the treasured portrait of George Dole.

From the higher ground at Punahou it was still possible in 1853 to see ships coming in or leaving the port of Honolulu. One day, wearied after baking and butter-making, Charlotte refreshed herself with a rest at her sitting-room window, where she kept thinking how her sister Sarah would have enjoyed the prospect across the gradual descent to the sea. Within the Punahou enclosure, the boys were hoeing beans and corn; beyond the wall, cattle were feeding on a grassy plain and natives were going to and fro along the road; a native house or a group of trees varied the scene, with broad fish ponds nearer the beach; on the ocean, whaleships lay off and on, with some days as many as fifteen of them under sail. At Charlotte's side stood George, marking little paper boxes with the names of land shells collected on rambles into the hills.

It is not surprising that this letter of Charlotte's lay for a week unfinished, while she was doing her share, as she was, for a family of thirty-six. Stockings to be darned—how many of them there were!—and all sorts of mending as well as her kitchen duties alternating every fortnight with Mary Rice; and, in addition, there was the very welcome arrival of Sister Lyman with her four youngest children, the three older boys being already on hand as boarders. Their mother had come down from Hilo to stay the rest of the term until General Meeting in May. Possibly this visit was planned to consider the suggested change of installing Brother Lyman at Punahou to fill the place of

Brother Rice, whose uncertain health was beginning to necessitate a change of work. In the end, however, the Lymans concluded to remain at their old home in charge of the Hilo Boarding School for Boys.

On all the Islands the year 1853 was marked by the calamity of smallpox, said to have been brought to Honolulu in a bundle of old clothes from San Francisco. Mission brothers worked hard to vaccinate all they could reach, but it was impossible to find some of the natives who fled to the valleys in fear.

During the influenza epidemic Brother Rice had succeeded in mustering enough hands and materials to finish Punahou's first school house, still in use a century later as Old School Hall. And the same year, 1852, he had helped Hawaiian church members to build Moiliili Church, a mile to the south of Punahou. This too, in restoration, is filled with a native congregation now of many races, who appreciate his devotion to the people. Because of the smallpox epidemic, camps for the sick were established: one near the beginning of the town at Alapai Street; another on the eastern boundary of Punahou near the present Wilder Avenue. Mr. Rice went day after day to visit the distressed and dying people, carrying special foods like wine whey and *pia* (arrowroot) prepared for them in the Punahou kitchen. His children recalled that every night during the epidemic their father never failed to bathe and change his clothes before coming into the house. The opening of school was delayed many weeks.

In April Sanford Dole was as happy as a lark on his ninth birthday, but Mother Charlotte wondered whether he would always see such sunny days. One evening he and four other little boys were sitting in her room around the lamp on her table, reading and talking, when one of them looked up and asked if the explorer, Sir John Franklin, had been heard from in the Arctic. Eight years later, on a June day in 1861, this boyhood question may have been recalled by seventeen-year-old Sanford, when he learned that the widowed Lady Franklin and her niece were to be his fellow passengers on the steamer *Kilauea* along the Kauai coast from Nawiliwili to Koloa.

On another evening Daniel Dole had gone to the village with the older boys to deliver a lecture on physical education, having given quite a number of evening lectures that year. The town was changing. With greater numbers of transient seamen crowding the Bethel services, some of the more permanent residents formed a new church body, called the Second Foreign, later the Fort Street Church. Brother Cooke was a deacon, and the congregation was made up of all sorts and sects. In the course of a few years some four hundred frame buildings had been put up by the government, foreigners and natives, and water from a good spring had been brought down in iron pipes from Nuuanu Valley to the harbor where new wharves were in use. Some of the natives were earning more and had better-furnished houses than formerly.

In June of 1853, to Sister Sarah whom she had not seen for seventeen years, Charlotte sent something more valuable than a letter, nothing less than two daguerreotypes: one of Daniel and herself for Sarah, and another of George and Sanford to be sent on to their Grandmother Dole as soon as convenient. She hoped to hear that they had arrived safely and marveled at the skill of the artist in creating the image of absent friends. Would Sister Sarah not try again to have her own likeness taken to send out to them? These from Honolulu were paid for by the sale of butter and cheese from Charlotte's old cow. Fortunate indeed were these Mission colonists to have cows and pasture for them. In the reorganization underway, following the famous Seventh Resolution from the American Board, some of the brethren were trying to obtain acreage for pastures, especially at the urging of Chief Justice Lee and the Privy Council, who, alarmed at great areas left vacant by depopulation, begged responsible men to take up land at low rates.

Even with the pestilence about them, over a hundred pupils and friends had gathered at Punahou for the annual examinations in May, and Charlotte baked hard Indian bread to feed the multitude. A little later, at the examination of the Royal School in the courthouse at the village, young ladies took part in singing and reading compositions, apparently an unheard-of exhibition in Charlotte's experience. Was it the practice, she asked, for young ladies to appear on the stage in the evening? Was it actually done in good old Connecticut? If so, Punahou was behind the times and young ladies trained there might be too modest. Also, the Royal School charged entrance fees for the evening, the avails to be devoted to the Charity School. Perhaps the end justified the means. The house was crowded with all sorts of people, among them the drunkard, the gambler, and the libertine. What young lady, Charlotte asked in consternation, would wish to appear before such a promiscuous assembly? This was not like a quiet New England village. No doubt it would be the town talk here for weeks to come.

After General Meeting was over in June, Charlotte sighed with relief that Punahou had obtained from the government a charter for a college. This was at the express request of the American Board in Boston, for it gave the school a basis on which to build up an institution, by endowing professorships and obtaining necessary teachers. They were now to be called Home Missionaries, added Charlotte, though some of them must receive support from abroad as always. Perhaps when new teachers came out, the earlier ones might be able to go home to the United States. They could not go now, but must stand by, or the school must be given up. The king had appointed June 15 as a day of fasting and prayer, for deliverance from the pestilence which threatened to sweep through the land and decimate his subjects. All looked dark and uncertain. Yet the Doles must both take some vacation this summer. They must do what seemed duty and leave the result with God.

Before the end of the month a way to vacation seemed to be opened by Captain Dornin of the sloop-of-war *Portsmouth,* a Navy commander who had been a frequent visitor at Punahou. One of his officers was said to be very attentive to eighteen-year-old Laura, one of the Judd twins. Captain Dornin offered the four Doles, with Mrs. Judd and two daughters, passage to Lahaina on Maui. Of the Dole excursion to Kauai three years before only brief mention occurs; but to nine-year-old Sanford, traveling aboard an American man-of-war was an event of a lifetime.

Due probably to the prevailing epidemic, the *Portsmouth* lay anchored off Honolulu harbor, and was proceeding to Maui in the hope of shore leave there for the crew, since no cases of smallpox were known to have occurred on Maui. In Honolulu harbor the passengers were taken out in the ship's boats under sail and a fine sail it was, at least to the two Dole boys. Getting under way was elaborate and exciting to watch, the call of the bugle sending men streaming up the rope ladders to unfurl required sails. Some of the sailors manned the capstan and raised the anchor.

This was Saturday evening. Not wishing to beat through the channel between Molokai and Lanai, the captain decided to sail to the leeward of Lanai. On the southern side of the island the ship naturally found itself in calm waters when trade winds were blowing. And as foreign captains were nervous about being too close in shore with their valuable ships, the distance of fifteen to twenty miles from land cut off all advantage of sea-breezes by day and land breezes by night. Here they lay Saturday night and all of Sunday. Toward morning on Monday the vessel crept slowly out of the calm streak on the eastern coast of Lanai and from there it was only a short stretch across to reach Lahaina anchorage early on Monday.

Captain Dornin was most attentive, giving up his own deck cabin with two sofas to the comfort of his guests. And they repaid him ill, reflected Charlotte Dole, most of them being desperately sick from the very outset of the voyage, and this in spite of the unwonted luxury of a steward to attend them. Young Sanford however was all over the ship, climbing ropes and talking with any of the two hundred and sixty crewmen he could reach, among them a fifer and drummer of his own age. At sunrise on the Fourth of July, a second man-of-war, the *St. Lawrence,* having likewise sought refuge at Lahaina, both ships fired the customary salute to the great day.

To get up the hill to the Alexanders' at Lahainaluna was a real pleasure, genial Brother Alexander laughing over their having escaped the so-called quarantine by arriving in a man-of-war. Two cases of smallpox, however, had occurred on Maui before their arrival. At Lahainaluna the boys had other boys to play with, and spent some time trying to discipline two broody hens intent on laying in the same nest. It created so much fun that Brother Alexander persuaded George to write a dialogue of the two hens. Later came a visit to the Baldwins near the shore where the surf kept up a constant roaring. Most of Dr. Baldwin's time was being spent trying to protect Hawaiians from the disease which had not begun to spread rapidly on Maui. A third visit was with the young Sereno Bishops. He had just returned to the Islands with his bride and located at Lahaina as seamen's chaplain.

Then came a long horseback ride over a sandy and stony trail to Wailuku where the Baileys and Condes, shipmates of Charlotte and Horton Knapp on the bark *Mary Frazier,* made the Dole family doubly welcome.

One great joy in all these Maui visits was to meet Punahou parents who were pleased with the work conducted there for their children. Also, Charlotte's persistent cough improved and almost disappeared in the warm, mild air of Lahaina. At one place on the mountain ripe peaches were a treat; at another, fresh strawberries which Charlotte and the boys hulled for breakfast. At Wailuku, to an exile from New England, fields of wheat white to the harvest were of vivid interest, as also cane fields and two sugar mills. A ride up the lower slope of Haleakala brought them to Makawao, the home of dear Mary Green, the missionary daughter who had recently been teaching devotedly at Punahou. Her father was the pioneer wheat grower in the Islands, and both he and his wife were overjoyed to have the Doles under their roof.

Back again at Lahaina after three weeks of journeying and visiting, they attended native meeting on the Sabbath where a Hawaiian played an excellent seraphina for equally good congregational singing. Later this musician was invited aboard the *Portsmouth* to play for service there. Tall coconut trees surrounded the native meeting house at the back, with *kukui,* much resembling New England maple. To Charlotte, the pretty spire added a touch which made it look very homelike. There was about Lahaina a feeling of relaxation, protected as the village was from strong trade winds, and singularly beautiful with its groves of shining green breadfruit trees, luxuriant grape vines, and great patches of broad-leaved banana trees unwhipped by the wind.

Perhaps the crowning luxury of the three weeks' vacation came in the offer from the captain of the *Portsmouth* to convey the Punahou family back to Honolulu. An uncommon act of kindness this was, wrote Charlotte, for him to take so many passengers on board such a ship, not the least of the privileges being the freedom from traveling by a crowded little schooner with possibility of infection. Moved by the graciousness of Captain Dornin and his officers, Daniel Dole wrote them a note of appreciation which he inserted as a card of thanks in *The Polynesian.*

More than seventy years after this eventful summer Sanford Dole still told of it with a boy's enthusiasm and the eye of a true yachtsman. There was the very formal dress parade by Marines aboard ship, which enlivened the tedious Sunday when becalmed off Lanai; there was the Hawaiian governor of Maui, who was also aboard and of course was escorted ashore at Lahaina in considerable style, with a proper salute before any other passengers left the ship. And above all, there was the return voyage when the two war vessels left at the same time. It was a stirring sight to see them, like two great sea birds, scudding down wind through the Molokai channel under full sail. The frigate *St. Lawrence* was smaller, but both ships carried studding sails. It was almost a personal triumph for George and Sanford to be aboard the *Portsmouth* when she won the channel race next morning after sunrise at Honolulu.

September brought to the Rices a baby girl, who was named Anna Charlotte for Mama Dole, as the Rice children called her. With a family of five lively children, it was not strange that Sister Rice too was warned of the necessity for a shifting of burdens to a home of her own. Here again was a Mission family beginning to feel that they must perhaps go home to the United States. But Chief Justice Lee, one of the ablest of the men who spent their lives for this adopted land, had long interested himself in two vital issues: keeping Mission families in the Islands to help build up the new economy; and the new venture of a sugar plantation at Lihue on the island of Kauai. When a manager was needed there, Judge Lee asked W. H. Rice of Punahou to take the job. To Harrison and Mary Rice this seemed an uncertainty, yet one that must at least be attempted. To Charlotte Dole the trial of losing their associates, the Rice family, would be no slight one.

A sense of change pervaded the air. June of 1854 saw the last General Meeting and the transformation of the Mission into the Hawaiian Evangelical Association. The Oahu College became an independent corporation, its trustees looking for a president to direct its future course. In the government, Dr. Judd had gone into private practice after resigning as the king's Minister of the Interior. Difficulties with French demands gave rise to a rumor that annexation to the United States might take place before the end of the year. At Punahou, children of others than Mission workers were now admitted, among the first being two sons of the former French consul, Mr. Dudoit, who begged the Doles to be very strict with his boys.

For Daniel Dole, it meant busy weeks of vacation plowing with native workmen to plant and harvest crops of beans, Indian corn, squashes and peas, all in great demand when the whaling fleet would visit Honolulu in the fall and again in the spring. Not a little profit from the sale of this farm produce served to cancel a large part of the debts against the school. For Charlotte, it meant doubling her work. But she went at it calmly, in the sure knowledge that the Doles too must soon find a change of location. She was not unaware that some parents wished a younger man to take Daniel's place, but undue concern availed naught, duty must be done and the future left with God.

To many, even to call Punahou a college seemed premature, but the charter had at last been obtained for the Oahu College. There would be sport enough made of such pretensions, thought Daniel, who, however, rejoiced that the trustees had called young Edward Beckwith to be its first president. He had been so successful as principal of the Royal School for three years that over fifty of his students there, many of them Honolulu Mission children, transferred to Punahou with him. In September 1854, at the courthouse in town, a formal ceremony with solemn addresses and prayers installed the new president of the Oahu College.

At one stroke the daytime population of Punahou was thus doubled, although an actual college existed only in name. Edward Beckwith taught all the forenoon, adding work in singing which became very popular. The young president enjoyed it all too, especially the early morning jump into the bathing pond; and for two months early in 1855 he even took afternoon classes at the Royal School to tide over that excellent institution until his youngest brother could arrive from Massachusetts to take charge of it. Besides classes in Latin and Greek, Daniel Dole took over Mr. Rice's work, which included building a long section of stone wall below the school. For Charlotte Dole, these changes presented increasing cares which she found herself less and less able to meet with her wonted efficiency. Her letters lay long unanswered; at times she was unable to walk from one courtyard to the other.

But under the troubled surface of her thoughts there ran the comforting reflection that Mission friends at Koloa on Kauai had more than once asked Daniel to open there a small school for the "foreign" children of that island.

In June 1855 Daniel formally brought to an end his fourteen years as Punahou's first principal. Several of the trustees opposed acceptance of his resignation, and a number of other Mission brethren felt entirely unreconciled to the proposed change. But both Charlotte and Daniel knew it to be duty. And so the turn was made into a new road.

Wedding of Kanehemeha IV and Emma Rooke at Kawaiahao Church in 1856. Sketched by Jessie Shaw Fisher from the memories of Sanford Dole and with his assistance

Chapter III

KOLOA
1855–1866

TO GEORGE and Sanford Dole the summer of 1855 brought a prolonged holiday marked by no ordinary vacation voyage. This time they were all going, not for two or three weeks, but to build a house and stay, stay for keeps, and at Koloa where wild ducks came, where there was sugar cane to eat and a whole countryside for playground. What was more, Father had paid a hundred dollars to charter the schooner *Maria* to carry down freight for the new house. What a phenomenal vessel she must be, thought Sanford, to take all the lumber for a whole two-story house!

They disembarked at the first port, Nawiliwili, to land the horse and carriage taken especially for Mother who had become more or less of an invalid. Driving the ten or twelve miles by way of Lihue through the mountain gap across to Koloa, the carriage, probably the first on Kauai, proved quite a novelty to everyone they met. The road was narrow, of course, and rough, but seemed to them fairly good; there were bridges over all the smaller streams and fording the larger ones was a simple matter in dry summer months.

During those early years Koloa had been growing more rapidly into a settlement of foreign homes than Lihue, which is today the county center. Until the beginning of the plantation there in 1851, Lihue had remained as scattered groups of Hawaiian houses including the home of Governor Kanoa above the bay at Nawiliwili. Koloa, however, during fall and winter months, was an important port-of-call for fifty or sixty whalers which might put in for fresh vegetables, sweet potatoes, beef, pigs, and firewood, the vessels anchoring in the roadstead while a good offshore trade breeze prevailed, or laying off and on, if a change of wind threatened. It was an opportunity for Hawaiians to sell their produce; foreigners too had begun to make their homes there as early as 1835 when the Reverend Peter Gulick and his wife established a Protestant mission station, and the first commercially successful sugar manufactory in the Islands was then begun at Koloa.

In 1842 Dr. James W. Smith had settled at Koloa not only as Protestant missionary, but also as the only physician on the island, and his growing family was soon fully as eager as the Rowells at Waimea, the Rices at Lihue, and the Johnsons and Wilcoxes at Hanalei, to have a boarding school at Koloa as the most central point on the island. To be welcomed again by the Smiths at Koloa was to Charlotte Dole like coming home. For Sister Smith had been Melicent Knapp, Horton Knapp's own sister, and all during these island years had been as close as an own sister to Charlotte. Then too, to help Melicent in her home school for Hawaiian girls, still another Knapp sister, Deborah, had recently braved the long voyage from Connecticut to become a part of the big Smith family.

To the Koloa community as a whole, both Charlotte and Daniel Dole were drawn by ties of long association. As early as 1839 Charlotte, with her young husband, Horton Knapp, had visited with the Gulick family there at the Mission and also in Manager Hooper's thatched house, leaving then in Brother Whitney's double canoe to see the Waimea Mission Station. Again in 1842 when the Smiths had first come to Koloa with little knowledge of Hawaiian, Horton and Charlotte Knapp had escorted them from Honolulu on a tiny schooner. Until the Gulick Mission home could be made ready, the Smiths stayed with the D. H. Goodales who had come out in 1841 as shipmates of the Doles, Bonds, and Rices and on upper Koloa lands were experimenting with *kukui* oil. The kernels of the nuts were ground and pressed, with an output of fifty gallons a day, in the hope that the oil might prove superior to linseed oil as a paint base.

Other prospectors like Jarves and Marshall, also Peck and Titcomb, had tried out cotton, coffee, and silk culture with luxuriant plantings of mulberry trees. These however were so soon blighted by dry weather that Jarves and Marshall had already sold their lease from Ladd & Company to Charles Tobey and Dr. R. W. Wood of Honolulu. And the Knapps rode across the island to Waioli, where they found Charles Titcomb's second coffee plantation and his silk cocooneries tended by Hawaiian women.

Sugar-growing and -making which remained the practical project for Koloa, had been started there in 1835 by the Honolulu commission and mercantile firm of Brinsmade, Ladd & Hooper, called Ladd & Company, or *Lada ma,* as Hawaiians phrased it. Peter Allan Brinsmade and William Ladd were both from Hallowell, Maine; William Hooper from Boston. Brinsmade had been appointed United States Consular Agent at Honolulu in 1838, and he it was who in 1840 gave the happy picnic there in Manoa Valley, a day so thoroughly enjoyed by many of the Mission family, Emily Dole among them.

The three young New England partners of Ladd & Company had succeeded in obtaining the king's permission and leases for 980 acres of land at Koloa. Primitive Oriental mills of heavy granite base with vertical rollers had been imported to Koloa and Waimea very early, and continued to be operated there by Chinese. Ladd & Company lost no time in sending to China for men of long experience in boiling sugar.

Perhaps a third of this area covered by Ladd & Company leases was fertile soil for cane culture; the district was a quiet corner of the island not too exposed to interference from chiefs unfavorable to the new mode of life; and, in addition, the new leases gave convenient access to a landing for small ships. To the king, Kamehameha III, the regular annual rental of three hundred dollars in cash from a comparatively small area seemed a distinct advance over the taxes in labor, hogs, tapa cloths, or canoe paddles formerly received from the entire district.

In the vicinity of the mill and fields, with the great new adobe church hard by, a village began to grow up where a quiet, orderly Sabbath was begun by the ringing of the church bell. But the day before always brought holiday. The Saturday morning market was early thronged by natives "in rude attire or none at all," chaffering for dogs, pigs, chickens, and other produce. Long familiar with the art of barter, Hawaiians were rapidly adjusting to preference for "Kauai currency," tokens printed in Hawaiian on small cards, paid out at the rate of a *hapawalu* (twelve and a half cents) a large sum then, for a day's work on the plantation, and quickly redeemed at the trading center for calicoes, needles, or flints. James Jackson Jarves, who was unable to produce silk at Koloa, proved to be the one to leave us in his *Scenes and Scenery* this inimitable picture of the morning market place. And a Koloa boy, W. O. Smith, added the colorful afternoon of Saturday when all the Hawaiians went riding bareback through the village, some of the women wearing long *pa-u* of bright calico, all shouting and laughing as they dashed past.

The first year of the plantation saw twenty-five acres planted to cane and thousands of coffee trees started. Many thatched houses for laborers were set in order as well as forty-eight taro patches to supply their food and even a long stone barracks, which Manager Hooper considered far superior to the flimsy grass houses of native construction.

All this activity presupposed mechanics, carpenters, stone masons, a cooper, blacksmith, and wheelwright. One by one these too were added to the village, some of them sailors settled ashore, men of sterling worth who with their Hawaiian families became an integral part of the community.

For the proprietors, hard work and discouragements were the order of the day. None of the three partners was experienced in agriculture, but by dint of perseverance and Yankee ingenuity a dam was built for water power and with a two-foot head "the koa logs hunted for in the mountains at Hawaii were *turning themselves round at the rate of twenty-four times per minute."* On November 14, 1836, when the mill actually went into operation, with four men to feed cane into it, "there was no stop to it. The natives were completely taken aback and thought the Mill one of the seven wonders of the world." Only molasses was attempted the first year and the wooden rollers had soon to be replaced by iron. The second mill was discovered to be inadequate even before it was completed, but it produced coarse brown sugar which was marketed in rawhide-handled bags made of rushes by native women for three cents apiece.

Some of the chiefs and other Hawaiians grew cane to be ground on shares at the Koloa mill. New settlers began to plant small plots of cane on the same terms, among them Dr. Lafon of the

American Mission, who served also as plantation physician; the Rev. Reuben Tinker, earlier of the Mission; and later Dr. J. W. Smith and his Hawaiian congregation to help defray the expense of a new church building. Also, Charles Tobey and Dr. Wood devoted the Jarves & Marshall leasehold to cane culture.

Dr. Wood was a native of Augusta, Maine. He had been engaged by Peter Brinsmade in 1838 to take charge of the Hospital for American Seamen at Honolulu. Later Dr. Wood started probably the first drugstore in Honolulu and long conducted a private practice there. In 1839 his sister, who had accompanied Mrs. Brinsmade to the Islands, married Manager Hooper of Koloa, where she lived for a number of years and whither she afterward returned on a visit, to Charlotte Dole's great pleasure.

By 1841 a larger new iron sugar mill was ordered for Koloa and put into service near the Waihohonu stream, where its great square smoke-stack of stone may be seen today, bearing its date of 1842. Demands on capital expenditure were heavy; in 1844 a too-ambitious program of expansion was attempted. Dr. Wood, who already held a mortgage on half the lease, bought in the other half from the Hawaiian government. In 1848 he therefore became owner and proprietor of the new fifty-year lease covering a total area of 2,200 acres. At the centennial of the plantation in 1935 Arthur C. Alexander laid us all in his debt by gathering these facts and many more into Koloa's first formal history.

When in 1850 the Dole family of four made a Punahou vacation visit to Koloa, Daniel took keen interest in the projects of these Maine compatriots. In 1855, when the Doles moved to Koloa to live, Dr. Wood's partner and manager was his brother-in-law, Judge Samuel Burbank, still another Maine man, a young lawyer who by good fortune had been bred a farmer. All of these young New Englanders were men of character and integrity which set a high level in the new community. While some of their projects had failed of success, the pattern of Hawaiian plantations on an extended scale, conducted and financed by a Honolulu mercantile firm as agent, housing and caring for their workmen, had been set as early as 1835.

In setting his course for Koloa in 1855 did Daniel Dole realize that to grow up as neighbors of this agricultural enterprise was to be a distinct asset to both of his sons?

The new Dole home began at once to take shape as an extension of the earlier Mission center. For Daniel Dole put up his first cottage on the Mission grounds a little *makai* (toward the sea) of Dr. Smith's steeply thatched adobe house built by Brother Gulick twenty years before and in 1855 still attested to by the names of various Gulick sons cut in several of the inner doors. Very likely it was felt that the *haole* or foreign school, as the children called it, was in the nature of an experiment. Certainly it began on meager funds, and consisted of two rooms and a garret, with a cook house built as usual a little separate from the living rooms. There were only mat partitions at first and in the garret only tiny windows at the gable ends. Watching the carpenter at work, George and Sanford thought that their house was going very slowly. They were to occupy one end of the garret, and part of the other end was to be a little room for Maria Rice who was overjoyed to be getting back to school again after more than a year at home in Lihue.

Indeed, the whole Rice family had been as eager to see the Doles as the Doles were glad to be coming to Kauai. At the outset Harrison and Mary Rice had urged them to make their home at Lihue, but Daniel and Charlotte, perhaps because of her poor health and the advantage of being near a physician, had finally made the decision for Koloa. During the first two years the Dole family lived in their own cottage, but boarded for the most part with the Smiths, in order to relieve Charlotte of housekeeping until she grew stronger.

While the school was to occupy most of Daniel Dole's time, his Kauai neighbors had begged that he preach to them in English, alternating Sundays between Lihue and Koloa. In this way the Kauai Foreign Church, with Harrison Rice as deacon, gradually came into being. Every other Saturday, even before his house was finished that first summer, Daniel would set out on horseback with his boys for Lihue, often holding service in the Rices' Koamalu home. And on alternate Sabbaths all who could come from Lihue or elsewhere would join the Smiths and Doles for service at Koloa.

By November of 1855 Maria Rice had apparently become the first boarder in the new school, writing home to her mother from "Students' Garret," Koloa. Here she helped Mother Dole with the cooking and housekeeping in the prettiest little white-plastered house she had ever seen in her life. Little by little a garden grew up about it, Daniel and the boys cultivating vegetables in the back yard with flowers about the front door. One day when Sister Rice rode over with Emily to call on the Doles, she was dismayed upon leaving to find her small daughter strewing destruction in the front garden, striking out with a long stick and whipping off heads of lilies and roses alike to the tune of a rhythmical monotone: "Us-ain't-got-none-such, Us-ain't-got-none-such."

Before very long more rooms were added to the Doles' little house, for Willy Rice was old enough to be promoted from school at home to one of the garret rooms at Koloa with Edward Wilcox from Hanalei who studied alone with Father Dole, preparatory to going on to college later. William Rowell too was added to the boys' garret where surreptitious games of *konane* (Hawaiian checkers played with flat stones on a little Niihau mat) were now and then substituted for study hour. In good time Father Dole quietly regulated proceedings by confiscating the Niihau mat. From Lihue, Maria, Emily, and Willy Rice rode over Monday mornings, an hour on the way, and went back Friday afternoons.

From Waimea, a longer and harder ride, came four Rowells, Melvina, William, Clara, and Marion, who went home only at vacation times. Of the Smith household Emma, a few months younger than Maria Rice, was already helping Mother and Aunt Deborah in the Hawaiian girls' school at home, but with her sister Charlotte and brother Willie Owen, attended the Dole school as day pupils. Later there were three part-Hawaiian children, Hattie Fredenburg, with Henry and Sophia Heywood, children of the stone-mason.

One of the little girls of this Koloa school, Mary Burbank, daughter of the plantation manager, still recalled it seventy-five years later, if people asked her about it. Across the road from the Smiths' was the big adobe Hawaiian church, built in Father Gulick's time; just above that was the large Hawaiian school taught by a Hawaiian teacher. Below it, on the site occupied by the present public school, was a thatch-roofed house with clapboard sides. Here the new Dole school opened, in a thicket of indigo bushes, with a clearing to the road in front where the boys played a bat-and-ball game called wicket. The schoolhouse was a simple one without a ceiling, all the rafters in the interior exposed where not covered by blackboards around the sides.

Mary Burbank and her little brother Samuel could very well have walked the short distance down the stream from their home in the old stone house, for in those days the Koloa mill stood not far above the Hawaiian church and the Mission houses on the corner of the main road to Lihue. And the Burbank children liked to go through the mill on their way home to get pieces of the candy crust that formed on top of the boiled juice in the coolers. Mary, however, was terrified by the long-horned cattle often to be met with on the plain, especially when the whole plantation herd of five hundred head was driven into the branding pen near the mill. Mr. Burbank told the children always to keep near the winding stream and to jump into it and wade or swim home, if danger seemed to threaten. But it was found better for them to ride to school as they always did, one behind the other on the same horse.

Several years after the school was opened Aubrey Robinson and Francis Gay came as pupils from across the Niihau channel; and before that, from four channels away to the windward, Father Bond, formerly of Hallowell, Maine, but, by adoption, of Kohala, Hawaii, sent his three oldest children, Ellen, George, and Cornelius, to the care of his former shipmate, Daniel Dole. Soon Alfred Wight, also from Kohala, joined the Bonds. From Maui came Jimmie, Lizzie, and Sam Pogue, with James Robertson, and George and Mary Richardson.

Maria Rice seemed much the oldest to little Mary Burbank who followed her with adoring eyes. When Clara and Marion Rowell came from Waimea, Mary was delighted to have playmates of nearly her own age who could make a trio with her at recess time. Maria often talked with them, one day studied the palms of their hands one by one and next day brought each a little folded paper with their fortunes on them written in her fine, neat script, learned, she said, from Dr. Smith who taught penmanship in the little Koloa school. Maria had only three years there, leaving to help with the Lihue plantation bookkeeping as her father's strength slowly failed.

It must have been during Maria's last term at school that

Mother Rice asked Mother Dole to visit her at Lihue, leaving Maria in charge of the housekeeping for the school, with Sister Deborah Knapp to look in now and then to consult in case of need. When it came time for church meeting at Lihue, Mother Dole addressed a note to fourteen-year-old Master Sanford B. Dole, Koloa, thanking him for his letter, cautioning him to start for Lihue immediately after prayers if Father thought best, to have everything ready beforehand, to bring a clean suit for the Sabbath, to wear George's pants to ride in, but not to wear a ragged shirt, one without a bosom would do, and to bring his meeting shirt without fail. Also to tell Maria to be sure to make the butter salt enough, since it must be sent to Honolulu as soon as the largest pail could be filled; thanking them for getting off the other butter tub in season, his affectionate mother, Charlotte Close Dole, reminded her son to be a good boy and try to do right in everything.

Before long so many children were asking for a school home in the Dole cottage that plans looked forward to enlargement. In 1857 Dr. Smith deeded to Father Dole for one dollar ten acres of land directly south and *makai* of his own home. And the Doles' house was moved bodily, a team of oxen no doubt hauling it on rollers down the road the short distance, where it was set up with the addition of still more rooms for boarders. It stood on the site of the modern Kauai mortuary now under big monkeypod trees almost opposite the teachers' cottages of the present government school. These ten acres were no doubt part of Dr. Smith's homestead area deeded to him in 1855 by the American Mission Board.

In five years the need of a schoolhouse too became as urgent as of a chapel for the little English-speaking or Foreign Church of Kauai. As principal of the one and pastor of the other, Daniel Dole circulated a subscription for a thousand dollars to put up across the road from his home and below the big Hawaiian Church a small building to serve as a church on Sundays and a schoolhouse during the week. This stood for many years on the grounds occupied by the present public school and actually became part of the public school itself, when English was made the language of the schools all over the Islands. In 1860 when it was built it served seven days a week as both chapel and schoolhouse. A bronze bell, perhaps from some ship, hung in a little cupola on the roof and was rung for school and church. In 1908 the building was taken down, having served its time, but the bell is still in use on the veranda of the present school where it rings loud and true.

By 1860 George Dole at eighteen was working early and late on plantation jobs, with less time to join in the farm work at home, such as milking the cows, caring for the horses, and weeding the garden. Sanford, at sixteen, often wished, especially when company came, that he had a sister to help Mother with house chores like dishes and cooking and sweeping, which made him feel like a fish out of water. But often at just such times there was the fun of picnics at Wailua River or in the woods, with horseback riding and mountain climbing. As the boys grew older and the school larger there were even more farm chores in dairy and field. For although their ten acres of homestead furnished more land than they could well cultivate even with native help, their table was amply supplied with corn, excellent sweet potatoes, beans and green vegetables, as well as the best of fruit like mangoes and peaches from the orchard.

Tall and strong, both boys delighted in getting off to swim, if no farther than to Maulili pool just east of the Mission premises, near where both early sugar mills had stood. Here George and Sanford found they could hold their own with the Hawaiians even in *pahia,* a sport often described later by Sanford as the graceful art of folding up like a jack-knife for the jump, then straightening out suddenly to strike the water with a boomerang curve and skim the surface to a feet-first presentation. Above the bridge near the old mill pond, where earth banks shelved steeply from a height of ten feet or more, a little water judiciously applied created a surface as slippery as glass. The boys' own bodies serving of course as toboggan sleds, the results to their skins may easily be imagined.

One game they all enjoyed was wicket, often watched by small Mary Burbank. *Aipuni,* the Hawaiians called it, or rounders, perhaps because the bat had a large rounded end. It was a forerunner of baseball, but the broad, heavy bat was held close to the ground. Every boy had a horse, a sturdy little beast that could scour the country far and wide, subsisting on anything from *pili* (thatching grass) to sweet potatoes. Willie Smith, known later always as W. O., recalled the satisfying taste of ship's bread or hard tack, simmered in hot milk and devoured with rich, dark molasses for supper; and the fun of having other boys ride over to see them and then of all riding down to the landing to watch whaleboats taking off loads of pumpkins which the sailors would store by stringing them up the ship's rigging.

The lure of wild ducks gathering every evening in the marshes and neighboring taro patches was strong. At last Sanford's father allowed him to borrow Dr. Smith's gun and off he went proudly the first evening to try his luck. "I did not get a single duck that time," he admitted, "but I brought down a black heron, known as *auku* by the Hawaiians. I was proud of that bird. He was not badly hurt and I bore him home in triumph; he was turned out in a marshy corner of the horse pasture, where he stayed for a week or two before flying away." He said also:

"Any further hesitation on my father's part was useless. I often went out late in the afternoon and really helped the family table along with wild ducks, either the common ones or the *moha,* which are better eating. This of course led to bigger game, and having with great difficulty procured a rifle, I began to frequent the steep bluffs on the sea between Koloa and Lihue, where I often camped out and in time became skillful at shooting goats. From this it was only a step to hunting wild cattle in the mountains back of Lihue and Waimea."

As a lad of seventeen, Sanford went to Honolulu with his father and mother late in May of 1861, and returned on the 13th of June to keep house during their absence. Punahou students were also going home for vacation, an event to be traveling by the new *Kilauea,* a sturdy clipper model, brigantine-rigged, Boston-built propeller, of which everyone was justly proud, as the first steamer built especially to withstand island storms and rough channels. The propeller, Sanford discovered, made more trembling than he had thought it would, for he could see people shaking in their berths. Off Oahu, when it was proposed that they go and eat supper, Will Rowell first "turned pale and then galloped up on deck, but when he had made room for his supper, he came down and ate it."

Shortly after sunrise Sanford went ashore at Nawiliwili with the Rices just for the round trip. His brother George, who was working at Lihue Plantation, met the ship's boat with mangoes from Paul Isenberg. The steamer "lay tossing about in the outer harbor" instead of anchoring inside for the short stop. This of course delayed the landing boats. Back on board, Sanford watched with interest for the next whaleboat, which everyone knew was to bring Minister Wyllie's party on board. And in this party was the English Lady Franklin with her niece, who had been visiting Hanalei and, having a desire to see Waimea where Captain Cook had first landed, were to take the daylight cruise along the west Kauai coast by steamer.

Sanford's reaction in his letter was laconic, with a democratic overtone: "They had to wait a good while for Mrs. Franklin, but I had a good chance to see her as she sat a good deal of the time on deck reading or taking notes." This was during the two hours' passage along the coast to Koloa where Sanford landed with the Smiths. At home, he reported all in order: the leaves swept off the back veranda; the turkey alive and twice as big as he had been in May; the hens all right; one of the roses had died, another was blossoming; the pig was fat; corn and beans picked, but too dry to plant more, very little water remaining in the stream after the mill had finished grinding. The Rowells went on home to Waimea in the *Kilauea* which returned the same night for Koloa freight and was to sail at noon next day, the 15th. Sanford's detailed letter to "Dear Parents" ends: "I will send two bags of potatoes and a pail of peaches and mangoes." Not a word of Lady Franklin's party having spent the night at Dr. Wood's and stopped in at Mrs. Smith's just before noon on the way to the steamer next day. But the boy had written a good letter and followed his parents' instructions.

With Albert Wilcox, who was just his own age, Sanford often exchanged letters across the Island. A number of those from Koloa, kept for years in the old Wilcox home at Waioli, today bring the year 1862 into unexpected focus. Having no school session on New Year's Day at Koloa, the Dole pupils organized a rifle company among Hawaiian boys for drill and target practice. Required uniform: blue woolen shirt, dark breeches, Bunkum cap.

Later an expedition into the woods with William Rowell of

Waimea netted a bunch of bananas plus sharp regrets that, on finding chewed *hala* nuts strewn about, they had not carried rifles heavy enough for a pig hunt. In August the two, with Eddie D., paddled a canoe down the Huleia River at Lihue two miles or so to the mouth, where they hoisted sail and with a spanking breeze shot back up river with high waves and fierce whitecaps. Once running aground, and again almost capsizing, only added to the fun.

By September, George Dole went over to Wahiawa to begin collecting taxes. In November, he made a memorable excursion of three days with Father Rowell and several Hawaiian guides to the summit of Waialeale. It was mostly through rain and mud, but all were amply rewarded by an instant's view from the top out over Wainiha Valley and even across to the little island of Niihau. Next year Albert and Sanford must be sure to make the same trip, he wrote.

One company of the Koloa Volunteers became a cavalry troop. Drilling was greatly stimulated, as Sanford wrote to his own cousin, Mary Dole in Maine, by the gift of eight old muskets with bayonets and one sword, sent over on the schooner *Excel* by Mr. Knudsen from the old Russian fort at Waimea. This armament consisted of flintlocks stained with the blood of Hawaiian soldiers in the Kauai Rebellion of 1824. By June 4, 1863, the company had been in existence seven months and numbered fifteen, most of them natives. The privates were armed with old flintlocks, some of them American pieces, some of them English tower muskets. The captain of this valiant band was Mary's "absent brother," Sanford.

Other volunteer companies had begun to drill in Hilo and Honolulu, especially at Punahou, and the First Hawaiian Cavalry in the town. Minister Wyllie expressed a sense of satisfaction that a volunteer spirit, among both the native and the naturalized subjects of the king had at last been awakened. Many young men were eager to enlist under the Stars and Stripes and some Hawaiian citizens already in the United States did do so, but those in the Islands had already been mustered under the Hawaiian flag.

During 1863, Charlotte and Daniel planned and saved in the hope that Sanford might have the whole school year at Punahou.

Seeing him off on the *Odd Fellow* in September, Daniel watched the schooner make its way up against the trade wind. While, from home, Charlotte could distinguish the vessel almost out to the horizon off South Crater. Later she found herself listening for the boy's familiar footsteps in the empty house, then wondering whether the fresh breeze would hold, or die down and keep him out in the channel for a week. But she must finish lining his coat for the winter, and write him that the linnets brought from Honolulu had flown over to lodge in the big trees at the Smith place. Loving, detailed letters followed Sanford, who noted on each the day of arrival. Those from his mother hoped to see his style of writing improve, and rejoiced that he had done so well in his first debate. His father reminded him to employ Mr. Lett to make him a pair of shoes, asked him whether he played his flute often, cautioned him not to let it fall; asked also about his work, whether he studied much by lamplight and whether he got enough exercise out of doors; reminded him to obtain either at Castle & Cooke's or the post office one dollar's worth of five-cent postage stamps, half-American and half-Hawaiian, putting one of each on the letter enclosed for his Grandmother Dole.

Sanford was twenty years old. With all the advantages of new and stimulating teachers under President and Mrs. Mills at Punahou, he wrote that the one thing he missed most was discussion with his father in the evenings. For one thing, he was eager to talk over every new phase of the war in America. In November, to know what the accession of Kamehameha V would bring to the Islands. And somehow Sanford must soon get to the United States to volunteer with the North in the Civil War. On this point his father replied quietly that Hawaii would need him still more, begged him to use the Hawaiian language at every opportunity, so that some day he might be able to preach in it; and his mother voiced her feeling that while romance was calling him to the colors, he would find little romance in freezing to death. On the other hand, were he actually needed by the Union, neither father nor mother would say him nay.

On Kauai, interest in drilling volunteer cavalry troops among Hawaiians was not aroused entirely by bugle calls from the war in the United States. Much of it expressed local disapproval of the new king's refusal to subscribe to the liberal constitution of his two predecessors. Throughout the Islands discussion was rife. At Koloa, cavalry volunteers designed their flag to display (KUMU KANAWAI) (Constitution) in outraged protest that the king should arbitrarily change what since 1852 had been the fundamental law of the land.

Returning from Punahou in the summer of 1864, Sanford kept bachelor's hall at home with George, while their parents enjoyed the rare privilege of seeing old friends at General Meeting in Honolulu. George and Sanford hoped that Albert Wilcox would join them at Koloa, but he was growing cane and collecting taxes. Sanford, too, was working with the plantation cooper. This was Charles Neumann, a skilled musician who had inspired pupils at Punahou and often gave lessons at Koloa or Hanalei, if summoned there for coopering. Today when sugar is shipped in bulk, even the day of jute bags is passing. In earlier times, when kegs must be used for packaging, a cooper was as essential as a sugar boiler; for no ordinary carpenter had the knack of fitting staves into a sound, tight cask, well hooped. When hundreds of these must be made ready for the grinding season, Neumann was glad of an apprentice hand like Sanford. And then there was often an enjoyable evening of music at the Doles' little melodeon. Neumann had a passion for music and was foremost in subscribing to a similar melodeon for the Foreign Church of Kauai at Koloa.

Plantation work at Wahiawa, in the beautiful hill country just west of Koloa, proved to be Sanford's first independent job. This was offered by Judge Duncan McBryde, in whose home Sanford would live during ten weeks, from August to November, until the plowing and planting of ten acres to cane was completed. A friendship grew up too, for later, at McBryde's early death, he left Sanford as guardian of his young children.

Although discouragements during this first job were not lacking, in the end a hundred dollars had accumulated toward Sanford's only year at Williams College. Hawaiians, who had agreed to help, left at the end of a week, so that with only two of Mr. McBryde's Hawaiians, Sanford held the plow himself a good deal. Then three natives from Lawaikai signed on and stood by. The best one to hold the plow was Davida, a young boy who had worked at Koloa for George. After plowing, came fencing;

by the time rails and posts had been hauled, the oxen were worn out and Sanford must hunt up two more pairs of steers in Koloa to make up a new team for harrowing. With Burbank's big harrow "which is awfull heavy," the whole team would be fagged out on hot days. Chains would snap and bowpins vanish, and once even the oxen were lost, while the plow had to be sent to the Koloa shop for repairs.

The Monday after finishing at Wahiawa, Sanford then started out to get laborers from Niihau for Mr. McBryde, and glad he was of the opportunity to see the island. Riding to Waimea, he had supper at Mrs. Rowell's where he borrowed a blanket and an umbrella; then set out at night in the Sinclairs' boat. Without a breeze the crew of five men had to row a long way out, on a painted ocean, smooth and brilliant with phosphorescence. When at last a faint land breeze sprang up, the sail was spread.

The boat, about half as big as a whaleboat, carried a large mainsail and a jib. Becalmed for a while, they at last met a steady trade wind, which increased toward morning so that another sail was hoisted. With a heavy load of *paiai* (hard poi) the boat shipped a good deal of water. At the south end of Niihau they passed so close to the bluff of Kawaihoa that Sanford could have touched it with a six-foot pole. The gray rock itself, one or two hundred feet high, seemed beautifully carved and fluted and polished, like the interior of some ancient English church. At its base, just above the waves, ran a wide level walk with two small springs of pure fresh water. As the boat coasted along the shore, it encountered a great shoal of porpoises. Sanford had a lively time leaning over the side, under a whitecap breeze, watching the water full of these agile creatures, leaping out from under the bow as the boat ran through them, others on all sides showing their flukes and spouting their little jets of water a foot or two high.

Landing at about eleven in the morning, Sanford found a horse and rode the four miles to the house where the Sinclairs were all very kind to him during the rest of the week. As he rode through miles of waving green grass two or more feet high, it seemed difficult to believe that there could be only rainwater on the island. In fact, it must be the best sheep ranch in the Islands. The 2,300 pastured there made no impression on the miles and miles of grass. Surely one hundred thousand head would not stock it. And with the wild ducks as tame as chickens, how he did wish he had a gun in his hand! Sanford's estimate of Niihau pastures, made in November after an unusually rainy summer, was perhaps unduly enthusiastic and indeed was reduced by half, in writing to Albert Wilcox at Hanalei about this time.

For all his leisurely visit at Niihau, Sanford remarked incidentally that he did not succeed in securing a single Hawaiian laborer for Mr. McBryde. He left Saturday morning by the same boat, from the Lehua end of Niihau, and it took about five hours to cross the channel, but the wind was rather ahead and, with hardly any ballast, the lee gunwale was several times under water; even with that spanking breeze they could only fetch Mana, and then it took till dark to row in to Waimea.

Riding home, Sanford naturally stopped at Wahiawa to report his failure at recruiting on Niihau, a disappointment offset somewhat by the pleasure of the visit and the satisfaction of finding his first cane planting coming up well in Mr. McBryde's field. "Today, November 8," he recalled as he wrote to Albert Wilcox, "is election day in the States. Heaven grant that Abe Lincoln will be elected, as I believe he will."

Life alone at home for a few weeks was enlivened by Sanford's moving the family melodeon into his own room for company. One evening too, Henry Alexander and Joseph Emerson came in for a *poi aha aina* (feed), out of a big *umeke* (calabash) of poi with salt salmon and wild duck. Henry and Joe were going to board at the Doles' while they learned sugar boiling at Koloa mill, which was about to begin grinding.

In December of this year, 1864, Sanford paid Albert Wilcox a visit at Waioli, riding over on horseback, taking the wrong turn several times, after crossing the Wailua ferry, but eventually finding Mr. Krull's dairy farm long after dark, he spent the night there, and proceeded on next day.

On Saturday afternoon, his love of sailing, coupled with ignorance of winter currents on the north side of the island, took him out into the bay at Hanalei in a canoe with Albert's two younger brothers, Sam and Luther. The sea was rough, but they paddled down the river to the bay and discovered a canoe swamped in the surf, the Hawaiian hanging onto it unable to make any headway. Fastening a line to the canoe, the boys towed him ashore. Pulling around a while, the boys ate oranges they had with them and waited for a stronger breeze.

At last, starting to run in on the waves, their own canoe was swamped in the strong current about half a mile out so that they could not hold the half-sunken boat and were washed out fast toward the open sea. Eight or ten Hawaiians, noticing them, came swimming out to help; leaving the canoe with sail and paddles to their rescuers, the three boys swam for shore, making slow work at first against the current and encumbered with clothes. The natives meanwhile had gotten a rope on their canoe and were slowly towing it in. The wind came up strong from the north, making tremendous waves in the bay which opens directly out under the North Star and can be very dangerous during winter months. People began to collect on the beach, Father Wilcox and Albert among them. At last they all got in near the Waioli River where the surf was not so heavy, the undertow however still very strong. Father Wilcox was obviously anxious, even though he had made a point of all his boys learning to swim. Sanford confided to George that he had enjoyed it, having as it did "just enough of danger to give a spicy relish to the adventure."

After working not only on the plantation, but at times as Port Collector, George had saved enough for a year's vacation and had sailed on the bark *Yankee* on July 7, 1864 to see the world and in particular the early homes of his father and mother.

The ship's course setting nearly north, windward Kauai was in sight all day with the Lihue Hawaiian Church and canefields easily distinguished by passengers Emily Rice, William Rowell, and George Dole. Several of the other Island passengers, including Mrs. Cyrus Mills of Punahou, contributed to one issue of the *Yankee Notion* which was read aloud to great applause, particularly the latest dispatches from San Francisco per *Booby Express*.

On the 29th of July, as they neared the latitude of San Francisco Bay in a dense fog, a pilot boat came bearing down upon the Honolulu packet, which needed no help, but whose passengers watched the pilot boat with interest. A beautiful clipper-built schooner about as large as the *Odd Fellow,* she carried towering clouds of canvas in proportion to the size of her hull.

The new world of California George found so entirely to be desired that he wrote, urging brother Sanford to come, and if he ever got away, to make no promise as to returning. The cooler climate was something that would improve his mother's health, George felt certain. If she and his father could only make the voyage they might enjoy, besides the treats of music and picture galleries, a rare feast—and the fun of lunching on coffee and pie for two bits. Yet with all this exuberance in the new world of California, one letter to Sanford ends with a peremptory: "Please never send me another letter with a page and a half *blank*. If out of thoughts, tell me anything about home, the garden, the horses, or my dog Colonel, and please do not insult him by calling him Kernel."

After the jungles of Panama, New York held its own fascinations, of course, for Island people, but beyond looking about a little and getting himself two suits of clothes, George decided not to linger. Greenwich, Connecticut, came next, with his Mother Charlotte's old home and family, who welcomed the tall nephew and cousin as no stranger to their kith and kin. A green, prosperous land of rolling hills and good farms, he thought. How could anyone ever think of leaving it?

George's letters went westward steadily to the three at Koloa, Father, Mother, and Beloved *Kaikaina* (younger brother), as he often addressed Sanford. Little by little the viewpoint in the letters changes, as their writer, perhaps in proportion to the distance, began to realize how keenly he watched for return messages from home, as well as for each number of the *Kuokoa* (*Hawaiian Independent*) to which he had subscribed in Honolulu.

The home folks, in their turn, looked with longing for letters during his long year's absence from home. Thirty-three letters he wrote, and it is as good as a trip to New England to read them over again today, over ninety years since he wrote them down. For well-written indeed they are, with their tale: first, of meeting Uncle Isaac Close, identified by his shawl and carpet bag, at the train at Worcester, where hundreds were gathered for the annual meeting of the American Mission Board. So many younger Hawaiian Mission "Cousins" appeared that they at once appointed a "cannibal" meeting where they sat on the floor and jabbered away in Hawaiian. All were greatly interested of course in the

Above: "Old 'Sixty-Seven" at Williams College. Sanford Dole (seated) is sixth from left
Courtesy Williams College Library

Right: Sanford Dole on his return from college in 1867
Courtesy Charlotte V. Hall

Sanford Dole about 1875

general meeting, and later when George met Dr. Rufus Anderson he was gratified to learn that the Prudential Committee of the Board had voted unanimously to continue Daniel Dole's salary.

The letters from New England were filled with pictures of the Connecticut homes which opened to young George Dole, of the seven aunts and great aunts, to all appearances older than the Pyramids and all seven miraculously living together under one roof; and at last also from Skowhegan (Bloomfield), Maine, where his own Grandmother Dole still kept the portrait of her young son Daniel over the fireplace and with her own hands now prepared grandson George's suppers of gingerbread, cheese, and pie, or of hulled corn and maple syrup. Here he watched small boys skating and the first snow falling; and here he crossed the Kennebec River to see aged Grandfather Bond in Hallowell and the brick Academy of Norridgewock where his own mother, Emily Ballard, had taught; then, retracing his steps, he visited his uncle, Captain Calvin Ballard, whose sons George and Sanford, in age, face, and figure much resembled their young Dole cousins of Koloa.

When Charlotte Dole's letter brought the first news of Sanford's Waioli adventure by canoe, Aunt Sally Close exclaimed, trembling, that the boy was nearly killed! Matter-of-fact George, even before reading Sanford's own account of it to himself, replied that he would as soon expect to hear that a fish had been drowned.

Perhaps it took the journey down the Ohio and the Mississippi— such rivers!—visiting sugar plantations in Louisiana, to convince George Dole that his real home lay in the Islands. For he concluded that sugar-making had been developed to a higher degree there, where the milder climate presented immense advantages. "Give me glorious Hawaii forever," he exclaimed, "and no more of these adulterated approximations labeled coffee."

New England called him for farewell visits. These included walking with Uncle Isaiah Dole out to the old home apple orchard where every tree was known by name and taste of fruit, and where they found, grazing in a meadow, some actual descendants of sheep which Daniel Dole as a boy had helped to shear; trapping and hunting with one uncle; sleighing, chopping wood, and butchering hogs with another; and in January of 1865 watching the cutting of Connecticut ice nine inches thick, 4,000 tons of it, being stowed away in great blocks weighing hundreds of pounds apiece. Finally, in April with Uncle Ike Close, George made a memorable visit in New York to join in the impressive mourning for Abraham Lincoln, "the best President we have ever had." From New York he wrote that the two State of Maine plows ordered by George Charman of Koloa had already been shipped and that he himself would be home by October.

NEW ENGLAND
1866–1868

MEANWHILE, in his turn, Sanford's thoughts were looking definitely toward New England. This had begun
even before George had set out on his pilgrimage. With
the younger brother the impulse seemed perhaps more deep-
seated; more an instinctive longing for the perspective of time
and distance, for space to think things out for himself. In some
way he had acquired a pair of steers and set to work, plowing and
planting, on nineteen acres of upland belonging to Dr. Smith and
not far from the ten acres which he had worked the year before
for Mr. McBryde at Wahiawa. Even with cane to be ground at
the Koloa mill, sugar was a long-range crop, but his hope of
possibly a year at Williams College kept his hand steadily at the
plow.

He worked too on the plantation as a *luna* (overseer) or setting
up kegs for Mr. Neumann, the cooper. Another venture was
keeping bees, the *Commercial Advertiser* of Honolulu noting
that, for neatness and purity, the beeswax sent by Mr. S. B. Dole
of Koloa was unsurpassed by the best imported. Queried the
editor: "Why may not our domestic trade be supplied by home
manufacture entirely?"

The year 1866 ushered in the radical change from sail to steam
between California and the Islands. The pioneer ship of the
California Steam Navigation Company, eagerly looked for by
young Honolulu "Cousins," was reported in their *Maile
Quarterly* on March 27 as the long-expected *Ajax,* which had
at last rounded Diamond Head, and was safely anchored in the

harbor, blowing off steam. Mary and Willy Rice, and Sanford Dole were leaving on her, not to mention notables like Princess Bernice Pauahi with her husband, the Honorable C. R. Bishop, as well as Dr. and Mrs. R. W. Wood of Kauai. The *Ajax* had brought young Mark Twain to Honolulu, and was to sail on the 4th of April, those first steamships often making long stays as contrasted with the modern schedule of in-and-out of port the same day. Undoubtedly Sanford would have enjoyed the still more leisurely voyage by sailing ship, but on the fourth day out he took pleasure in reporting the distance as already eight hundred miles from the Islands. He was chatting on paper with his father, thanking him for all he had done and was still doing for this younger son, who hoped to live so that his father would feel fully repaid.

The *Ajax,* a new propeller steamship of 1,355 tons, had some four hundred passengers aboard and not only set an excellent table, but also had most courteous officers and stewards. Entering the San Francisco Bay area by dark, they had passed so close to the Farallon Islands and lighthouse that the water seemed filled with thousands of birds something like ducks. Lights from the shipping and the long lines of gas street lights ashore were a beautiful sight, far more so than the town itself by day. In fact, when engulfed in its usual clouds of dust and smoke, it reminded one forcibly of the ancient city of Sodom. Mr. and Mrs. Titcomb, cousins of Daniel Dole, were, as with George two years before, most thoughtful and kind. She was planning to leave for New York by the *Sacramento* on the 18th of April, and Mr. Titcomb advised Sanford to do the same, since the steamer fare would surely have advanced by the next trip. Beyond visiting a menagerie, two museums, several stores and a market, with the modest purchase of a few collars, he left San Francisco for the return voyage.

Steaming out of the Golden Gate, the *Sacramento* was accompanied by hundreds of sea gulls about the size of pigeons, almost entirely white and so tame as to fly very near the deck. Whales could frequently be seen blowing. And near the Cliff House Mrs. Titcomb's opera glasses had shown numerous sea lions. Mr. Titcomb had obtained for Sanford the courtesy of first-class privileges except for eating and sleeping, both of which were excellent in second class. In fact, Henry A. P. Carter in first class was trying to avoid the late dinners by being allowed at the second-class table. The steamer *Sacramento* proved to be a large one of three thousand tons and so broad in the beam that there was but little motion even with quite a sea running.

Panama Bay, Sanford wrote home, was a beautiful place, dotted with thickly wooded islands, the low shores rising to bluffs and hills and gradually rolling ridges very like the hunting grounds of Pihanakalani on the windward slopes of Kauai. During the whole double voyage of five weeks less eight hours to New York only one sensation had exceeded Sanford's expectations and that was the strange exhilaration of riding in the train of cars at Panama. While waiting for the cars to start, the passengers had been accosted by scores of darkeys noisily offering their wares of everything from brandy and food stuffs to monkeys with pants on. The three hours' ride across the Isthmus was indeed novel. At first the young Sandwich Islander felt convinced that the whole contraption was running away, regardless of frail bridges no wider than the cars themselves. But the swift motion soon entered so wholly into his blood that, had he been the driver, he felt certain that he would be putting on full steam ahead and sitting on the safety valve.

The voyage from Aspinwall to New York was as smooth as from San Francisco to Panama—in fact, a common whaleboat would have been safe. The profile of Jamaica looked very like the outline of Kauai from the northeast. Entrance into New York harbor was very fine, coming in sight of the low sandy shores of New Jersey early in the morning, the wind blowing hard and very cold. We took a pilot, he wrote, from a pilot boat with a model just like our crack schooner, the *Nettie Merrill*, at home. Then we began to see tug boats and more pilot boats, then ships inward- and outward-bound, with schooners, brigs, sloops, and steamers, a most enlivening scene, till we neared the Narrows. The poor cholera ships were anchored at outer quarantine; then came the beautiful shores of Staten Island, with her noble villas amid trees just unfolding light green leaves. Beyond the Narrows came the forts and batteries on either side as we entered the quiet waters of the splendid bay, were detained perhaps ten minutes at quarantine, and then moved on to the big city behind its surrounding hedges of masts.

Once ashore on the sixth floor at Lovejoy's lodging house, clothes seemed a first necessity, since the young traveler had feared for some time that his old sack suit might give out. But his real pleasure consisted in seeing Island friends like Bill Castle, who went around with him the rest of the day, through the charm of Trinity Church and up its two hundred and eighty-four-foot spire to view the city, later riding all through the finest streets in the horse cars. Next day he took Dr. Smith's letter, and hunted a long time before finding the right tailor's shop on Bowery Street, but once found, in five seconds he knew by the eyes and shape of the face which of the two tailors was Dr. Smith's brother. After a long talk, he joined Castle again for a visit to the Brooklyn Navy Yard, boarding the two ironclads, *Puritan* and *Roanoke,* and watching some immense ironclads a-building.

Next came Connecticut and his mother's people, but he kept wondering whether his father had had any trouble with the steers, and whether he himself would not be hearing from home inside of a month. Yet he felt very much at home on the old farm at Greenwich, where Aunt Sally Close, who reminded him of Mother Bishop, met him with a kiss, and Uncle Isaac went to the store with him to post his home letters. Here Uncle introduced him as George Dole, but one of the girls there remarked that he couldn't come *that* over her. Soon Sanford was busy dropping corn for Uncle in a stony field south of the barn, saw robins for the first time and a whippoorwill in the woods, tried fishing down along the brook to the sawmill, but "nary fish"; went to see Uncle Maiah at the place where there were so many ancient aunts and the ideal big old-fashioned kitchen; made a boat for small cousin Bartow; gave Uncle a haircut and shampoo while he was playing his fiddle; saw the first blacksnake killed with a scythe; helped plow and plant pumpkins and sorghum; showed Uncle how to play *nia* and had games of dominoes with Aunt Sally; bought an ice cream at Port Chester; hoed corn, wrote letters and helped Uncle cut timber.

From Williams College came welcoming letters from Will

Rowell, who with Oliver Emerson rejoiced at the prospect of an accession to the ranks of the "Cannibals," told Sanford to have the stage driver bring him right to Room 5 in Kellogg Hall, and was glad to hear that he was to have another brother George, news of Clara Rowell's engagement to George Dole having reached him apparently before it had Sanford.

Friends recently made in the Islands were two young Boston men, William T. Brigham, a cousin of Judge Austin of Honolulu, and Horace Mann, Jr., son of the eminent educator. Young Mann was making a botanical study, which, as *An Enumeration of Hawaiian Plants* was first published from the proceedings of the American Academy of Arts and Sciences in September 1866 and was issued as a separate volume the following year. Brigham had remained in the Islands six months longer than his friend, collecting for him a number of valuable botanical specimens, while himself working on a study of volcanoes. This became a *Memoir* of the Boston Society of Natural History and was published in 1866 under the title: *Notes on Volcanoes of the Hawaiian Islands.*

In June of 1866, while on the Connecticut farm, Sanford received an appreciative letter from Horace Mann, Jr., thanking him for his trouble in assembling, presumably from the dunes below his home at Koloa, a collection of Hawaiian skulls and forwarding them to Cambridge. Very soon too came appreciation from Professor Wyman for whose work the skulls had been intended. In stating that they make a very important addition to their ethnological series, Mr. Wyman asked for any tradition or other data on the locality where they had been found and their condition on excavation.

Not so many years before this a box of Hawaiian crania sent home to his New England father by the young enthusiast, James Jackson Jarves, had met with caustic remarks from the parental pen. By Hawaiians young Jarves had been called *Po Kanaka* (Skull Man). Sanford Dole not only escaped such a reception in America, but, in 1868 when visiting the Agassiz Museum at Harvard with Will Brigham, was cordially greeted by Professor Agassiz himself, and learned that the Hawaiian skulls sent from Koloa were considered the finest and most complete collection of crania ever to reach Harvard. In Gray's herbarium Horace Mann, Jr. introduced Sanford to Professor Gray, and later they took dinner with Mrs. Mann. "That box of skulls was a lucky thing for me," wrote Sanford to his father, "especially in introducing me among scientific men in Boston."

By June of 1866 Sanford received his second batch of home letters, among them a very tender and loving one from his mother written on the 23d of April, his twenty-second birthday. It had not been easy to see Sanford go, but their hopes of him were high. On a visit in New York he had seen Uncle Nathan Dole, who asked him all about Brother Daniel, and introduced Sanford to Judge Lowth, who said he had known Sanford's "first mother." On returning to Stamford he met many Knapp and Close relatives who asked about his mother Charlotte, and he assured them that she would be visiting among them herself before many years had passed. One uncle was adding a room to his house for her and wished Sanford to write and ask her what color she preferred to have it painted. A great many fine residences impressed the Island youth at Stamford and elsewhere, yet, none had he seen so far with a prettier or pleasanter yard about it than his at home; he added in his letter to his mother: "I can see just how things look, how you look and I love you all better, if it is possible, for this separation." He wrote:

What a lot of old ladies there are here! They amuse me! Uncle Samuel sends his love to Mother. Sunday was foggy, but we went down to church at Horse Neck in the old carriage that has been running for the last forty years. Down at Port Chester the thermometer stood at 113°, so they said. We had ice creams, a special weakness of mine, but I believe good for the health. Often on the farm it is 98° when we are haying. But I enjoy it all, especially the farm and my pleasant north room upstairs. Sometimes it is so warm that I sleep part of the night on the floor by the open window.

And I do like Uncle Isaac very much. He is good company and just as full of fun and high spirits as any boy, and he can tell off the names of about eighty birds which abound in Greenwich. When we go to Sunday School, he and I sit back by one of the cold stoves and talk about the girls. He wishes me to come during winter vacation to help eat buckwheat cakes with sorghum syrup.

But I am in a hurry to get to studying. Think I shall get a book or two to study while I am at Maine, perhaps one on surveying. Who knows but what I may some day be engaged in the Hawaiian coast survey?

Perhaps I was in too much of a hurry to leave home. A month later would have left my canefield with less trouble for Father. But I am glad to hear that the men have been faithful. Solomon does so well that it may be easier to have him for *luna* over them all. Give my aloha to him and Lihilihi and all the rest. And about selling the cane or sugar, do just as you think best. And be sure that the men are well paid for their work.

On the way to Maine, Boston was the first stop. Here Sanford turned the sum of $8.00 gold, entrusted to him by Father Wilcox, into twelve currency and with that bought a clock from the same store as the Doles' clock. Sanford wrote home:

It is a good clock, of sound orthodox exterior, and I feel assured that Mr. Wilcox will be pleased with it. I left it a few days for the man to run and regulate, and then took it to Gould & Lincoln's to be shipped. I bought a book by Gillespie on surveying and like it very much as more practical than any other I have seen. In Boston too Will Brigham took me to the Natural History Museum, and to Cambridge where the buildings were interesting, but Commencement rather dull. Dr. Wood of Koloa Plantation sat on the platform with the dignitaries and when I made my way up after the exercises to speak to him, he looked as if he could not believe his eyes, but conversed benignantly with me and asked me to call.

After Cambridge, followed a few days at Grafton, Will Brigham's summer home. Arriving at the Boston station just as the Grafton cars pulled out, tall young Brigham sung out and broke into a run. "I followed," wrote Sanford, "both of us running very fast; they let us through the gate to the platform and off we galloped again; the hind car was just showing its heels, but we reached the steps and slung ourselves in, *pau ia pilikia* (the trouble was over). A short but furious thunderstorm met us at Grafton, also, with the carriage, Brigham's sister, a charming girl. And his father and mother and three brothers were all as kind as could be."

In a long talk young Brigham outlined to Sanford plans for building two large schooners of about 250 tons each with funds already partially subscribed for a thorough exploration of the islands of the Pacific; the ships, having been equipped for surveying and collecting, to be sent around the Horn for a two-year cruise, touching at Honolulu for supplies. It sounded too good to be true when he offered Sanford any post he wished in the expedition, and proposed taking President Alexander of Punahou as chaplain. This ambitious project did not take ultimate form, but its early suggestion by William Tufts Brigham, whose name, twenty years later, became almost synonymous with the Polynesian researches of the Bernice Pauahi Bishop Museum at Honolulu, carries more than passing significance, particularly also in view of similar expeditions conducted in the Pacific in more recent years.

From Boston Sanford took boat for Bath, Maine, only to find Uncle Ballard off on a cruise, but young Cousin Sanford quite ready to go in the cars along the Kennebec up-stream to Hallowell, a quiet little town where the two Sanfords had a swim and picked raspberries on the riverbank. Calling at the house of a cousin, they found her sister, Emily Ballard, who showed them an album signed twenty-five years before by Daniel Dole, about whom the legend had grown up that it had been his habit to prop his Latin book open on the handle of the plow, while at work in the fields. But of the Emily Ballard of 1840 echoes seemed few; even her own sisters were gone, yet somehow their letters from her at Honolulu had been kept, and later were given to Sanford and George as the nearest approach to the lost miniature of their own mother.

In August the end of Sanford's Maine pilgrimage came a little farther up the Kennebec at Skowhegan, where Grandmother Dole proved to be as nice as all grandmothers should be. The portrait of his father as a young man, which hung over the mantel, seemed at first entirely unfamiliar to Sanford, but, as with George, he soon began to find familiar lines in it. Grandmother's first gift to him was a pair of woolen socks she had knit for him, of yarn which she had carded and spun herself. And to watch her working at her own spinning wheel was worth coming far to see. He wrote:

She and Cousin Mary are much pleased with the scarfs brought from Koloa. Mary says there is no man she would rather see than Uncle Daniel, of whom she has heard so much. She proves to be a precise young lady, plays the piano well, and studies music seriously. But would she condescend to such a carnal amusement as chess? I have a set of chessmen and have spent a rainy forenoon making a chess board, in hopes.

In early times the name Skowhegan (watching point) marked the falls on the Kennebec, where Indians waited for salmon in the spring of the year. For young Sanford Dole, the best fun at Skowhegan was swimming every day in the Kennebec and teaching his young cousin Pearson to swim, the same cousin who was to appear in Honolulu just before the turn of the century. One day the two cousins went up the river in a boat with Uncle Isaiah to see part of the old farm and drink from the well dug by Daniel Dole as a boy; another day they went fishing and paddled down the river to the place where Sanford's father had been born. At the shoemaker's, old McPherson said, "Are you the son of Dan'l Dole that went to the Sandwich Islands? I used to know him well." And on their way, five miles up the river to Norridgewock, named for a famous Chief Norridgewog, Sanford was delighted to shoot one of the Kennebec ducks, not much like the Kauai ducks, and which his father had warned him were far too wild to shoot, but which nevertheless proved very good eating.

Ten days' camping at Moosehead Lake, going up on foot with Cousin Charlie, Uncle Nathan Dole's son, each carrying about 20 pounds, including blanket, gun, ammunition, and rations, were varied by finding good food at farm houses, shooting two ducks at one crack and a partridge apiece; also by taking the steamer for Mount Kineo and spending Sunday at a farm. At the outlet of the lake Sanford caught three trout, after which, on Charlie's advice, they struck out thirty miles across the swamps to the Forks where the Dead River runs into the Kennebec, but where no one lived except in logging season. Through lonely, solemn pine woods in heavy rains, they had the misfortune of losing their compass with the impossibility of finding the old logging roads, they took campers' luck philosophically and were glad enough to reach the outlet of the lake and finally the Skowhegan stage. "Tell George Rowell," added Sanford, "that the *auku* (night herons) at Moosehead Lake stand about three feet high. I have a wing feather of one of them which is eighteen and a half inches long."

Factories seemed to abound in the neighborhood of this Long-Land-Water, and Sanford watched, fascinated by the mechanical carding of wool or the shredding of poplar logs into fine husks for excelsior mattresses and doormats. And at the paper mill, out came his watch to time the processing of the soft wood pulp through the rollers and dryers, until wound off as finished paper ready for the printing press. Time: exactly one minute and a half.

In a skate factory he resolved soon to get himself a pair of skates, for he was convinced that he could not survive even one winter deprived of the zest of that sport.

On the way to college at Williamstown, Sanford went down the Kennebec to Bath, where he took the boat to Boston. Here he called at the law office of Senator Brigham, who was most cordial and gave him a letter of introduction to President Mark Hopkins of Williams College. It was the Senator's son, W. T. Brigham, a graduate of Harvard in 1862, who had spent three years in Hawaii, partly as an instructor at Punahou; returning by way of China, India, and Europe, he was admitted to the bar and served also as instructor in botany at Harvard.

Hardly had Sanford Dole reached Williamstown in 1866 before a very kind letter came from young Brigham, expressing regrets that Dole had not had time to give Brigham more swimming lessons on his way to college. Brigham wrote of having told Professor and Mrs. Chadbourne that something good was coming to Williams from Hawaii; also that he felt Williams ranked ahead of Amherst, and of all New England colleges had the best gymnasium, which Sanford would surely enjoy; and that Sanford was fortunate to be taking a university course, elective subjects from Senior and Junior years without entrance examinations, an improvement not yet current even at Harvard. He added:

I should like to know what you select for studies; remember the offer of half my bed whenever you can come, and know that while I am digging into dusty old law books, I shall be sorely tempted to covet your chances for rambles into the hills with Rowell and Emerson. Old Saddleback is not far, and looks enough like a crater to be homelike to Cannibals.

My *Volcanoes of Hawaii* has got on well and will be done this month, if Father Coan writes me about the last eruption. Queen Emma has been bundled off by her British exhibitors, who were afraid of the Boston influences on their protégé. So our Hawaiian Club has lost a grand spree.

September and October found Sanford well launched in his college work, but many a reminder of home took him back over continent and ocean. He wrote:

Your stockings, Mother, which you knit for me are tip-top, and will last me till I get home. Grandmother and Aunt Sally have given me a good supply of woolen stockings. I have been mending a rip in my pants, and shall henceforth appreciate such stitches taken for me.

A little boy brought some apples into my room this morning. I bought a few large ones, at about two cents apiece, and told him to bring me a peck next Saturday. I think I have not yet eaten as good apples here as we used to get at the Islands from Oregon. Pears are the fruit for me, the best raised in this country. But they cost too much! I long to be strolling through our Koloa garden while mangoes and peaches are ripe. I feel rich in the love of father and mother and brother, and think my home one of the best and pleasantest in the world. How high has my cane grown? A June copy of the *Advertiser* in Oliver Emerson's room has interested me in the doings of the Legislature in Honolulu, which I certainly hope will not pass the bill legalizing paper currency.

Williamstown is a pretty place, expecially the college grounds, well shaded with large maple trees already turning to gold and red, just as those in Maine were doing a month ago.

Calling on President Hopkins, Sanford had found him a kind old gentleman. Sanford's first Senior study, philosophy of rhetoric, seemed rather deep, but he wrote:

I have been running to grass too long and must reform my habits. We recite twice a day in rhetoric and shall be finished next week, the Seniors taking one subject at a time and rapidly. Every Saturday we recite to the President in the catechism. From our first hour last Saturday this promises to be one of our most interesting studies. Hopkins is a fine instructor, a little like Dr. Wood in appearance and voice, but without the dollar look of the latter.

I board with a club of eleven others, all fine Christian men. There is a prayer meeting with one of the professors at one every day, and class prayer meetings every Friday evening. On Sunday we attend morning and afternoon service in the chapel, and in the evening a discussion meeting of the Mills Theological Society.

In October Sanford was grateful to receive his overcoat by express from Greenwich, with a bundle of pears and a letter from Aunt Sally, who was pleased that Sanford had made up his mind to behave at college, "instead of helping to hoist cows into the belfry." Uncle Isaac, she reports, had made over one hundred gallons of sorghum syrup, and there would be good apples and "pumking" pies when Sanford gets home to Greenwich again.

At college Sanford had now three lectures a day on anatomy by the manikin, from President Hopkins, and one on zoölogy by Professor Chadbourne, all very interesting. In November, Senior elections for class-day honors proved a stormy affair, until the class president resigned and Sanford was elected to take his place for the remainder of the term. "I took no great part in the disturbance," he remarked, "but could not very well help being

drawn into it." Perhaps this is a foreshadowing of his ultimate
role as political peacemaker in Hawaii. On Saturday "quite a
row" enlivened the classic shades of the college, the Freshmen
hanging an effigy of the Sophomore class on a gallows on Kellogg
Hall and announcing that there would be a funeral later. The
Sophomores wrested the corpse from them, however. A second
effigy was promptly made, but the relics of this corpse too
were snatched back and forth, even in front of the President.
Hats were smashed and noses banged until some upper classmen
intervened and surrendered the ragged corpus to President
Hopkins.

This may have been an occasion on which most of the students
sported canes, as Sanford had explained in an earlier letter with
a sketch of his own Island cane. This had been much admired
after he had had it repolished in San Francisco, and topped with
an ivory head, perhaps a souvenir from some whaling ship. He
included a tiny sketch of the solid, square handle, and before very
long gave a diagram too of the Kellogg Hall rooms, where he
chummed it with William Rowell and Oliver Emerson. An over-
night guest with them was Sam, "Parson Damon," as they called
the Honolulu chaplain's oldest son. Parson had visited out West
and was in high spirits over it all, but content now to go back
to the Islands to live where "the horses don't trot."

One of their November excursions with some good stiff
climbing was to the top of Mount Greylock, called the highest
mountain in Massachusetts, though that was not saying much,
the Sandwich Islanders thought. "However, we were rewarded
by finding snow on the summit," exulted Sanford, "the first time
I had seen it to handle it. The thermometer stood at 26° Fahren-
heit at the top, where we had a fine view of Mount Monadnock,
the Fishkill and the Adirondack ranges."

At the annual meeting of the American Board of Foreign
Missions in Pittsfield in October, the Cannibals from Williams had
enjoyed two days of meetings and visits among friends. Of
particular interest were the Binghams, father and son, the younger
Hiram soon to leave for Honolulu in command of the second
Morning Star, sent on tours of mission stations in Micronesia.
A month later Will Brigham attended the farewell service from
Boston on the new ship which proved to be a pretty little yacht

rigged like the first one, everything about her new and clean. Dr. Anderson of the American Board, Father Bingham, and Captain Bingham all addressed the meeting; late in the afternoon the brig hauled out into the stream and next morning sailed into a north wind.

News of droughts in Koloa boded ill for any income from Sanford's canefield, but he was not unduly downcast, his chief concern being that his Hawaiian helpers should be adequately paid. At Christmas vacation he cured a heavy cold in no time, just by going to see Aunt Sally and Uncle Ike at the farm; tried out the gym at Harvard, but found it by no means equal to the one at Williams; and got back to college in January of 1867, arriving with other students in the cars about nine in the evening, five miles from Williams at North Adams, where they completely filled the sleigh omnibus drawn by two laboring horses. He wrote home:

"As cold as Greenland's icy mountains" it surely was, often the shout came, "Everybody out!" to dislodge the sleigh stuck in a deep hole, and a sudden pitch of the whole thing would send them all flying into a heap in a kiss-me-quick style. But even at 15° or 20° below zero it is all great fun; going to meals and classes through four feet of snow, the wind crusts our ears and cheeks with ice, oh, it is excruciatingly jolly! The temptation to throw snowballs is too strong to be resisted; several times I have gone over into deep snow in a tussle, but I generally contrive to have the other fellow underneath.

On the icy streets of New York at Christmas it was not easy to maintain an upright demeanor. But I did get to some of the best free picture galleries both there and in Boston where the galleries far excel those in New York. How I wish you would let me spend fifty or one hundred dollars in pictures for beautifying our home at Koloa. *Please!* Beside regular work in Political Economy and Geology, my choice in Fine Art is Landscape Gardening, as noble as any art, it seems to me, to create the beautiful results of one's labors with the aid of sun and rain and soil, to be sure, but rivalling even nature itself.

By February, Sanford was envying the men who had already settled on professions. He himself was especially concerned about being able in time to square the account with his parents. He had already talked personally with President Hopkins who impressed him more and more as "a clear and forcible teacher, a remarkable man, a deep thinker, in a word a Socrates. Moreover, he approves of dancing and on occasion has been seen at a ball," which was quite radical for a man who had been president of the American Board of Missions for the last ten years! Added to all this, Sanford told his father, "Prex is so dignified and yet genial, kind and fatherly. Why, he even called on us three Cannibals in our rooms the other day."

During spring vacation Sanford and Will Brigham visited Washington, Philadelphia, and Richmond, a treat indeed, especially the public buildings of the national capital: the Patent Office and Treasury Department, immense structures of white granite; the Smithsonian Institution with its collections in natural history and the fine arts; all set in such beautiful gardens, a splendid city in the making. On the Potomac, shad fishing was lively; wild swans waddled along the banks which were beautiful in bluff and slope and foliage, with a fair view of Mount Vernon and the forts on the Maryland banks.

Describing for his mother his room with Rowell and Emerson at Williams, Sanford spoke of hanging baskets at all the windows, his own supporting an ivy that ran around three sides of the room and "beats every plant the other fellows have." Other outdoor friends also added their cheer, especially on rainy spring days. These included a young crow as black as Othello; also a chipmunk with his revolving wheel, and a bull frog in a glass jar of water. A pair of robins had nested in a tree just outside the window and were beginning to feed their young ones assiduously.

Class Day would come in two weeks and Sanford found himself already regretting the inevitable partings. In recent elections for Class Day honors, he had been chosen to the Adelphic Union for one of the orations. For this he selected as his theme: "The Martyr Spirit." But the burden of his home letter of June 20 disclosed his decision to study law for a year in Senator Brigham's office and return to practice in Honolulu. The die was cast. With grief he realized that he must still receive financial help from his father and mother, although he had done his best to earn his own way; before many years, however, he planned to repay some of the very real help which they had given him.

Following Commencement, came a jaunt after his heart's desire, nothing less than a boat cruise down the Connecticut River. While he had remained buried in the snows of Williamstown, Brigham,

Jr., had pursued his long-cherished plan of having a flat-bottomed river boat built, eighteen feet long with two small lockers. This he had had shipped to northern Maine, where with Emerson and Folsom the four young men launched it early in August. Then they proceeded to pull the four hundred miles through Maine, New Hampshire, Vermont, and Massachusetts, clear to Springfield, spending all but three or four nights cooking over a fire and sleeping in their tent. Once they were taken for gypsies and had a merry call from some village damsels.

The only drawback had been that since Brigham could not swim, his father, denouncing the whole project as foolhardy in the extreme, had been in misery until the three weeks were over. Even deep, swift water in the worst rapids however had not succeeded in capsizing the boat. Sometimes they had crackers and milk to eat, occasionally Emerson or Dole would shoot a merganser duck for supper, and they lived well. Sanford's forearm gained half an inch in circumference, they were all as brown as Indians and voted the river cruise a splendid success, the more so because it was such a hairbreadth achievement to get through according to original plan and with the boat almost intact.

August was an eventful month too for brother George at home. Having become manager of Koloa Plantation at the beginning of the year, he had very soon begun to fit up the little old stone house which had been the manager's residence and was still in use by the plantation until 1955. To this stone house George Dole brought his bride, Clara Rowell, on August 17, 1867, with such promise of happiness that they always referred to it as Paradise.

By the 31st of August, Sanford had commenced his reading of *Kent's Commentaries,* finding the law a vast science, and looking forward to hard work. On Senator Brigham's advice and by his own choice, he would attend cases in the Boston courts instead of law school in Cambridge. His little room was cheerful with a fragrant geranium plant, a fuchsia and a begonia, also a hanging basket with a creeper. Here he was better off than at Williams, for he had excellent food and could get in his seven-mile walk every day. He had taken a class of boys in Edward Everett Hale's Sunday School, having been repeatedly urged to do it, and studied up the lesson in the life of Christ every Saturday night with Will Brigham. He would have liked to play whist occasionally, a game chiefly of skill, but deferred to his parents' wishes in the matter, although he confessed to a mental confusion as to the type of logic which would ban this, and yet allow dominoes and backgammon which were only card games of chance under other guises.

The Hawaiian Club of Boston, which was doing much for the Islands, especially with regard to the Reciprocity Treaty so much opposed in Congress, had elected young Dole a member. He found that most of the members were opposed to the annexation of the Islands to the United States. "How is the feeling on this at home?" he asked. Will Brigham was to deliver a course of Lowell lectures at Cambridge that fall on "Volcanic Phenomena." Sanford had heard for the first time the thunder of the big organ at Music Hall, as guest of Senator Brigham at a meeting of the Unitarian Association.

Dr. Edward Everett Hale, author of *The Man Without a Country,* and a Unitarian in freedom of thought, was nevertheless from the year 1856 pastor for forty-three years of Boston's South Congregational Church. His primary concern was a general betterment of human relations, social, political, personal. Young Sanford Dole he called one of his boys, welcomed him to church and often invited him to his home. In later years, Dr. Hale was to refer to himself as a Dole cousin, when he learned that his great-great-grandmother was a descendant of Richard Dole of Newbury, Massachusetts, the first of that name in America.

It seemed to Sanford that the Unitarian churches were far higher in the exercise of the Christ spirit than many of the so-called orthodox churches, which were often rent asunder with disputes. It might be that a merging of the best of the two, the liberals and the more orthodox of the Unitarians, would yet bring about the most perfect earthly church. Sanford felt that beliefs once held implicitly must be examined anew. "I can no more help this than I can help dreaming when I am asleep," he explained to his father. "Perhaps somehow in the last year or so I have involuntarily passed from boyhood to manhood. I think less of sectarian differences. I judge men, not by their creeds, but by their lives. While great and good theologians are perplexed, it were strange indeed if such young minds as mine were not troubled on these points."

It was now December, a clear, sunny day—with the temperature at zero. People rushed along, rubbing their ears and slapping their hands against their sides; horses trotted with icicles hanging from their lips and at every breath puffing great clouds of vapor like high-pressure engines. Sanford took a hasty bath every morning, the water so cold that he got out red and burning as if immersed in boiling water; then rubbed down and felt as if he could sit on the North Pole at least long enough to take a cup of coffee. He wrote:

Last week I heard Dickens read from *Nicholas Nickleby* as under teacher in Squeers school and also Boots at the Holly Tree Inn. A wonderful reader he is, very dramatic in his delivery. To get tickets for the Dickens lecture, one of the Andover men stood in line, in December too, from midnight until morning. I have been reading Mr. Pickwick, often with a hearty laugh. To me, he is one of the most philosophical men on record, and I already entertain a definite admiration for his character.

Cousin Charles Fletcher Dole, who had made the Moosehead Lake excursion in Maine with Sanford, was at Cambridge where the two often had long talks. They had made a long-range acquaintance in childhood, through an exchange of butternut meats gathered at Chelsea, Massachusetts, and sent in a missionary box to Honolulu, whence the box would in time return filled with "strange bits of coral and lava and pretty shells, ringing still with the surf-beat of the Pacific." This Charles recounts in his own story, *My Eighty Years*. His father, Daniel Dole's brother Nathan, had been an editor for the American Mission Board in Boston, and would sometimes take his small son on the steam-ferry from Chelsea to visit the American Board museum of curiosities. Wide-eyed, the child would gaze at all kinds and sizes of idols, "the false gods of the heathen," ferociously bejeweled with sharks' teeth.

Strange, thought Charles, that the tall Cousin Sanford of 1867 was totally unimpressed by these same images when he in turn visited the little museum with Dr. Rufus Anderson. But, countered Sanford, "I grew up with the most fearsome and ferocious of them all, the huge old idol that we hardly even noticed when we trudged past him a dozen times a day in Old School Hall at Punahou!"

As young men, Charles and Sanford often discussed their

mutual variance from the rigid beliefs of their fathers, both of whom were Congregational ministers of the old school, and both of them revered by their sons. Sanford had made his decision for the study of law; Charles had also made his, for the ministry, but with his own mental reservations. Sanford felt that his New England cousin was far ahead of him in the amount of classical learning with which he was armed, Harvard seeming to produce more learned, but perhaps less scholarly men than Williams: "that is, they really know more, but do they know it as well?" Charles, in his turn felt that Sanford was "already quite open to liberal thinking."

One never-to-be-forgotten evening the cousins called by appointment on the young Dr. William B. Wright, whom Sanford had come to admire and love. Charles placed him as the minister of a very ugly brick church, known for its steeple as the "Holy Corkscrew." Never had these two ministers' sons heard the gospel as it was when Dr. Wright gave it to them, "with such simplicity, such enthusiasm, and on such broad lines of sympathy," wrote Charles, adding, "I needed to see such a man as that, who believed in his religion!"

In his letters home Sanford wrote of Will Rowell as at Brooklyn, New York, expecting employment from Nevins Armstrong of Hawaii. The latter, experimenting in the distillation of turpentine, would, if successful, send Rowell to the Carolinas to ship pine logs.

John Burbank, formerly of Koloa Plantation, is apparently to make his home in Maryland, did not buy a farm, as he wrote me he might in West Virginia. I went to hear a young preacher recently who had started out as a dentist; his sermon was so narrow-minded and dull, it seemed unfortunate for the world that he did not stick to pulling teeth. Dickens I have grown to consider one of the great moral influences of the age; few have done so much to make humanity more humane. I am continuing to read his works in the evenings, and have begun reading in the Hawaiian *Kuokoa*, the life of Kamehameha I by Kamakau.

Sanford's keen interest in birds had begun to culminate in the study of ornithology. Tuesday evening was set apart for this, when he went with Will Brigham to the Museum of Natural History. Sanford wrote:

Brigham is studying Geology and has a room warmed on that evening, so I have the advantage of a library on ornithology, many of the volumes costly and beautiful. Part of July I spent collecting specimens of birds near the farm at Greenwich. At no place have I found so great a variety of small birds, as there are around the old farm. I shot my first wood-cock there and was quite proud of it, for it takes a quick hand and eye. They are less than half the size of mud hens, and jump up out of the bushes and whirr off like a flash.

A winter of busy days and nights ensued. By April 28 Sanford had shipped his fowling piece home. In May he enjoyed much the Boston visit of Cousins Annie Ward and her mother, Mrs. Titcomb, from Newburyport, particularly hearing with them the oratorio *Samson* at Music Hall. Sanford was appointed joint editor with Brigham and Hunnewell, Jr., for the quarterly published by the Hawaiian Club. He went rowing on the Charles River, and saw *Uncle Tom's Cabin* played. Sporting summer suits and straw hats, he and Brigham drove off in a buggy to enjoy the charming countryside of Boston, Roxbury, Brookline, and Brighton. There came also happy visits at Newburyport with boating on the beautiful Merrimac River as well as the ocean; and a Hawaiian Club spread at General Marshall's Riverside home in honor of General Hartwell, an able young jurist and member of the Massachusetts legislature, who was leaving an assured career in his native state, to try his fortunes in Hawaii as Associate Justice of the Supreme Court.

Rejoicing in a special remittance from home for the purchase of law books, Sanford wrote from an overflowing heart to acknowledge the gift and to regret the inevitable costliness of such volumes. He had even thought of borrowing from Hunnewell for the purpose, and hoped that his parents were not denying themselves for his sake. "With my new suit I may seem like the son of a rich man," he tells them,

but if you could only know with what solemnity I buy a pair of gloves, or how I have resisted sore temptation to spend my, or rather your, money on fruit or candy or beggars or soda water or ice cream. Still, I have faith that my profession will some time square the account. This is a June day as hot as Purgatory, too hot for the law, and I am writing in my room in the whitest of Chinese cotton pajamas, and touching only on the calmest and most unexciting subjects.

But you first of all must know the good news which has reached me through Senator Brigham: I am to have the chance of going into Judge Austin's office when I start in Honolulu. This is quite unexpected, and I thoroughly appreciate the advantage it offers me. Cushman Jones of Honolulu, a cousin of Mr. Austin and another Bostonian, encourages me too. I had expected to nail up my shingle and trust in Providence alone.

For all his preoccupation with the law, however, Sanford's thoughts turned often to his friends, the Hawaiians, and their needs. He delighted to hear that his mother and George's wife were able to visit more among the natives in Koloa. It had been a mistake, he reflected, to drop so much of the intimate calling from house to house, especially among those regarded as the *poe aia,* or black sheep. Thundering at them from the Sunday pulpit, and then shunning many of the younger and wilder ones on week-days, seemed to have in it little of real influence and true religion. He wrote:

At Greenwich recently the superintendent persuaded me to open the Sabbath School with prayer, which I obediently did, but absent-mindedly, with one glove on. Here in Boston I attend the Berkeley Street Church more than any other, thinking of their pastor, Dr. Wright, quite a young man from Chicago, as my own pastor. For live Christian preaching I prefer him to any other man I have heard in Boston. Before leaving for a visit to England, he asked me to breakfast one morning. Heretofore, he has been a loved and trusted teacher, but this time I at once took him to my heart as a brother. I have watched and listened to that man with increasing wonder; and what my mind and soul have gained from him I consider as not less valuable than a college year of study. I expect that he will become famous. He is young yet, and is growing fast. He has more refinement than Beecher, with equal eloquence and originality. If I could be a preacher like him, law might go.

Like this new friend, Sanford Dole, though young yet, was growing fast. It is a rewarding study in the course of these two New England years, to turn and turn again the pages of his letters, all so methodically dated in his father's hand as they arrived at Koloa. Week by week one watches the young mind unfolding, reaching out in new directions, while not his thinking only, but his very handwriting too grows clearer and more incisive, surer and more mature. Undisturbed by the conviction of many, including Aunt Sally Close, that he is destined to return to New England as a preacher of the gospel, he forges quietly ahead on his own unhurried way. As he himself more than half suspects, the boy who had left Koloa two years before has become a man.

In July, Harvard Commencement was attended in weather resembling far too closely Nebuchadnezzar's fiery furnace. At Williamstown there was his own class anniversary, with the real pleasure of seeing one of his best friends, Sam Buck, and at Commencement earlier graduates like Sam Armstrong, who had been an older boy at Punahou. After the experiences of three years during the Civil War, he was still known everywhere as General Armstrong and did not at first recognize Sanford Dole, perhaps because his mind was still with his reconstruction work among freedmen at Hampton, Virginia. Soldiering, he said, had set him to thinking; he was not made for a preacher, he would rather minister than be a minister. "Set the people to work," he said, "and the ministers to chewing tobacco, if necessary, to make them like other men, not still and mannerish, but open, hearty and happy. A good healthy laugh is as bad for the devil as some of the long nasal prayers I have heard, yes, worse."

In Maine, came the celebration of Grandmother Dole's eightieth birthday and a final attempt on Sanford's part to know his cousin Mary; by letter the two maintained a friendly exchange, but beyond that, all continued prim and formal. At Greenwich he made a last visit at the farm with Will Rowell whom Aunt Sally found irrepressible with his jokes and tricks. In Boston, Sanford called on Dr. Anderson of the American Board, and talked with him about Father and Mother Dole making a visit to their New England homes. "Before very long," Sanford assured them, "I shall have a home in Honolulu for you on your visits to the Capital."

On September 10 Sanford passed his law examination, wishing he had read more Blackstone than *Kent's Commentaries*. On the 12th he was admitted to practice law at the Suffolk County Bar, and received his diploma. His room that day he found filled with congratulatory flowers from the hands of beauutiful Cousin Annie Titcomb Ward. As to his year's labor and its immediate result, Sanford made the significant comment that he was pleased, though not entirely satisfied. For a young man setting out on a career the year of college followed by only one year reading law must indeed have seemed inadequate even then, but Sanford's versatile interests and zest for life had absorbed much in that short time. In particular, his acquaintance with such men as Senator Brigham, Professor Agassiz, President Mark Hopkins, Captain Hunnewell, Dr. Rufus Anderson, Dr. Edward Everett Hale, and Dr. Phillips Brooks, whom he heard in Philadelphia, as also his own young pastor, Dr. Wright, was to give him unexpected stimulus for all of life to come.

Many of his immediate contemporaries, like Will Brigham, Sam Buck of Williams, and of course home folks like young Gulicks, Armstrongs, Rowells and Emersons, were to bring him close friendships and joyous comradeships. All his life he kept a letter from Albert Judd, a slightly older Mission son, who in 1868 was already in very successful law practice at Honolulu. Judd urged him to return to the Islands, but cautioned him against certain abuse in a profession which was often stigmatized as dishonest. Vexations and obstacles were legion. At the Islands, however, the opportunities of being really serviceable to many were so numerous that he himself had never regretted his choice of returning to practice in his own home town.

All these weeks Sanford continued his serious study of Hawaiian birds, encouraged by Will Brigham who even contributed his own notes, and urged Sanford to send on any corrections, as soon as he got back to the Islands; for the list, the first such study to be made, was to be printed in a few months by the Boston Society of Natural History, of which Sanford was now a corresponding member.

Boston itself, as it began to recede in his thoughts, became increasingly stimulating. "Were I not a Hawaiian," he confessed, "I think I would be a Bostonian." He and Brigham had desks in the latter's father's office at 35 Court Street and both of them had gradually learned to decipher the old gentleman's writing, which resembled turkey tracks and at first seemed quite as blind as Minister Wyllie's notorious hand. Other Boston, or rather Charleston friends, were old Captain Hunnewell and his son. By invitation, Will and Sanford had walked over one evening to take Kona coffee with them, finding an elaborate spread, and, towering over it all, their huge silver urn filled with delicious coffee. Hunnewell Junior showed them his many valuable curiosities. The Captain was an indefatigable talker, with endless tales of the first Kamehameha. He later sent Sanford his picture autographed six years before on his 74th birthday, but with the explanation that at that time he was not ornamental as later with a flowing beard. A similar photograph he had had placed in the Hawaiian Club album.

Many ties drew Sanford homeward. "A returning Prodigal Son," he signed one letter.

But it is not going to be easy to leave my New England friends. Sam Buck, for instance, the most congenial of my classmates, who writes often and always with affection, asks if I have not begun to contribute to the *Atlantic Monthly,* which in Boston is accounted the chief end of man. Then there is the whole Brigham family, with their Sunday night sings, especially when we sing "That Sweet Story of Old;" nothing so takes me back to the time when Mother used to sing that to me; it was the first hymn I learned, when I was four years old. Now when I get home, George's small son will soon be singing it. Will Brigham is delighted that George has put the name Walter Sanford to his boy, and says that if he had a son himself, he would call him Sanford Dole Brigham.

At last, all the goodbyes were said. Sanford, at their request, joined his cousins, Mrs. Titcomb and Mrs. Ward, with little Emma, in New York to sail on the 9th of October for Panama and San Francisco by the fine new 4,000-ton steamship *Alaska.* A Punahou schoolmate, Emily Alexander, was also among the passengers. And quite a group came to wave them off: Nat Emerson, William Gulick, Brigham, Rowell, and even Uncle Ike from Greenwich. A very smooth sea carried them on, little Emma Ward blowing kisses to all, "a perfect little imp and a good deal of trouble, but a general favorite on board." A seabird alighted on one of the ship's boats and Sanford, with an eye to natural history, crawled up and caught it by one leg, getting ferocious bites in the attempt, but he skinned it and preserved the skin.

As they approached Monterey Bay at the Pacific end of the voyage, wild ducks and sea gulls were seen flying about the ship, whales and porpoises sporting on the sea. Reaching San Francisco at midnight on the 3rd of November, they were met by the happy husbands, Titcomb and Ward. After many visits and having bought himself a saddle, Sanford sailed for home on the 18th by the steamer *Montana.* Maui was sighted on the 30th and on the 1st of December Sanford disembarked at Honolulu.

He called at Father Damon's, also on Judge Austin; afterward on Mother Chamberlain, and on Father and Mother Bishop, spending a happy afternoon driving out to Waikiki with Mollie Rice. Born at Punahou when Sanford was five years old, Mollie was one of the girls whose acquaintance he most valued of all those whom he knew anywhere. When he had written her the year before on the death of her sister, Maria Isenberg, she had replied, as always, to "dear brother Sanford," using the Hawaiian transliteration of his name, *Kenapi,* for Sanford.

On the 3rd of December, the young lawyer made a rough crossing of the Kauai channel in the little schooner *Hattie*. On the Nawiliwili wharf stood George Wilcox, who took Sanford home to lunch with him at Grove Farm. Then, riding over the hills toward the west, the homecomer caught his breath and reined in his horse at the top of the ridge, where the green slopes of Koloa came in sight. Koloa! Very few moments in life ever gave any joy equal to the sheer delight of that instant.

In Paradise, the Koloa manager's home, he found George and Clara and baby Walter, but tarried only a few moments. At long last, home to Father's. One may well imagine the welcome awaiting him there. Even the gray cat and sedate Colonel, the old dog, thumping his tail on the veranda, were part of it all, with Crusoe stretching his head over the pasture gate, neighing for sorghum. And within the house were the two whose love and blessing and prayers Sanford always felt to be his rich inheritance.

In the evening, George's family joined them. And it seemed as if New England could not be far away, when they heard of Brother Will Brigham's family; of the untimely death of young Horace Mann; of Will's taking over the keys to his herbarium and his Harvard classes in botany; of Will's longing to come out to the Islands with Sanford; and of his almost gnashing his teeth at having missed the recent eruption from Mauna Loa, which he had himself predicted; and finally, when they read Will's letter of disappointment, at not being able

to go down to Koloa with you, Sanford, to share your joy in getting home, a joy, which can never be repeated, but I know you enjoyed it enough for both. And although you have not wasted your substance in riotous living, Sanford, you will no doubt be quite as welcome to your home, and your elder brother probably will not refuse to see you. How I wish the plantation would send George on here so that I could see him again! I cannot get you out of my mind today, and I tell you, Sanford, if I could do anybody as much good as you have done me, I should be content, and consider my chance of canonization in one heart secure. What greater treasure can a man have than a friend?

The next two months brought happy days in the island garden, Kauai always to remain to Sanford Dole the best island of all for a breath of fresh air, when cares of business or state pressed heavily. The two months of December and January were spent mostly in the open, surveying with George Wilcox for the Kamooloa ditch to Koloa, leveling in the gap, shooting ducks at Mahaulepu, hunting pigs at Halemanu, branding cattle, on Sundays often reading sermons for his father who was not very well; above all, Christmas dinner and long talks with his father and mother in the evenings, almost always on New England themes.

During these two years and more New England had grown into the very texture and substance of his being, had become, not an adopted country, but almost as integral and intimate a part of his thought as the Islands themselves. And long afterward, with the quiet ease characteristic of him even amid all the repercussions of the Hawaiian Revolution and with a mounted guard patroling his Honolulu home, Sanford Dole was to tell a representative of the *New York World* that, indigenous though he himself was in this island world of almost perpetual summer, nothing in his life had affected him more intensely or more strangely than his first experience of New England emerging from its dark, frozen winter of leafless trees into the glow and bloom of spring. The very air seemed to soften and brighten toward a mystic change, filling one at times with a strange enchantment, an unreal, dreamy state of the senses, indescribable and delicious. There was about such a transformation something unearthly, beyond even the reach of dreams.

Chapter V

HONOLULU
1869–1873

BETWEEN its backdrop of climbing green mountains with open valleys and its foreground of changeless, yet ever-changing blue ocean, the straggling village of Sanford Dole's birthplace and boyhood bore only distant resemblance to the busy seaport and capital city where he was to spend the rest of his life.

As a lad of twelve, from the slight elevation of Punchbowl Hill, his eyes had once followed the lines of Honolulu which looked, he concluded, like nothing so much as a dull checkerboard of dusty lanes and cross lanes marked here and there by a few houses, bare of green leaves save lines of coconut tufts or groups of spreading *kou* and *wiliwili* trees near the sea, with here and there thickets of *hau* arbors; also the feathery *algaroba* at the Roman Catholic Mission on Fort Street with its many seedlings scattered out across the plains as wispy shrubs of wild *kiawe* along paths where Punahou boys, taking cows back to the village or out again to Manoa pasture, had thrown broadcast out of·their pockets seeds from the Cathedral parent tree. Slender mangoes were growing taller, also two young monkey-pod trees of about Sanford's own age—one still shading the Library of Hawaii even today. Shade was at a premium in the dusty village of a hundred years ago. Even then, however, the tall lad of twelve, gazing down from Punchbowl, saw too with his mind's eye the transformation which the magic of *Ka-ne* (benevolent god of hidden waters) might some day create on that arid, yet sheltered lee shore.

In the forenoon of Saturday, February 6, 1869, as the schooner *Nettie Merrill* approached from Kauai, passengers on her deck could make out many shrubs, and taller trees beginning to stretch up above the houses, especially in the palace grounds and in front of the Queen's Hospital; also in Marin's garden on Vineyard Street, and just above along the Nuuanu stream at the home of Dr. Hillebrand, now Foster Gardens, with its giants of tropical forests. For Dr. Hillebrand was the young German physician of the new hospital, who, after he had regained health in searching mountain and valley for his *Flora of the Hawaiian Islands,* had received a commission to serve as immigration agent for the government and the Royal Hawaiian Agricultural Society. He sent five hundred Chinese coolies as plantation laborers and then shipped back from India and the Orient such varied immigrants as mynah, rice bird, linnet, quail, and pheasant; along with flowering shade trees, also seeds and seedlings of some of our present tropical giants of almost a century's growth; and camphor, cinnamon, mandarin orange, jackfruit, *litchi,* Chinese or Java plum, and banyan.

The underground half of this picture is plotted in by Thomas F. Sedgwick, an industrial chemist and hydrographer. Reporting in 1913 for the Territorial Survey of Water Resources, he goes back to the beginning of need for water in the town; tells a matter-of-fact story of the tedious loading of sailing ships from water casks sent on small boats up the Nuuanu stream to be filled at the king's spring and then floated down to the hot, parched, sun-beaten wharf. He remarks that the site of the king's spring is no longer known; tells of the relief brought in 1847 by the first "leaden pipe" to the harbor from a spring near Fort at Beretania Street and follows the successive laying of larger and longer iron pipes by the Honolulu Water Works. He traces too a graphic picture of Sanford Dole's boyhood dream that, almost as if at the waving of a magic wand, the bare and dusty checkerboard village of 1856 would vanish forever.

Now, thirteen years later, this boy was grown to manhood, had chosen his profession and of his own initiative was coming back to cast in his lot with his native town. From childhood it had been a peculiar delight to follow this familiar coastline and its every valley. On this February morning of 1869 there was a sharpness to the ridge outlines and in himself a peculiar eagerness of interest which noted changes of even more than young tree growth. On the lower levels the dark, rich green of Hawaiian

taro patches, which from time immemorial had followed the
fresh water in irregular terraces even well up onto the valley
slopes, was being replaced by the brighter green of Chinese rice
fields. And nearer to the low deck of the schooner, no sailor's
eye could miss the new buoys laid to mark the deepwater channel.
With a special buoy and anchor for the new steamship *Idaho*
plying between Honolulu and San Francisco.

In the inner harbor the process of dredging, long under way,
was depositing surplus sand and coral to fill in new land below
the Custom House of coral stone at the foot of Fort Street. It
looked to be as much as two acres already reclaimed from the sea
for wharves along the Esplanade, as it was hopefully named. A
three-thousand-foot frontage of wharves would soon make the harbor safe for a hundred vessels. Some of the old wooden wharves
were being replaced in stone, according to reports to the Minister
of the Interior; and at the west, on the edge of the reef, a new
separate wharf for landing cattle instead of herding them in clouds
of dust through narrow city streets.

Best of all, on the inner reef a new lighthouse and a second
light tower on the Esplanade, to sight in line with incoming ships,
had at last made the deepwater channel safe for working vessels
into the harbor at any hour of the night. Miracles, it seemed, had
been wrought.

At the wharf, when one stepped ashore, there was a permit to
be obtained for landing baggage, and a two-dollar tax to be paid
toward expenses of the Queen's Hospital. Then one was free to
stretch long legs in walking uptown and on up the valley, Nuuanu,
to the cottage offered for a while by Cushman Jones. A hack
could have been taken for the two miles, but no extra quarter
of a dollar was jingling against another in the pants pocket of the
young cub lawyer just landing to seek his fortune.

His brief journal entries chronicle the days. On Sunday morning
he returned to the congregation of his boyhood in the Seamen's
Bethel; in the evening he attended Fort Street Church, mentioned
by his Mother Charlotte as one of the first offshoots springing
out of the crowded Bethel fifteen years before. Monday: "Commenced office life" with Judge James W. Austin in the upper
story of the old government building, Honolulu Hale, over the
post office in H. M. Whitney's store. This was on Merchant
Street at the head of Kaahumanu Street, next to the corner where

Honolulu's first concrete building for the new post office was just being constructed. Tuesday: "Admitted to the bar." The following day his first client appeared, Mahuka by name; and young Dole inserted his business card in both the *Advertiser* and the *Kuokoa* (the *Hawaiian Independent*).

Thursday ushered in the Chinese New Year festival, bringing a round of calls with Judge Austin among Chinese merchants; in the afternoon dinner at Waikiki in the home of Judge Lawrence McCully, clerk and interpreter of the Supreme Court. Friday: calls on the families of Rufus Lyman and Judge Austin. Saturday: an assignment and a petition to draw up, then an evening visit at Punahou with President Alexander's young family.

The pattern of his life, slowly changing, still followed such familiar lines as calling on Mrs. Chamberlain, Mrs. Bishop, Mrs. Dimond; or watching for the night with young Levi Chamberlain, who, like his father, was being claimed by tuberculosis. Occasionally there was an evening party like a church bazaar or the Mission Cousins' Society to which he escorted now this young lady and now that, but the calls were decorously noted as made on their mothers or fathers. When a free afternoon hour presented itself, Alfred Castle, a Mission Cousin of nearly his own age, joined him in taking a rowboat out into the harbor around the bell buoy. Once they rowed down to Waikiki inside the reef; another day to the Kalihi landing; once they pulled out through the surf to board the *Nettie Merrill* for "a poi scrape"; again, they raced with a whaleboat and won. When sailboats were to be had, three of them started to race one day just as a squall struck, capsizing Castle and Dole who imperturbably took seats on the submerged keel of their boat to watch the result of the race between the remaining contestants.

On March 9: "Attended Julia Dimond's wedding [to Henry Waterhouse]. Walked home with Miss Dickson." One wonders how large the young monkey-pod tree had grown which Father Dimond, Mission bookbinder, had planted in honor of his daughter Julia's birth in 1844 and which more than a century later still stands guard over the Library of Hawaii, for this young Cousin was the "lovely Julia" whom Albert Wilcox had admonished Sanford to hurry back to win, lest Henry Waterhouse or some other step in ahead of him.

On Sunday, March 31, Cushman Jones invited to his house

Sanford B. Dole and Thomas Rain Walker, a young English friend who became vice-consul for Great Britain, to discuss the founding of a Young Men's Christian Association. On rainy afternoons there was a gymnasium to frequent, where Sanford could take Captain Johnson of the *Syren* who had had dinner with him. Drafting the constitution and by-laws of a Y.M.C.A. took time and care; in April young Dole "had the honor of being chosen as its first president." April 23 noted such events as racing with MacFarlane's boat, getting "our mast and sail blown overboard. Emma Smith's wedding rehearsal. Castle, Bailey, and Dillingham at my rooms." This was Cousin William Bailey who had hoped that Sanford would choose to begin his law practice at Wailuku on Maui. And Dillingham was, of course, the bridegroom at Emma Smith's wedding three days later. Cousin Emma, a childhood friend a few weeks younger than Sanford, had taught music at Punahou and the Royal School, and was director of Kaumakapili Church choir, as well as the efficient designer and seamstress for her own wedding gown of white tarlatan at a cost of four dollars. Henry MacFarlane was a member of her wedding party in which Sanford Dole served also as groomsman in the guard of honor of several couples who escorted her up the aisle of her father's old thatched church at Kaumakapili.

Meanwhile practice and study of the law progressed in due order. Looking back on its beginning from across the years, Sanford told of it almost as if it had been an everyday experience. At the time, he had made notes of many of his cases, adapting them as "Unprofessional Briefs" in *The Hawaiian,* a small quarto which appeared in 1872. And all of them served him well, when, in his eightieth year, he began to dictate his reminiscences to Miss Uecke of Punahou. Casual though his own story may seem at times, it represents actually the day-by-day process of adjustment to earning a living, according to an orderly plan to help where an honest citizen might, as new conditions arose. There was February 9, 1869, when with a friend he proceeded to the courthouse on Fort and Queen streets for the ceremony of his formal admission to the Bar:

A case was going on in the criminal side of the Supreme Court. A sleepy jury sat under the rather sensational harangue of the counsel for the defense. A dozen or two spectators were scattered among the audience

From a little-known daguerreotype of Bernice Pauahi and
Charles R. Bishop about the time of their marriage

Above: Old Royal Palace, built in 1845 on the site of the present one. Here five kings of Hawaii reigned

Below: Kawaiahao Church in the late 1880's

seats, the impassive looking Judge patiently sitting upright calmly chewing his tobacco as if proof against fate.

The clerk was mending pens; the day was hot; half a dozen lawyers sat in the Bar, the best listeners the animated advocate had. My friend and I came in and sat within the Bar; my friend whispered to the Clerk; the Clerk conferred in a low tone with the Judge who immediately cut short the fiery flow of eloquence pouring forth from the prisoner's attorney, by requesting a few moments' delay in the case for the ceremony of admitting a new member to the Bar. I was called; the members of the Bar stood. I read in an earnest and serious tone the elaborate professional oath and was sworn by the Clerk. The Judge, who had taken occasion to replenish the contents of his cheek, announced that the case might proceed.

The defense counsel, rested and refreshed, took up his argument with renewed enthusiasm; the Jury settled themselves in new and comfortable positions as far as was possible in jury seats, and my friend and I, having received the diploma licensing to practice, with the great seal affixed upon it, passed out, my friend remarking that this admittance through the criminal side of the court was ominous of future distinguished criminal practice. I tenderly and carefully stowed my diploma in my inside pocket and my friend and I bowed ourselves out.

Weeks passed. Now and then I was cheered by having my services in demand, a deed of land to draw up or a title to be searched, even a question which might cause me much intellectual calculation and trouble, but was supposed to be free gratis. After a few months Judge Austin retired from practice in Honolulu and I moved to an office over Richardson's shoe store at Fort and Merchants Streets. This had an outside stairway at which I put up my attorney's sign in English and Chinese, with the Hawaiian alliteration, *Loio*. The Police Court was then located in the old Court House, which is still in use as the American Factors warehouse, where the Supreme Court was likewise established. My first humble Police Court case I remember I won. This did not always happen, but I acquired much more than I had learned during my student days in Boston.

And my first fee, a gold eagle, I can never forget that, nor the sensation of power and independence it gave me! What new hopes it brought and how strange it made me feel as it lighted up the days of initiation! I had it bored and wore it for a charm on my watch chain, though I needed it for bills.

When my fellows of the Bar dropped in to smoke my cigars and inquire as to my business, I replied cheerily that I had never expected to get it all first thing. "Well," said one, "sit and keep your mouth open, something is sure to drop in!"

On a subsequent day this friend who was learned in the law, and had the treasury of long experience, was sitting with me at the noon hour. One of my clients came in with a question very puzzling to me. I held my friend in great esteem and considerable fear. It was a critical moment. I wished him anywhere else, feeling that my answer would raise or lower me in the opinion of this grim advocate. Summoning to my assistance all my self-control, my learning and my judgment, with one eye on my friend's face, who sat impassive, looking at the smoke rings from his cigar, I proceeded carefully, yet with an attempt at ease and careless self-possession, to give my opinion. My client, impressed and contented, departed, and I looked enquiringly at my friend, who after a moment of deep thought arose with the remark, "You were right, but how did you happen to hit it?" Then with a profound smile he went out.

Day after day I advertised myself by my thoughtful presence in the different courts, watching difficult cases, now and then making a note in my memorandum book with a sage and professional air. This did not go unrewarded. Clients became more numerous, some impelled by the not entirely groundless belief that I would work for almost nothing, others who were glad to help a beginner, expecting to discount their fee on the strength of this encouragement.

Once, interrupted in my study of the law by a slow step on the stairs, a dilapidated-looking Chinaman asked me to "sue one kanaka, he pepehi me too muchee. How much dala you do?" Arrived in the Court however, we found the defendant, a middle-aged Hawaiian, walking with a limp, his head tied up in a bloody handkerchief, his clothes torn and one arm in a sling.

I groaned inwardly as new light broke slowly on my inexperienced soul. The attorney for the defense was a prominent member of the Bar who delighted in desperate cases and was an accomplished fighter in the forum of Justice. This man arose and stated to the Court that the case needed thorough examination, so strangely did suspicion point to the informant, Young Lit. My enthusiasm almost evaporated, although my first witness, Ah Chow, made it clear that Young Lit had been attacked in his kitchen by A-i, the Hawaiian yardman, with poker, shovel and gridiron. A-i then testified that when chatting amiably with Youngy Liky, who was playing some outlandish instrument, he had remarked that the Chinese was not an accomplished musician; whereupon Youngy Liky called him a damn kanaka and knocked him down with a stick of firewood, and Ah Chow rushed to the defense of his countryman. A-i, finding it necessary to defend himself, employed the nearest weapons, meanwhile retreating as rapidly as he could from the scene of action.

Other witnesses for the defendant followed with such confused testimony that the judge finally said he had no patience with such disgraceful quarrels, and discharged both parties on payment of costs. I marched back to my office a wiser man and told my disappointed client he should be thankful to get off as lightly as he had done.

These were still my days of inexperience. I got into all the courts— sometimes won, sometimes lost cases, as with most lawyers. Enthusiasm and devotion in the little I have had to do have brought me some reputation and increase of practice, with consequent increase of fees. Less often have I been tempted to dispose of the golden eagle, my first fee, which hangs on my watch guard, for some of the more practical and less sentimental requirements of life.

Letters from friends weave a very vital thread into the texture of these early professional days. Always there is the quiet, loyal pride of mother and father on Kauai, comments from Daniel varying through pleasure that Sanford has shown "go-ahead and gumption" in a bankruptcy case, to the timely warning on punctuality as a habit, one of the most essential traits of the successful lawyer. And on the 23rd of April Daniel recalled tenderly the day when, twenty-five years before, little Sanford Ballard had appeared at Punahou, the joy he had brought first to his own mother, later to his new mother, and to his father and brother George who had prayed and worked for Sanford's future usefulness in life. From Waihohonu, the plantation home at Koloa, came occasional word from George and Clara, often with a box of mangoes or pears. From Boston Will Brigham wrote, longing for Sanford's return. Sam Buck, his Williams classmate, wished him well, and wrote of his own law study. Both correspondents remarked on the new velocipede craze, "this unmanageable hybrid which is the greatest nuisance we have; our village fathers have been obliged to put a stop to its antics in the streets, whereat young America doth greatly rage and fume."

At this time Sanford had taken a Sunday School class at Kaumakapili Church and in June was chosen to lead the joint procession on Sunday morning from Kawaiahao Church, marching through Fort, Beretania, and Nuuanu streets, back to Kawaiahao, each squad with its own particular banner.

Days in the Honolulu of 1869, however, were not all work and no play. Young men obviously enjoyed watching the old year out at Haleakala, the beautiful home of Mr. and Mrs. C. R. Bishop, where the Bank of Hawaii and Bishop Street now mark modern city ways; and young men very frequently joined late afternoon gatherings of the sewing society, where once on a day in June it is chronicled that "custom was departed from in a frolic on the lawn" at the H. M. Whitney home by the cool spring near King and Piikoi streets. Four days later, while Sanford's father and mother were visiting on Maui, a calico party at the Mac-Farlanes' apparently had no sedate precedents from which departure needed to be taken or noted. At the annual Punahou alumni meeting "Emma Dillingham was appointed poetess, Henry Parker essayist, and myself orator for next year."

And days of office or court work were so often followed by afternoon adventures on the blue and sparkling waters of the harbor that on the 23rd of June the Honolulu Yacht Club was organized with Charles Spencer president, Henry Castle secretary, and Sanford Dole soon a very active member. The glorious Fourth falling on Sunday, its celebration took place next day in one of Honolulu's first regattas, during the course of which Dole sailed in the *Cara Bell*, "the winning yacht, and went in P.M. with Dillingham to Waikiki for sea bath and spread." One afternoon when their boat pursued a westerly course out of the harbor, Dole Point was inadvertently christened upon their running aground in what their friends often described as an "attempt to sail overland into Pearl Harbor."

The *Punch Bowl*, Honolulu's new periodical, reported with spirit the tension of excitement that gripped the entire town over the long-awaited arrival of His Royal Highness, Duke of Edinburgh, second son of Queen Victoria. Telegraph arms on the watch tower signaled a steamer passing Koko Head—"expectancy burned into irritancy"—finally the signals called "man of war, this at last bringing the soberest citizens to their doors and gossipers to the street corners." Still the Duke did not come. Especially impatient were ladies who had bought new finery. At last, quietly at ease outside the reef, her draft too great to allow safe passage through the channel, the trim British man-of-war lay at anchor where she was to remain the fortnight of July 21 to August 2.

The Duke, her commander, was received with royal honors, the residence of His late Highness, Governor Kekuanaoa, being converted into shore quarters for Ke Keiki Alii (the royal duke). Editor Dole was among the king's guests at a brilliant palace ball where pledges and toasts were exchanged; and where the Duke's piper enchanted all with his airs which soon skirled into a Scottish reel vigorously danced by experts. At the wish of the Duke to see ancient Hawaiian dancing, an elaborate *luau* and hula were offered by Mrs. Dominis at Waikiki, the Duke arriving early to see the imu, and especially delighting the Hawaiians with performances of the ship's band.

Young Dole seems to have moved with ease among such scenes, but apparently enjoyed quite as much rowing out one afternoon into the harbor around Her British Majesty's ship *Galatea*. With interest too he must have viewed the prodigious *hookupu* (gift-bearing) to the honored guest of the kingdom, who stood for hours gallantly and democratically shaking hands with each donor, as thousands of Hawaiians, decked in their gayest, trooped to his shore residence on Queen Street. One portly woman carried a fat pig clasped to her bosom; hundreds brought chickens, pigs, coconuts, mangoes, besides an aggregate of two tons of taro, a ton each of melons and sweet potatoes, not to mention exquisite mats and polished wooden bowls. All of these, some eight or ten tons, were sent on board the *Galatea* next morning in two scows. Visiting royalty from England was a rarity in the Sandwich Islands.

Meanwhile Sanford Dole had had his parents as Honolulu visitors, coming for General Meeting of the Mission in June, vacationing then on Maui, and returning for a few days in July. Father Dole preached in the Bethel pulpit, as he had done twenty-seven years before and often in the interim, and enjoyed visiting Sanford both in his rooms and in his office. Both father and mother regretted that they were not able to fulfill their long-cherished hope of thanking Judge Austin personally for his kindness to their son. This early professional association was of undoubted value, since Austin, as characterized by his contemporary, Judge Hartwell, was distinctly judicial, a peacemaker who habitually discouraged litigation by bringing two factions together.

Judge James W. Austin, having decided, after fifteen years of a responsible practice in the Islands, to return with his family to their home in Boston, had left in May. At his Honolulu auction Sanford had "bought two whatnots for Mother, and a carriage for Napua in Koloa." Occupied largely by the settlement of involved estates among Hawaiian nobility, Judge Austin had in 1868 been appointed Second Associate Justice of the Hawaiian Supreme Court, whereupon his private practice was perforce discontinued. With Justices Allen and Hartwell he had sat in hearings on the revision of the Penal Code. The original law, drafted by Judge Lee in 1850 in what he termed a "chrysalis state of the nation," could not by any possibility have anticipated the changes which nearly twenty years had brought to the people of the Sandwich Islands.

Accustomed from childhood to discussions at home on many angles of community life, Sanford Dole had even as a lad of nineteen shown active resentment at the refusal of Kamehameha V, on his accession, to subscribe to the Constitution of 1852. This continued critical interest increased while Sanford was at Williams College and may very well have thrown weight into the scale of young Dole's choice of a profession. Certainly the conviction became intensified as he grew older, since almost his first public move was to foster an independent monthly journal for un-hampered comment on matters of community interest. With him in both informal and printed discussions was of course young Al-fred Castle, Registrar of Public Accounts; as also another Mission Cousin and friend of Punahou days, Curtis Lyons, surveyor and land expert, who for a time lived at Saints' Rest cottage with Dole and used Dole's office as an address in his own advertisement for clients. Part of the time Sanford took his dinners with the Dilling-hams. Once when both Walker and Dole were dining regularly at Emma Dillingham's hospitable table, Dole's diary notes trying the Canton House as a boarding place, adding the terse comment: "gloomy prospect." In October of 1870, when at the Bethel com-munion service the Dillingham baby was baptized: "Mary Emma behaved creditably."

With Dole and Lyons was also the young Englishman, Thomas Rain Walker, who entered with zest into their lively sessions. At one time Walker and Dole together established a social center, a series of semi-public readings introducing the new bachelor home which became the scene of pleasant evenings for men about town and officers from visiting ships. On less formal evenings, with other Island men, mangoes and watermelons provided re-freshment, forerunners of the huge papayas and New England Sunday breakfasts at the later Dole home on Emma Street. These early quarters were several times moved, once as far out as Makiki near Punahou and always designated by such names as Saints' Rest, The Rookery, or Hawthorne. Once Daniel and Charlotte Dole were guests at Hawthorne for several days; a little later George and Clara Dole.

In July, 1870 when their new journal was launched, the cottage occupied was still at Emma Street on the lower slope of Punchbowl Hill. This may have had some bearing on the selection of *Punch Bowl* as the name for their new monthly. When describing their aims in the first issue, the three young editors trusted their fate might not too closely resemble that of the "three wise men of Gotham who went to sea in a Bowl." The editor of *The Friend* considered their choice of a name strangely out of place. Outside contributors there were, including Sanford's father in Koloa, and all, though serious enough in their comments, had a good deal of fun out of it, their printer and publisher, Mr. J. H. Black, assuming entire responsibility, having some ado to keep the little sheet anonymous, but enjoying it none the less.

The leading editorial in the August number of the *Punch Bowl* voiced severe criticism of the king's appointment of Mr. H. A. Widemann as Associate Justice of the Supreme Court. He was a German naturalized citizen of the kingdom, a man of strict probity and excellent local knowledge, of good education, and with some experience as a circuit judge on Kauai, but of no formal legal training. Upholding the dignity of the Supreme Court, the ardent young writer felt quite justified in very sharp remarks, unmollified by Mr. Widemann's modest approach to the responsibilities of the position as successor to Judge John Ii, whose training had lain wholly in the realm of Hawaiian common law. Contemporary journalists noted the violence of the attack in the *Punch Bowl,* and characterized it moderately as something of a tempest in a teapot, one commenting in general that if the young editor continued to write as promisingly as he had begun, he would no doubt attain to an enviable standing in the community. At one session of the Legislature Dr. Hutchison, the Minister of the Interior who had retained S. B. Dole for government investigation on Maui, but who apparently had no idea that Dole was a joint editor of the *Punch Bowl,* waved a recent copy of that newspaper in the air before the legislators, shouting denouncement of its hostile criticism of government policies.

On August 3, 1870, came Dole's first work in the fourth circuit of the Supreme Court, when he sailed for Nawiliwili, Kauai, as defense attorney on a forgery case. Justice Widemann presiding, Kahalai, the defendant, pleaded guilty; Dole addressed the court in his behalf and succeeded in getting for his client a sentence of only sixty days. Attorney General Phillips, was the prosecutor for the Crown and Honorable Duncan McBryde sat with Justice Widemann as Kauai's Circuit Judge.

Court week at Lihue was an event. Judges and lawyers often stayed with G. N. Wilcox in the old Grove Farm thatched house, originally the home of Mr. and Mrs. Widemann. Not so many years later, after Sam Wilcox's family had joined his brother George there, court week often saw twenty or more at table for meals. The children of the family never forgot the big crocks of hard-boiled eggs pickled in vinegar and gradually assembled in preparation for the occasion, canned goods and hotels then being items of the unforeseeable future. But the children's own special treat was a big glass jar of shining hard candies which one of the Honolulu lawyers, especially W. O. Smith, was always sure to produce.

When the twelve cases on the 1869 Circuit Court calendar closed at the ninth day, Sanford Dole remained for divorce cases in the local court, driving over in his brother's gig, or with Judge McBryde, to spend the night in his old home at Koloa with father and mother. On Saturday there was the zest of a hunt for wild cattle at Wailua. The following Thursday and Friday, G. Wilcox, W. Rice, and G. Rowell took Sanford with them to Halemanu and Milolii for goats and pigs. On Friday Sanford gave a picnic for everyone in the woods at Kaluahonu. Evidently he had waited over to represent his brother George in a trespassing case brought by Akau, a Chinese. On the 1st of September Judge Lilikalani decided the suit in favor of Akau, and Sanford sailed for Oahu the same day, but not before he had received a letter from editorial colleague Walker who thus upbraided him: "Perfidious man, where are contributions to the *Punch Bowl?* This month's issue promises to be all Castle, Saturday Review, Walker, and advertisements! Authorship begins to leak out. Pray be quick back, or something may happen."

Quite as likely as not Dole reached Nawiliwili wharf after other passengers had gone aboard and the last shore boat was pulling out. Riding unhurried down the long hill, Dole left his horse with some friend, dropped his big saddle into the rocking whaleboat, and stepped down easily himself from the wharf. "We all saw this happen year after year," George Wilcox used to tell, "and someone would be sure to remark, 'There goes the late Mr. Dole.' Yet he was never known to miss that last boat." Once however, so the story goes in reverse, Attorney Dole failed to appear when the Honolulu steamer arrived with the judge and attorneys for Court Week. But just as they were all sitting down to breakfast with the Wilcoxes, in walks the imperturbable Mr. Dole who, in default of the steamer, had fortunately caught a schooner and a brisk trade wind across the channel.

Very soon after the accession of Kamehameha V in 1863 a planters' society had been organized largely to increase the supply of laborers. The government wished to co-operate, but with a view toward encouraging other Polynesians to ship as workmen, that the Hawaiian race might be increased by cognate peoples from the South Sea Islands. This project proved more idealistic than practical. The Bureau of Immigration, created in 1864 with Dr. Hillebrand as its special commissioner, received the next year more than five hundred contract laborers from China. The expiration of their five year contracts, due in 1870, gave rise as early as 1869 to much discussion of the contract labor system and in 1868 to the first company of Japanese laborers.

At a planters' meeting in the courthouse on October 9, 1869, Sanford Dole spoke against this system of contracting for workmen. Two days later at the adjourned meeting Dole gave additional points in opposition to the assignment clause which allowed transfer of laborers from one employer to another regardless of the wish of individuals involved. The same week in October 1869 a citizens' meeting debated the question, and a similar meeting of Hawaiians at Kaumakapili Church was held the following Friday. Dole's journal entries note still a fifth labor meeting, and yet again on the 26th of October, "a lively labor meeting at Kauma-kapili Church." All of this was a part of the life in Honolulu reflected in the daily press and more briefly recorded in Sanford Dole's diary.

After Alfred Castle's marriage on New Year's Day of 1870 there were frequent visits among the young people, once a surprise party on the young couple; one November evening: "Castles and Dillinghams called on us, a good lark." Again it was a velocipede race at the circus, or a Y.M.C.A. meeting in the Sailors' Home; officers from the British man-of-war *Chameleon* called, or a capital time was enjoyed at a party aboard the *Mohican*. Again:

I escorted Miss Bella Holden to a sociable; took Miss Dickson to the ball at the Court House; spoke against the popular idea of revivals at a prayer meeting at the Fort Street church; made purchases for Koloa Christmas tree at the auction. December 24th attended Christmas services tonight at the St. Andrews and Roman Churches, and the 25th attended services and feast at Kawaiahao Church. January 13, 1870 Judge Widemann gave his decision in the Bernard Bankruptcy case in my favor; Judd opposing attorney. Sunday, 16th: baptism of infants at Fort Street Church, Carter, Jones, Waterhouse; Carter baby squalled. Wed: Election caucus at Thompson's office.

While interest in politics was coming to the fore among Sanford Dole's preoccupations, his love of the outdoors ran now as always a close second. Its expression became indeed almost a creed with him. His August number of the *Punch Bowl,* read by many Honolulu citizens and cheered on from afar by Buck and Brigham, opened with a fervent plea for health in outdoor sports for women as well as men. In the days of hoop skirts this must have sounded revolutionary. He deplored the tendency to let a spiritless canter or quiet carriage drive take the place of the frequent horseback rides of his boyhood, mountain air being the best of stimulants, and a pull at an oar on the waters of the harbor a better tonic than a pull at a flask of plantation bitters. "We believe," he thundered from his editorial pulpit as vigorously as his older contemporary, Sam Armstrong—"we believe in manly sports as a means of grace. We believe in a muscular Christianity."

It may have been at this time that someone made for him, apparently of *koa,* the extra long but graceful Indian clubs which he enjoyed using of an early morning until after he was eighty years old. Later given to Punahou, these clubs were sacrificed on the altar of war during Punahou's occupation by the United States Engineers in 1942. Dole prepared too a little printed pamphlet of setting-up exercises which he distributed gladly. In 1870, as soon as he could find a friendly Honolulu pasture, he sent to Koloa for his horse Dan and had him shod for the coral-paved roads beginning to lead out of town, particularly past the jail at Iwilei and on for several miles through Kapalama and Moanalua toward Ewa.

A contemporary Honolulu newspaper, *Bennett's Own,* noted with pleasure the appearance of "A Synopsis of Birds of the Hawaiian Islands," recently published in the *Proceedings of the Boston Society of Natural History* by a corresponding member, S. B. Dole. A present-day journalist, Jared G. Smith, once declared reminiscently that Dole's boyhood hadn't been wasted, "for he knew every mountain trail; the native birds, their song and habits; the ferns and landshells—collector's items for school boys in the long ago; and all of Hawaii's beaches. He was a powerful swimmer and sailing was another of his favorite sports. He was a man's man!"

Again collaborating with his friend Brigham, who had encouraged him to go on with this early scientific listing of seventy-seven Hawaiian birds, Dole had also prepared, in the extensive Hawaiian collection of the Harvard College library, a catalog of works there relating to the Islands. The younger James Hunnewell assisted him in the collaboration, particularly with reference to the *Missionary Herald,* and the resulting paper had been published in the proceedings of the Hawaiian Club at Boston. In November, 1869, the *Punch Bowl* of Honolulu noted a reprint of this valuable bibliography of Hawaiiana, an edition in quarto, limited to one hundred copies, and rushed through the press in honor of the aging Captain James Hunnewell, who had long sustained the liveliest interest in things Hawaiian.

Other contributions by Sanford Dole to the *Hawaiian Club Papers* included translations from the Hawaiian historian, Joseph Kamakau: one on the *Long Voyages of the Ancient Hawaiians;* another on the story of the first priest, Paao; not to mention the amused memory of very early missionaries preaching earnestly in a canoe shed on Hilo Bay to a concourse of dignified warriors, women, babes, little boys clambering up the posts above the heads of the listening multitude, and, still farther up, shining eyes of the more venturesome small boys peering down through holes in the roof thatching—when suddenly all were routed by a six-foot hog charging in from the noon heat to his wonted straw bed at the center of the *halau,* swinging his tusks in utter contempt of the

common people, since as *puaa anana,* (sacred hog) he was taboo
to all but the queen regent, Kaahumanu.

For more than a year young contributors to the Honolulu *Punch
Bowl* continued their pointed comments on the injustices of the
system of contract labor. And for the year from October, 1869,
to September, 1870, they were actively seconded by Major C. C.
Bennett in his contemporary monthly. Not content with comment
alone, Curtis Lyons carried active opposition to the floor of the
1870 Legislature in which he sat as Representative for Kohala,
Hawaii. His short, comprehensive bill called for repeal of the
law under which for twenty years persons had hired themselves
out to labor for others. Objection to the proposed change ensued,
spearheaded by the Hon. Charles C. Harris, with the warning to
consider well an act that would admittedly cause complete disruption of existing economic conditions.

Another Cabinet member, Attorney General Stephen H.
Phillips considered dispassionately the vital importance of the bill
for repeal, the personal rights of large sections of the people, and
the obvious fact that the existing law was not perfect; considered
too its repeal which would throw out of gear not only many
tax-supported institutions, but also ships, mechanics, and all
classes of trade and people. Everything considered, he must vote
for indefinite postponement of the bill for repeal of the Masters
and Servants Act.

Lyons, in closing the debate, spoke as a Hawaiian, his own
interests having always been identical with those of Hawaiians
among whom he grew up at Waimea, Hawaii. His strongest
defense of the bill before the House was his hope of increasing the
power of the people by constitutional methods. Indefinite postponement, however, was the fate of the bill, leaving contract labor
in force for another generation.

In May of 1870 the death of Judge John Ii marked the passing
of the old order of chiefly influence so long a definite economic
factor. The years 1855 and 1857 had seen the passing of High
Chief Paki and his wife, High Chiefess Konia, parents of Mrs.
Bernice Pauahi Bishop. In 1868 Laiana (Father Lyons) wrote
from isolated Waimea, Hawaii, that the entire nation mourned
the death of "His Highness, Governor Kekuanaoa, father of two
kings and a bulwark for righteous dealings." And now Judge Ii

was gone. Of a lower order of chiefs, he stemmed from the days of Kamehameha I who had assigned him as companion to his young son, Liholiho. Early a student under the Binghams, John Ii had become a valued councilor of Kamehameha III whom he had served as hostage on board the French frigate *L'Artemise,* as a Christian gentleman commanding general admiration. From the inception of the House of Nobles John Ii was a quietly forceful member, receiving royal appointment also to the treasury board, the Privy Council, and the commission to draft the Constitution of 1852, likewise to the Supreme Court as Associate Justice. Here he was a dignified figure, less familiar, it is true, with the laws of foreign countries, but well versed in the intricacies of the common law of his native land. A consistent Christian for nearly fifty years, Judge Ii had the confidence of all, retiring at last to his own lands at Ewa, where he served as pastor in the Hawaiian church until shortly before his death. To assist his widow and daughter, young Sanford Dole was appointed one of the executors of his estate.

Outstanding in the chronicle of 1870 was the arrival of the British steamer *Wonga Wonga,* twenty-three days from Auckland. Pioneer of the Australian line, she came as far north as Honolulu, and was subsidized by the Hawaiian government for carrying the mail. Activities thus stimulated brought about publicity looking toward the erection of a first-class hotel, a new venture in the little seaport city. A year later Dole escorted Miss Dickson over the new Hawaiian Hotel, forerunner of the present Royal Hawaiian, and still later attended its opening ball. Dole's journal mentioned for the first time in June 1870 that he attended the band concert at Emma Square.

And this month of June celebrated the fiftieth jubilee of the Hawaiian Protestant Mission, during the course of which young Dole was called upon to read in Fort Street Church the reminiscences of his neighbor, Mother Whitney of Waimea, Kauai. Vigorous Mother Thurston was more than equal to the task of reading, for an hour and a half and audibly to the large congregation, parts of her own pioneer story, later embodied in the spirited account of her *Life and Times* which has seen three editions. Since in 1870, however, it was still considered unseemly for the voice of a woman to be heard from the pulpit, this valorous Mission wife, mother, and teacher was accorded the privilege of reading from the steps leading to that eminence sacred to the male persuasion.

The *Punch Bowl*—odd name for such a connection—published Sanford Dole's account of the Mission,

to which we owe all our civil, commercial and religious prosperity. The Jubilee festival closed with a great meeting and ahaaina, feast, at Kawaiahao Church, when His Majesty and his ministry, the missionaries of all denominations (including we are pleased to observe, clergymen of the Anglican Mission), the Nobles and Representatives of this country, and the diplomatic representatives of the United States, all united in personally paying respect to the occasion. Never were the troops called to attention on a more worthy occasion and the marshal of the day and his lieutenants ought to feel honored in their duty. The Jubilee, as it deserved, was highly successful; and the whole emphasized very forcibly the national motto, *Ua mau ke ea o ka aina i ka pono.*

Business in Dole's office was looking up. The summer of 1870 saw his second visit to Kauai for the Supreme Court session; in Honolulu he had six Supreme Court cases and for a time was acting under power of attorney for A. F. Judd during his absence in the United States and Europe. At one time came an assignment to investigate complaints against the government at Hana, Maui. Ministers Harris and Hutchison attempted to persuade young Dole to act as interpreter for the Legislature. Judge Austin returned for a residence of two years, occupied his old office and often appeared in court on cases with S. B. Dole. Not infrequently the latter had an article in the *Pacific Commercial Advertiser,* of which Mission Cousin Henry M. Whitney had for fifteen years been editor, owner and publisher. Wishing to take his family to the States, he sold the paper to Black & Auld, printers. Henry Carter, Adams, Green, and Sanford Dole discussed the advisability of joining the venture, but apparently did not do so. Dole, asked to edit the paper, felt obliged to decline, but wondered whether the little old *Punch Bowl* had perhaps begun to show results.

The summer of 1871 was to see another dream come true when Daniel and Charlotte Dole, escorted by son Sanford, sailed on the old steamer *Ajax* as far as San Francisco, whence he saw them off in the "Cannibal Car" for six months in their strangely unfamiliar homeland of Maine and Connecticut.

Sanford meanwhile enjoyed visiting with the Titcomb family

and often with Marion Rowell. Young Rev. Charles F. Dole in the East, after seeing his uncle, Daniel Dole, for the first time, wrote to Sanford that he never before had known a man so completely of the old Puritan type. From California Sanford returned to Honolulu aboard the *Moses Taylor* whose auxiliary engine burst en route, killing six men.

It was often said in the Honolulu of 1870 that everyone knew everyone else. And true this was, partly because people often walked and the walking distances were not great. Coming down Emma Street, for instance, it was only natural for young Dole to turn a few steps to the north on Beretania to see Laura Judd and her husband, Joshua Dickson, with their family of four small daughters, including also Grandma Dickson and daughter Hessie from New England. Naturally it was croquet of an afternoon or even a moonlight night, backgammon of an evening, or escorting Miss Hessie over to Fort Street Church or to make calls on friends, some of whom were the Ned Adams family around another corner on Kukui Street. Edward P. Adams of Castine, Maine, had come from the gold fields of California, settled in Honolulu as a commission merchant and auctioneer, married Miss Caroline Wright and before long possessed a family of six children. Genial and hospitable, he loved filling his home with family and friends.

One evening in October of 1870, slipping away from a crowded German fair at Olympic Hall, Dole escorted Hessie Dickson home, she intimating that she had a surprise in store for him. For her brother and Laura had just returned from a trip East and had brought back with them Ned Adams' niece, who had agreed earlier to come out to the Islands for a visit. Now since the recent death of Carrie Adams, Niece Anna fitted easily into her uncle's busy household as older sister to the motherless children.

And Anna Prentice Cate proved indeed a surprise. With the freshness of the spring in her native New England she greeted one, a lovely person, keenly sensitive to beauty. Born in the old seaport town of Castine at the head of Penobscot Bay, she knew and loved also mountain, forest, and flower. A lover of literature, with an unusual memory for poetry, she had had joy in teaching high school and normal school young people of her home town. Modest, unassuming, her vivacity and grace of manner won homage even from the king, Kamehameha V, who distinguished her by the presentation of a royal feather lei. Even more personally devoted did Sanford Dole become, his diary noting frequent calls at the Dickson or Adams home, walks into the hills, or rides to the beach.

The year 1871 continued business as usual during the day, once on a rainy day riding with Father Damon to Ewa to see about Dr. Ford's children. For the third year S. B. Dole accompanied the Supreme Court to its Kauai session. On Sundays he superintended the large Sunday School at Kawaiahao Church, where his friend and Mission Cousin, Henry Parker, was pastor. Here too Mrs. Dominis, later Queen Liliuokalani, was choir leader and organist for the new pipe organ which Will Brigham had seen and heard in Boston in advance of its shipment to the Islands. Many in the small town could hear the town clock in the stone church tower and many, including Mr. and Mrs. Charles R. Bishop, lived within sound of the church bell and heeded it of a Sabbath morning. Once when he needed an extra teacher, Sanford Dole stopped at the Bishops' on his way to Sunday School and easily persuaded Mrs. Bishop to fill the gap, although she was often a member of the choir as well.

On October 23, 1871, the whaler *Arctic* arrived, Dole noted in his diary, with news of the loss of the whaling fleet, some of the ships owned in Honolulu. This was a disaster, Mrs. Austin added in a letter, as severe as the recent fire in Chicago:

All Honolulu merchants depend upon the fleet in some way. There will be no business done here this autumn, and probably many failures. Large ships are chartered for freight, and no freight for them. Cushman Jones, besides his ships, has lost all his profits, his season's business. He could not eat a mouthful of breakfast this morning, and hardly spoke a word. The ships were enclosed by ice in August, and thirty-two went down, seven or eight escaped. Whales were plentiful and the ships filling up rapidly. Very few were insured. Every body is as blue as indigo.

In August of 1872 Ned Adams planned to take his oldest daughter Lucy to Castine, Anna Cate to accompany her after a visit in Honolulu of over a year. Perhaps this was in the nature of an emergency and served to bring Sanford Dole's feeling to a focus, his diary for the 30th of June noting neatly: "Sunday School Concert at Kawaiahao. Evening, betrothal of S.B.D. and A.P.C." And the next day he placed his ring on her finger. This pleasure no doubt contributed to his success on July 4th in winning the amateur boat race, Castle and himself oarsmen, steered by J. Robertson.

A week after the engagement of Sanford to Anna Cate, he took his father and mother to call on her at the Adams home. Then day after day, anticipating her departure, the engaged couple drove of an afternoon to Waikiki or rode farther around Diamond Head. One morning early they rode horseback with the newly-wed Frank and Agnes Boyd Judd, calling on the Wilders and breakfasting with the Judds. On the 30th they drove up Nuuanu and then down to the Castles to call on Father and Mother Dole. Next day the Doles returned to Koloa and on August 1st Sanford saw Anna off for the East with her uncle and young Lucy on the steamer *Idaho*.

Idleness did not follow however in Honolulu, for business at the office was brisk and must be combined for the fourth year with work in the Supreme Court session on Kauai. Again in Honolulu, much visiting took place and there were many evening parties with cards or dancing. Weddings too seemed to be the order of the day. In September Sam Damon and Hattie Baldwin were married by Pastor Frear at Fort Street Church, with a reception at Father Damon's in Chaplain Lane nearby. Mary Water-house was one of the bridesmaids, she who had made the sensation of the evening not long before as peasant woman in the vestry of the church at a benefit fair for a new piano. And within six weeks vivacious Mary herself became the bride of Willie Rice of Lihue. After Ned Adams returned on the *Idaho,* Sanford Dole moved back to Emma Street to live in the Adams family until later, when Adams made another trip all the way to Maine for his second wife. This was Ellen Fisher, who had succeeded Anna Cate in the normal school at Castine, and later, like Anna, became one of Honolulu's accomplished hostesses.

George Dole meanwhile found himself not too hopeful about the future of Koloa Plantation on Kauai, where he had been manager for four years. Labor was increasingly hard to get and no prospect of any reciprocal trade treaty with the United States was yet in sight. When Dr. Wood sold Koloa to Paul Isenberg, George Dole resigned in January of 1872, took Clara and the three children to her old home at Waimea, and moved temporarily to his own old home with father and mother in Koloa village, while finishing a five months' contract just over the hill on the McBryde ranch. His eager wish to purchase this beautiful Kauai estate failed of fulfilment. He auctioned off his cattle and land for some eleven hundred dollars, and took his family to Honolulu. Here he had accepted a position with the Board of Education, as principal of the Industrial and Reformatory School at Kapalama. Cousin Mary Parker had for several years been its successful principal, and had hoped to continue, had indeed engaged the assistance of Cousin Lottie Smith of Koloa, when Judge Hartwell, long a frequent visitor at Koloa, carried Miss Lottie off as a bride.

This Kapalama School in Honolulu, with Mr. and Mrs. Kauhane as native assistants, was more one of guidance for mischievous boys than one of correction. The land occupied by its workshops, schoolhouses, dwellings and gardens lay in a large undeveloped area opposite the present Kaumakapili Church on North King Street. Some sixty Hawaiian boys, beside having class work in Hawaiian and English, cultivated the school *taro* and vegetable patches, did carpentering, and made their own clothes in the school tailor shop. At many points the work must have been reminiscent of early Punahou days to George Dole, as well as to his brother, Sanford, who often rode out to Kapalama from town on his horse Dan of an afternoon or evening.

From Sanford's early boyhood in the Koloa home no week had been complete without the arrival by schooner of the *Commercial,* as they often called the *Advertiser.* Eagerly were the contents of its columns scanned and discussed in the Dole household. A distinctly home product published in Honolulu, this paper was owned and edited by neighbor Henry M. Whitney, a Kauai boy born at Waimea and sent to New England while very small, like other very early Mission sons. Employed on the *New York Commercial,* he had been recalled to the Islands as printer for the Hawaiian government, and in 1856 had established the *Pacific Commercial Advertiser* as an independent weekly. In modern times this has become our indispensable daily, the *Honolulu Advertiser,* although a century ago and for many years thereafter it bore the earlier and broader title.

Until 1870, when Whitney sold the *Advertiser,* he frankly opposed the contract labor system and continued to do so in his

Ka Nupepa Kuokoa (Hawaiian Independent). For an estimate of this newspaper symposium Hawaii is indebted to Ralph S. Kuykendall's second volume of *The Hawaiian Kingdom,* where this is considered "a public discussion of more than ordinary significance." Yet even under new owners and a reversed policy of favoring the system of contract labor, the *Pacific Commercial Advertiser* opened its columns to writers both pro and con.

Here Sanford Dole, at twenty-eight, crossed swords with a nimble adversary whose articles were signed only Weltevreden. This signified, as most people knew, the "scheming, dreaming genius," Walter Murray Gibson, who in the course of other fabulous adventures had continued his education as a man of thirty in the Dutch prison of Weltevreden in Batavia, Java. Born at sea of English immigrant parents, Gibson had grown up among American Indians, later teaching school in South Carolina and educating himself beyond his marked facility in history, languages, and folklore. In a recent book, *Tall Ships to Cathay,* Helen Augur pictures vividly some of Gibson's adventures which were declared by Nathaniel Hawthorne not to have been equaled since *Gulliver's Travels.* With a fascination equivalent at times almost to mesmerism, Gibson had come to the Hawaiian island of Lanai as a Mormon missionary in 1861, when his scheme for a Mormon Empire of Borneo had been shrewdly discounted by Brigham Young. Excommunicated by the Mormon Church in 1864, Gibson, with a sharp eye on his own worldly advantage, bent his many skills toward Hawaii for Hawaiians and later even Polynesia for Polynesians. His five articles in the *Advertiser* of 1872 were very persuasive.

During the year 1872, until the death of Kamehameha V in December, the subject of repopulation and field workers took leading place in the public mind. Many foreign mechanics and tradesmen joined Hawaiians in resenting further introduction of Chinese and Japanese laborers. Walter Gibson went so far as to advocate as the sovereign remedy the transformation of Hawaii into a colony of Malaysia, the land from which he claimed that the ancestors of Hawaiians had turned the prows of their ocean-going canoes.

Of the many printed discussions on population and labor, Sanford Dole's contribution is considered by Kuykendall as the most important from every standpoint. In fact, it is an able presentation under six headings: "The Problem of Population"; "Immigration"; "Inducements to Immigration"; "Homesteads and Citizenship"; "Population and Land Policy"; "Systems of Immigration and Settlement." It was printed serially in the weekly *Pacific Commercial Advertiser* from September 28 to November 16, 1872. A more detailed discussion of this newspaper symposium finds place a quarter-century later in Chapter XV of this present story.

Following his instinct for sound economy, Sanford Dole was watching with concern the spread of a general business depression. Fewer and fewer whaleships were arriving at Island ports; workers on sugar plantations were becoming more and more scarce. Finally, the Honolulu Chamber of Commerce, founded in 1850, went so far as to request the government to fix by legislation the value of English sovereigns at more than three per cent above their par value.

Such an extraordinary proposition was more than young Dole could endure in silence. Parts of his discussion as printed by the *Advertiser* on November 15, 1873, stir one to thought even at the distance of eighty years:

> It was common once to fix wages and prices by law, but such measures have been succeeded by the law of supply and demand, a principle adequate to regulate wages and prices upon the exact basis of intrinsic values. To fix a fictitious value is the same thing as fixing the price of any other commodity and more objectionable since money is a more universal commodity than anything else.
>
> We have had a season of loss and misfortune. We have not got a plenty of coin; and we have no more right to it than a farmer to profits when he has lost his crops.
>
> If simply more of gold coin is needed, the deposit of silver with the Government, in exchange for silver certificates, supplies the want perfectly. These certificates are always redeemable and can even be used for payment of foreign debts if necessary, as the Bank of California receives them at a discount less than the present rate of exchange.
>
> But the results of the proposed change [in the value of the English sovereign] would be mischievous in every direction. The credit of the Government at home and abroad would suffer both by direct loss to its creditors and want of confidence in a government liable at any time to lower the standard of its currency.
>
> Our obvious and intelligent course is to agree with our nearest commercial neighbors. In a word: to adopt American coinage in all its features. As we

do the greater part of our business with them, it follows that their coinage must be the best adapted to our needs.

If English money is preferred, let us make pounds, shillings and pence our national currency, but avoid the absurdity of trying to convert sovereigns into half-eagles, and save ourselves the censure and loss of prestige resulting from such a masquerading attempt to create values by legislation. In a year's time our exports will be greater in proportion to our imports and the national profits will restore the money equilibrium.

Personally, as well as politically, the year 1873 marked a Sanford Dole milestone. In April, with W. G. Irwin as cabin mate, he sailed on the *Dakota* of the United States, New Zealand, Australian Steam Mail line; crossed North America for the first time, noted from the sleeping-car window the varied mountain scenery, scars of old mining camps, Piute Indians, snow-covered hills in Utah and "an Indian camp of the picture-book kind"; telegraphed to Rowell from Ogden; called on Emily Rice de la Vergne at Omaha, on Clarks and Lymans at Chicago; crossed the Canadian border, his Honolulu companion, Mr. Henry May, appreciatively sniffing the English air there; crossed Niagara bridge; reached Boston without his trunk; but was enthusiastically greeted by Will Brigham; changed to steamer at Portland and found a warm reception at Castine, Maine. For he and Anna Cate were to be married.

Will Brigham arrived to stand as best man and to bring the bride a beautiful set of brooch and earrings. "She deserves everything lovely," noted Sanford, "for she is one of the best women that ever lived." And even though many in the Cate and Adams families had known Daniel Dole years before, when he supplied in neighboring pulpits, it was not surprising that they regarded young Sanford with close scrutiny. Up for inspection as it were, and a bit trying, but he admitted to his father, "it is all very kindly, and they make me perfectly at home."

Then too I have more enchanting matters to occupy me. Tremendous operations are going on here in cake baking, sewing and packing of boxes. But Anna and I have had one snow-balling contest, for snow banks still lie on the hills and in the woods. Castine is one of the most lovely waterside places I ever saw. Boating is very good, both in the bay and up the river, though the tide did once desert our boat and the wedding party walked home, leaving the boat for Brigham and me to fetch back later with another sail down river.

We are to be married on May 19th, using the Episcopal service of the American prayer book, in the Cate home, a capacious house of the plain New England type. It promises to be a sunny day! There are springtime flowers everywhere, the little birds are singing and new leaves are budding on elms and maples. The ceremony will take place at half-past twelve. Later we take the steamer for Portland and Boston where the Hawaiian Club is to give us a reception. And we should be home in Hawaii by the fourth of July!

With shopping in Boston; a sermon from Dr. Wright; a side trip to Lake Champlain where the Unitarian cousin, Charles F. Dole, was ministering to his first church; a farewell visit to Castine; and the great majesty of Niagara Falls—with all this the honeymoon was so full that Sanford's hoardings for the trip were exhausted by the time Honolulu harbor spread out once more before them. Their first sight of friends was Uncle Ned Adams on the pilot boat coming out to their steamer, the *Costa Rica*. And then, beside George and Clara with their two little boys and two little girls, Father and Mother Dole had come up to greet them, to stay a few days and then return to Kauai to receive the bride and groom for a fortnight in the old Koloa home. Picnics, calls, dinners, drives, rides, swims "to our hearts' content," noted Sanford. Hawaii was home. What matter if the family purse was empty? These two were facing the future together!

THIRTY HISTORIC DAYS
1872–1873

SANFORD DOLE himself wrote the definitive account of political events at the turn of the year 1872 to 1873 while he was living through those momentous thirty days or shortly thereafter. Six years earlier, while a student at Williams College, he had foreseen this moment when, at the death of Kamehameha V, the Hawaiian people would become king-makers through their own right of representation. Now as a man of twenty-eight young Dole was beginning to make his way as a citizen of his native land. When he wrote the account which forms this present chapter, he with others rightly looked forward to constitutional liberty. Before his paper was first printed however, a scant year later, these hopes were dying with the new sovereign. Could even Sanford Dole have then foreseen what political changes the next twenty years were to bring?

Printed in five weekly installments in the *Pacific Commercial Advertiser* of January, 1874, this study was read by request forty-one years later before the Hawaiian Historical Society. And in 1936 it became, by Sanford Dole's own earlier selection, the leading article to introduce his series of nine papers prepared to complement Lorrin A. Thurston's volumes on the Hawaiian Revolution. Its first and third uses therefore span the half-century of his life from fledgling lawyer to distinguished statesman. Here, it foreshadows Dole's interests and long public career.

THIRTY DAYS OF HAWAIIAN HISTORY
(*Verbatim from 1874 edition*)
By Sanford B. Dole

History derives less interest from the magnitude of its events than from the principles involved therein, less from the numbers of its hosts than the causes and character of their movements. The uprising of a small people may be as inspiring as the uprising of a great nation.

To the lover of liberal institutions the accession of King Lunalilo to the Hawaiian Throne was full of propitious omens. A step toward popular government, even in a comparatively insignificant State, belongs to the world and is part of the universal progress. To Hawaiians it will ever be an era of great political moment. It was a serious crisis in affairs and fortunately terminated favorably for Hawaiian citizenship.

A brief review of a few of the most important circumstances in Hawaiian History will assist to a better understanding of the interesting events connected with the election and installation of King Lunalilo in January, 1873. The Hawaiians had rapidly advanced from the very complete feudal system of the time of their discovery by Captain Cook, to the liberal constitutional monarchy of the reign of Kamehameha III. The common people had passed in a single generation from the condition of serfs, retainers and tenants, to that of citizens and land-holders, with personal freedom and a voice in the government. Upon the death of Kamehameha IV, his brother, Prince Lot, proclaimed himself King and took the Government in his own hands. Then, calling a convention of the people to amend the Constitution, which he found inconsistent with his own ideas of Government, he addressed them in a dignified and liberal speech in which he made use of the following language:

"It has been the traditional policy of my predecessor to whom the kingdom is indebted for the liberal reforms that have been made, to lead the nation forward and to watch over its welfare. My subjects will find in me, as they did in him, a jealous guardian of their liberties, and an earnest promoter of all measures calculated to increase their happiness and to check the evils that tend to their destruction."

Five weeks later, after much parliamentary sparring, the King, being roundly defeated in a proposed amendment fixing a property qualification for the voting privilege, which was a favorite measure with him, abruptly broke up the convention, and in the following words fell back upon his last resort against the liberal institutions of the country:

"As we do not agree, it is useless to prolong the session, and as at the time His Majesty Kamchamcha III. gave the Constitution of the year 1852, he reserved to himself the power of taking it away if it was not for the interest of his Government and people, and as it is clear to me that the King left the revision of the Constitution to my predecessor and myself, therefore as I sit in his seat, on the part of the Sovereignty of the Hawaiian Islands, I make known today that the Constitution of 1852 is abrogated. I will give you a Constitution."

He kept his promise. In a few days he gave his subjects a Constitution proclaimed through the streets of the capital at the head of an armed force. The new Constitution fixed a property condition of suffrage, merged the two houses of the Legislature into one, and introduced several other features of absolutism into the Government. The people submitted not without protest to this infamous act. The King ruled with a strong hand. He gathered around him vigilant and resolute counsellors. He easily controlled the one-house Legislature. Nine years pass away, years of political suppression—and growing alienation between King and people. A period not devoid of commercial prosperity but yet attended with alarming national decay. Nine years, and then the end came.

The King's Birthday.—Wednesday, the 11th of December, 1872, like most tropical days rose bright and warm on Honolulu, the Hawaiian capital. It was the birthday of Kamehameha V., the King, and preparations for its customary observance as a national holiday were in full progress in the early morning. Flags fluttered from the government and private masts and shipping in the harbor. Business houses and shops were closed, and working men of all classes rested from labor. Parties of townspeople were starting out into the country to enjoy the holiday in rural festivities, while a scattered army of natives on their half-trained horses galloped gaily into town over the various roads, from all parts of the island, men, women, and children, and even the horses crowned and garlanded with flowing wreaths of the fragrant *maile,* all eager to join in whatever of merrymaking or excitement the city had to offer.

In the meantime while these signs of festival and pleasure were thus prosperously progressing, a scene of quite a different character was taking place at the Palace of Iolani. Before light the principal Government officials and the most intimate friends of the King had been hastily sent for, as he had been failing rapidly through the night and had at length gone into a state of stupor. Shortly after sunrise his consciousness returned, and those around him took immediate measures to have a will drawn up for him to execute. After some general conversation in regard to the succession, in which no positive conclusions were reached, and a few allusions to the distribution of certain items of his personal property, the Governor of Oahu taking down in writing his words, he told his friends that he was not so sick as they thought he was, and that they all had better have breakfast before going on with the will. Some of the company then left the room, and the King with assistance got up and walked around a little and ate a small quantity of food; then reclining again on his couch, in a few minutes without sign of approaching dissolution, he suddenly and quietly expired, at twenty minutes after ten o'clock.

The public was aware that the King had been seriously ill for many months in spite of the studied concealment on the part of the administration of the fact and the repeated statements in the Government Gazette that His Majesty was in "excellent health," but as to the nature of his malady or the severity of his illness they had to content themselves with the vaguest and most indefinite rumors. Still the fact of the King's absence during the preceding two or three months from the public drives and all state occasions left them not wholly unprepared for the report which was made through the town about breakfast time, that the King was dying. Here and there in the yet quiet streets, knots of people gathered and anxiously discussed the event with its possibilities. At about nine o'clock in the forenoon the King's Chamberlain passed through the business portion of the place and told people that His Majesty was better, and was eating his breakfast. This news greatly relieved the prevailing anxiety and changed the hush of gloomy anticipation which already brooded over the community, to the more lively and noisy scenes belonging to the anniversary of a King's birthday. But before half-past ten o'clock, the guns of the Puowaina battery above the town, which had been loaded to give at noon the royal salute, began to thunder forth in mournful minute guns, the announcement that he, whose birth the people were then commemorating, was dead; national festivities scattered over many a league were checked and hushed with the ominous warning, and the echoes of the death peal reverberating among the cliffs and crags of the mountains bore to the distant parts of the island a vague hint of the brooding of a public crisis.

The deep feeling caused by the event of the King's decease was rather alarm at the situation and its possibilities than regret for the dead. No royal testament had been signed. No successor to the throne had been appointed and proclaimed; the King left no nearer kin than Ruth Keelikolani, Governess of the Island of Hawaii, his half-sister and not in the line of royal descent. It was a crisis without precedent in the history of the nation; it was impossible to divine the temper of the people or guess at the line of action which different claimants to the throne might adopt.

As the country revellers of the morning straggled homeward in the evening, now mourners perchance, and many of them true to the ancient customs which made the days of mourning days also of absolute license, badly intoxicated, and spurring their jaded steeds up hill and down at a reckless speed, hugging their unfinished gin bottles with affectionate fondness as they rode, singing, shouting and swearing, would reply, if questioned as to their views on the succession, with an air of surprise at the question, that they supposed as a matter of course Lunalilo would be the new King.

On the next day the dead King lay in state in the throne room of the Palace while his Ministers, his Staff, and the Chiefs of the realm kept watch over him, and sombre *kahilis* waving at his head beat a sad and silent deadmarch for the crowds of people, subjects and aliens, who continuously filed through the apartment for a curious, farewell glance on the last of the Kamehamehas.

The Succession to the Throne.—On the day after the King's death, his Cabinet Ministers issued an order, calling a meeting of the Legislature for the eighth of January for the purpose of electing a new king.

The possible candidates for the office were Prince William Charles Lunalilo, Mrs. Bernice Pauahi Bishop, Queen Dowager Emma and Colonel Kalakaua. Of these, Prince Lunalilo held the highest rank and influence, his countrymen generally according him the position of highest chief by blood in the kingdom. He was about thirty-eight years old, had never married and was an educated and accomplished gentleman. During the late reign he had been unpopular with the administration, having been studiously slighted by the King and deprived of all honor, emolument, or participation in the government. His only official position remaining was the hereditary one of Noble, which gave him a seat in the upper side of the Legislature and which the Government was powerless to affect.

Mrs. Bishop ranked among the highest of the chiefs of the kingdom. She was the wife of Mr. Charles R. Bishop, an American living in Honolulu, and enjoyed a wide popularity among the people.

Queen Emma was well known throughout the civilized world, and popular among the Hawaiians.

Colonel Kalakaua belonged to a family of rank and distinction among the chiefs of the kingdom. He was a man of education and industrious habits and during the late reign had held some civil position under the Government and had a commission in the Hawaiian army as a colonel.

During the first few days after the King's death there were many indefinite rumors afloat in regard to these different individuals, about what they said; what others said about them; what they wanted and hoped for and what they did not want and hope for. Naturally also they became the subjects of much criticism. Their lives were reviewed, their characters were weighed and compared, and their respective capacity for guiding the ship of state, discussed in all the possible relations of such questions. In all this agitation Prince Lunalilo appeared to hold the first place in the popular heart.

A large mass meeting which was held at the Kaumakapili church in Honolulu for the stated purpose of passing resolutions of condolence to the sister of the deceased King, after having performed that pious duty, proceeded at once to what was evidently the real object of the meeting, and passed a resolution amid general applause nominating the Prince as the successor to the throne. In other parts of the islands also many impromptu meetings were held and generally with the same result. No immediate step was taken by any of the candidates and the days succeeding the royal demise passed anxiously. There was no precedent in Hawaiian history for such an emergency, and many were alarmed lest during the interregnum, under the excitement of opposing political interests, with the large numbers of people who flocked to the capital, lawlessness might arise and acts of violence be perpetrated, and the more especially as in old times the death of a ruling chief was the signal for a carnival of unrestrained license of every kind; but the only instances of any remnant of this custom were the nightly mourning orgies in the Palace grounds, and a feeble mutiny in the national prison at Oahu on the day of the King's death. On this occasion, some of the prisoners rose on the jailer and attempted to escape, arguing that with the King's death law had ceased to exist, and logically concluding by virtue thereof that punishments also properly came to an end.

Business went on through these days, apparently as usual. The courts of justice remained open and transacted their special duties; criminal cases were prosecuted in the name of the King the same as while he was living. Still, though there was no standstill in affairs, the shadow of a great crisis rested on the land. Vague, indefinite, and unknown, all men felt its gloom and looked anxiously forward to the end. Trade drooped under it and heavily and sullenly dragged its task through the hours of each slow passing day. A hush of waiting for some uncomprehended solution muffled the din of traffic and forbade the merry music of festive reunions. Every evening from seven o'clock till midnight the spacious Palace grounds were open to the natives who thronged thither in crowds to offer their tribute of mourning for the dead King, who lay in his coffin in the throne room of the Palace, guarded by detachments of the royal troops. Nightly, till the funeral, the sound of these lamentations rose on the air in every variety of requiem from civilized psalm-tune chorals and sad, plaintive melodies of their own composition to the regular *kanikaus* and hopelessly despairing wails of the olden time, with their accompaniment of hula drums, gourd and bamboo time-beaters, and weird gesticulations.

Lunalilo's Manifesto.—Matters continued in this unsatisfactory condition until the morning of the seventeenth of December, six days after the death of Kamehameha, when a manifesto was issued by Prince Lunalilo and scattered with the assistance of the press to the uttermost parts of the kingdom. In the following terms this chief submitted to the people his claims to the throne, and promising certain liberal measures, asked for their vote:

TO THE HAWAIIAN NATION!

William C. Lunalilo, son of Kekauluohi, the daughter of Kamehameha I., to the Hawaiian people, greeting:

Whereas, The Throne of the Kingdom had become vacant by the demise of His Majesty Kamehameha V., on the 11th of December, 1872, without a successor appointed or proclaimed; and

Whereas, It is desirable that the wishes of the Hawaiian people be consulted as to a successor to the Throne; Therefore,

Notwithstanding that according to the law of inheritance, I am the rightful heir to the Throne, in order to preserve peace, harmony and good order, I desire to submit the decision of my claim to the voice of the people to be freely and fairly expressed by a plebiscitum. The only pledge that I deem it necessary to offer to the people is that I will restore the Constitution of Kamehameha III. of happy memory, with only such changes as may be required to adapt it to present laws, and that I will govern the nation according to the principles of that Constitution and a liberal constitutional monarchy, which, while it preserves the proper prerogatives of the Crown, shall fully maintain the rights and liberties of the people.

To the end proposed, I recommend the judges of the different election districts throughout the islands (thereby appealing to their ancient allegiance to the family of the Kamehamehas), to give notice that a poll will be opened on Wednesday, the 1st day of January, A.D. 1873, at which all male subjects of the kingdom may by their vote peaceably and orderly express their free choice for a king of the Hawaiian Islands as successor to Kamehameha V. And that the said officers of the several election districts, do, on a count of the vote, make immediate certified return of the same to the Legislative Assembly summoned to meet at Honolulu on the 8th day of January, 1873. That if any officer or officers of any election district shall refuse to act in accordance herewith, or if there shall be a vacancy in said officers in any district, the people may choose others in their places who may proceed in conformity to law in conducting the election.

Given under my hand this 16th day of December, 1872.

"God protect Hawaii nei."

An appeal so moderate, just, and democratic could hardly fail of being well received, and under the circumstances of Lunalilo's existing popularity and the prevailing anxiety for definite measures, no other step could have been taken with so favorable an effect upon his fortunes. The independent press warmly espoused his cause, and numbers of influential people committed themselves positively in his favor. The news of the reception of the manifesto on the other islands showed a similar enthusiasm for the Prince in every part of the group, and it began to be a settled thing in the minds of men that he was the unanimous choice of the nation. Still, however, some anxiety was felt as to the possible action of the Legislature in the matter, lest they might be influenced by other candidates to ignore the wishes of the people. As yet no open opposition was made to the popular feeling by his rivals, though some of them had their adherents, who did not hesitate to support them as opportunity offered.

During all this agitation, Prince Lunalilo kept himself closely at home, where he freely received those who, now that his star was rising, hastened in no inconsiderable numbers to pay their respects, to tender advice, and to ask favors of him who had till lately lived in comparative obscurity and neglect. With much patience and good nature, he would listen to his new friends and when they were ready to go would personally bow them out with that unfailing courtesy which was a prominent trait of his character.

Electioneering—Mass Meeting.—A few days after the appearance of the manifesto, a paper printed at the Government press for parties who were anonymous was distributed secretly by night through the streets of Honolulu, of which the following is a translation:

This Is the Truth!

On the 16th day of the present December, a proclamation was issued in this city commencing as follows: "I, Wm. C. Lunalilo, the son of Kekauluohi, the daughter of Kamehameha I., to the Hawaiian Nation, greeting."

"Let the genealogists see, and they testify this: Kekauluohi was not a daughter of Kamehameha I. as asserted in the publication. But her line is after this manner: Kaleimamahu lived with Kaheiheimalie and Kekauluohi was born thence; and Kekauluohi lived with Charles Kanaina and thence was born the Chief Wm. C. Lunalilo.

"On the other side this is the real truth: Kamehameha I. (after the birth of Kekauluohi) lived with Kaheiheimalie and thence was born Kinau; Kinau lived with M. Kekuanaoa and thence was born the two Kings now deceased. But in regard to the relationship of Kamehameha I. to Kaleimamahu it is as follows: Keoua lived with Kekuiapoiwa thence was born Kamehameha I. Afterwards Keoua lived with Kamakaheikuli, and thence was born Kaleimamahu, the father of Kekauluohi. This also is the truth: Kamehameha I. lived with Kaekapolei thence was born Kaoleiohoku, a male, the first born of Kamehameha I. Kaoleiohoku lived with Keoua, a female, and thence was born Pauahi, which female chief lived with M. Kekuanaoa, thence was born the sister of the late King, Ruth Keelikolani. Kaoleiohoku further lived with Luahine, thence was born Kalani Pauahi.

"Oh people, you here have the truth, and the relationship of these chief families to Kamehameha."

By the SKILLFUL GENEALOGISTS.

N.B.—By the foregoing genealogical accounts it will appear that the Chief Wm. C. Lunalilo is not a descendant of Kamehameha I.

No satisfactory conclusion can be made from the genealogical authorities of the Hawaiians. Jarves makes Lunalilo the grandson of Kaiana, the brother of Kaeo, an ancient King of Kauai, and Dibble makes Kaeo the uncle of Kamehameha I. and he and the "skillful genealogists" agree in making Lunalilo the grandson of Kaleimamahu, who was the son of Keoua and half brother to Kamehameha I.

Whatever of truth or probability the foregoing publication may have contained, it was regarded by the people as a mean attack upon their favorite; and the secret manner of its distribution with its anonymous character added to this feeling. This evidence of opposition unknown in strength and working in secret had the effect very materially to stimulate the Lunalilo party, and the signs of its power and growth became more positive every day.

As the tide of popular feeling for the Prince increased, efforts to swell it to the utmost that it might sweep away all opposition assumed a more public character. The independent newspapers in both languages were covered with leaders and articles absolutely committing themselves to the fortunes of his party, and in which they boldly charged all opposition in such positive terms as to assume the enthronement of their candidate as a *fait accompli* and all hostility thereto as already treasonable. In the streets, and in the fish market at Honolulu, where at certain times large numbers

Sanford B. Dole and Anna C. Dole about 1886

Entrance to the Emma Street home and interior view

of people congregated, stump orators from hitching-posts and fish counters harangued willing listeners and easily drew enthusiastic applause by a judicious use of the magic word, Luna-lilo.

Many who had hitherto wavered and refrained from supporting any candidate, and some who had openly opposed the Prince, now one by one declared in his favor. These changes of base by which discreet individuals endeavored to preempt in the fortunes of an inevitable destiny caused much irreverent amusement among the sagacious ones who had adhered to him from the first utterance of his claim.

About this time it was reported that the rival candidates, with the exception of Col. Kalakaua, had waived all claim to the Throne in favor of Lunalilo. There does not appear to be any evidence that Queen Emma made any effort toward the sovereignty or that she troubled herself at all about the matter or regarded her own prospects, and it conveys a false impression to speak of her as a candidate. And so far as definite report goes, the same is true of Mrs. Pauahi Bishop, for as much as the King in his last severe attack just before his death, distinctly, but informally, proposed to her that she should be his successor, which flattering offer she declined.

The number of people in Honolulu was materially increased during these days by additions from the other islands. Every steamer and sailing vessel that came into the harbor was crowded with men, women and children attracted thither by the political situation and the coming funeral of the late King.

On the evening of the twenty-sixth of December, a mass meeting called by a number of white and native citizens through the newspapers, was held at Kaumakapili church. This building had been used a number of times during the interregnum for political meetings until it had acquired a character like that of Faneuil Hall in revolutionary days. When its bell, which hung in a low belfry of wood near the churchyard gate was rung out of the usual hours, the natives all through the town would throw down whatever they had in their hands and leaving their work or amusements would run for the church, such was their interest in the politics of the times. On this occasion as the bell sounded forth its call, the people began to collect and at the appointed time half an hour later the church was filled with a dense crowd of which the great majority were natives. The stated object of the meeting was to take measures for the election on the first of January called for by the manifesto of Lunalilo, and for such consultation upon civil matters and such expression of opinion as might be appropriate. After the meeting was organized, two resolutions were passed referring to the vacancy of the Throne and the proposed election and calling upon all citizens of the district to assemble at the polls, according to the suggestion of the manifesto, on the first day of January to choose their King. The second resolution recommended that a committee of thirteen be chosen, who should make all necessary arrangements for the election, which was immediately acted upon, and the committee, including both natives and foreigners, was appointed by acclamation. A third resolution was then offered which read as follows:

Resolved, That this meeting acknowledging the justice of the claims of His Highness Prince W. C. Lunalilo to the Throne of the Hawaiian Islands as the successor of His late Majesty Kamehameha V. and approving of his guarantee to restore the Constitution of the Hawaiian Islands, and to "fully maintain the rights and liberties of the people" as stated in his manifesto of the 16th of December, 1872, express their hearty support of His said Highness Prince W. C. Lunalilo, as a candidate to the Throne of the Hawaiian Islands.

After several speeches this was passed with much applause. Next followed a motion by Mr. Whitney, editor of the *Kuokoa,* a native weekly newspaper:

Resolved, That we the people do hereby instruct our four Representatives in the Legislative Assembly to vote for Prince W. C. Lunalilo for King, and for no one else.

This was instantly adopted with the most uproarious enthusiasm.

Mr. Whitney then related an incident of the infancy of the Prince:

Mr. Bingham, who was about to perform the ceremony of baptism, asked, "What shall we call the child?" "Kanaina," the father replied, "William Charles Kanaina." "No," objected his mother, the noble Kekauluohi; "he is the highest chief in all the islands, therefore his name shall be Lunalilo," or "out of sight above," as Mr. Whitney translated it.

This little narrative "brought down the house" in a wonderful manner; all present stood up, swinging hats and handkerchiefs and shouting in the most tumultuous way. And then the work of the meeting being satisfactorily accomplished, with three grand cheers for Lunalilo, the great audience broke up. The effect of this assembly was healthy in its influences upon the politics of the time. It was significant of the earnestness of the people and helped to silence those who ridiculed the idea of a popular election for a King.

Kalakaua's Manifesto.—Two days after the meeting, a manifesto was issued by Col. Kalakaua, copies of which were liberally distributed in Honolulu and forwarded to the other islands. It was worded in the old figurative and poetical style and is interesting as a specimen battle-call of the Hawaiian pre-civilized age.

It was of no use. This elaborate message fell upon the community without effect. It was a failure as a proclamation and only valuable as a curiosity. The time had passed for attempts of such a nature against the widespread feeling for Lunalilo. After his master stroke—his liberal manifesto—with his previous popularity, something more than a printed circular was essential for successful opposition. This effort of the Colonel, made just before the first of January, was without doubt intended to defeat, if possible, the carrying out of the election on that day.

The Plebiscitum.—The Committee of Thirteen were not idle after their appointment at the meeting of the 26th of December. Prominent advertisements and posters in both languages proclaimed to the people of the district the necessary information and called upon all Hawaiians, native-born and naturalized, over twenty years of age, the age of majority for men, to cast their ballots for their King at the polls of the people, upon the first of January. In the late regime a property qualification had been a condition of the voting privilege, but on this occasion citizenship was the only requirement.

There were still, on the eve of the election, enemies and skeptics who sneered at the enterprise and prophesied a failure. They asserted that the people would not respond, with the exception of a few partisans, and that their vote, even though unanimous, would express nothing as regarded national sentiment. These individuals, moulded under the ideas of the late despotic reign, were unable to appreciate the principle of civil power originating with the

people or to understand the force of united popular will; and they
doubted the influence of the election even if it should be universally attended.

The first of January arrived and being a national holiday, the
only business carried on was that of voting. Even the usual festive
observances of the day were neglected for the one matter of absorbing interest. Early in the forenoon a crowd had gathered at the
polling place and the balloting went quietly and rapidly on, and
in a manner full of earnestness and determination, many prominent citizens and high officials of the Government depositing their
ballots along with humble kanakas fresh from their ancestral
taro-patches. In the afternoon the voting slackened somewhat,
and the crowd around the polls were alternately instructed and
amused by the delphic utterances of impromptu stump orators
who found it easy work to sway the popular mind in favor of the
hero of the day. There was little or no open electioneering for Col.
Kalakaua, and the supporters of Prince Lunalilo seemed to have
things all their way. About the middle of the afternoon a company of the Household Troops marched down to the polls and
deposited their ballots. At five o'clock the voting ceased, and the
crowd who had passed the day in unfailing good nature, remained
to hear the result. Every minute increased its numbers till at half-
past six, when the counting of the ballots was completed, the
street was filled with a dense mass of people, natives and foreigners, quietly waiting for the announcement of the vote.

When the judges of the election came out at last and proclaimed
the casting of a number of ballots, larger than had ever been polled
in the district during the late reign, and all for Prince Lunalilo,
the feelings of the listening crowd broke forth in repeated and
enthusiastic shouts which rang from the street, where they stood
almost unobservable in the gathering darkness of the night, and
proclaimed the news of the victory far and wide over the city.
The excitement of the people was intense and they were in a mood
to finish the work of conferring royalty by immediately marching
in a body to the residence of the Prince, in order to carry him to
the Palace of Iolani and install him there as King by popular
acclamation. But the Prince having feared some manifestation of
this kind had sent word to the judges of election that they should
request the people to go quietly home and wait till the election in

the Legislative Assembly, after which he would be happy to receive them at the Palace. An uproarious cheer was their answer and then the main part of the concourse started off through the streets, hallooing and singing, as noisy and demonstrative a rabble as the town had often seen.

The returns from the other islands exhibited similar unanimity and enthusiasm in almost every elective district. The whole nation with but a few scattering exceptions had united in nominating Lunalilo for King.

The Legislative Election for King.—As the eighth of January drew near, rumors began to circulate to the effect that Col. Kalakaua was making every effort to influence the legislators in his favor, and much uneasiness was felt lest the election of the first should be reversed by the action of the Legislature, in which case there seemed little doubt but that serious civil disorder would ensue. On the afternoon of Monday, the sixth, these rumors developed into definite reports, and it was stated that Hon. Mr. Kipi, a member from Hawaii of considerable influence, had been gained over by Col. Kalakaua. Later in the evening several more members were reported to have followed Mr. Kipi.

Kalakaua had staked his hopes on the legislative election. It does not appear that he entered the election of the first of January as a candidate, but simply strove by his proclamation and in other ways to cause its failure.

Tuesday had been appointed for the funeral of the late King, but after the troops and people began to assemble for the procession, the clouds which had been gathering on the mountains through the morning darkened the whole sky and poured down a copious shower which scattered the gathered mourners and caused the funeral to be postponed till Saturday. In the evening the accounts of the recreancy of representatives became more definite and alarming, and it seemed doubtful whether the election of the Prince could be carried, especially as it was believed that a considerable number of the Nobles were unfavorable to him. The excitement in the city of Honolulu both among natives and foreigners was great, and the morrow was awaited with anxious foreboding.

The eighth of January opened with a bright, calm morning. All business was given up to the one work of the day—the settlement of the succession to the throne. During the forenoon the streets were filled with groups of people of all classes and races, eagerly talking over the coming event. The latest rumors as to the position of the different representatives were discussed with discouraging conclusions. The nobles were weighed in the balance of public opinion, but without brightening the prospect. Actual fighting was regarded as inevitable should the election reverse the vote of the first. Many prepared themselves for emergencies by arming.

Early in the morning Prince Lunalilo with a number of his friends debated the events of the day and their possible results. Little satisfaction was gained from this consultation. They were unable to count enough undoubted supporters in the Assembly to ensure the election. The Prince was grave and anxious. He was aware of the spirit of the people and that it was their resolute determination to greet him as King that day. No one could divine all that might happen.

At the same time quite a different scene was taking place at Kalakaua's house. The gallant Colonel was preparing himself and his friends for the fortunes of the day over the viands of a well-appointed breakfast, to which a number of the representatives and others had been invited. The affair was generally regarded as a political move, but whatever may have been the intention, the meal passed off in an ordinary manner, and little was said about the claims of the rivals to the throne. The number present was small.

Noon was the time fixed for the sitting of the Legislature, and as it drew near the current of movement in the streets tended toward the Court House; many of the crowd were armed with stones and cudgels and some with revolvers, borne with a grim determination to see the question settled immediately and their choice proclaimed as King in one way if not in another. They thronged into the Court House square and surrounded the building, where they quietly waited for such instruction as events might afford. When the doors of the audience division of the Legislative Hall were opened, those nearest thronged in and filled it at once. At noon the Assembly was called to order. Nearly all of the members were in their seats. A few moments later a tumultuous cheering from the crowd outside announced the arrival of the Prince, who had walked over from his residence with two or three friends. When he entered the Hall, the audience arose and welcomed him with hearty shouts.

Business was opened by the presentation and reading by the [late King's] Cabinet of the documents relating to his demise and to their subsequent official action. The motion was then made that the Legislature proceed immediately to the election of a king from among the chiefs of the kingdom, according to the provision of the Constitution for a vacancy in the succession; when this was passed, Lunalilo left the Hall, and awaited the result in an adjoining room. As the members had taken their seats they had each received a duplicate letter from Col. Kalakaua, stating his claim to the throne as being a member of an ancient and honorable line of Hawaiian chieftains, and requesting their votes in the ensuing election. The letter was manly in its tone and couched in simple and appropriate language quite different from his gorgeous manifesto of the twenty-eighth of December. He was not present through the proceedings, but remained at the Palace with the military on guard over the still unburied corpse of the late king. Another paper printed over the signature of "The People" was also distributed among the members reminding them of the national decision of New Year's Day and suggesting that they should all sign their names to their ballots that it might be known who, if any, should try to thwart the wishes of the people.

For the more successful carrying out of this suggestion, Mr. Simon Kaai, member from Hawaii, made the extraordinary motion that each member should sign his name to the back of his ballot. After some trifling opposition from Mr. Kipi and one or two others, the motion was carried with little or no dissent in the show of hands. It is undeniable that the threatening and determined aspect of the concourse of people in and around the building awed the positive opposition, which certainly existed, into apparent compliance.

The balloting took place immediately upon the passage of this resolution. The members being called off by the clerk went up one by one to the table and deposited their votes. Then one of the tellers read them off with the signatures endorsed upon them. It was a thrilling moment. The audience in the Hall and the great crowd outside were as silent as the grave and almost breathless with excitement. The first ballot was told off "Lunalilo for King." The next was the same; and the next. As each one was reported, the result was telegraphed by those who thronged the open windows to the people below. So the telling went on in the hushed stillness of the great assembly, till, as the number reached a bare majority and thus far all for Lunalilo, a cheer came up from the grounds, and, gathering strength, burst in a deafening roar which rose and fell like the crisis of a storm; the outskirts of the crowd took up the refrain and the streets leading into the square sent on their answering shouts. Never before had the capital been the scene of equal enthusiasm. The whole city echoed with the triumphant acclamations, and suburbans miles away listened to the hearty welcome of the new King.

When the counting of ballots was over in the Hall, showing a unanimous vote for Lunalilo, the audience arose and hailed the result in a manner which was an echo of the outside enthusiasm. In a few minutes the King appeared on the western balcony of the Court House and was vociferously welcomed by the dense throng of his new subjects below. He made a short speech both in the Hawaiian and English languages; and then, dispensing with the carriages that were awaiting him, set out for Iolani, the Palace, on foot; but he did not go alone; there was indeed no military cortege; no drums and bugles announced his progress; no uniforms and feathers lent their glory to this triumphal march. Bareheaded and reverently the King walked, with the Chancellor of the Kingdom at his side, while the people did him honorable escort. The great crowd who gave him his first welcome as King, surged around him in solid mass as he went, and thus the imposing procession moved through the streets, citizens all, vanguard and rearguard and heralded only by the hearty hurrahs of the populace.

When night came the town blazed with illuminations, and a huge torchlight procession, organized by the patriotic German club, wound its dazzling way through the place for hours.

The thirty days are almost over. Their work is accomplished. Hawaiian citizenship is vindicated. A step upward is achieved. It remains but to mention the attendant ceremonies of the opening of the new regime and the closing of the old.

The morning comes with the usual tropic brilliancy. The whole community is astir. Everybody is out for the grateful work of the day. Flags flutter gaily from staffs and masts. The interior of the great stone church shines with flags and flowers. The people, their guests—the commissioners, navymen and strangers from other lands, their nobles and rulers, themselves, the king-makers, with their wives and children gather in the pews and galleries and throng the aisles and fill the churchyard. The soldiery of the kingdom make a lane to the church door. At noon the King with a few officials of high rank and attended by the glittering staff of the late king, comes on foot to the church and passes up the aisle to the platform; his arrival is greeted with acclamations. The ceremony is rather like the inauguration of a president than the coronation of a king. The Hawaiians have no ancestral crown, but the splendid emblem of sovereignty, the royal feather robe, is laid over the throne, and seated upon its shining folds, Lunalilo the King receives the glad recognition of his subjects, while discharges of artillery from Punchbowl and the men-of-war add their loud acclaim. After the oath of office is sworn, the King delivers addresses to the Legislature and to the people in both languages. It is an impressive scene: the young King, dressed in plain black, with his fine and commanding figure and dignified bearing, surrounded by the attendant officials in brilliant uniforms, and the enthusiastic assembly in holiday attire. The aid and blessing of the King of Kings is besought in earnest words of prayer, and then the venerable old church is left to its own week-day solitude.

Again the city is wholly given up to rejoicing. Again as the sun goes down, lights flash from villa and cottage and the army of torches drives the night before it through the streets.

One more day. The remains of His late Majesty are on the way to their unseasonable burial. The procession is imposing with military display, and well-appointed arrangements. Home and foreign officials tread the dead march in their places with manner of appropriate solemnity. Stately *kahilis* move in gloomy majesty around the funeral car. Out from under the black pall which half hides the splendid coffin, flashes the golden sheen of the royal feather cloak. The national band lament the dead in classic strains from the old masters. And yet few unofficial mourners follow the pageant. The people are there as spectators only and line the roadside instead of making a part of the procession. Joy rather than sorrow is the popular expression, and as the new King passes as chief mourner, scarce can the shouts of the roadside throngs be restrained in spite of the solemnity of the occasion. When the funeral ceremonies are ended, the last prayer said, the volleys fired, the black *kahilis* placed standing before the Mausoleum door, then the prevailing joy and gladness break forth and Lunalilo rides back to his Palace and the duties of his reign with the jubilant acclaim of a spontaneous ovation from his subjects.

HONOLULU
1874–1879

ALL THE LOYALTY of his people, however, proved powerless to extend King Lunalilo's reign beyond the threshold of its second year. Beloved for his kindliness, his skill in music and his democratic habit of talking personally with his people, they had shouted, "This is our King." He promised and planned amendment of the Constitution of 1864, but before this could be approved by the Legislature, his life was cut short by tuberculosis.

Again minute guns from Punchbowl sounded a king's requiem. It was Wednesday, February 4, 1874. Good King Lunalilo this day lay in state from ten in the morning until two in the afternoon.

This sovereign had been the people's leader, even before they had acclaimed him in the old Stone Church, seated on his mother's great cloak of golden feathers. This ceremony seemed to Sanford Dole "rather like the inauguration of a president than the coronation of a king." Rightly Lunalilo lies buried beside that church in the heart of the town at Kawaiahao. With him lie entombed the hopes of many good men.

The thirty days of Hawaiian history, so aptly pictured by Sanford Dole, echoed sadly on February 6, 1874. At a meeting of the Hawaiian Bar on that day Mr. Justice Hartwell's measured estimate of Lunalilo struck home when he said: "I think we have all felt that in his hands Constitutional liberty was safe. This is saying a good deal of any sovereign. But it is saying the simple truth of Lunalilo." And unanimous approval passed S. B. Dole's resolution that "the Bar do wear mourning for thirty days and that the Court Room be draped."

On the very afternoon of the 4th citizens had crowded to a mass

meeting at Kawaiahao to nominate for kingship Colonel David
Kalakaua, descended from councilors of Kamehameha I.

And next day, February 5, Queen Emma, mother of the late
Prince Royal of Hawaii and widow of the late Kamehameha IV,
issued her manifesto as candidate for sovereign. On the 9th
"Queen Emma men" filled the open yard of Rooke House, her
childhood home on lower Nuuanu between Chaplain Lane and
Beretania. It was a huge mass meeting, acclaiming her with
shouts as the choice of her people. She was loved and respected
by Hawaiians and foreignors alike. Since the establishment of
the Hawaiian-Anglican Mission, however, and her own long
visit in England in 1865, her sympathies and interests looked
primarily toward England and the English.

To Americans and many Hawaiians, Queen Emma's day as
sovereign had passed. Nothing remained but to make a virtue
of necessity and favor Kalakaua as candidate for election.

Tension grew acute. Fears of a riot, or even civil war, marked
the approaching day, which was set for a special session of the
legislative body on the 12th of February. The Honolulu Rifles
were called to their armory at the foot of Nuuanu, not far from
the courthouse where the Legislature met. American Minister
H. A. Peirce arranged for signals from a ship at the wharf to two
United States war vessels in the harbor for landing-parties, should
need arise.

Sanford Dole's reminiscences describe crowds of men, mainly
Hawaiians, gathering about the courthouse on Queen Street near
Fort. At first they formed a cheerful mob, but once it was
whispered about that of forty-five votes only six had been cast
for Queen Emma, threats began to be hurled at legislators thought
to have voted for Kalakaua.

A committee of the Legislature delegated to convey word of
his election to the new king, was headed by dignified Major
Moehonua of Maui. When they stepped into his carriage to
deliver their message, the carriage was seized and literally torn
to pieces by the mob, which barely let the committee escape into
the courthouse.

Front and rear doors of the building were closed and the
legislative hall cleared of spectators by Charles Reed Bishop,
Minister of Foreign Affairs. With him as aides were Luther Wil-

cox and George Dole of the Honolulu Rifles. David Dayton, Deputy Marshal, and well liked by Hawaiians, was gently lifted "high above their heads and passed out horizontally to the outskirts of the crowd." Surging into the courthouse with clubs and improvised battering-rams, the rioters ransacked both police and Supreme Court rooms. Judge Harris, attacked with a chair leg, "picked it up and politely handed it back to the one who threw it." Legislators, where they could be found, were savagely beaten, furniture broken to pieces, papers scattered to the winds. One of the members was thrown out bodily; at least one man died of injuries a few days later.

Sent in haste by Mr. Bishop to Queen Emma's residence at Rooke House, Sanford Dole discovered her retainers in a state of such hysterical excitement that he could not even get an audience with Queen Emma, to enlist her aid in pacifying her supporters. On his return, he found the courthouse a shambles and within the heavy railing two last legislators defending themselves with chairs as shields. They were a father and son from Maui. Spreading out his arms, Dole made a firm stand against the attackers, amongst whom he met little teamwork; but with this instant's respite the two victims escaped by the inner stairway.

At last, but summoned too late to quell the fury of the mob, sailors and Marines from the American men-of-war were seen marching up Fort Street from the wharf and making arrests among the rioters. A giant sergeant of Marines, capable of holding two average men with one of his enormous hands, called out in high spirits, "Bring on your gonakas!" British Marines were detailed to guard Rooke House, and other men from the British gunboat *Tenedos* patrolled the town for a few nights. But all troops were withdrawn to their ships within the week.

The next day Queen Emma conceded the election and advised her followers to do likewise. Kalakaua, a timid man, was found by C. T. Gulick and Dr. Trousseau in hiding under a wooden house opposite the palace. Although assured of safety, the new king preferred to postpone taking the oath of office. This was duly administered, however, and Kalakaua was proclaimed king at noon on the 13th of February in the presence of the Diplomatic Corps, the Cabinet, the Privy Council, and members of the Legislature.

Reluctant to appear before the Legislature next day, the king issued a commission to his chancellor, Chief Justice Allen, to prorogue that body in his stead. On hearing of this plan, Sanford Dole went to the king at his quarters on Richards Street and pointed out to him its bad form. Whereupon the king acted with due ceremony in person, most of the Legislators appearing with bandaged heads or arms. A number of rioters, tried in jury sessions of the Supreme Court, were sentenced to longer or shorter terms of imprisonment. On the 17th the king appointed his first Cabinet: W. L. Green, for foreign affairs; H. A. Widemann, for the interior; P. Nahaolelua, for finance; and A. S. Hartwell, attorney general. For some time Kalakaua was apprehensive of further disturbance, but none occurred.

This account of the election difficulties is largely in Sanford Dole's own words, set down many years later. At the time, the *Advertiser* of February 21, 1874, printed his frank discussion entitled: "The Lessons of the Riot." The disgrace of the situation he felt to be "indeed grave; the national credit was shaken, confidence in the government destroyed, the very existence of Hawaiian independence endangered, some already looking to see our civil system under the protection of some foreign power.

"There is but one way of escape from such a fate. The path of prosperity and safety now lies in resolution and vigilance. We may not atone for the past, but we can guard the future.

"We look to the new reign for the policy and leadership which shall avert the threatening evils."

Whether Sanford Dole's New England bride considered a thorough-going riot more than she had anticipated in making Honolulu her home, she did not say. Instead, she wrote quietly enough to Mother Dole on the 4th of February of going to see King Lunalilo lying in state amid almost fearful wailing; of hearing as she sat at her desk, shouts from Queen Emma's followers who were making loud and determined efforts in her behalf.

The Sanford Doles were boarding on Fort Street at Chaplain Lane with Mrs. Irwin, mother of young William G. Irwin who sometimes went sailing with Sanford. Irwin's sister often played sweetly on the parlor piano, while Anna, in her upstairs rooms, was busy training her German ivy to wreathe itself around the pictures on their walls. Some day, she wrote, Sanford was to take her to Pele's Place in the valley to find ferns and mosses to plant in a new wire basket for her veranda. She was taking as much delight in it all as Will Rowell and Sanford had done in their rooms at Williams College. But Anna had the joy of an upstairs veranda where she and Sanford were training vines up to the roof to temper the afternoon sun. Directly across Fort Street, which was then only a narrow carriage-way, branches of an old algaroba tree in front of the Roman Catholic Church had at first given their Irwin veranda pleasant shade, but priests had had the tree trimmed back severely, although it was the first of its kind in Honolulu. Such homely news gentle Charlotte Dole on Kauai found heart-warming to receive from her new daughter, who was willing to write the little things that a woman longs to hear.

Later a letter from Anna told of the actual day of the 12th, a beautiful, quiet day until small crowds began to appear from nowhere along Fort Street. Anna then suddenly recalled Sanford's having said that, in case of trouble, he would "pitch in for law and order, but for nothing else." That afternoon Mr. W. F. Allen arrived from town, pale and excited, with the keys of the custom house, lest the mob surge in there for liquor. Uncle Ned Adams hurried in too, begging Anna to go over to his house and stay with Nellie and the children, which of course she was glad to do.

But oh, the relief when Sanford later rode up to the Adams' house on horseback to take her home! He was a good deal excited. It seemed as if he had been through something too dreadful to describe. It had begun with Moehonua's carriage being literally torn to pieces before his eyes and every window in the stately courthouse being shattered by stones and clubs, the powerful natives with their flashing eyes and dark skins looking the very impersonation of fury. "It gave us a certain sense of security to see the British sailors guarding Queen Emma's home," added Anna, "but it was a long time that night before we could compose ourselves to sleep."

Ordinarily the days chronicled for Mother Dole passed quietly enough. Once Lottie Smith, now young Mrs. Hartwell, came to call with her baby, who was very bright and so pretty, they must be proud of it, thought Anna. Then came the day the firemen

paraded, when Sanford looked so grand in the procession with
his blue flannel shirt and pioneer's axe. The reading club in the
evenings, sometimes at Uncle's or the Jones's or the Parkes's, was
always so interesting and the young Doles looked forward to it.
On Sunday afternoons they often drove out to Moiliili or Waikiki,
branch churches of Kawaiahao, where Sanford held Sunday
School and church services in Hawaiian. One Saturday evening
they enjoyed attending Emma Widemann's home wedding to
Henry Macfarlane, Father Hermann officiating; a gay evening
followed, with supper and dancing.

During the month of May Father Dole wrote that Mother
had been taken with a slight paralytic seizure while sitting at
table. Sanford at once went by the *Kilauea* to return with them
to Honolulu on the 30th. His father and mother drove over
the road through the hills from Koloa to take the steamer at
Nawiliwili, much as they had taken their first drive to Koloa
nineteen years before. And next day they were comfortably
settled in George's roomy house at Kapalama School. In June
there were happy days together at first, and later when Mother
Charlotte grew worse, Clara took baby Charlie home to Waimea
on Kauai, while Sanford and Anna moved out to stay with the
family at the school.

Mother Charlotte's strength slowly failed. On the 4th of July
another stroke followed. Next day George's journal chronicled
her death as a blessed deliverance for her. Sanford's brief diary
recalled that Sunday as one of beautiful weather. So too was the
day following, when Mother was buried from the old Stone
Church at Kawaiahao in the little Mission plot and very near
Mother Emily's grave of thirty years before.

When Sanford wrote of this to Will Brigham in Boston, that
staunch friend answered: "I am glad I was in the Islands ten years
ago and could know so many of the older missionaries. How fast
the saints are gathering in that little Kawaiahao churchyard!"

Anna Dole told her husband that when she first knew him, the
one who came most swiftly to her mind was his beautiful young
Mother Emily from Maine; but little by little she had come to
realize what his Connecticut Mother Charlotte had brought to
his happy childhood. Something too of what the small boy had
put into Charlotte Dole's life, while she patched his clothes and

watched him play, had sung itself into Charlotte's heart with a lilting refrain of words. "I have a little step-son," she exulted,

> . . . the lovelist thing alive,
> A noble sturdy boy he is, and yet he's only five . . .
> His days pass off in sunshine, in laughter and in song,
> As careless as a summer rill that sings itself along . . .
> . . . of our home, that in the summer hours
> Stands in its simple modesty half hid among the flowers,
> I have not said a single word, nor of our mines of wealth;
> Our treasures are *this little boy,* contentment, peace and health.
> . . .
> And many a courtly pair, I wean, would give their gems and gold
> For a noble happy boy like ours, only four or five years old.

That home at Punahou remained a bright memory. And now, just as Sanford and Anna were beginning to make their home together in Honolulu, the old one at Koloa was coming to its close.

Going down with his father on their sad errand of change, Sanford had with him the older boy, Eddie Adams, and small Johnny for a few days at Koloa before they went to Lihue for their vacation. They sailed slowly along in the schooner *Jennie,* Sanford of course sleeping on deck with the two boys. Both Anna and Sanford were so fond of children that she took particular delight in Sanford's letter telling of Johnny's starting up suddenly, in mid-channel with no land in sight, to ask: "Mr. Dole, where are the Sandwich Islands?" And waking again later, he had asked anxiously whether yesterday was past. This was the same small Johnny who, after Anna had left them in Honolulu to go back East, had in a single breath added to his nightly prayer: "God bless Cousin Anna and let her come out all safe and don't let the sword fish make a hole in the vessel and take care of Mr. Dole when he goes after her."

When Daniel and Charlotte Dole had gone to visit "among the Yankees" in 1871, the little cottage at Koloa had been sold and good old Crusoe, the horse, had found a new home where he was loved. Now still greater changes must come. Full of association as they found everything, Sanford wrote to Anna:

Mother's little keepsakes, needle-work not quite finished, her chandelier furnished with new wicks, her store of sheets—the pain of it is that the reality of this home life is over. Father is cheerful, but does not say much.

Kuike and Kauhane, and others came, wept and stayed—all hard enough. George Charman will buy the place, for which I shall draw up the deed to send to Father from town. Perhaps brother George will bring it when he comes down to help Father with the auction of furniture. The Smiths are kind. Mr. Rowell came over and spent the night. We have plenty of milk, vegetables, poi and Mother's canned fruits. Eddie Adams and I rode over to Lihue to the Rices' to get our horse Winona, he is getting to be a real steady horse, Eddie rode him back. On Monday Eddie and I are going on a grand pig hunt in the woods *mauka* of Lihue. Today we have had an early swim in the stream and are going out after ducks. At the moment he and Johnnie are fishing in the brook.

Father sends love. The boys send theirs to you and to Uncle and Nellie. Eddie was going to write, but forgot, and now we are going to ride. Good bye, Darling.

Even Charlotte Dole's Koloa garden was to become a thing of the past. One who kept that bright memory was Dora Isenberg, who as a girl of eight would often drive her own horse over from Lihue in the little carriage to take Grandmother Rice to call. Father Dole would make a delicious drink of Chinese oranges for them; Mother Dole always had a new rose or lily to show them. And her sun dial! No one else had a sun dial, and Dora did long to ask how it worked. Mother Dole's lilies too where quite different from other people's lilies. And there was sorghum, perhaps from the Connecticut farm; a stick of it was so sweet to chew, although it was meant for the cows, but no one else grew sorghum in the Islands then. A little girl must not ask questions when visiting, so while the older people talked, Dora would run up to the little garret room where her own mother had slept as a school girl. There were heaps of old magazines there to read, and in the boys' room Sanford's training sword and boxing gloves hanging neatly on a nail.

After Sanford returned from Koloa in August he moved their own furniture, both from the Irwins' and some stored also at George's in Palama, to a cottage near the Cushman Jones's in Nuuanu. Mrs. Jones was Kitty Hall, a Mission Cousin who joined her husband in making Anna Dole welcome and asking her to live near by, as Sanford had done earlier.

Now the Doles were to have the fun too of keeping house in the Jones's own home while they went to Washington, he the bearer of dispatches with regard to the Reciprocity Treaty. Anna looked forward eagerly to this Nuuanu cottage, thinking as she wrote to Father Dole in September:

It will be almost like a home of our own where I can have my own things at last. The ivy and fern baskets look so well in it already. The two front rooms are newly papered and painted, with fresh Chinese matting on the floors, and I have had a boy to help clean house. It is not stylish, but just to have it clean is a comfort, even though you pointed out to Mother Dole and me, when we were cleaning the chandelier at Koloa, that cleanliness being next to godliness is *not* found in the Bible!

But we can have you to dinner, with George and Clara, and at last use my beautiful plain silver spoons that Uncle gave me, also the crystal vase in its silver stand that my Sunday School class brought to me in Castine just before our wedding day.

Thank you, Father, for saving many of the books in the Koloa home. They are too hard to get to part with easily. And we may, before another year, actually begin to have room for some of them at our own homestead. There is a good piece of land on Emma Street—the agricultural gardens just below Mr. Brown's—going at auction soon. We must take a mortgage on it at first, but will be very happy to begin planting and laying out a piece of land for our own home which you must come and share with us.

I felt badly that Sanford did not get the police judgeship. It was because of his letters in the paper after Kalakaua's accession to the throne. Many men wished Sanford to have the judgeship, and I have felt more disappointed about it than Sanford himself, I think.

For the last six months of 1874, we are both on the editorial board of the *Maile Wreath* for the Cousins' Society, and sometimes I can help Sanford by writing, as I did last month on the works of George Macdonald, a writer whom I admire. Sanford did a paper on Prayer Meetings with free and critical remarks on being called upon to pray. Our Cousins' meeting, at the McCullys', did not give time to discuss Sanford's pointed comments which were good. However, he had spoken his mind and many will read it in the Cousins' *Maile Wreath*.

Longing for her mother and friends in Maine, Anna Dole had enjoyed setting her uncle's home in order and taking flowers to it for Nellie Fisher Adams when she too came out as a New England bride. Anna recalled only too vividly what a tug it had been, even in her own new happiness, to leave Castine and all its memories. And now what joy it is to have Sister Isabel's letters, telling of Anna's mother, of the babies and of the family not liking to think of the Islands without telegraph or even a daily mail, such an out-of-the-way place that they must depend on sailing vessels to hear from Anna. "And Della says, 'poor benighted people, I suppose Cousin Anna don't even know that now they wear the hair low in one braid. But Brother Sanford will take us to task again if we even think of those islands as dark and heathen!'"

Brother Sanford, however, was engrossed in trying to arrange his business so that he could take his wife to Maui late in September, first to the Baileys' at Wailuku and then to board at the Andrews' in Makawao. There he had to leave her, hoping that the change might offset the effects of a fall she had had months before on Christmas morning while riding side-saddle. It had left her terrified of horses, as well as of cattle. On Maui she began diligently to ride every day on a slow, plodding horse. She had grown very thin, with a persistent cough which improved, yet brought the shuddering fear that she might be going into what was then called consumption.

Desperately homesick letters she wrote, although she did her best to interest herself in gathering and pressing ferns for the pretty album sent by her husband for just that purpose. "People are kind, so kind," she wrote to Father Dole, who was preaching in Hilo, "the Greens, the Andrews and dear Miss Carpenter among her Hawaiian girls at the Seminary." From Grove Ranch Kate Grey had invited Anna to visit for several days; Mrs. Henry Baldwin had come to call and ask her down to Sunnyside for a week; but first she must be stronger. And indeed strength was returning, but if Sanford would only come and take her home! This he did in November, to their mutual joy.

While editor of the Cousins' magazine, the unexpected death of his friend, Alfred Castle, was significantly chronicled by Sanford Dole. As with young Levi Chamberlain in a temporary illness years before, Dole had watched with Castle at night. He had seen him bear torture with unassuming heroism, until at last he had given up to the inevitable, but only after completing for the Legislature the detailed work assigned him, his biennial report as Registrar of Public Accounts. Tortured too, Castle had been by finding himself unable to subscribe to rigid Puritan tenets of church membership. "But Thank God," concluded Sanford, "that His own Universal Church is not limited by earthly ecclesiastic ties, and that Heaven with its blessed gates wide open, is over all."

Law business, although not very remunerative, had at length begun to dispel Dole's cloud of doubt as to the necessity for removal to California. In 1873 such a course had seemed imperative, but presupposed a non-existent capital. He and his wife had worked along together, boarding and economizing where they could. Anna told Father Dole that it had been entirely her own great idea to teach at Punahou, but even the suggestion of such a thing had been met by Sanford with a decided No. Yet she did enjoy her occasional groups of young girls who came to study English classics. And now at last in 1875 it was becoming feasible to buy the Emma Street lot, possibly on a mortgage, yet reserving enough margin to put up on this lower Punchbowl slope the plain cottage with its steep front steps like those so often favored by Hawaiians.

Enshrined forever in Sanford's memory was picture after picture of that first home and of her who made it tasteful and attractive. Anna, he told, was in all impulses of inclination an enthusiastic home builder. This was her dominant mood and into the making of our own home she entered with all the heartiness of her enthusiasm.

I well remember our careful study of plans. One evening our friend, Tom Walker, came with pasteboard, and skilfully constructed a model of the cottage as we had dreamed it, building it before our eyes on a small scale to study. We had to plan according to our slender purse, yet nothing cheap met acceptance for that reason. It was a little house of four rooms, but we moved into our own home at last with heartfelt satisfaction.

At first we had only two helpers, an unskilled Chinese and the yard boy. Anna herself cared for the table and the rooms, perhaps beyond her strength. She delighted in having guests, especially if they had a baby that she could hold in her arms. Beautifying the home became her deepest joy: flowers, pictures, furniture and rugs, draperies, statuary. During the early days of housekeeping we put aside a little change every week until we had amassed a fund for a blue parlor rug. Loving all flowers, and roses with passionate delight, she worked at their cultivation as my mother had longed to do in Koloa. When the Japanese beetles destroyed most roses, Anna concentrated an intensity of affection on the few that she managed to raise. Our home truly owed much to her rare taste in arrangement and adornment. Nasturtiums I remember Anna always had, delighting in their perfume as well as their color.

With a home of their own Anna's heart longed for a church home as well. On her request to Pastor Ives of the Congregational

Church in Castine, Maine, she was commended to the fellowship of the Fort Street Church in Honolulu. Sanford received his father's dismissal from the Foreign Church of Kauai. Uncle Ned joined them and together the three came before the examining committee of Fort Street Church. "Somewhat frightened at first, and we stayed until about 10 o'clock," Anna admits to Father Dole; "but after long discussion they concluded to let us enter, as we had asked to do, on confession of the Apostles' Creed." Sanford, however, expressed his uncertainty as to the doctrine of the Trinity and grave doubts as to eternal damnation. In writing to his father, he explained something of these doubts and of his feeling of dishonesty in subscribing blindly to others' creeds: "I believe that the supernatural is in the highest sense natural, and man can appreciate it by no better means than the natural logical methods we should use in explaining other subjects." He and Anna did not therefore become formally members of the Fort Street Church, but maintained such cordial relations with it and its successor, Central Union, that many thought of them as members of the church body as well as congregation.

George Dole, meanwhile, having decided to work on the weekly *Hawaiian Gazette,* with H. M. Whitney, put in his resignation as principal at Kapalama, and bought Captain Dudoit's old house in the Maemae region of Nuuanu Valley, south of Nuuanu Street and the smaller cemetery there. Later this site became part of the T. H. Davies home for many years. Ke-one-ula (Red Sand), the Dole home at Kapalama, had been a good home to the five children and had brought them a new sister, Emily Charlotte, named for both Dole grandmothers. Now to be moving up the valley and into their own home brought new adventures and special delights. Mother, of course, was busy with carpets and cleaning, but always had time for the children. Walter and Herbert had only to cross Nuuanu Street to the stimulus of Mrs. Lowell Smith's Valley School; then the Nuuanu stream was near and best of all with Father who enjoyed the swimming as much as everyone else. And often Uncle Sanford and Aunt Anna would drive up from Emma Street.

The house was a friendly, rambling one of added-on rooms and long verandas, one of these making a central hallway with a low window where it was easy to jump through into the bedroom.

The true story of this window, and its function in the murder of Captain Dudoit, is told by Charles Warren Stoddard in his eerie tale, "My Late Widow," but the dark thickets of weeds and lantana had long since been cleared away from the sunny hillside, and to the Dole children their first home was never a haunted house. Marion, first Dole daughter, had just (1953) made a happy pilgrimage to the site, recalling the mangoes from the one large, well-shaped tree; the avenue of strawberry guava trees with their small glossy leaves; and playing on the cemetery wall with next-older brother Herbert. Often, too, little Carrie Parker Green—companion on the recent pilgrimage of 1953—would come up from Judd Street to play, and then Marion and her little sister Clara were grateful that they need not call her Iu-bi-le, as loyal Hawaiians had promptly named Carrie when she was born on Maui in 1870, the year of the Mission Jubilee.

There weren't many other children to play with them, and the best fun of all, when Carrie came over and Mother could go with all three little girls, was to run down through the pasture to swim and splash in Nuuanu stream, which the three, after the lapse of all these years, still call Alekoki. For Alekoki it was, that mountain pool among the ferns, trysting-place of young Prince Lunalilo and little Princess Victoria Kamamalu, until the sad day when, forbidden by her brother, the king, as well as by her devoted foster-father, Judge John Ii, she came no more. Waiting in disappointment, Lunalilo threaded together like flowers those Hawaiian words of hurt and longing, his lei aloha for her, of words which to this day are sung and danced and loved in memory of that quickly-rippling pool in Nuuanu, *A-le-koki*.

One who knew Lunalilo from childhood, A. Francis Judd, later Chief Justice, related that the young prince and the little Princess Victoria Kamamalu were to have been formally betrothed during the reign of Kamehameha IV. The two were of equally high rank, gifted, and greatly loved by the people. As sovereigns, with Lunalilo's avowed intention of restoring the liberal constitution of Kamehameha III, how different might have been the later course of our Hawaiian monarchy had Lunalilo's aimless existence held some measure of happiness and a definite focus of interests, rather than apparent neglect on the part of his royal cousins, Kamehameha IV and Kamehameha V! Even this seemingly reasonable charge lays too much perhaps at the door of the last two sovereigns of the Kamehameha line. It is difficult, however, not to recall that in primitive times any high chief like Lunalilo would have been rigidly disciplined, even while a boy, for public responsibility. In the breaking down of the old order no substantial new one had yet emerged.

Journalism seems to have been an inborn instinct with Daniel Dole and both his sons. Even so, it is surprising that with all his personal as well as professional preoccupations Sanford Dole found long evening hours for work on yet another newssheet. Anna often helped too with book reviews. Appropriately named *The Islander,* this new journal appeared every Friday from March through October of 1875. With Thos. G. Thrum as business agent, J. H. Black as printer, and many signed articles, it proceeded, as did the *Punch Bowl,* without acknowledged editorship. Its subtitle: *A Weekly Journal Devoted to Hawaiian Interests, Scientific Researches, Literature, Home and Foreign Affairs,* sounds inclusive and thoroughly characteristic of its semi-anonymous young lawyer-editor. During six years since the adventures of issuing the *Punch Bowl,* he had grown, but was still moved by the same thoughtful absorption in the world and the people about him.

Whether, as seems probable, this assembling of local and foreign items in a small newspaper was primarily a means of sharing with the public Judge Andrews' ripe scholarship, the editor did not admit. His brief prospectus however implied as much, in introducing Andrews' notes and translations, as containing until then unknown examples of Hawaiian literature, destined to lend personal and permanent value to files of *The Islander.* For Judge Andrews, of all the American Mission workers, was preeminently a student of Hawaiian, and a man after Sanford Dole's own heart. Literature must go hand in hand with religion, believed Andrews; science and literature must expand the mind and religion must sanctify. "How is it that we have been preaching so much and teaching so little? It is our business to teach these people their own resources, mental, moral and physical." With this in mind, Andrews first taught himself to engrave on copper and so imbued his Hawaiian students with the joy of creation that even the exacting labor of polishing the copper plates was considered a "favored recreation."

The Rev. Lorrin Andrews, dying in 1868, had indeed filled full his measure of forty years' service to his adopted land. While founder of Lahainaluna Seminary, Seamen's Chaplain at Lahaina, copperplate engraver, translator of Proverbs and other books of the Bible, Associate Justice of the Supreme Court, as well as presiding in other Honolulu courts, and secretary of the Privy Council, his independent and inquiring mind had put together the earliest standard Hawaiian dictionary. Beloved of the chiefs, he had early felt obliged to decline their request to become their legal adviser. During his last years the Legislature accorded him an annual pension. His enviable scholarship was devoted to notes on the structure of Hawaiian poetry and translating the difficult song prophesying Kamehameha's conquest of the Islands. Eager to leave also a translation of the *Mele of Kualii,* fabled king of Oahu, Judge Andrews had delegated this to S. M. Kamakau and C. J. Lyons. The translations of these two *meles* with copious notes appeared serially under Dole's editorship in *The Islander,* their publication and editing alone serving as a distinct contribution to things Hawaiian.

In fact, when, almost fifty years later, Thomas Thrum edited the Fornander collection of Hawaiiana purchased by Mr. C. R. Bishop for the Bernice Pauahi Bishop Museum, Judge Andrews' translation, as presented by Dole, was incorporated in the new publication. This called forth a letter printed in the fourth number *The Islander,* written to its business agent, Thomas Thrum, by Judge Fornander himself. Encouraging it was to young journalists like Dole and Thrum to have his commendation of their enterprise in publishing *The Islander,* particularly when Judge Fornander hoped to read in their columns more of the past of these Islands, a past as interesting, he wrote, as that "which Homer sang to listening Greeks—as the past of any other people that had grace enough to commemorate the deeds of their ancestors." For in memory no doubt of his own Swedish ancestry Judge Fornander began to gather songs and stories from his wife's Hawaiian forefathers, and thus himself became an acknowledged authority in Polynesian folklore.

To the columns of *The Islander* is due likewise the publication of C. J. Lyons' classic presentation, "Land Matters in Hawaii." As a lad with other early Mission sons Lyons had carried compass and chain in heat and cold, often all day through pouring rain, into steep valleys like Waipio and across uplands down to rocky or sandy shores, in surveys which followed the king's *Mahele* (division of lands). Few could know so well the glories of the lands which they were eager to see kept as *kuleanas* (individual plots) by the Hawaiians, who of themselves had neither tools nor skill for such technical foreign surveys. Other such young workers, like Henry Lyman, Munson Coan and Sam Armstrong, had settled in the States. Curtis Lyons, remaining to grow up with his native Islands, had become preeminently fitted to discuss ancient units of land, their subdivisions, the sincere attempts to untangle local difficulties of fixing recorded titles among a primitive people. For they were a people accustomed to moving about: to using logs for housebuilding from *mauka* (uplands), thatching from open kula lands, and fishing along the *kahakai* or lands marked by the sea; a people who moreover had dire need at times to shift when two crops of upland taro, for instance, necessitated letting those lands lie fallow for a long season of rest.

Not a few notices in *The Islander* mentioned the natural history museum in Aliiolani Hale, the present Judiciary Building, opened in 1874 for the sessions of the Legislature. Honolulu's first public library was also housed there, and a second room was used for quarterly meetings of the Natural History and Microscopical Society with its purpose of extending and arranging collections of stones and calabashes, even feather capes. Under chairmanship of His Majesty, King Kalakaua, such officers as W. L. Green, C. R. Bishop, A. J. Cartwright, Dr. G. Trousseau, and C. J. Lyons, showed constructive interest and co-operation. Membership was limited to one hundred.

From Maui Father Bailey sent to *The Islander* enthusiastic notes on Hawaiian cryptogams. Feeling himself a novice "in ferning," Mr. Bailey hoped that *The Islander* might be enriched by abler articles of scientific interest. Editor Dole found the fern papers most valuable and looked for more, even though the little newspaper, having hopefully expanded from four to eight pages to accommodate not only translations, but in the "Song of Kualii" the original Hawaiian text as well, had not begun to pay its way financially.

In the realm of politics *The Islander* was just in time to chronicle in April 1875 "less dismal talk on Queen and Kaahumanu streets," due to the arrival of the British steamer *Macgregor* with its bunting all flying to announce passage by the United States Senate of a reciprocal trade treaty with the Hawaiian Islands. This mutual remission of many import duties for seven years between Hawaii and her nearest continental neighbor had been agitated at intervals for almost thirty years. In 1855, Judge Lee had secured endorsement of such a treaty in Washington, only to have it defeated in the Senate by Louisiana sugar planters. Kamehameha IV and his successor had favored it only as a lesser evil than annexation to the United States. In July, 1868, when members of the Hawaiian Club of Boston were working diligently toward its passage in the United States Senate, young Brigham wrote Dole that it had been "tabled by its friends to save it for the next session, as it could not get a ⅔ vote."

By 1873 Hawaiian planters were beginning to ship part of their sugar to British Columbia, and even to Australia and New Zealand, in the hope of lower tariffs in those distant quarters of the globe. At the urging of his ministers, Lunalilo even agreed to negotiations for the use of Pearl River lagoon as a United States naval station, but in the final decision the king refused his consent. Kalakaua's well-timed visit to Washington in 1874 with American Minister H. A. Peirce, also Chief Justice Elisha H. Allen as envoy and H. A. P. Carter as special commissioner, lent to the whole negotiation, commented *The Islander,* "all the characteristics of dignified international regard."

Kalakaua, the first king ever to visit the United States, was received as the guest of the nation by President Grant and all the members of Congress. When he returned, unannounced after three months, on the United States warship *Pensacola,* elaborate preparations to welcome him were rudely shaken. But the three United States ships of war lying in the roadstead displayed every pennant at full dress at nine in the morning, as the *Pensacola* steamed slowly in, Dr. Baldwin of Lahaina noting in his journal that as the royal passenger landed at ten all four men-of-war manned their yards with proper salutes, to which the guns of Punchbowl battery duly replied.

Next day, February 16, 1875, Anna sent word to Father Dole on Maui:

We heard the three guns about sunrise. Disgusted that the mail steamer had not brought advance notice, Sanford, who was chairman of the welcoming committee, went off on board while the warship was steaming along fast in mid-channel. But His Majesty preferred not to wait. People on shore did what they could, got up a very good procession, but only one of the three arches was decorated. It was too bad. But in the evening Honolulu's finest illumination greeted the King. Aliiolani Hale, the Government House, literally crowned with transparencies, bore a large crown and KALAKAUA in capital letters, with two strings of red, white, and blue lanterns from the top of the tower to the lower roof, and all its windows were alight with candles. I have never seen anything in that line look better. Rockets and fireballs were sent up, a torchlight procession came into the palace yard . . . and listened to a few words from the king. As soon as Sanford could leave, he came home for me. We saw a hula on the steps of the king's house. And Sanford did well in his speech which will be in the paper. In the morning we had gone into the king's house and shaken hands with him and other members of the royal family.

Looking beyond immediate concerns, *The Islander* showed a keen sense of relative values in the issues at stake. Exclaimed its editor:

Hawaii, now perhaps more than ever before, needs the help of brave, patriotic citizens. The Treaty cannot make us securely prosperous without people, while a large population would bring independence with or without foreign assistance. Whatever the importance of reciprocal measures with our neighbors, it does not compare, as a state necessity, with increasing the population, or Hooulu Lahui, as our King terms it. Immigration is of the first importance to Hawaiian politics.

The treaty could not go into effect until 1876, but far-seeing planters had long before begun to increase acreage and purchase new mills, many from Scotland. Certainty of an export market duty-free began to bring American, British, German and even Chinese capitalists, speculators, and adventurers, many of whose projects were of course short-lived. Journalist Jared G. Smith tells of this, remarking on the Molokai planter who ventured a sugar mill driven by erratic wind-power. Production of rice kept almost even step with sugar, which in fifteen years more than trebled the government revenues.

Sanford Dole's home on Emma Street was meanwhile taking shape. A small adjoining lot had been obtained to allow more space for mango and avocado trees, and Anna wrote to Father

Dole of Sanford's already finding not a little exercise mowing grass on the first plot. By April 28, 1876, the house was furnished and next day they moved in, starting their first hearth fire on May Day. On Sunday the Adams family were their first guests at lunch. Cousin Henry Parker, a lifelong bachelor, congratulated his friends on their new home, presenting them with a "theological squash" and watermelons from his Kawaiahao parsonage, with a stick or two of sugar cane to show them what he had been able to grow.

Best of all, perhaps, to Anna were the boxes on board the *Syren* containing a twelve-foot-square rug and a pretty little armchair from her mother, who felt she must send something, knowing the ship was to sail. "Now, Anna," she wrote, "you need not save up any more for a parlor rug, I enjoyed so much getting it and the little armchair. May the winds and the waves bring them safely to you. How I wish I might send vines and roses from our old house in Castine!"

The Honolulu of 1876 and 1877 was for the most part a very simple one of small, unpretentious homes. Lady Anne Brassey pictured it when she landed there at the end of 1876, with her husband and children in the yacht *Sunbeam* on a round-the-world cruise. At dawn she watched a twenty-ox team, driven by a man in a cart, hauling on a rope a fourth of a mile long, to draw in a large ship through the opening in the reef, the driver and the cattle being on the coral. The tug *Pele,* whose duty it was to tow ships into the harbor, was up for repairs and the *Gazette* announced that for some six or eight weeks this antique plan of towing vessels in and out must be resumed. The route of the tow path was straight inland up the lane now called Richards Street, the tug ship Hawaiians called a *kolo moku.*

On Saturday afternoon, a holiday always, Hawaiian men and women still came galloping in to town, chattering and laughing, dressed in the gayest colors and wreathed with flowers. "All the women," remarked Lady Brassey, "sit their horses very well, astride like men, with long riding dresses of the brightest cottons." Canoes full of natives were out fishing, one great double canoe arriving under sail from Maui. Coming down to the beach to swim and fish like everyone else were the king and queen and the king's brother, Prince Leleiohoku, all of whom, but separately and in state, paid formal visits to the English yacht. At Hilo the Brasseys, returning from the volcano, had found their yacht wreathed with flowers, the masts tipped with tall feathery sugar cane plumes for the Christmas festival. At Honolulu, church choirs came out to serenade the yacht, a formal ball was given them in the Hawaiian Hotel. And one of the visits Lady Brassey enjoyed most was at Aliiolani Hale, the new government building, with its excellent English library and a good natural history museum.

In the new home on Emma Street Sanford and Anna Dole found a persistent shadow. Every day Anna seemed thinner, in spite of her happiness, and again her anxious husband took her on an interisland voyage, this time to Hawaii. Her delight in the pastoral poem of Hilo with its sounds of gentle rain, its kindly people and rich tropical foliage, followed by the fern forests and desert wastes of Kilauea, punctured with sulphurous fire fountains, she tells well in a description printed in the *Advertiser* many years later. Mindful of Will Brigham's interest, Sanford sent him their record of the crater, drained as dry as an ash-heap by a vigorous outbreak of lava just the day before their arrival, but with avalanches of rock still thundering down the sides.

Through Puna they traveled too, and then crossed to Maui for ten delightful days at Rose Ranch, Captain Makee's dreamland home in Ulupalakua, on the lower western slope of Haleakala. Here he had introduced among others the first eucalyptus trees in the Islands, all vividly pictured in Charles Warren Stoddard's *Lazy Letters from Low Latitudes:* "many thousand saplings rooted under his very eyes, acres and acres of choice cuttings, many of them set out with his own hands. Cane planting was the Captain's business, but tree planting was his pleasure." Deep joy must Sanford and Anna have found in this "tropical garden in the midst of Alpine groves upon a plateau commanding breadths of earth, and sea, and sky." Yet all this island wonderworld failed to bring the wonted sparkle to Anna's eye and color to her cheek; and Sanford, unable to go farther, was forced to see her off from Honolulu to try the benefit of a long visit with her mother in New England. This was in June of 1877.

George Dole was planning to take his family back to windward Kauai where, at Kapaa, Captain Makee of Maui was starting one of the new plantations stimulated by the Reciprocity Treaty. Eager to work on a plantation again, George Dole gladly accepted the Captain's offer of the managership with the option of gradually buying in twenty shares, one-fourth of the stock. While the new house on the hill at Kapaa was being built for them all, Clara took the three boys and three girls to her old home at Waimea with Father and Mother Rowell, and Father Dole visited the Smiths at Koloa near his old home.

Sam Hundley, master stonemason, supervised the building of the new home at Kapaa. Born of English parentage in Roanoke, Virginia, he had come from California to put up the square smoke-stack for Makee Sugar Company; and later also the far-famed Valley House brought, cut and fitted, for Captain Makee in the small sailing vessel *Merrie Swan,* all of it landed in boats on the windswept rocks at Kapaa. Sam Hundley had been the first to meet George Dole when he came ashore at the same spot, where no vessel puts in even for freight in this year of 1956. This is still told by Hundley's daughter Bernice, veteran school supervisor, whose lovely Hawaiian mother Sam Hundley had married in her home at Anahola; here the Hundleys continued to live for years, no very long horseback ride from his plantation work.

By June 1878 the house on the hill, where Miss Hundley lives now, near the Mahelona Hospital, was ready for the lively Dole family. Hoping to keep them all at home as long as possible, George and Clara made arrangements with different people, some-times a couple, to live with the family and teach the children several hours a day. One of these governesses was Mary Burbank of Koloa. Father Dole lived with them too, growing frailer in health. Occasionally Sanford, coming down for court week, would find time to take the older boys out hunting.

When the mill was starting to grind and water was turned into the flume, the Dole boys perfected a technique of swiftly collecting enough cane trash to make a passable seat in the narrow flume, and then riding on the stream with shouts of glee as near the mill as they dared. Legends of course grew up about precarious chutes atop the stalks of cane during grinding season, but this their father distinctly forbade. Their sister Clara still remembers older brothers waiting in the pasture at a low place in the flume to see younger ones safely off before it dropped to the mill level below.

Part and parcel of the sugar venture at Kapaa was in 1877 a

companion one sponsored by King Kalakaua, for the benefit of some of his courtiers whom he hoped to see established on the fertile lands of Kauai. The name of the project, *Hui Kawaihau* (Ice Water Society), was carried over from a choral society at court where obviously many were leading idle, worthless lives. Captain Makee, Governor Kanoa of Kauai, Governor Dominis of Oahu, High Chief Koakanu of Koloa, and a number of others lent their enthusiastic support in establishing the thirty-two resident members with their families at Kapahi in Kealia, Kauai. For these new residents bullock teams, lent by George Charman of Koloa and W. H. Rice of Lihue, hauled two miles from Wailua-kai the little Hawaiian church which for seventy years served Hawaiian congregations on the flats at Kapaa.

Theoretically, the king was planting cane under the direction of Captain Makee and Manager G. H. Dole, the latter often called in to assist Governor Kanoa in adjusting difficulties and to advise the inexperienced cane planters. Wrangling persisted, however, and coupled with ignorance, was no doubt partially responsible for ultimate disruption of the *Hui*.

Yet the *Hui* members worked hard for success, and city men though they were, their first year netted a fair profit. The second year a cane fire discouraged them, but they went at it again with *ratoon* crops, only to find themselves *poho* (in the mire), and completely disheartened. By 1881 the members had moved away, and little record of their story would have sifted down to us through the years but for the interest of Charles S. Dole. He was one of the small boys who rode the mill flume and always recalled with zest the opening *luau* of the *Hui* at Kapahi, a gala occasion which every Kauai notable attended and to which even the king lent his presence.

Sanford Dole in Honolulu, after a busy office day, would work in his garden, wishing his wife were there to enjoy it with him. He thanked George for young *hala* trees, writing that he was gardening seriously to give Anna a floral welcome. Under a doctor's care in Boston she wrote despairingly to her husband, wondering how their home looked, whether the young trees had grown, whether the carriage house was even partly hidden by vines.

About this time Sanford bought in under mortages one-fourth

Left: Queen Liliuokalani wearing the Order of Kalakaua

Right: King Kalakaua in full dress uniform

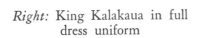

Courtesy Archives of Hawaii

Princess Kaiulani for whom Sanford wished a
regency established

of Grove Ranch plantation on Maui. Writing to his father in March of 1878, he mentioned this purchase; hoped his father's health was improving, and enclosed a picture of himself to keep his father company, adding that he was pretty lonely himself, and in a great hurry to have his wife again. In spite of his father's health, Sanford decided early in the summer of 1878 that he must go East to see for himself whether perhaps Anna might not have improved much more than she realized. A photograph just received showed her, he told George, in much better health— handsome, as she used to look when she first came to Honolulu. But when he met her at her mother's home in Castine (where he enjoyed boating, some driving and even a little shooting), they both felt that another winter in the East was the wise course for her to pursue.

By the 9th of October Sanford had returned to what seemed a rather forlorn home in Honolulu. Part of this came to the surface in his first letter to brother George on Kauai: "I heard nothing from the Islands until, on arriving in San Francisco, Mr. McCully told me of Father's death, the same day I received your letters which had been to Boston and back. I was shocked and saddened —I can hardly realize that Father is gone. The memory of his pure-hearted and unselfish life will always be our rich inheritance."

Daniel Dole died quietly in the early morning of August 26, 1878, just two weeks before his seventieth birthday. He was buried on the hill of George's home at Kapaa. Ten years later, when the George Doles all went to live in California and the Sam Hundleys bought their Kapaa home, George and Sanford, at Mother Rice's invitation, removed their father's grave to the Rice family plot in the Lihue Cemetery.

For his sons, Daniel Dole's death marked the final leave-taking from their nearest friend, but they knew, as George said, that he had stepped from darkness into light. Sanford's associate, Thomas Walker, wrote him from Honolulu by the first boat to San Francisco: "We must try to follow in the footsteps that the saints have trod." To George from far Illinois came an echo out of the past, written by no other than his good foster mother of Punahou, Miss Marcia Smith, who had ever held Daniel Dole in high esteem. W. D. Alexander, one of the most brilliant scientific minds among the early Punahou boys, had, while Daniel Dole yet lived, written

him more than once of their debt to him as a sound scholar and
a teacher gifted in showing young people how to study and think
for themselves.

On the 15th of September, from the pulpit of the Seamen's
Bethel in Honolulu, where Daniel Dole himself had often spoken,
Chaplain Damon gave public tribute in his sermon to this holy
man of God, who, though not perfect, nor brilliant, nor prominent, had quietly pursued his long course of consistent well-doing.
Studious, scholarly, and a reading man, who delighted to interpret
the Sacred Scriptures, his preaching had been peculiarly instructive
and searching; " 'simple, grave, sincere; in language plain, in
doctrine uncorrupt.' A certain stately air in his walk and intercourse indicated that the Puritan element had not become extinct."

Said the chaplain:

> I regard it as an unspeakable privilege to have been, during more than
> a third of a century, on the most intimate terms of Christian friendship with
> the Rev. Daniel Dole. I have known of him in trial and affliction, when
> called upon to resign a position which many believed him peculiarly well-
> qualified to fill, but I cannot recall one bitter or acrimonious remark which
> fell from his lips. Upon the minds of the children of the American mission-
> aries to these Islands he has left an indelible impression for good, while the
> community at large derives a lasting influence from his holy walk and godly
> conversation.

Solitary evenings in the Emma Street home were occupied by
Sanford in revising his earlier study of Hawaiian birds. In January
of 1879, when sending his brother George a copy of this newly
printed list, Sanford considered it a great improvement over his
first, printed in Boston ten years before; and remarked too that
very recently in Palolo Valley he had seen an entirely new bird,
a snipe, something he never before saw or heard of in the Islands.

This second edition, published in Honolulu by T. G. Thrum and
reprinted in his *Hawaiian Annual* for 1879, contains two additional birds known to naturalists and four "new to the books."
Of these four, Dole named one for his wife. This was the rare,
and now probably extinct *Ula-ai-hawane,* the red bird that feeds
on the *hawane,* a Hawaiian *Pritchardia* palm. Mr. George C.
Munro, in his *Birds of Hawaii,* 1944, states that Dole, mistaking
it for a finch, classified it as probably *Fringilla Anna;* but that its
proper generic name, now used, still carries the specific as *Ciridops
anna (Dole).* A bird of remarkable beauty, in its harmonious

combination of red, black, white, and gray, it frequented the higher slopes of Hawaii, was wild and shy, and seldom taken by hunters. The only example of the species which Dole had seen was in the choice Mills collection at Hilo, which he had listed for the Centennial Exposition of 1876 in Philadelphia. This renewed interest in birds no doubt stimulated Dole's revision of 1879, which Mr. Munro states was the only list of Hawaiian birds available here in 1890 to the Rothschild expedition for the study of Hawaiian *avifauna*.

Much as Sanford Dole regreted leaving his business again so soon, he wrote George from San Francisco before the end of February, 1879, that he must do his best to help complete Anna's recovery. Crossing through the Rocky Mountains by railroad, he wished more than once for freedom to be stalking large herds of antelope quite close to the train. In Boston Anna was greatly improved and eagerly awaiting him. Snow flakes were still flying, but not enough to give Anna a real sleigh ride. Cousin Charles Dole they heard in a thoughtful sermon on anger, and Cousin Nathan was still working on his translations. Brigham was most cordial, enquiring especially for George. Anna and Sanford went to theaters often, Sanford convinced that plenty of laughing was good for her health.

Dr. Edward Everett Hale recognized him, even after eleven years, and invited him and his wife to dinner. Sanford said:

The hearty, unrestrained expression of these unsectarian Boston ministers, is like going from a close room to a mountain top where the trade winds are blowing in all their ecstatic freedom! At a social of the Teachers' Club Mr. Hale asked me to tell about the Hawaiians and to sing a couple of hymns in Hawaiian. At the Hales' home at dinner, Brigham also present, the doctor went in for plenty of fun and did his share, his son doing an Arabian song with drum accompaniment, while I did a little of the Hawaiian sit-down hula with a big pasteboard box for a drum, while Dr. Hale sat on the floor too to be more in keeping with the performance.

On Sunday I heard Dr. Wright in the morning and Phillips Brooks in the evening. Bicycles are popular here, magnificent machines on which one can beat a horse in the long run. I am learning to ride them and may bring one out. Before leaving Boston I bought the printing press with ink and type which you asked me to get for your boys.

On the way West the Doles spent many weeks in Denver with Anna's married sister Isabel, and enjoyed a pleasant sojourn at Colorado Springs near Mother Rice and her daughter Emily's family; one week, to Sanford's delight, they camped out in Cheyenne Canyon, at the edge of the Rockies, although it was too early for hunting. He wrote: "The mountains are bold and beautiful, similar to some ranges of Hawaiian mountains. Pike's Peak is in plain sight, its summit partially covered with snow."

By August George's letter of welcome met them on the steamer in Honolulu harbor before landing. As Sanford replied:

It did us good. I rely on your letters, George, and feel I must have them. Anna is quite enthusiastic about things and I am very glad to be back at work again. Are the boys out of patience? They must bear up. I may be able to send the printing press next week. Let the boys be preparing their editorials to convulse Kauaian society. I send you two boxes of young fig trees and one box of apples. Thank you for the chickens and bread fruit. Our carriage has come, but now we want a horse. There is much illness here, typhoid very prevalent. Grove Ranch has been doing well. They are planting now, but will soon be grinding, in November, and should make a dividend this quarter.

Cousins' Meeting Saturday was a solemn affair. Something must be done to make them laugh. As one of the *Maile Wreath* Editors I already begin to feel mischievous. At our Kawaiahao Sunday School concert we had Berger at the organ and four brass instruments, so our music at any rate was quite a success.

I went to Molokai Monday in the Mokolii, on business. Visited at Bal's, Beckleys', McColgan's, with the natives at Kawela, and a night at Meyer's. Shot ducks at Kawela, goats in the mts., pigeons at Meyer's.

I think of running for the legislature from Waimea District. Anna and her friend Miss Davies attended to the Christmas presents. Anna would like to visit you, but thinks that now she has got me again, she will stay by me. I am still pressed with business; employ a boy in my office to write. I expect to attend the Feb. term of court at Kauai, and shall enjoy visiting you again. Is young Alfred to be Alfred the Great? Which one is going to make a lawyer and come to study law with me by and by?

Tomorrow, Dec. 31st., there will be a grand blow-out at the laying of the corner stone of the new Palace.

Always Sanford Dole recalled wishing as a college student that he might have heard the new pipe organ for Kawaiahao Church, when in Boston Will Brigham had gone at Captain Hunnewell's invitation to hear its trial exhibition. Father Bingham, first pastor of Kawaiahao, was also present, remarking changes at Honolulu in the thirty years since he had made architect's drawings for the Stone Church there.

In 1879 the old church walls echoed back a Sunday School

concert with Captain Henri Berger at the organ and four brass instruments. Fond of music and disappointed at earlier attempts, Kamehameha V had sent to Germany in 1872 and invited Berger to form a Hawaiian band. Success was immediate. King Lunalilo, himself longing to wield the bass drum, always took the band with him even on expeditions by canoe. At Kalakaua's election in 1874 the band played gay and cheerful tunes to quiet the excitement of the riot; and during the seventeen years of his reign Kalakaua encouraged Captain Berger with genuine interest.

After the return of Sanford and Anna Dole to Honolulu in 1879 they felt at last that they were in their own home. "To be sure," he told his brother, "our white cat Nimrod and Hiram the Cochin China rooster are both deceased—and Hiram stands as high as a table. But we have a Chinese cook and a yard boy for help. And although Anna is not entirely strong yet we can have guests, and Anna works at her easel again in front of the banana trees in the yard."

From faraway Castine, Mother Cate wrote of her delight in Anna's gift of violets, while another painting she had sent, the "Aurora," was the pride of her mother's New England parlor; "whatever you do for me," she added, "I shall doubtless consider the *perfection* of painting. I only wish you could see our garden of damask and blush roses, pansies, pinks and heliotrope."

Even before Anna's return Sanford had begun to wonder whom they could have in their home, a cheerful, intelligent young girl perhaps, who would be quick to understand the needs of a semi-invalid. One morning, as he reviewed the big Sunday School at Kawaiahao, he suddenly realized that alert young Elizabeth Napoleon might be just the one. He had known her there since she was six, and she was now thirteen, old enough to be a friend and companion to Anna. Her own home was at Mililani, just across the street *makai* from Kawaiahao Church. He would go over and see what her mother, Pamaho'a, thought about it.

Pamaho'a was a tall, fine-looking Hawaiian, a younger cousin of Kanaina, Lunalilo's father. Hers was a simple, roomy Hawaiian house, full of children, and, as usual among the *alii* (nobility), each child had his own *kapa moe* (sleeping quilts and kapas), with a special *kahu* (attendant) to care for him. The house stood, unbelievably today, in a big yard on the site of the present

Territorial Tax Office, but at that time under a spreading mango tree, and chained to this a lively monkey, brought probably by some sailor.

With quiet dignity Pamaho'a told Mr. Dole she was willing that he and Mrs. Dole should take Puiki, as Elizabeth was called at home by nickname; but Pamaho'a would sign no papers of legal adoption—no, that would be like selling her child, and that she would not do. She realized that Puiki would grow up into a world very different from the old *Hawaii nei;* and she was glad that one of her children should live with Americans, speaking English and leaving her Hawaiian ways in the old home beside the church.

To Puiki however, with a child's innate pride and reserve, the new way of life was utterly foreign. Try she did to work at the household tasks set her by Mrs. Dole, sweeping and dusting, setting the table, making beds and tidying bedrooms, chores any New England girl would naturally do—but be a servant Lizzie could not and would not. One day she vanished, and as suddenly Puiki reappeared under the old mango tree at home, her fine dark eyes snapping resentment and rebellion. In her mother, however, she was dealing with the old order and a matriarch, no command of whose was to be lightly disregarded.

At that moment a steady, quiet step brought Sanford Dole to Mililani. Sitting down beside the tense, slender figure, he told Lizzie how much he needed her to help Mrs. Dole get well, how they both loved having Lizzie in their home, which was really her home too. Instinctively the child began to trust him and soon was walking up Emma Street with him, to tell Mrs. Dole she was sorry and would try again.

Not once or twice only did this scene occur under the mango tree at Mililani. Each time Sanford Dole's gentleness and understanding gave Lizzie a growing sense of being wanted and needed in a place where she was safe and secure. To the childless couple she became with the years a loving and loyal daughter. Nor was her first home forgotten, for today her beautiful Hawaiian *kapa moe* (quilts) are cherished possessions among her children and grandchildren. True, the Anna Dole of 1879 was an ingrained New Englander who often found herself at a loss among Hawaiian thought-ways. But when Sanford's gentle voice would say: "Now, Anna!"—could one do less than take pleasure in his pleasure?

TOWN MEETINGS
1880–1883

SIGNIFICANT of public unrest in January 1880 is Sanford Dole's thought of possibly running for the Legislature from Honolulu. Although the time for this action was not yet appointed, more than one trend in public affairs gave cause for anxiety to citizens who still hoped for a representative government. Early in March Dole's position was clearly outlined in writing to his brother: "The currency question waxeth hot in the papers. The Bank assists the *Advertiser* in its leaders on the subject. We intend to fight it out if it takes all summer. We particularly oppose the *Advertiser* upon general and miscellaneous impeachments. It has laid itself open of late to straight thrusts and of course we must use the opportunities."

Evidently these straight thrusts from the *Gazette* were severe. By May, Dole had switched off from the *Gazette* and was to have full control of the literary output of the *Advertiser,* Black, the publisher, acceding unconditionally to his terms. But after two weeks this agreement had to be canceled: Gibson, Dole wrote, appeared to be the real editor; at least, Dole's material was revised, "corrected or suppressed at somebody's sweet will; now I am fancy free; Hartwell is very anxious to transfer the *Gazette* to me or to someone else, but I don't bite worth a cent."

The king was beginning definitely to show his ambitions, bearing out Nevins Armstrong's comment that representative government was an unknown quantity to Kalakaua. Flattered both by Gibson and an Italian adventurer, Celso Caesar Moreno, Kalakaua had by various means assembled enough "King's men" in the Legislature to pass a bill subsidizing Moreno's plan for a steamship line to China. When other and still more dangerous bills failed of passage, His Majesty prorogued the Legislature, and within the hour, as Thomas Thrum recorded in his "Retrospect for 1880," dismissed the Cabinet and appointed Moreno Premier and Minister of Foreign Affairs.

Excitement aroused by this act of tyranny was so intense, states Professor W. D. Alexander, as to unite the discordant elements of the community, supported for the first time by a large proportion of the Hawaiians themselves. Even the three highest and most influential chiefs, Queen Dowager Emma, Ruth Keelikolani, and Bernice Pauahi Bishop, joined in condemning the king's course, just as they had disapproved of the king's coronation as one step in his schemes toward an absolute monarchy. The diplomatic representatives of the United States, England, and France "raised their respective flags over their legations, and declared that they would hold no further official intercourse with the Hawaiian Government as long as Moreno should be premier." King's men harangued crowds of Hawaiians, instilling fear of foreigners, yet describing "Way-up Celso Moreno" as a naturalized and true Hawaiian devoted to the salvation of the people.

Announcement of His Majesty the King's unprecedented action had been made on Saturday, August 14, 1880. On Monday evening following, the great assembly hall of the old thatched church at Kaumakapili was filled to overflowing with Hawaiians and foreigners. Called to order by Henry Waterhouse, the meeting proceeded to the appointment of chairmen from both races, G. W. Pilipo and W. R. Castle, and the purpose of the meeting was stated. S. B. Dole's resolution, which as reported by the *Advertiser,* he "supported with a vehement but sound speech," was adopted; namely, that His Majesty's recent action, inconsistent with the principles of the constitutional monarchy as handed down by the Kamehamehas and Lunalilo, is therein hostile to the permanence of Hawaiian independence, the perpetuity of the Hawaiian race, and the security of life, liberty, and property in the Hawaiian Islands. Discussion brought out both sides of the question, but hisses and groans forced supporters of Moreno into a speedy retreat. Thirteen gentlemen were appointed as a committee to wait on His Majesty with the resolution. These included Messrs. G. W. Pilipo, Nawahi, Kunuiakea, W. R. Castle, Dole, Waterhouse, Hall, Adams, Pfluger, Kaulukou, Keau, Kalama, J. W. Moanauli.

The four reports of this committee are brief: For the morning and afternoon of Tuesday, when G. W. Pilipo and S. B. Dole were delegated to convey the communication, the king sent word by his Chamberlain that he would consider it after receiving it through his Minister of the Interior. No answer having been obtained on Wednesday, the main committee awaited the return of Dole and Pilipo, who were informed by the Attorney General that the king would soon reply; adjourned till Thursday noon.

The same evening a second mass meeting was convened in the Bethel Church to consider the disturbed state of public affairs, many of Honolulu's ablest citizens assembling quietly with grave faces. Just as the meeting opened, Mr. A. J. Cartwright, entering in unusual haste, announced that Mr. C. C. Moreno had resigned his cabinet post and that his resignation had been accepted. Loud cheers woke echoes in old Bethel, mingling with shouts of "Long Live the King!" Mr. C. R. Bishop moved that a committee be appointed to wait on His Majesty immediately, and to thank him.

About the same time news of the public announcement of the change reached the special committee of thirteen. At its adjourned meeting Thursday noon it was therefore voted that the proceedings of the committee be printed in the Hawaiian and English newspapers. The four reports are signed: S. B. Dole, Chairman.

Cleavage of the community into two parties was beginning to appear. The *Gazette* thanked God that there was a party "in opposition" to many of the acts of the king. As was only natural, another mass meeting at Kaumakapili summoned by posters in Hawaiian, expressed aloha for the king, who had been alarmed by the first meeting and sent his soldiers to attend this Hawaiian one. J. M. Kapena was called to the chair, with Henry Waterhouse and John Kalama as secretaries, and S. B. Dole as interpreter. The chairman intimated that the work of the first mass meeting had been the plotting of a faction which must now be undone. Dole introduced a resolution to express thanks to the king for listening to the voice of the people and removing Mr. C. C. Moreno from office. Dole's speech aroused feelings pro and con, but "was received with the greatest enthusiasm." Political cleavage seemed not yet complete.

Robert W. Wilcox, a young Hawaiian from Wailuku, Maui— not related to the Abner Wilcox family of Hanalei and Waioli,

Kauai—shouted that foreigners were stirring up confusion for their own evil purposes, particularly *na keiki o na misionari* (sons of the missionaries). Mr. Pilipo requested Mr. Wilcox to direct his remarks to the business of the evening. At this, pandemonium broke loose, hats were hurled, shouts rent the air. Mr. Kaai succeeded in speaking for fifteen minutes, his resolution expressing aloha for the king, censure for the resolution of Monday, and gratitude for the king's release of Mr. Moreno from the office of Minister of Foreign Affairs. Had he remained in that office, many complications would have arisen, since some foreign powers might not have recognized his appointment. Confusion ensued and the meeting broke up in disorder.

Actually, as Sanford Dole recalled, this Hawaiian mass meeting had been hastily organized by His Majesty himself, to be held at the same place as the first in order to neutralize its effect. But the Royalist party discovered later that conflicting resolutions had been passed, the first not at all consonant with the king's expectations. Resulting contradiction but served to render this second gathering ridiculous. Other projects of the king, such as borrowing money from the treasury on his personal note, had to be refused even by his own ephemeral cabinets. A recollection of Dole's, concerning Attorney General Nevins Armstrong, pictured that official coming out of a Cabinet meeting, rubbing his hands and crying out, "Hell to pay!" The king, remarked Dole in retrospect, seemed about as fit for his position as some of the fellows who tried to run the fishmarket.

And yet, continued Dole's clear-sighted musing, with all the king's faults, it must be said that he was possessed of a great deal of polish, good manners, and natural dignity. He had a fine presence, was tall and well-built, and on the whole was temperate in the use of liquor. A good host, genial and courteous, he was perhaps at his best in receiving official guests from other countries.

Another and apparently the final mass meeting in the interests of Moreno, was called for Saturday afternoon at the fish market where all and sundry were sure to congregate for that half-holiday. As reported by the *Commercial Advertiser:* "No one would speak until Moreno arrived, and then nothing was said." Called upon for a show of hands on wishing Moreno retained in office, Robert Wilcox and his followers held theirs up amid groans and hisses, mingled with laughter.

Dole's contemporary comments to his brother George were eagerly read on Kauai: "August 30: Robert Wilcox is an empty-headed youth, probably egged on by the king; he, Wilcox, appears to wish the destruction of white men; doubtless the king wishes the extinction of all independent men and the suppression of all free discussion. Moreno went in the steamer yesterday with three half white youths including Bob Wilcox, ostensibly to educate them abroad, really, as is believed, to make his own travelling expenses out of the appropriation."

On September 1, 1880, the *Pacific Commercial Advertiser* was bought by Walter Murray Gibson with funds advanced by the Minister of the Interior. As reported in the *Hawaiian Gazette* of October 6, 1880, this new move was planned "to support the Hawaiian Government and its policy and pursue a line of discussion best calculated to carry out the measures of His Hawaiian Majesty; to be invariably loyal to His Majesty."

Associated with Gibson was a California sugar refiner named Claus Spreckels, who, after opposing passage of a reciprocity treaty for Hawaii, hastened to the Islands once the measure had gone into effect. Soon he was growing cane on formerly Crown lands above Wailuku in the fertile plain of central Maui, and by means of a personal loan to the king obtained valuable water rights for a second irrigation ditch almost twice as long as the first one achieved by Alexander & Baldwin. With Gibson "to conduct, manage, and edit" the *Pacific Commercial Advertiser,* Spreckels too was soon in high favor with the king.

"Those opposed" lost no time in giving public expression to their thoughts, which of course were not welcomed in the columns of the *Advertiser*. For his brother on Kauai Sanford Dole gave sidelights on the situation:

You will be pleased to hear that a new paper, the *Saturday Press,* was started last week, September 4th, in opposition to the *Advertiser* under Gibson. I have ordered it for you. It is owned by the leading business firms here; it is well supported from the start, as you will see. A great many have taken away their advertising from the *Commercial* and given it to the new paper, and many have stopped their subscriptions to the former. I trust that Gibson will be starved out before long.

The King has been removing [as] obnoxious persons from various offices, such as Henry Waterhouse from being agent to acknowledge contracts, Adams, Cleghorn, and others from the Privy Council; the Boards of Health and Immigration have been upset and new men put in. Gibson is put into everything; now that Moreno is away, Gibson's persevering and humble bootlicking is producing its fruits. It is rumored that the King intends to get McCully off the Bench next time the legislature meets. Kalakaua seems to be entirely given over to the devil.

The first number of the *Saturday Press* invited remarks and suggestions of planters, practical or speculative; would find room for notices of shippers and shipping, public works and private enterprise, and ideas tending toward improvement, agricultural or mechanical. Managing Editor Thrum remarked that the king must see for himself that those who advised him in experimental directions were disloyal both to him and to his country. "We have the unpalatable task of translating Gibsonese into English when on September 8th those differing from rulers are called *disloyal;*" on the 15th these had risen to the status of *rebels;* and "pernicious rubbish" was being circulated in the Hawaiian columns of the *Wednesday Express.* Emphatically, asserted the Editor, "we are drifting or being driven toward the fatal shores of absolutism. The Privy Council has demanded and obtained from the Minister of Finance the sum of $1,200 avowedly for resistance to possible riots."

Without doubt the early issues of this new paper more than paid their way. Thrum's Retrospect of 1880 summarized the public meetings of that year as having met an almost unanimous response throughout the Islands, which was echoed back from foreign lands; and added that the outspoken tones of the *Saturday Press,* a paper got up virtually by the people, for the people, together with the earlier consistent course of the *Gazette,* had done much to save the country from ignominy and disgrace.

By the end of September the private lines from Emma Street to Kapaa, Kauai, read:

The new cabinet find the government finances in as rotten a state as they could well get in six weeks; 5 or 6000 dollars paid to Gibson in advance for what he could perhaps never do, such as furnishing 300 copies of the *Advertiser* for a year to come; furnishing a lot of sheep that were mortgaged to Campbell; printing the *Civil Code* in the dim future when prepared and passed by some future legislature; and generally for supporting the government in his paper. It is rumored on the street that the coronation appropriation of $10,000 has been drawn from the treasury. The more they investigate, the more the whole thing stinks. The demands on foreign governments to remove their representatives are likely to cause considerable difficulty.

It is believed that Gibson will have to retire to his sheep pasture on Lanai; his finances are in a bad way apparently and the *Advertiser* is an expensive luxury for him. He applied to Spreckels for aid, but didn't get it.

Pfluger has made a contract with Spreckels for next year's sugars based upon the New York rates of Cuban sugars and thinks it a good thing, which it must have been from the way Spreckels stormed and threatened before he came to terms.

The U. S. war steamer *Ticonderoga* arrived this noon. What her plans are, and if she is going to make the Hawaiian government walk Spanish, I do not know. She has just fired a salute of 21 guns, but I fancy it must be for Minister Comly who probably has gone aboard, as there is no reply from Punchbowl, which I suppose shows that the Hawaiian flag is not being saluted.

We are invited to a birthday party for little Princess Kaiulani, by the Cleghorns for Saturday night at Waikiki. Mrs. Cleghorn as Princess Likelike, and Kalakaua's youngest sister, is one of the political malcontents.

[Before the end of October:] An English and American man-of-war are in port, the latter lately from Samoa. I suppose the *Ticonderoga* has sailed. The political horizon is quiet, but not promising. The King is busy drilling an undue number of troops by night in the Palace grounds. He can't be trusted "further than you can shake a dead bull by the tail," as Cecil Brown sometimes laconically remarks. Yesterday the last fight for the Kanaina estate took place. After dark we got a verdict against the new claimant who said he was Kanaina's nephew. The King was interested in the case and had the new claimant been successful, doubtless the King would have pocketed the bulk of the estate.

Other more personal matters than politics sift through in Sanford's weekly letters to his brother. Will Brigham, who was lecturing in botany at Harvard, wrote:

Judge Austin and Father Damon both advise me to spend the summer in the Islands. A vacation in Europe would be less costly, but there is more useful material in Hawaii. Will you not go to Kauai up Waialeale with me, Sanford? I shall try to go to Kilauea, up Loa and Kea, to Waipio and Kohala, Lanai, Molokai, West Maui and on Oahu up Kaala range; to make plans of all the *heiaus* I can get to; see all the idols; get measurements of 100 typical Hawaiians 14–40 years old. No such record exists of these important proportions. This would be a great feather in my cap in Europe. Young Ed. Adams has been measured here as a Hawaiian, and found remarkably well formed. I like him very much.

Whiting, who has lung trouble, a nephew of Austin, will probably go with me; also the artist Charles Furneaux, to sketch scenery and plants. I want also to get some hill lobelias and tree ferns, and last but not least to see my old friends once more.

It may be that in preparation for this visit another room was added to adjoin the guest room in the Doles' Emma Street home; and Sanford spent a rainy afternoon in the parlor laying Chinese matting, that cool, fragrant carpeting of almost every Honolulu home seventy years ago. Then the parlor furniture was relocated in new and unexpected places, making quite a different room of it.

No account appears as to whether achievement crowned all of Brigham's hopes for the summer, which were listed in his letter like projects for a then non-existent Bernice Pauahi Bishop Museum. But many years later he told in a Bishop Museum *Memoir* of hastening to the Islands in June of 1880 at the call of a slight summit outbreak on Mauna Loa, prelude, he felt, to a great eruption; told too of climbing Mauna Loa and finding such changes at Kilauea that his careful survey of 1865, accepted later by the trigonometrical survey of the Hawaiian government, was long since out of date; also of his being forced to return to Boston in September and of leaving Furneaux to preserve for scientific study "those appearances that the camera does not retain and which are so difficult to describe."

Another visitor of 1880 to the Islands was the vibrant personality, General S. C. Armstrong of Hampton Institute, Virginia. He addressed a Hawaiian congregation from his father's pulpit at Kawaiahao, stirred citizens to an even keener sense of public responsibility, enjoyed to the full horseback rides by moonlight to Waikiki and a visit to Maui, his birthplace, with an expedition to the crater of Haleakala.

His older brother, William Nevins, had been called to the Islands from law practice in New York at the behest of his old school fellow, the king, who appointed him his Attorney General. Convinced before long that the time had come to prosecute a journey around the world, His Majesty made Nevins Armstrong his Commissioner of Immigration for the expedition. And so the new Commissioner, quite unimpressed by pomp and circumstance, set out with the king, likewise Colonel C. H. Judd, the king's Chamberlain, Robert, the king's German valet and linguist; also though well secreted when not needed, the ancestral feather cloak of Hawaiian royalty.

Instantly accorded royal salute by foreign warships in the Bay of Yedo, amid the roar from two hundred and seventy-three cannon in dense clouds of smoke, Kalakaua began to realize from new angles the importance of being king. In contrast to all the splendor of an Asiatic empire, one of his visits was made by special invitation to the Kaigan Church at Yokohama, a little Protestant chapel partially built by a fund sent from Hawaii in 1854 after Commodore Perry's courier had reported in Honolulu the successful opening of Japan's long-closed empire. Within the church the royal party felt a moment of homesickness to see the greeting Aloha in the decorations and in the welcome from Dr. Theodore Gulick, a native of Hawaii.

Published long after Kalakaua's death, W. N. Armstrong's story, *Around the World with a King,* makes good reading today. It throws much into logical perspective, particularly certain encounters in Italy with His Majesty's erstwhile Premier and Minister of Foreign Affairs. Meeting their steamer in the Bay of Naples, Signor Moreno at once assumed prerogatives as master of ceremonies, ushering the bewildered Hawaiian king into a landing boat and ashore, leaving his retinue on the steamer's deck "kingless and dumbfounded."

Alone and unable to speak Italian, the suite departed for shore in pursuit of their abducted monarch. At the hotel the king, fearing for his faraway throne, if he persisted in such dependence on Signor Moreno, received his Chamberlain and Attorney General to their rightful offices. The Italian welcoming committee, amazed that the strangers spoke English, were also under the impression, given by Signor Moreno, that the king of Hawaii had come to see his natural sons, the three Hawaiian youths, studying the arts of civilized warfare in Italy. King Humberto regretted this error due to Moreno's craftiness and Kalakaua at last followed the advice of his retinue to compromise himself no further with so unscrupulous an adventurer.

Quietly pursuing the homely round of life in Honolulu Sanford Dole sent his brother his grey horse Winona, also young fig trees for planting, and thanked for breadfruit per schooner from Kauai; told of Bel, his California setter, walking aboard the *Likelike* "on her own hook" as a stowaway and making the round trip to Hawaii, a record beaten by Walker's dog who, also a stowaway, had made the round trip by steamer to San Francisco, and after five weeks' absence came trotting into the yard on King Street quite content to stay at home for a while.

Interested too in family news from Kauai, Sanford asked after the pigeons and requested the boys to send him a copy of the first newspaper from their little hand press. And exchanged items about his own black cow which had calved and was supplying "more milk than we can afford to buy at 10 cents a quart; with another cow to calve in two months we shall supply ourselves with milk and cream, and soon with butter. I have purchased a Jersey bull from Dillingham, rather an old one, I think, but he will do for my small herd. Expect a cow from Rice soon. Bel, my setter, has eight black pups. November 26th Jake Brown and I plan to go to the Waianae mountains and camp out for a couple of nights."

Grove Ranch, the Maui plantation in which Sanford had told his father that he hoped some day to own a fourth share, had been started by Captain T. H. Hobron. It covered more than three thousand acres of good cane land adjoining Paia Plantation, with which it was later merged. By 1880 Grove Ranch began to pay good dividends and was incorporated. W. O. Smith of Kauai was manager, indeed had there found his bride Mary Hobron. Later Alfred Smith came as a *luna* and finally took his brother's place as manager. Judge Hartwell and his wife were also interested in this development on Maui. S. B. Dole's dividends were promptly paid in on the interest and principal of his mortgages. While attending court week on Maui in the summer of 1880, he enjoyed staying at Makawao to ride about the plantation when time permitted. He found it in fair condition, but needing men. He wrote:

Spreckels' cane looks well; he is building himself a large store at Kahului where he will also put up a bank and probably build himself a home, though for that Kuhului seems an infernally dusty spot. Makawao by contrast is delightful in its elevation and climate. So far, Grove Ranch has only 350 acres under cultivation with 110 men and 110 yoke of oxen.

Back in Honolulu, Sanford found Anna very happy in her painting, with frequent lessons from Brigham's friend, Charles Furneaux. By great good fortune the artist had not only witnessed,

but lived with Mauna Loa's spectacular eruption. From its first
glow at the summit crater in November, 1880, Mr. Furneaux had
followed its every phase for nine months, from the Kawaihae
desert to its last long finger of fire growing cold in the forest only
half a mile above Hilo town. For months Furneaux camped on
the Olaa slope close to the edge of the flow in a dense growth of
ohias, tree ferns and wild bananas. For want of canvas he often
painted his scenes on broad shingles of California redwood. Later
he made a part of this jungle his home and left it on his death
for the benefit of Punahou School.

Furneaux' Honolulu studio was in the tower of Aliiolani Hale,
the new government building which Anna Dole had so delighted
to see illuminated on the night of Kalakaua's return from the
United States in 1875. Here it was that Anna worked as a pupil
with Furneaux and here in August of 1881 he held an extensive
exhibition of his oil paintings of the volcano now treasured by
collectors, particularly the Bishop Museum.

When evening brought a little leisure, Sanford conned over a
lecture on co-operation for a meeting of the Library Association.
In a day when the term co-operative was little known and its
power largely undeveloped, here was a young Sandwich Island
economist looking forward to its benefits in the Pacific.

This was only 1881. Citing foreign examples of the growth of
this social force, Dole stressed the achievement of seventeen
English weavers who, in 1884, pooling meager supplies of butter,
sugar, flour, and candles, and at first keeping their co-operative
shop open only two evenings a week, had expanded in twenty
years to payment of over a million dollars in benefits to 9,000
members. Many had made themselves independent of capital
which, from being their master, had become their obedient servant.

Then, bringing the suggestion to bear directly on Honolulu, the
speaker said pointedly: "Not one of us feels that he can afford this
library of several thousand volumes as a private luxury, yet by
uniting, every man in this town owns it for fifty cents a month."
[Actually, this early reading room served as a man's club, even
excluding women and children from its membership.]

"We ought to have gymnasiums and public baths," added the
practical speaker, "a good hall for meetings and merry-makings,
a picture gallery or art museum. And each family ought to have

its own home. All these and more we could have, but none of
them are we likely to have unless we co-operate."

Bits of home news often appear as postscripts in Sanford's letters
to his brother:

For your boys I have ordered a combined jig and buzz saw and turning
lathe. But don't tell the boys. We thought Bel, my setter, was lost again,
but she has staidly returned. When she disappeared on steamer day, we
concluded she had stowed away for San Francisco.

My law school begins in November, meeting twice a week for two
winter terms of forty-eight lectures each. Also, I am to preach at
Kawaiahao Church when Henry Parker goes around Oahu. Riding out
to Ewa the other day with Judge Judd on Ii estate business, I looked in at
Bishop and Needham's poi factory, where the mill of your invention,
George, is working successfully by horsepower with a daily output of
several tons of good *paiai* [hard poi].

I have begun to vaccinate in the smallpox epidemic. Kauai people deserve
credit for stamping it out on your island. There is less activity even on
the streets here; business seems to be affected, though most of the cases
are light. My high Boston bicycle has arrived—rather a spirited animal
which threw me several times before I could master it.

"Ceremonies for laying the cornerstone of the new Lunalilo
Home on Makiki slopes have taken time," chronicled Sanford,
who was one of the administrators of Lunalilo's estate which had
been left to found a home for aged Hawaiians.

"But," he adds, "the best fun out is *Pinafore*. You will see my
account of it in this week's *Gazette*. I have been to every performance. The choruses are very attractive; Walker is capital as the
Admiral, and Atkinson as Boatswain is decidedly stimulating;
the ladies appear remarkably well and improve every time. Anna
stayed in bed all day to be able to see the opening performance
and is going again. Last Saturday she and I drove to Waikiki,
where quite a few summer houses are being built; we went to
carry Mrs. W. R. Castle a magnolia bloom. If Anna and I ever
have a little girl, we shall name her Magnolia Dole."

In 1881, when Punahou School was forty years old, S. B. Dole
served with S. C. Damon and W. R. Castle on the endowment
committee. Driving out to the celebration in June, Sanford and
Anna stopped on Punahou Street to gaze without envy at the
mansion being erected by Claus Spreckels on land he had recently
bought from Punahou for five thousand dollars. On the great

lot 800 feet deep with a 400-foot frontage, this elaborate Victorian palace stood for many years within its formal enclosure of heavy black-iron-filagree fencing.

Stirred by early Punahou memories, Sanford signed his June letters to Kauai with his school nickname, Sanballat, adding: "In memory of father I go in for putting up a building at the 50th anniversary of Punahou in 1891. Think, however, I should prefer a gymnasium to a chapel, but we'll see."

While Kalakaua was still on his world tour, Chief Justice Harris died suddenly. "It is fortunate," remarked Dole, "that David, the King, is away, but the Regent, his sister, Mrs. Dominis, will not act to fill the vacancy unless there is urgent need. If it can be done without consulting David, choice will probably lie between Hartwell and Judd.

"Hartwell," noted Sanford in August, "has stopped taking the *Advertiser* on account of its remarks about me last week. I think Gibson has hurt himself instead of me by his foolish attacks on me. I believe that he is nearly stranded. If Gibson insists on sending you his paper, George, let them accumulate in the P.O. as waste paper, and take no further trouble about them."

Very anxious as to George's health, particularly a wound slow to heal, Sanford shipped him by the *James Makee* a hundred pounds of ice, hoping it might be refreshing and useful. Later Sanford reported an isolated case of smallpox smuggled ashore from a ship bringing Chinese immigrants. Marshal Parke sent instructions to George to "look sharp after his new Chinese workmen from that vessel, the *Cassandra:* better isolate them in work and housing, have them inspected at least once a day, and rigidly quarantine every case of fever and pain in the back."

No dividend beyond a keg of sugar this year was the Grove Ranch report from Maui:

We shall devote our force to raising cane to be ground at Paia, and hope to work up the crop to 12 or 1,500 tons in two years; we have also leased to the East Maui Plantation Company a field of 124 acres above the line of the ditch for a term sufficient to raise one crop of cane, they to pay us 1/12 of all the sugar they make from the crop. The rest of the land above the ditch line we shall devote to stock raising.

The year 1882 saw the operation of the Planters' Labor and Supply Company as a separate organization, taking the place of the Planters' Association organized about the same time. S. B. Dole explains this merging as a necessity after the members adopted the charter of the Labor and Supply Company and the objects of the two societies became identical. Scientific investigation in cane culture did not at once form a large part of the work of the association; the first issue of the *Planters' Monthly,* edited by three lawyers, W. R. Castle, S. B. Dole, and W. O. Smith, appeared in April, 1882. For the July number Dole asked his brother to send from Kauai an item as to the Kapaa plantation crop, the time of grinding, tonnage, and dividends; also a statement of prospects for the next crop as to acreage and probably tonnage.

In the long roster of fifty-five men assembling from all the Islands for the meeting in March 1882, which affected the merger of the two societies, most of the names were familiar as of men having the best interests of the Islands at heart. In fact, a special noon meeting with His Majesty the King was scheduled in Aliiolani Hale, and took place with due ceremony. Renewal of the Reciprocity Treaty, due in 1884, had been a vital force in calling these men to conference. All realized that to bring about the right kind of prosperity it was going to mean a long pull, that it must of necessity be a strong pull, and a pull all together. In discussions as to types of laborers, one planter wished to go on record as opposed to bringing in any cannibals from the New Hebrides; another spoke highly of the Portuguese for promptness and efficiency in field work; also of the excellence of the Chinese in mill work; still another reported some Chinese as finding it difficult to cope with large animals that hooked at one end and kicked at the other.

Toward the passage of the first treaty of reciprocity David Kalakaua's visit to the United States had been of material assistance. As to the renewal of that treaty after seven years the king seemed to be growing indifferent, if not directly hostile. "I suppose the chances are," mused Sanford Dole as he chatted with his brother, "that David Kalakaua will terminate his existence as a private gentleman. He may be somewhat proud of the treaty, but at present his thoughts run to what he can make, if it comes to an end. As he told Dr. Hutchinson the other day, he is going to buy up a lot of the bankrupt plantations and import a lot of immigrants with the ten million loan to run his plantations with, and so make his fortune."

Such dreams reflected no doubt the ambitions of Gibson, who became Kalakaua's Prime Minister in 1882 and dominated both king and cabinet for years thereafter. Claus Spreckels too obtained title to valuable cane lands and legislative authority to superintend the minting of Kalakaua coins, a transaction netting a handsome fortune for Spreckels' own pocket. This same Legislature of 1882 repealed restrictions on sale of liquor to Hawaiians and swelled the appropriation bill to twice the estimated government income, including besides $30,000 for Hawaiian youth in foreign countries, $10,000 for a Board of Genealogy and $30,000 for coronation expenses, nine years after the king's accession. This last project, meeting with disapproval even from some of the best Hawaiians, aroused some pleasant memories in Boston, whence General J. F. B. Marshall, long a friend of Hawaii, wrote to Father Damon: "How our good friend, the late 'Laird of Rosebank' [Minister Wyllie], would have revelled in the correspondence and diplomatic acts and ceremonies which this coming coronation will necessitate!"

The island kingdom of Hawaii was indeed expanding to grandiose proportions under its new premier and the first sovereign ever to make a journey around the world. In his reminiscence Sanford Dole pictured long afterward the center of this Pacific drama, the new palace, at a cost to the taxpayers of some $343,595:

His Majesty, who was very fond of publicity in recognition of his royal position, prepared for a very ceremonial coronation. Money was appro priated by the willing legislature, crowns were made in Europe for him and his queen, Kapiolani; a showy pavilion was built in front of the palace for the event. An elaborate procession was arranged, exhibiting some features of Hawaiian primitive life with evidences of its progress in trade, and the affair came off in good weather before a brilliant assemblage of some 8,000 people with apparent great success. In this coronation the elected king crowned himself, and then the queen. This occurred February 12, 1883.

One of the King's ambitions was this new palace, the construction of which had been under way upon his return from his trip around the world. The old palace was a substantial, suitable building of coral rock, comfortable and adequate for the work of a little kingdom like that of the Hawaiian Islands at that time; but not sufficient for Kalakaua's somewhat magnified dreams, the display in European courts probably having had its influence on him. The erection of the new palace continued until its completion shortly before the coronation with the fine results existing today.

The throne room has been recognized by persons acquainted with European palaces as in a way unexcelled by similar halls in other parts of the world. Of course this building and its beautiful throne room added much to Kalakaua's satisfaction with his position. The occasional receptions and royal parties which were held there with some splendour and pomp appealed directly to the King's appreciation of his situation as a sovereign with a brilliant court and the prestige of formal occasions in surroundings of beauty and splendour. In addition to a very conspicuous ceiling of elaborate work in plaster of Paris, there were chandeliers with a great abundance of pendants of cut glass, producing brilliant and beautiful effects when lighted at night, [and reproduced with joyous exuberance by Hawaiian women of all the Islands in their original quilt designs].

The hall was hung with portraits of Hawaiian Kings and Queens, all of life size, with one or two royal magnates of European courts, conspicuous among which was one of Louis Phillipe of France, which was landed in Honolulu on the day that its original was driven from Paris at the termination of his short reign. The French government, having seized the Hawaiian yacht and other property of the government of that time, it has since been conscientiously moved to make occasional reparations in the way of national portraits, silver and china.

Newcomers who enjoyed state occasions under the dazzling new magic of electric lights in this throne room, as also parties in the king's bungalow, were Isobel Strong and her husband, the California artist commissioned by John D. Spreckels to paint Hawaiian landscapes for his San Francisco office. Mrs. Strong, daughter of Mrs. Robert Louis Stevenson, herself made many a sketch of Kalakaua's coronation, and is still recalled in Honolulu by older people who as children accompanied their mother for painting lessons at the Nuuanu cottage lent to the Strongs by Mother Parker of the American Mission.

Welcomed by official Honolulu as a gay addition to the local community, the Strongs remained for several years. After her second marriage Mrs. Strong's story, *This Life I've Loved,* gave many a bright anecdote of the monarchy. Their small son Austin would often sit at their wicket gate where Hawaiians riding up the valley would stop to drop a lei of flowers over the little boy's head and water their horses, while Austin gazed sadly at the shabby old horse tub. Boys of the neighborhood, who all had brightly painted watering tubs filled with goldfish, were quick to hurl taunts at the Strongs' leaky half-barrel.

Who that heard it, or read it years later in the *Atlantic Monthly,* could ever forget Austin Strong's picture of the king's victoria and outriders nearly running down small Austin one evening near the duck ponds at Waikiki? Furtively clutching the wriggling top of his straw hat, the boy stood tongue-tied at thought of his head being chopped off when His Majesty should discover under that hat crown an Imperial Japanese goldfish purloined from the pool in royal Kapiolani Park. But the king, having no immediate execution in mind, rescued both boy and fish, and delivered them safely to the Nuuanu studio, where the Strongs shouted with laughter at their son's appearance. To save face for those poor parents, Austin plunged the grand duke of a goldfish at once into their old horse tub, there to flaunt the brilliant court train of his gleaming tail for neighbors all and sundry.

Next morning, a dazzling equerry, dismounting to water his horse, bowed low to present small Austin with a great square envelope bearing the royal crest, enclosing full permission to fish in the royal park for life, and signed: Kalakaua Rex.

Other royal visits occurred at the cottage when the king, in his suit of spotless white and his hat of fine, closely woven peacock quills with its wide band of tiny sea shells, came to ask Mrs. Strong whether she could paint a saltwater fish in fifteen minutes before it faded; and when often in the early morning the king's fishermen would arrive with their catch and wait while Isobel swiftly caught undersea brilliance in paint and paper. Half a century ahead of his time, the king was working with Mrs. Strong on designs for what are now known the world over as aloha prints. He hoped that his Queen Kapiolani and sister, Princess Liliuokalani, would adopt and adapt these suggestions for becoming regal *holokus* to wear at Queen Victoria's Jubilee in 1887, in place of conventional basques and tightly draped skirts already on order in Paris. True to their own more artificial age, however, the royal ladies declined to set a new mode. To cover disappointment, King Kalakaua, in solitary state in the new throne room, bestowed on Isobel Strong the broad blue ribbon and star of the Order of Oceania.

While a young aide at the court of King Kamehameka IV, Colonel David Kalakaua had in 1861 graciously and efficiently served as courier to Lady Franklin and her niece in their tour of Hawaii as the king's special guests. The two English ladies wrote home of their enjoyment of Colonel Kalakaua's unfailing courtesy and faultless English, particularly his manner of address and conversation during leisurely breakfasts while visiting Princess Ruth on the Kona coast. In Hawaiian, and among Hawaiians, Kalakaua was equally at home, and amused no doubt, as was Lady Franklin herself, at the foremost outriders in her calvacade. On approaching a village, these couriers would inevitably charge ahead, shouting: "Make way, make way, for the Queen of the English!" Instinctive deference it is true, paid to the *alii* of a foreign country on these long rides through Olaa and Kau. But, fond as Kalakaua was of ceremony and display, might not the repetition of this exaggerated title have fed his own longing for future display, should the turn of the years favor him in the royal succession? Certainly Mark Twain in 1866 found this same Colonel Kalakaua a man of dignity who "would do no discredit to the kingly office."

No wonder then that King Kalakaua desired the formal ceremony of being invested with a crown. According to original plan, the coronation ceremonies of 1883 were to conclude with the unveiling of the new statue of Kamehameha I. Storms of rain however delayed this, and of course convinced many Hawaiians of the high rank of the great *alii*. The *Hawaiian Gazette* heaved a sigh of relief, announcing that the P.C.A.— for years the *Pacific Commercial Advertiser,* but latterly dubbed the Premier's Coronation Advertisement—"has informed us that we may begin to give our attention to other topics" than the coronation. Two days after that event the newly crowned king, at the invitation of Premier Gibson as master of ceremonies, did unveil the golden cloaked statue of the first Kamehameha, in the open square before the Government Building, facing the palace gates.

Other schemes began to take shape, such as sending Colonel Curtis P. Iaukea as a special envoy, with a secretary, to the coronation of the Russian czar, and to bear His Hawaiian Majesty's regards "to the Sovereigns and Heads of States who have so signally honored Me and My State." Commissioned also to study immigration to Hawaii, this special envoy was graciously received at the courts of Great Britain, France, Russia, Austria, Italy, and Servia, with a roving commission which brought him home by way of India and Japan.

Plans ripening for an Empire of the Pacific, to center in Kalakaua as Protector of all Polynesia, commenced with official protests to foreign powers against any interference in the Pacific.

Perhaps in the hope of crippling all comment in the columns of the *Saturday Press,* a libel suit was instituted against that paper by Dr. George L. Fitch, agent of the Board of Health and personal friend of the king. The presidency of the Board of Health, among his many other political offices, was held by Premier Gibson. Admitting only rudimentary medical training, Dr. Fitch not only held responsible public offices, but built up false hopes that leprosy was not seriously contagious and was undoubtedly curable. With citizens eagerly crowding the courtroom, with Chief Justice Judd on the bench, two attorneys for the crown and S. B. Dole for the defense, the case came to trial in July, 1883. T. G. Thrum, proprietor of the *Saturday Press,* represented that paper as personal defendant.

Dole's line of defense stressed the importance of a free press, if for no other purpose than the discussion of such pernicious statements from a government official. "It is not only the privilege of a newspaper to comment on public inefficiency, it becomes a manifest duty," declared the defense attorney, mustering every available point in his statement to the jury. "The very liberty of the press is on trial. Public health is at stake."

In his charge to the jury Chief Justice Judd reiterated the vital nature of the trial. The result was acquittal of the *Saturday Press* on the indictment of libel, and on the part of the public increased awareness as to incompetence in public officials.

Repercussions on points of tension in the little mid-Pacific kingdom were not slow to reach Sanford Dole even across ocean and continent. From Boston Will Brigham, on his way to start a sugar plantation in Guatemala, wrote: "How is Anna? and has she got through the coronation in safety? Our newspapers contain many hard cuts at the 'kanaka koronation' folly, and I think the estimation in which the Islands are held has fallen greatly in this community."

And Thomas Rain Walker, traveling with his wife in England,

evinced the liveliest concern for his adopted land in the far Pacific, chatting with his dear friend *Loio* (lawyer), much as had often been their wont in Honolulu during a stroll to the top of Punchbowl nearby with "the light manila" in hand. Having met Curtis Iaukea several times in his European travels, Walker commented: "There is no excuse for the extravagant nonsense which sent him abroad; but, this being said, they could not have sent a young Hawaiian who would comport himself more creditably. He has earned golden opinions on all sides."

And by the end of September Walker was moved to remark:

It is months since we thought that each tomorrow would see our friend Gibson tumble from the premiership of the Pacific; and now really the octopus-like manner in which he hangs on to his various appointments is beginning to inspire me with admiration; he is a remarkable man. The recent circular advising all foreign powers to keep their hands off the Pacific is a surprising achievement. The Reuter's telegram which I saw stated that the circular had been issued without a communication of its contents to the representatives in Hawaii of countries concerned; this however I can hardly believe, for so glaring an insult to the three diplomatic personages must either suggest a change at Iolani Palace or threaten to plunge the civilized world into warfare.

A copy of the extra edition of the *Saturday Press* reporting the celebrated libel suit of Dr. Fitch against that Honolulu paper, found Walker even in Scotland "heartily glad that the right of public criticism of official people and measures has been maintained." Dr. Wright, Dole's Boston pastor, likewise received a copy of the *Saturday Press* and even while on a fishing jaunt in Maine sat down and read aloud to his companion the entire account of the case, every word with deep interest. "Your plea was masterly," he wrote Dole, "and when I saw the ability with which you handled your witnesses, I realized that you had won the case before your argument. Then you did just the right thing; avoided vituperation at great provocation, when its use would have won you a brilliant reputation at the expense of your client. You did the best thing and did it superbly."

This whole libel suit with open sessions on subjects of acute public concern brought about in effect a successor to the early Town Meetings of colonial America. Such gatherings in New England, in a new, untried political form, evolved logically as actual governing bodies; these mass meetings of discussion and protest in Honolulu took place within the framework of an already established monarchy. Still more primitive parallels are not far to seek. For before the name Honolulu appeared, the lee shore of Oahu, with its groves of spreading *kou* trees, was known as *He Awa o Kou,* a sheltered beach safe for canoes bringing folk to talk over public matters in the shade of *kou* trees. Now, in a later time of grave anxiety, another such meeting convened in Aliiolani Hale, the House of Nobles at Honolulu, where groves of *kou* trees had once stood. Now Justice and attorneys were spokesmen; the eager public attended, listened, and applauded the verdict. The purpose remained the same: preservation of the common weal.

Chapter IX

IN THE HOUSE
1884–1886

A MONG rumblings of public discontent, appeal was made
before the Supreme Court at Honolulu in mid-December
of 1883 for an injunction on the illegality of Kalakaua's
silver coinage. Presented by three lawyers, W. R. Castle, S. B.
Dole, and W. O. Smith, this test case, on which high hopes were
built, met defeat on a technicality. Editor Atkinson of the
Hawaiian Gazette remarked that these three gentlemen had
acted in accordance with their legal rights, and that "the cabinet
has committed an illegal act to prop its failing fortunes, because
the ex-Mormon mis-manager can keep his seat in no other way—
that leader who deadens the Royal ear with honeyed phrases.
Alas, Hawaii, a millstone has been hung around your graceful
neck which it may take years of struggle to remove!"

Expressions such as these must have at last so affected the
Premier that, from his auxiliary post as president of the Board
of Education, he summarily dismissed A. T. Atkinson after five
years of excellent service as principal of the Fort Street School,
deeming it "inappropriate to maintain in the Board's service one
engaged in journalism who derides the Sovereign, and endeavors
to bring contempt on the Government."

By 1883 the renewal of the Reciprocity Treaty was being
discussed. After having granted to the Pacific Mail and the
Occidental and Oriental Steamship Companies the privilege of
bringing in Chinese immigrants, this favor was abruptly withdrawn and promised to Claus Spreckels. Public protest began to
mount. On December 10, 1883, a mass meeting of Honolulu
citizens to consider this unexpected action on the part of Premier
Gibson was called by S. B. Dole, W. O. Smith, P. C. Jones, Jr.,

174

A. T. Atkinson, W. L. Holokahiki, G. W. Pilipo, B. W. Kawainui, and J. Kalama. All classes in the community were represented among the three hundred people present. Emphatic statements stressed the danger to national independence. In a forceful speech S. B. Dole branded Gibson's official deed as a breach of faith with an American firm and likely to endanger Hawaii's treaty relations with the United States at a crucial time.

Amid applause, those present expressed lack of confidence in the king's cabinet and proceeded to nominate candidates on an independent ticket in the coming election campaign. If even a small majority for the House of Representatives could be returned, it might mean some gain in opposing legislation barely defeated in the incredible session of 1882 and sure to be revived in 1884.

Among such bills were the huge loan of ten million dollars; a lottery bill; and a proposal to license opium, all three as nearly disastrous to the people and their islands as any that could have been framed by their bitterest enemies. Editor Atkinson of the *Hawaiian Gazette* needled the administration with a question as to whether even the Hawaiian crown, bought "on tick," had yet been paid for or must linger on as a public disgrace—a detail, perhaps, but significant.

One thing was certain, S. B. Dole would run for this next Legislature, not to represent the district of the government center at Honolulu, but from his boyhood home district of Koloa and Lihue. To free some of his working time he engaged H. E. Avery of Kapaa to join him as office assistant at Honolulu. Well-known though Dole was on the island of Kauai, he was urged by his brother to come down early, before the election in February. Will Rowell too was planning to visit Waimea in the hope of being chosen to represent his old home district.

W. H. Rice of Lihue, with his familiar command of Hawaiian, supported his two school-fellows, Dole and Rowell. Mrs. Rice, formerly Mary Waterhouse of Honolulu, was eloquent too in their behalf. In fact, Mary and Willy Rice joined heart and soul in the election excitement, with open house at Hale Nani, their simple, hospitable home at Lihue.

Results for both Dole and Rowell were hard won, and gratifying. W. O. Smith, resident at Grove Ranch, also was returned to represent Wailuku, Maui. In January the *Saturday Press* had urged voters to return independent Representatives with stout hearts and thinking brains; in its February report of total returns for the election the *Press* noted that Oahu, Molokai, and Lanai, as expected, had voted in favor of the administration, a result due largely to the use of free rum, religious favoritism, race prejudice, and freedom for lepers. But even this centralization of power had been offset by returns from Maui, Hawaii, and Kauai, for in the total of 15,146 votes cast on all the islands, Independent candidates had polled a majority of 680. Of the 28 men to sit as Representatives, 11 would be men representing the Administration men, 17 Independent or Opposition. This per-haps seemed slight, but it spelled that hoped-for wedge of majority in the House at least.

Before the session, however, almost three months were to elapse, giving time for Dole to organize his office work and get in a short vacation where interested comment followed him and was eagerly read. From Honolulu his wife confided fears and rumors active in the public mind, particularly in the matter of leprosy. "Do wear gloves, Sanford," she begged, "and don't eat any raw fish. People say that against Dr. Fitch's advice Gibson let out sufferers from the dread disease even at Kakaako detention hos-pital, and that a hundred or more are at large in Honolulu streets alone. Dr. Trousseau describes the results and revelations of the past two years as terrifying in the extreme."

From Michigan Miss Marcia Smith echoed out of the past with the amazed realization that Sanford, the little boy she had known at Punahou, was now a man in middle life, shouldering his share in active work, and joined by other Punahou boys in making a fearless stand for honest government. From afar she watched anxiously for the outcome of the crisis at the Islands. And she offered to fulfill her promise to forward to Sanford the early portrait of George which to glance at took her back almost half a century.

Officially, and personally, from the Hawaiian Legation in Washington, D.C., Minister H. A. P. Carter shared timely thoughts with S. B. Dole as of April 5, 1884:

The most damaging thing now in our currency is that a Gov't can, as a favor to a private individual, permit him without legal sanction to flood us with whatever he pleases and make it legal tender, and make $150,000 out of it. What limit is there to such proceedings? Both law and public opinion seem paralyzed. There was not a shadow of warrant for it in the coinage act. Probably the next move will be to declare photographs of Mr. Spreckels legal tender to any amount.

I hope the Legislative Assembly will pass the most stringent laws forbidding any further trifling, and taking away from the Privy Council the power to make legal tender of mere brass—or any other material.

To become a new cog in the wheel of the Hawaiian Legislature was no insignificant matter. Just turned forty, after fifteen years of interpreting laws, Sanford Dole was now chosen by his fellow citizens as their spokesman in the legislative body of 1884. From the angle of practical politics, he must see his native land with the eye of a law maker.

On the 25th of April George Dole and his ten-year-old son Charlie took the steamer *Iwalani* from Kauai, arriving at dawn the next day, and going at once to Emma Street for breakfast and to accompany Anna Dole to the formal opening of the Legislature in Aliiolani Hale. This was an occasion, personal as well as official, of which no slightest detail was left unchronicled by the daily *Pacific Commercial Advertiser* thus: "On Saturday, the 26th April at 12 o'clock noon and pursuant to the Royal Proclamation, the session of the Legislative Assembly of 1884 was duly opened by His Majesty the King in person." Nor was any item of stately decorum and elaborate pageantry lacking in the entire proceeding.

Foreign ministers and consuls were received with due honors and conducted by ushers to their allotted places in the grand hall. For hours the general public, including numerous ladies in gay, rich dresses, continued to arrive from all directions until the body of the hall was well filled. The spacious balconies on the upper floor were crowded with ladies and children, while the entire grounds and vicinity presented a joyous company of natives and foreigners, alike eager to miss nothing of the long-awaited spectacle.

A few minutes before noon the Royal Hawaiian Band, in front of the Kamehameha statue, played "Hawaii Ponoi," the national anthem. Headed by six *kahili* bearers and the chamberlain, His Majesty the King, in the full dress uniform of a German cavalry officer, resplendent with numerous European and Asiatic orders, walked from the palace between lines of royal troops who presented arms as he passed. Accompanied by Governor Dominis of Oahu, and the Honorable A. S. Cleghorn, His Majesty was followed by the staff officers. A royal salute announced arrival at the hall.

Following closely in an open barouche was Her Royal Highness Princess Liliuokalani with her ladies in waiting, all in full court dress.

As the king entered the hall and mounted the royal dais, the assembly rose. The king was accompanied by his sister, H. R. H. Princess Liliuokalani, and staff.

Arrangements were perfect. To the right of the royal dais stood the royal family and the ladies of His Majesty's ministers. On the left, gentlemen wearing royal honors, and their ladies. Directly in front of the dais stood the Cabinet Ministers. On the right, members of the Diplomatic Corps, and on their left the Justices of the Supreme Court. Behind the Ministers were the Nobles of the kingdom, and behind them the Representatives. To the right of these were members of the Privy Council and of the Consular Corps, with their ladies, the general public being accommodated in the middle of the hall.

The ceremonies were opened with solemn prayer by the Reverend Alexander Mackintosh of St. Andrews Cathedral. A portfolio containing the royal speech was handed to the king by his chamberlain, Colonel C. H. Judd. Clearly and audibly His Majesty read his address to the Nobles and Representatives, in the Hawaiian first, and afterwards in the English language. A long and pleasant speech in which improvement and prosperity were highlighted with satisfaction, no least mention appearing of serious overdrafts on the national treasury nor of growing undercurrents of unrest throughout the entire realm of eight islands.

The complete legislative body, meeting regularly in joint session, comprised two groups: the Upper House of 18 Nobles and 4 Cabinet Ministers who as appointees of the Crown were chiefly "king's men," although a few voted as they chose; and the elected House of 28 Representatives with its slightly larger group of Opposition or Reform members, to whom many good citizens looked for constructive action. This thin wedge in the House lost no time in getting into action, as Sanford Dole later recounted:

His Excellency.
John L. Stevens
  Envoy Extraordinary and Minister Plenipotentiary of the United
States of America;
      Sir,
        Believing
t we are unable to satisfactorily
tect life and property, and to pre-
t civil disorder in Honolulu and
oughout the Hawaiian Islands, we
eby, in obedience to the instructions
the Advisory Council, pray that
u will raise the flag of the United
ates of America, for the protection
the Hawaiian Islands for the time
ng; and to that end we hereby
fer upon the Government of the
ited States, through you, freedom
occupation of the public buildings
this government, and of the soil
this country, so far as may be
cessary for the exercise of such
tection, but not interfering with
administration of public affairs
this government.
   We have the honor to be your
   Excellency's obedient servants
        (servants)

(Servants).

Sanford B. Dole
President of the Provisional Gov[ernment]
of the Hawaiian Islands and [Min]
-ister of Foreign Affairs -
J. A. King   Minister of Int[erior]
P. C. Jones   Minister of Fina[nce]
William O. Smith   Attorney Genera[l]

Honolulu, Hawaiian Islands,
January 31st 1893-

Original letter from President Dole and his Executive Council
requesting the raising of the Stars and Stripes over Hawaii.

The slight majority of the Opposition gained a considerable advantage on the first day in nominating the Honorable Godfrey Rhodes, one of the Nobles, as President or Speaker of the session. Rhodes was a liberal, in harmony with the program of the Opposition Party. And with the office of President went also the appointment of legislative committees, an advantage which gradually became apparent to the Palace Party as a sharp thorn in their side.

Since 1882, as Professor W. D. Alexander stated in his study of the crisis, "A considerable reaction had taken place among the natives, who resented the cession of Wailuku Crown lands to Spreckels, and felt a profound distrust of Gibson. In spite of the war cry of 'Hawaii for Hawaiians,' and the lavish use of government patronage, the Palace Party was defeated in the elections generally, although it held Honolulu, its stronghold. Among the Reform members that session were Messrs. Dole, Rowell, Smith, Hitchcock, the three brothers, Godfrey, Cecil, and Frank Brown, Kauhane, Kalua, Nawahi, and the late Pilipo, of honored memory."

On the second day of the session S. B. Dole was appointed chairman of a committee to reply to the king's speech at the opening of the Legislature. At the appropriate time a dignified, detailed reply was made, agreeing with the king at many points, particularly in his satisfaction that the estimates of the expenditures "have been placed within the amount of revenue for the last two years"; and "feeling that not only national credit but national existence as well, depends upon a faithful and intelligent management of expenditures."

Early in the session a resolution introduced by S. B. Dole, inquiring into the income derived by the king from Crown lands, was at once challenged by Attorney General Neumann. Dole replied with some heat, quoting Hawaiian law, attacking both the Premier and the Attorney General, and stating that people were not proud of much that had taken place in the past two years. President Rhodes expressed agreement with the charges of Dole, whose fluency in Hawaiian evidently nettled Neumann, a recent appointee of the Crown. Neumann would "get even" with Dole in another two years, expressions such as his "boyishness," and "fractious spirit," "the tender corns of the member from Lihue," suggesting more than surface irritation.

When it was announced that the commissioners of Crown lands declined to report to the assembly on receipts from Crown lands, the member from Lihue introduced a second resolution that the question be referred to the judges of the Supreme Court. The *Bulletin* of June 13, 1884, considering the matter of prime importance, gave ample space to the substance of Mr. Dole's remarks upon his resolution.

These remarks presented with cogent logic the facts that while some members of the House might be willing to work in the dark, Dole himself was not; that the Assembly could hardly vote intelligently on the king's biennial salary without knowing what his Crown revenues were. But, since "there is an honest difference of opinion as to our right to demand this information, it becomes the proper and dignified thing for us to leave the matter to the Supreme Court as our umpire. If this resolution should be passed and the opinion of the Supreme Court should differ from mine, I would submit; and I do those members who disagree with me the justice to believe, that should the opinion of the Supreme Court differ from theirs, they would also gracefully submit to it."

This resolution too met prompt defeat. Yet every avenue of action was not closed, for the member from Lihue and Koloa received appointment to the Foreign Relations Committee and as chairman of the Judiciary Committee; later also as a member of the Police Commission and of a select Committee on Waterworks.

Dole's next step was the bold one of a resolution expressing want of confidence in the king's ministry. With the ministers themselves voting against it, the resolution failed of passage, though by only a narrow margin. But the feeling had been publicly voiced.

More than one resolution decrying waste and unauthorized public expenditures went down to defeat, but the eyes of many were opened to misuse of public funds. When Minister of Foreign Affairs Gibson explained the presence of such items as turkeys, shawls, corsets, and bustles in the finance report as gifts to ladies making coronation *kahilis,* Dole remarked that for gobbling up public funds this might well be known as the "turkey cabinet."

A bill for $18,000 to build a new stable on the palace grounds met derision at the hands of the *Bulletin:* This sum would pay for sidewalks for the whole city, or a turnpike to Kapiolani Park.

For a private stable the amount was at variance with the king's own message to the Legislature, urging economy. Yet, when complimented on that message, the king replied that Mr. Spreckels had been responsible for it. Strange anomaly!—a royal message from the president of the California Sugar Refinery!

Application by Mr. Spreckels for a national bank charter, which lacked most of the safeguards of the American banking system, "was riddled both in the House and in the Chamber of Commerce and indignation meetings of citizens were held until the King was alarmed; finally it was killed on second reading by an overwhelming majority."

After friendly discussion however, the sugar king accepted the situation, in Professor Alexander's account, "and a fair general banking law was passed providing for banks of deposit and exchange, but not of issue."

With determination Dole fought both the lottery bill introduced by a Louisiana company, and a bill to license opium. "Pursued with liquor and leprosy," he cried from the floor of the House, "and now assailed with opium, what chance is there for the poor Hawaiian?"

All in all it was a hard, tedious fight during four long summer months. At its end the *Pacific Commercial Advertiser,* the Administration paper, but often boasting its political neutrality, commented: "Throughout the session Mr. Dole's speeches have been the most moderate and most logical of any delivered by the active members of the Opposition."

And a public evening reception was tendered the Reform members by three hundred citizens of many races in the Lyceum, gaily decorated with the Hawaiian coat-of-arms, also Hawaiian, American, English, and German flags. Large pictures of the king and queen, were hung above the platform, and selections by the Royal Hawaiian Band lent the brightness of musical color.

P. C. Jones served as master of ceremonies, accompanied to the platform by J. O. Carter, the Reverend A. O. Forbes, and T. R. Walker as spokesman in appreciation of service rendered by Reform members in the 1884 legislative session. Resolutions proposed by Judge A. S. Hartwell were unanimously adopted. Enthusiastic and vociferous applause greeted the appearance of Godfrey Rhodes.

Long known among Hawaiians as Kapena Loke, Captain Rhodes, of Hanalei, the liberal president of the Legislature just past, had watched with interest the participation of his three nephews, Godfrey, Frank, and Cecil Brown as Representatives in the work of the session. From the time when the Dole family— Sanford aged three—had made their first vacation tour around Kauai, S. B. Dole had known the Thomas Browns, the "little sister Alice and her polite English brothers," in their beautifully paneled English house with its "secret chamber for hiding in case of attack by savages." Latterly the Thomas Browns had lived in Honolulu, their father in government office as Registrar of Conveyances for almost thirty years, and their sister Alice as wife of the Reverend Mr. Mackintosh, chaplain of this 1884 session. Dole's recollections of their English home at Wailua Falls on Kauai were colored too by George Wilcox's story that when the Wailua estate had finally reverted to the Crown, King Kalakaua had had the house removed to the lowlands on the Wailua River, dreaming of a country mansion for himself which never materialized.

Suddenly recalled from these reveries to the actuality of 1884, Sanford Dole heard Chairman P. C. Jones calling on him to address the audience of the evening reception. Rising to the occasion, Dole pointed out the debt of Reform members to the timely election of Godfrey Rhodes as president of the session, "a success felt most keenly by our opponents," he added, with acknowledgment of the strong backing of public opinion during the entire session. In fact, he remarked to the amusement of his listeners, "the Government Banking Act was so easily killed that there was no fun in it. We have, it is true, secured no such boon as the overthrow of misgovernment, but we have made such clear exposures of their misdeeds as they can never get over. Dark transactions were coming to the surface right up to the last. It looks as if we were going back, but there are some defeats better than victories. In five years we shall be better able to weigh and test the results of the present session's work. I have great confidence in the power of truth."

As final speaker came the Reverend George W. Pilipo, often called the Lion of North Kona, "eloquent among a nation of orators," and an outspoken foe of corruption and peculation in office, definitely feared by his compatriot, the king. Not knowing whether he might again join with his Reform colleagues, Pilipo struck this note of timely warning: "Gentlemen," he said, "we have been swimming against the tide. But I urge you, let there be no faltering, no slackening. Let us work for a majority of true men in the Assembly of 1886. Only then can we say that the tide has turned."

Even the tangle of a legislative session, however, must come to an end, and gradually life resumed its everyday pace. In his daily walks down and back again up Emma Street Sanford Dole thought with pleasure of Bernice Pauahi Bishop and her husband as living now in the mansion which Princess Ruth had built the year before. Pauahi and Luka (Ruth) had been like sisters. And Bernice's natural kindness of heart had often taken her to Ruth's bedside in illness. They were cousins, and spoken of as the last of the Kamehamehas.

In May of 1883, when Princess Ruth was reported mortally ill in the house where Kamehameha himself had died at Kailua in Kona, Bernice Pauahi and Queen Dowager Emma at once boarded the little steamer *Likelike* for Kailua. And while they sat beside Luka, she composed her own *a-a,* her lament, her *kanikau* (farewell greeting) as had Liholiho's queen, Kamamalu, on setting out for the far land of Britanee whence for her there could be no return. So now Ruth chanted her own threnody of leave-taking from the great mountains of her favorite islands, from the waves of the ocean, from the beaches, familiar places, houses and friends.

Arriving too by the steamer *Likelike* had been His Majesty Kalakaua, but finding Princess Ruth somewhat improved, he had proceeded on to Hilo. She herself had known better; her time of farewell had come. The three highest *alii* in the land were to make their last journey together, Bernice and Emma as royal escort to the late Princess Ruth, Captain J. A. King of the *Likelike* paying them all such courtesy that the Honorable C. R. Bishop wrote him a grateful letter which has been kept these seventy years by Captain King's family. And Luka was to lie in state in the elaborate mansion for which she had exchanged her patrimony of the beautiful Kipu lands of Nawiliwili, Kauai, the mansion which she had but rarely occupied, much preferring to contemplate its high steps and foreign grandeur from the comfort of her big, roomy, one-story house under the fruit trees behind her new palace.

And now in 1884 Bernice Pauahi Bishop as Ruth's heir had moved into Ruth's ornate brick and stucco palace within its high stone wall like Iolani Palace on King Street. It could not have been easy for the Bishops to leave Haleakala, their own home on King Street, a simple, two-storied house of coral blocks, spacious and cool, surrounded by verandas. This had been built by Mrs. Bishop's father, High Chief Paki, and was for thirty years one of the most hospitable homes in the town. Wide gardens and old trees covered the ground later paved as Bishop Street. Even a tennis court formed one of its attractions and when foreign warships were in port, officers could be seen from the McGrews' fence, where young Kate and her brother Tarn would climb up to watch the trim Navy men playing tennis with Honolulu girls in hats and long, full skirts. "Not done these days," commented Kate McGrew Cooper in 1953, as she recalled two other "lovely grass lawn tennis courts" of her girlhood, one farther out on King Street where the Thomas Rain Walkers lived, and the other at the Dowsett home on land now part of Washington Place.

Loving children and young people, Bernice Pauahi Bishop often had them about her, devoting herself for years to her class of girls at Kawaiahao Sunday School. Untiring in her visits to the sick and unfortunate, she worked too in the Strangers' Friend Society. Sanford Dole remembered Pauahi as merry-hearted, yet dignified; high-spirited and very loyal to constituted authority, with character and personality which quite overshadowed her high rank. Both she and her husband were genial hosts, their home was full of books and they gave a ready welcome to stranger as well as friend, with many a picnic too at the Waikiki home. Will Brigham and Ellen Armstrong Weaver delighted to tell of Mrs. Bishop's dinner for young Horace Mann, that scientific Boston child "brought up on Silliman and Agassiz instead of Grimm and Mother Goose." In Honolulu Mrs. Bishop treated him to Hawaiian dishes, fish from her ancestral ponds, leis of green, fragrant *maile,* a bearer with a tall *kahili* at each corner of the table, and sparkling through it all, brilliant, delightful talk.

While young Mann and Brigham were living on Alakea Street

in a rented cottage, the Bishops' parlor was a frequent meeting place for their Reading Club. Or when they dropped in to call after dinner, Mrs. Bishop would suggest charades; the young people would run upstairs for costumes and to plan their parts, while the Bishop retainers would be sent through the little town to invite neighbors informally, with the result that the players found the parlors full of amused friends ready to overlook any shortcomings; then came cakes, jellies, and lemonade without ice, and by ten all had scattered through the dark streets, unless the moon lighted them. When the moon was full, there were horseback rides to Punchbowl or Waikiki, or rowing parties about the harbor in the king's or the governor's boat, with Mrs. Bishop and Mrs. Dominis, who had been brought up as sisters, and other *alii* as guests, all singing to the strumming of guitars. In earlier days there would often be a formal concert at the Bishops' with the amateur Choral Society, and Mrs. Bishop's beautiful contralto in solo. Both Lady Franklin and her niece, from London in 1861, were charmed by such an evening and by Mrs. Bishop herself, who, they were certain, would have graced any court in Europe.

In October of 1884 Bernice Pauahi died in the new mansion on Emma Street. "The whole nation is in mourning," wrote Father Lyons in distant Waimea, Hawaii; "it will be a great and solemn day for Honolulu; we had services here at Imiola Church." And young Henry Castle watched the forming of the long procession from Emma Street, the funeral carriage surrounded with two hundred clustering *kahilis,* his ears "filled with the sound of wailing which, now full and piercing, now dying down, rose with uncertain cadence from every part of the yard. Nature was full of life and the pomp of life. Every breath that stirred the leaves sent the pulse through the veins with a fuller throb, rousing the heart to a fuller consciousness of feeling and being. As the band passed with slow and measured tread, every note of that funeral anthem flung upon the summer air seemed to blend with the thousand impressions of sight, producing something new, something sad, solemn and strange. I cannot express it, nor explain the feeling with which I saw the funeral carriage pass on its way to the wind-swept resting-place at the head of Nuuanu Valley."

In April 1885 the unexpected announcement was made of Queen Dowager Emma's death at Rooke House. Many realized that she was not yet fifty, and recalled the strong stand against absolute monarchy that she had taken with the other two high *alii,* Princess Ruth and Bernice Pauahi Bishop. After Queen Emma's death the Honorable Paul Isenberg wrote: "The last fear that Kalakaua had is now passed away."

To many, it was as if the end of the world had come. Not a thing was moved in Emma's childhood home at Rooke House, on lower Nuuanu between Beretania and Chaplain Lane, where for two weeks she lay surrounded by torches and waving *kahilis,* crowds of mourners constantly present, every steamer bringing more from Niihau to Ka-u. Because the new Episcopal Cathedral was not yet completed, *kahilis* and flaring torches guarded her stately removal by night to the old Stone Church at Kawaiahao where she and Kamehameha IV had been married thirty years before. Here the one week of lying in state was lengthened to two by heavy storms of rain and thunder, all in keeping with her high rank. After the Reverend Henry Parker's Hawaiian address, King Kalakaua and Queen Kapiolani, in heavy mourning, assembled with the Court in the organ loft above the pulpit, facing the Diplomatic and Consular Corps, Nobles and Privy Council. At one o'clock, at no outward sign, the great *kahilis* suddenly came to life, standing erect to present arms for the arrival of the Anglican Church cross, with robed choir boys and men. Special police guards took up the casket, and the procession, over a mile and a half long, with two thousand mourners, cavalry, and foot soldiers, made its stately progress of three hours up Nuuanu Valley.

A young physician, L. Vernon Briggs, in the service of the Board of Health, marveled at the great *kahilis,* some sent by the king, none equaling in splendor the brilliant colors of Emma's own, in gleaming black feathers of the *o-o* bird, blue of peacock, scarlet of parrot, and long-tailed *koa'e,* in barbaric magnificence, while hopeless wailing echoed and re-echoed, torches and *kahilis* flashing crimson, white, and yellow above the hearse. Many of the *kahilis* had such personality that they were named: Malulani and Laiku having been given to Emma as a child; the peacock plumed one, Kaneoneo (Silence) having an intricately carved jointed handle of human bone.

The old Hawaii of wise, far-seeing *alii* had passed. The ruler of Hawaii in 1885 was one to whom his princely heritage of Polynesia meant little or nothing except as exploited by European glitter of crown and throne. In addition, as R. S. Kuykendall ably points out, Kalakaua sincerely believed that as king he literally held the right to rule as he chose, to dismiss and appoint counselors at will, as also to bring pressure on voters before, during, and after elections. In this he was a champion of some of the beliefs of Kamehameha V and was but laying new emphasis on that monarch's still-existing Constitution of 1864. Also, Kalakaua was not alone. He had among his subjects of many races a large and devoted following of Royalists. Even among Reform Legislators and their supporters were many who believed in the Hawaiian monarchy; but with this distinction, that to them it seemed the wiser course, as in England, gradually to train the people to share administrative functions, while reserving great dignity to the sovereign.

When in 1884 the small majority among Reform Legislators had succeeded in making slight headway, the king and his Prime Minister were definitely alarmed, especially by the one commoner whose native eloquence had won him the sobriquet, "The Lion of North Kona." After studying at Hilo Boarding School and for three years at Lahainaluna School, George W. Pilipo had first taught a school of his own and then in 1864 had been ordained to the Christian ministry in Mokuaikaua Church at Kailua; here for seven years he had worked as Father Thurston's assistant, then became pastor of the peoples' church at Kaumakapili in Honolulu. And not from the pulpit only did this Hawaiian prophet denounce corruption and dishonesty, but early and late during seven sessions of the Legislature from 1868 to 1884. He was a power among his people. At all costs, therefore, he must be silenced.

It is a matter of record, as stated by both W. D. Alexander and L. A. Thurston, that Kalakaua himself proceeded to Kona a month or so before the election to spend his whole time electioneering against Pilipo; the king sent, in addition, numerous cases of gin and the entire Royal Guard, including minors, to be entered on the polling list, and to vote solid against Pilipo on election day; the king himself, seated in an armchair at the polls, solicited each voter to cast his ballot for Pilipo's opponent.

Defeated thus by a bare, illegal majority, Pilipo, a sick man, used every exertion for the interests of law and order in the face of an incipient riot at the polls. As Sanford Dole himself had pointed out in 1884, some defeats are more significant than victories.

At many a point during this political contest Opposition candidates must have heard again the eloquent voice of George W. Pilipo calling to his colleagues of 1884 never to slacken their efforts toward reform in the Assembly of 1886. Talking informally by letter with W. O. Smith in California, S. B. Dole wrote on February 10, 1886, from Honolulu:

> The election news is not reassuring. We have 10 seats in the House instead of 14 as at last session. The Ministry carried on a corrupt and bitter campaign, freely employing gin, fraud, bribes, promises, intimidation, and a perfect freshet of lies. Dr. Wight is elected in Kohala, Kauhane in Kau, Castle in Wailuku, Dickey in Makawao, Kalua in Lahaina, Thurston and Paehaole in Molokai and Lanai, Cecil Brown in Koolauloa, Anakalua [Kauhi] in Ewa and Waianae and yours truly in Lihue and Koloa.

The majority of 117 which returned the member from Lihue and Koloa was won by loyal support and hard work on the part of Hawaiian friends as well as boyhood companions like G. N. Wilcox and W. H. Rice, themselves veterans of earlier legislative sessions. In a letter of January 22, 1886, Rice had urged Dole to come down soon, especially to go to Koloa and make some headway against 16 cases of gin already circulated by his opponent. With G. N. and A. S. Wilcox, Rice had engaged the Nawiliwili coffee shops for election day, and Carl Isenberg, manager of Lihue Plantation, had joined in for a general *luau* and holiday the Saturday after election. There would be two lively bands, one of Hanamaulu men who were already practicing with their tin fifes and would march over to Lihue for the great day. "Be sure," Rice added, "to get your ballots printed on good, slim pasteboard, blue on red, something that they cannot fold up and that we can spot. A. S. Wilcox will stand this expense with *kou haahaa*—your humble servant. Even if the Mormons vote for you, it will be a hard fight, the Government people are at the last ditch and will die hard. We will do all we can, but you must come down and help."

The whole Rice household was alert with the biennial excitement, Mary Rice on her white horse out over the district urging voters; ten-year-old son Charlie watching the hay being moved out of the barn loft to make room for the big *luau;* coffee and sandwiches being made to send down to workers at the courthouse above Nawiliwili. Soda water was served at the Rices' open house until it gave out and resourceful Mary made gallons of lemonade, laced with a dash of Enos fruit salts to simulate soda. Son Charlie still tells of going to Nawiliwili without permission, and seeing one Hawaiian come up to the polls so alcoholically confused that he could not give his own name, stammering only "S. P. Kolo"— the Hawaiian equivalent of "S. B. Dole." And Kolo this particular Hawaiian was always called thereafter, even to the second generation. One of his grandsons, when signing up recently for work with C. A. Rice, had no idea as to the meaning of his family name, until Mr. Rice told him of its origin almost seventy years before.

Sanford Dole's Honolulu office of 1886 was a busy place. His assistant, H. E. Avery, during this year admitted to the Bar, was of great help in the numerous accounts, investments, guardianships, and estates involved in Dole's work. Anna Dole, very anxious as to her mother's health, had gone East in October to care for her, and ended by spending a year there. The Emma Street house was closed except for Sanford's own room; his meals he took at the British Club where since 1878 he had been one of the non-British members. Driven with other people's business in addition to his own, Dole's brief letters to his brother include in November of 1885 a surprising bit of news from Italy:

"The *Australia* brought a mail. Caesar Celso Moreno sent me the first chapter of his new book, the chapter entitled 'The Ministerial Crisis in Hawaii in 1880.' It abuses many people and succeeds in being laughable, though it is not intended as a comic work."

From the height of the election campaign and during the long session Dole sent word to his brother:

Honolulu 26th Jan. 1886. W. H. Rice writes from Lihue that the enemy waxeth strong. My opponent took down 16 cases of gin last week and that probably accounts for the spurt. Hope they will drink it all up before election day.

25th Mch. 1886. Your hopeful views as to renewal of Reciprocity are probably correct, but it behooves us as prudent men not to stake what we cannot afford to lose upon what is generally considered a business uncertainty.

13th April 1886. Shall take a vacation from the office if possible, and there is no place I had rather spend it than Kapaa. I cannot do my best work when I am driven.

Spreckels says the Legislature will last only one month; he seems to have cut and dried matters quite to his satisfaction.

20th April. The Chinatown fire—the fire of prophecy because of neglect in supplying adequate water—has at last come off. The papers will tell you about it. There was great anxiety lest it pass Bethel and Merchant streets and clean out the Post Office, Schaefer, the Bank at Kaahumanu Street and all that part. I placed money and papers in Bishop's vault and took home a lot of papers, books and pictures, including the portrait of you, George, received lately from Miss Marcia Smith. Bethel Church is gone, but the trees *makai* saved the Sailors' Home.

26 April 1886. It might be a good idea for you to buy the Haleakala Ranch if you could raise the funds. Go up and look at it. There is fine land for good crops of corn in the spring. Thurston says there is enough water for the stock. In your hands the property would doubtless increase rapidly in value.

Anna writes that she is enjoying Boston, taking lessons in painting, going to theatres, &c. I suppose she ought to live in that climate several years for her health alone. Brigham wants me to join her, open an office and live there.

10 May 1886. I congratulate you and Clara on the new arrival. Walter says now there are nearly enough Dole boys for a base ball nine.

The legislature goes on smoothly. The Govt. are putting up a great number of rather respectable bills, most of them of rather minor importance. It looks as if they were trying to work up some moral momentum before they launch their damn nonsense.

13th May. It hardly looks as if you should tackle Haleakala Ranch alone. You have already involved yourself all that you prudently can in buying a further interest in Makee Sugar Co. Together we might, if Wilcox would join us.

Aloha to the tribe, especially Clara and the eleventh.

18th May 1886. Matters in the Legislature are getting a trifle more interesting; it is still however like a Sunday School.

26th May. Haleakala Ranch sold to E. H. Bailey at the upset price of $50,000. It was not worth more probably.

8th June, in the Legislative Assembly. We have occasionally a little fun, but for the most part it is slow work. The majority can vote us down every time, and sarcasm and vituperation is about all that is left to us.

June 22nd. The King sent a message to the House yesterday requesting that the Appropriation bill be revised in the direction of economy. Gibson, though taken aback, tried to cover his mortification in a hypocritical speech recommending economy. Then Thurston pitched in and we had a merry time.

25th July 1886. You will notice that we have defeated Hayselden's obnoxious bill,—the ministerial tax bill. This is a great relief and a great victory.

I don't think it would be sound to take the children out of school for a year; we must prevent that, if possible; for no better inheritance can be given them than a good education.

Glad you enjoyed the alligator pears. Hope I can send you another lot, but not by the *Makee,* she is so irregular.

Shall be glad to turn my face toward Kapaa. Never was so driven before.

Legislative Assembly. 10th August 1886. Work resumed after two weeks recess, and is moving as usual slowly. I hope to get down for a fairly long visit with you when we adjourn.

Friday forenoon, to Maui on business: I inspected Grove Ranch pasture land and herds and stud, over 700 cattle, and about 150 horses of all kinds.

Anna wants me very much to join her immediately at Castine, but I cannot see my way to it. She is better, also her mother.

22 Aug. I am glad you are continuing to send the children up to Punahou to school. We will talk it over when I go down. Sorry my visit has been delayed so long as to miss the boys' company.

I have had Miss Tuck bring Lizzie Napoleon home here for a while. They board at the Lacks'. Lizzie is very dear to me,—almost as if she was my own child—and she is a good, conscientious girl. I want to give her all the protection and good influence I can. Although it is very pleasant to have my house open again, inhabited and taken care of, I would not for a moment consider that, if it were not right for Lizzie. Her sister, Emma Mahelona, will begin housekeeping again before long and then Lizzie will have a place to go to beside here. I would not let Lizzie go to her mother's. She has been boarding with Mrs. Deverill who is matron in charge at Lunalilo Home.

Anna is still anxious about her mother and it reacts unfavorably upon her own health.

Carter is coming back from Washington—may go into the Cabinet; then I rather expect Gibson will take his place in Washington, or get a roving commission to Europe. The present cabinet is to all appearances a temporary affair and will disintegrate shortly after the close of the session.

7 Sept. 1886. The legislature gives no symptoms of dissolution. I am afraid that nothing but a charge of dynamite will do it.

Legis. Assembly 14th Sept. I have almost made up my mind to go to Kauai next week without waiting for the Legis. to adjourn. They will hold right up to the Oct. term of Court, I think, and I want very much a little rest before the work of the term.

I am thinking of buying into the *Hawn. Gazette* and editing it, and giving up the practice of law. After the Oct. term of Court I shall have to give up practice anyhow for a while. May go to S. F. to meet Anna, if she comes in November. I have strongly urged that she return immediately. I don't think Duty calls her to sacrifice her health to take care of her mother, while her sister has a home for her nearby.

5th Oct. 1886. The Legis. is as crazy as usual. Excuse a short note. Send up a petition signed by natives by return mail against increase of taxation, they are trying to increase taxes to one per cent.

18 Nov. Immensely rainy today. The historical procession for the King's birthday (Govt. appropriation $15,000) did not come off, the performers doubtless afraid of taking cold in their decollete costumes of *pa-us* and *malos.*

San Francisco 5 Dec. 1886. Anna and I are here at the Grand Hotel. She is pretty well. We have a fire in our room every day, and a pile of visiting cards on our table from friends.

I have purchased Clara's sketching supplies. The President's message to Congress contains strong and positive recommendations in favor of a seven year extension of Reciprocity.

Honolulu. 28th Dec. 1886. Glad to hear of the continued prosperity of the tribe at Kapaa.

We had a smooth passage from S. F., Anna quite well and strong. Thanks to Lizzie's devoted enterprise, with some assistance from Mrs. Allen and others, our house was open and blooming with flowers, creepers, *maile,* and other decorations. Anna was full of enthusiasm at getting home again.

W. O. Smith and family return next month to remain. As near as I can learn he has lost a good part of his property in Hobron's silver mine.

Sitting for 129 days from April to October, the session of 1886 had witnessed several changes of cabinet and long, acrimonious debate. S. B. Dole's contemporary and later notes mention the fact that, taking a leaf from the session of 1884, the king's adherents had at the outset in 1886 elected as president of the Assembly the Honorable J. S. Walker, long a Noble, a conservative in close sympathy with the Royalists, which naturally made it difficult for the Opposition. At one juncture when the king had at last wearied of domination by Claus Spreckels, the Opposition effected an alliance with the king and his party, and expressed distrust in the existing Cabinet. Gibson went on his knees to the king for reappointment, but Spreckels, "as mad as a wet hen, sought comfort with the Opposition," called on the king, returned all his decorations, and shook the dust of Honolulu from off his feet.

The phenomenal alliance of king and Opposition subsided as suddenly as it had occurred; yet two Cabinets were dismissed by the king and replaced. When finally several Reform members had to get home to private business, the Royalists seized the reins and by a bare majority passed an opium license bill which was signed by the king in spite of outspoken public protest. The general appropriation bill of this "Long Parliament" totaled far in excess of estimated income.

Remarked Dole on the 23d of October,

> The Government feel very shaky without a local capitalist to support them, and with their Hawaiian cabinet headed by Gibson. Today, as I hear, Minister Kaulukou has been replaced by Neumann; so they stagger to their final ruin.
>
> I have some thoughts of buying a ¾ interest in the *Hawaiian Gazette* and thus becoming a school of morals. But the prospect is faint. I should be investing in a hornet's nest. The affairs of the company are in a snarl, and nobody seems to know just how they stand.

In the midst of more than one type of hornet's nest, a New England letter, reaching Dole early in 1886, brought glimpses from another world. Written by his friend and older colleague, Judge Hartwell, it told of taking his family East for a stay of indefinite length and of plans for sharing a Boston office with Judge J. W. Austin. Also that the Hartwells were hoping soon to have a visit from Anna Dole; and that, although enjoying the cold, they were really homesick for the freedom and gentle climate of the Islands.

Recently the *Hawaiian Gazette* of November 24 had brought some excellent writing, apparently the work of "Dole's fist." Boston offered bright, agreeable people; the children were under stimulating influences, and all the family were relieved to be far from Honolulu's political corruption. Actually, however, Hartwell himself missed this, for working against it had become second nature to him. "It is man's work," he wrote, "of the best kind, which one can do in and for Hawaii."

Recalling "friend Walker's repugnance to the white fences of Honolulu," Hartwell had in a short two months been entirely won over to the coloring, architecture, and landscape gardening in and around Boston; and he hoped that George Dole might some day be able to bring his family for a year of "this elder civilization." On Hartwell's meeting one day a classmate of George and Sanford's father, this Dr. Leigh had asked in amazement, "What, did you know Daniel Dole?"

Much, however, as he loved the land of his father and mother, Sanford had long ago made his choice to remain a part of his native Hawaii. And now, agreeing with Hartwell as to its being man's work, he was putting his shoulder to the wheel of a government which sorely needed honest men.

For some time more or less anonymous pamphlets had occasionally made their appearance, testing out government resistance to ridicule. The roistering rimes of the *Gynberg Ballads,* for instance, had been embellished with caricatures as comic as the words, not sparing even "His Highness, the Grand Duke of Gynbergdrinkenstein, Herr von Boss, a millionaire, and Nosbig, Minister of State. Wisdom and Wit are Little Seen, but Folly's at full length," was the terse comment on the back cover of the *Ballads.*

An unsigned pamphlet entitled *Vacuum,* a farce, had first been seen the year before, when its author, S. B. Dole, must have been driven at the mere prospect of another long legislative session to seek relief in comedy. He may even have set down notes for it during sessions in 1884, for he sent his brother George a manuscript copy in November 1885, begging him not to "let on about it." Soon it came out in print, a modest sixteen pages of rollicking take-off from the Palace of the Flying Fish, where Skyhigh, Emperor of Coral Reefs, Sand Banks, and Blue Big Sea ponders the inefficiency of his firemen, who must put out a great conflagration armed with air alone in their fire hose; where the dismayed Emperor, on the lack of gold in his Treasure Room, finds His Extravagency Palaver, aided by Sir Silvergilt, paying the Imperial Salary in debased silver coins bearing the Imperial Image; and where the four Extravagancies, Palaver, Cockade, Calabash, and Picnic—one of them already dozing—fumble about at fixing a policy, only to find themselves summarily dismissed from office before anything can be accomplished.

Historians may find little of importance in these satires and extravaganzas, but among others, Editor Atkinson, of the *Hawaiian Gazette,* long cherished a copy of *Vacuum,* and Riley H. Allen, editor of the present *Honolulu Star-Bulletin,* has made for the Honolulu Social Science Association an admirable and delightful study of this social-political pamphleteering. Also anonymous, and its text no longer extant, was the popular "Chun Hook, the Murderer," a minstrel show actually staged in the old opera house which rocked the town with its lampooning of the recent opium bribe and caricaturing of "Emperor" Kalakaua's famous embassy to Samoa, aboard the decrepit Hawaiian warship *Kaimiloa*. Riley Allen adds that Jack Dowsett, Faxon Bishop, Billy Hoogs, and many another man, then juvenile and spry, played the exaggerated roles, armed with huge nickel-plated revolvers and badges slightly larger than dinner plates.

Escape literature and horseplay? Surely, and a normal reaction to pompous pretense and downright fraud, relief from utter exhaustion in the face of incompetence. Yet "a very shrewd purpose" underlay the bubbling spirit of comedy which created these little trial balloons and sent them out to test the public temperature. Pamphleteers and their caricatures, minstrels, and mock policemen met with "no outburst of indignation from an enraged populace" in defense of their sovereign's dignity. The time was ripening for more serious business.

REVOLT AND COUNTER-REVOLT
1887–1889

NOTWITHSTANDING attempts by Reform members of the 1886 Legislature to vote money in reason and proportion, national debts mounted. Not only was a round sum devoted to celebrating the king's birthday, but $20,000 was expended on purchasing a ship, with three times that amount for outfitting her as the *Kaimiloa,* a man-of-war, to promote Kalakaua's ill-fated embassy to Samoa. J. D. Strong was to go as artist of this expedition. Meanwhile roads on every island went from bad to worse; landings and wharves became dangerous; even for needed dredging of Honolulu harbor funds could not be had. Government debts increased with apparently no plan for reducing them.

In twos and threes thoughtful men began to consider ways and means for honest expenditure of public funds. As S. B. Dole expressed it in his account of the Hawaiian Revolution:

Dissatisfaction grew. With no legal way of overriding the King's veto, there seemed no hope of desirable reforms by legislative methods. Late in 1886, the feeling became so intense that a proposal to organize developed. Mr. L. A. Thurston, meeting me on the street, said that Dr. S. G. Tucker had urged upon him the importance of organizing without delay. Arrangements were made for them to meet at my house, and for two or three others to be invited. Dr. Tucker, Mr. Thurston, W. R. Castle and I attended, perhaps others. A scheme for an organization was blocked out.

Nearly all the persons selected received the plan heartily. Adherents grew rapidly in numbers, and meetings were held in different parts of the town. Delegates, going to the other islands, extended information to chosen persons; and the response was cordial. So the Hawaiian League increased steadily in numbers through early 1887. Some effort was made by the police to gather information about the league meetings, which were generally held at evening and rarely twice in succession at the same place.

Sanford Dole's letters to his brother George on Kauai carried not only personal items, but also frequent mention of mounting public opinion:

8th Feb. 1887. News from the United States by schooner yesterday deals with the renewal of the reciprocity treaty. Pearl River seems likely to become an important item.

24 Feb. 1887. I have settled the Punahou School bill for the children.

4th May 1887. I feel relieved at getting through the April term of court so satisfactorily. The Insurance case has weighed on my mind. I can't make plans yet. Many thanks for your kind invitation; I don't see how you can conveniently make room for us; am considering the question of journalism again, if the proprietors of the *Pacific Commercial Advertiser* will sell her upon reasonable terms, which is not yet clear.

Am thinking of going in a week or two to Molokai to hunt deer on Mr. Bishop's preserves.

Fred Smith is going to resign the management of Grove Ranch on Maui. Would you care to consider the position? We pay $3,000, probably cannot raise on that.

I received a copy of Ned [E. P.] Dole's law book, well and learnedly written; writing law books is a satisfaction which Honolulu lawyers are pretty much deprived of. I have looked forward to writing a text book upon Hawaiian water rights, which have some features peculiar to these islands, and interesting.

Lizzie Napoleon sailed for San Francisco by the *Australia* yesterday for six or eight weeks, mainly with friends.

I ship my canoe to you by *Waialeale,* masts, sails &c locked inside, key enclosed here.

17 May 1887. I send you a copy of the new satire. This week's *Gazette* is decidedly libellous against royalty,—unless its statements are true. Poor royalty is rather abject and seems to take anything from Chinese bribes to Anglo-Saxon contempt.

The *Kaimiloa* cannot get to sea. Her officers are deserting and there is a pretty steady carouse on board; they can't get the crew together long enough to weigh anchor and bend the sails. Seafaring people say that the ship as rigged is unsafe, and if she goes to sea, is likely to capsize.

31st May 1887. I took Dr. Emerson with me for a fine trip to Molokai. He carried off the honors, shot a fine buck. I had a good chance at an antlered buck, but missed him, shot two goats. All very hospitable at Meyers' home. We brought the deer down and distributed the venison.

Politics are getting warm. The rifle companies are filling up with good men evidently induced by the possibilities of genuine work ahead. Today's *Gazette* gives the Govt. a broadside, throwing them into confusion and to seek comfort—but to find none—at the Supreme Court. The trouble is that charges against the Govt. are too true to be combatted.

Obviously the king himself realized this truth. Aware for some time that undercurrents were at work, he prepared impregnable defenses about the palace which he regarded as a central fortification, according to vivid, authentic description by L. A. Thurston. Behind the thick eight-foot wall of coral stone and concrete surrounding the palace grounds, a patrol platform was built for sharpshooters to pick off any advancing force. Should such a force break through the main gate it would be met by rifle fire from the platforms under the palace steps, loopholes in the iron grill work still to be seen today. Attackers would work under the initial disadvantage of Honolulu's first electric arc lights, trained every night on all streets outside of the palace, eleven 2,000-candlepower lights burning from dusk till dawn to illumine the enemy and protect the defenders by darkness.

Mention in S. B. Dole's letters of the king's acceptance of Chinese bribes focused on rumors beginning to circulate before the ink had dried in Kalakaua's signature of approval on the opium bill. This is the sordid story from contemporary sources:

Hardly had the "Long Parliament" of 1886 closed in October, when one Aki, a Chinese rice planter of Pearl City, Oahu, appeared toward evening at the king's palace bungalow, bearing in a little basket gold pieces totaling $20,000. Eager to purchase the coveted license for selling opium, Aki was trying to meet twice the sum of $30,000 established as the legal price by the new law; for a courtier had told him secretly that he must hurry to bring the larger amount. Two or three evenings later a smaller basket was delivered to Kalakaua personally. Finally two more little baskets, together with the courtesy of a little baked pig, completed the sum demanded.

Thereupon Aki was told that he must speedily bring yet another $15,000, lest a second Chinese syndicate outbid him. With great difficulty this demand too he met, only to learn that others bidding $80,000 had taken the precaution to obtain the license before parting with the exaggerated purchase price. The courtier acting as go-between received as reward royal preferment to the responsible position of Registrar of Conveyances in the Land Office.

Aki had lost both his license and his money. A personal appeal direct to the king met the curt reply that Aki was lucky not to be jailed for bribery. Overcome, the rice-planter blurted out his pitiful tale in a series of affidavits; turned his face to the wall, and died.

When at the end of May 1887 these affidavits were published in the *Hawaiian Gazette,* a storm of public resentment burst out over such bare-faced extortion in a so-called Christian country. S. B. Dole told his brother that the government had opened incoming freight to search for arms and ammunition, which when found it seized: "an act having no legal warrant and one which will tend to unite the community still more against the government." By the 7th of June the *Gazette* hurled another broadside. On the 13th Dole shipped to his brother his own hunting rifle with cartridges and belt, that George might have another gun in case of political unrest. Added Sanford:

> Things here look like an early issue with the Govt. *June 21st.* Rex is very clearly *scared*. When he drives out to Waikiki he has a squad of mounted armed police around him. There is a good deal of feeling against the Govt. which is bad enough for any fate. I do not however favor taking the initiative against it. The *Gazette* is pungent today.

Like a spark the opium bribes acted on the fuse laid by a long trail of misrule and extravagance. Resident citizens of the United States, Great Britain, and Germany addressed formal memorials to their governments, "declaring the condition of affairs to be intolerable." The Hawaiian League of a thousand men consulted in grave earnest. Volunteer "Rifles," well drilled, under Col. Volney V. Ashford, expected to march upon the palace, and League members on the other islands favored radical action with prompt annexation to the United States. As S. B. Dole later described it:

> In the community generally there was a strong undercurrent of anxiety; in the League, a vigorous sentiment in favor of overthrowing the monarchy by force appeared and increased, to an extent that caused two members to withdraw from the directorate: Mr. P. C. Jones and myself.
>
> Finally the League adopted a plan of giving the King a chance to hold his position by acceding to its demands.
>
> A mass meeting was called at a large one-story building near the corner of Punchbowl and Beretania Streets which was used as the armory of the volunteer companies. If arrangements could be made, it became desirable that these volunteers be under arms in control of the town. Such action, without authority, would of course be a revolutionary step. Fortunately, the authorities ordered the companies out, which relieved the situation for the time being; while the troops were patrolling the streets under nominal

orders of the Government, they were actually under orders of the League until the crisis was over.

On the 29th of June posters in English, Hawaiian, and Portuguese announced the mass meeting for the next day. By 1:00 o'clock on the 30th all business was suspended; machine shops closed, wharves empty. Long before 2:00 o'clock men of all creeds and classes began to throng quietly toward the armory: mechanics, merchants, day laborers, planters, professional men; Americans, Britons, Colonials, Germans, Hawaiians, Portuguese, Chinese, Japanese. More than two thousand entered the hall; another thousand stood without the walls; all "united in sentiment as never before or since." Accounts of this event in the *Gazette,* the *Advertiser,* and the *Herald* were ably summarized in a pamphlet by A. M. Hewett, stationer and newsdealer of Merchant Street, Honolulu.

The great mass meeting was called to order by S. B. Dole. P. C. Jones, elected as chairman, felt that this was the largest and most important meeting ever held on these islands. It was time to make things short, sharp, and decisive. "In a voice that reached to the outer limits of the assemblage" L. A. Thurston read five resolutions all centered on requesting the king to take the advice of a new and responsible Cabinet in securing a new Constitution; to repay his debt to Aki's estate; and to pledge himself not to interfere with election of Representatives or with the making of laws by the legislative body; nor to interfere with the constitutional administration of his Cabinet, nor to use his official position for private ends. A Committee of Thirteen was appointed to present these resolutions to the king, requesting that personal answer be returned within twenty-four hours.

At the resolution requesting the king to dismiss Walter Murray Gibson from office, this great, orderly gathering burst into a storm of cheers that swept through the building.

C. R. Bishop, Privy Councilor and member of the House of Nobles, rose to read a letter which had reached him at 1:00 o'clock. A simple, direct letter from the king, offering to call upon W. L. Green to form a new Cabinet and promising himself to concede any reasonable guaranties. This letter was a capitulation, in advance, and a complete surprise to all present.

Applause frequently interrupted Attorney W. A. Kinney as

he read a Hawaiian translation of the five resolutions. In passionate English he asserted: "It is time that the Crown were addressed in the language of truth." He called for a new Constitution, and that speedily. With intense earnestness he declared, "No man can stay this movement now. The sails are set, the ship in motion; we cannot go back. Push her forward into the open sea." Cheers resounded.

More quietly but with equal force, Attorney S. B. Dole, when called upon, made his points: "This meeting is called to give the King one chance, just one chance, to fall into line for political reform. I need not detail the fact of bad government: the King has sold his sacred oath of office to the highest bidder. We are here for no unlawful purpose; we have assembled to consult upon the common good. And from the talk I hear along the street, opposition to political reform is in the public mind something akin to treason."

J. A. McCandless, in charge of digging Hawaii's first artesian wells, believed he spoke as representing his 1,500 workmen, disfranchised for no reason but that they were white men. "It is time," as Abraham Lincoln once said, "to set the foot down hard."

C. R. Bishop, one of the most conservative of men, said he came to the meeting as a Hawaiian, sure of a new constitution or material reforms to be discussed peaceably, needing no threats.

Henry Waterhouse, who had often spoken from the pulpit in the people's forum of Kaumakapili Church, said in Hawaiian: "Let us stand by these resolutions. Go before the King without fear and make our demands without fear."

As for Attorney Thurston, he too spoke as a Hawaiian and for many Hawaiians who had been deserted by their leaders. "Let there be a new Constitution, a new contract. If the King and the people agree to change it, there is no violation of constitutional rights, and no revolution. But there are no cheers today for the King who has three times promised good government and economy, in 1880, 1884, and 1886. Let a new Constitution now be insisted upon."

Paul Isenberg urged that a new Constitution be done legally.

Alexander Young, of the Honolulu Iron Works, was proud to look so many honest men in the face, not one a coward. "Do not wait," he urged, "strike while the iron is hot."

Cecil Brown said in Hawaiian: "I am a Hawaiian, born under this flag, and under it my bones shall be buried. We want the King to think of the public good. We want a new Constitution."

E. M. Walsh, manager of Paia Plantation, Maui, said: "Let us prepare a new Constitution. This is what we must have."

J. M. Vivas read the resolutions in Portuguese and spoke straight to the hearts of his countrymen.

W. H. Rice of Kauai said in Hawaiian: "From Hawaii to Niihau we want to clean up the government. Asking for bread, shall we be satisfied with stones?"

The last speaker, C. W. Ashford, came to the platform armed and in uniform of the Honolulu Rifles commanded by his brother, V. V. Ashford. His company marched in to hear their comrade while the great assembly gave three rousing cheers and a tiger for the "boys." Personally, Ashford had found Kalakaua a pleasant friend, but the time had come to take concerted action.

On motion of W. R. Castle to adopt the resolutions, seconded by N. B. Emerson and many others, a roar of "Ayes" met the question; dead silence when the chairman asked: "Contrary minded?"

At once the Committee of Thirteen waited on the king. He gave oral reply that he would accede without the twenty-four hour delay. The committee would not change the requirement, desired moreover a reply in writing. Next day the king calling in the representatives of the United States, Great Britain, France, and Portugal, offered to transfer to them the powers vested in him. Declining to accept this trust, these gentlemen advised him to lose no time in forming the new Cabinet and in signing the new Constitution demanded by the people. That very afternoon the king's formal acceptance of the demands was forwarded from the palace to the citizens' committee.

For two days the city had been substantially under martial law. Yet banks and business houses had opened as usual. Without the instant support of the Hawaiian League and the corps of Honolulu Rifles under Volney V. Ashford, this security of life and property could not have been maintained. Because of the power and determination to sustain it the revolt was short-lived.

Characterization of this great mass meeting by S. E. Bishop, editor of *The Friend,* included: "Such quiet force, such repressed but stern displeasure. The applause, the responses of Yes! and No! were short, but sharp, united, and as the seven thunders.

"We never have felt so sure of good, stable, economical, honorable government in Hawaii,—the tawdry show of coronation pales before the stately majesty of the righteous will!"

Sharing some of his thoughts with his brother across the Kauai channel, Sanford Dole gave inside views:

July 6, 1887. It has been an exciting week beginning with the mass meeting last Thursday. The seizure of arms by the *Mariposa* on Friday was a bold and successful move which took the government completely by surprise. The town was in possession of the Rifles all day and night, was in effect under martial law. Gibson and Hayselden were arrested early in the forenoon by the Rifles, simply so far as I can learn because it was the logical thing to do. The new cabinet having been appointed, Gibson and his son-in-law were arrested later in the day by the civil authorities under charge of embezzlement.

From Friday evening till today, Wednesday, we have been working night and day on a new constitution, which is probably now under consideration by the King, for his signature and oath. If he doesn't accept it, he will be promptly attacked, and a republic probably declared. This is all I can write now.

11th July. I was rather used up the latter part of last week. We worked over the new constitution seven or eight times. Friday night about midnight we had an alarm that the guards at the Government house were about to be attacked, so we broke up our own work something as did the revellers at Brussels when they heard the beginning of Waterloo. We went to our homes, shouldered our arms and marched to the scene of supposed danger, but found that it was only an alarm and nothing more.

12th July. Gibson fled this noon by the schooner *Claus Spreckels* for foreign parts. I suppose the government allowed him to go. It would probably be difficult to make a case against him, and to try him and have him acquitted would be very undesirable. Let us trust that we have seen the last of him.

I have had a good letter from Alapai of Koloa and have just replied to it. He says there isn't a single man in Koloa on the side of the *"moi lapuwale, a me Kibikone aihue dala"* [good-for-nothing king and money-stealing Gibson].

18 July. Don't name your new baby after me unless it is a unanimous vote. It would be an immense compliment to me. I had not thought of such a thing, have been quite satisfied with my name for Walter Sanford, especially in view of the way he is turning out.

We shall be very happy to have Clara junior and Emily with us for a few weeks. Lizzie Napoleon may be back by August 1st, but she will have her own room and they will have the guest room.

I am now refusing nearly all new court business and have been for some time. Shall hope to close up my affairs by the end of Sept. and then to visit you for some time before leaving the Islands. Grove Ranch makes over 2,000 tons this crop and will pay $30,000 or more.

28 July 1887. The steamer arrived this forenoon with Kapiolani and Mrs. Dominis [Queen and Heir-Apparent, having attended Queen Victoria's Jubilee]; no demonstration at the wharf, not even a respectable cheer.

Lizzie did not come, but will leave San Francisco Aug. 16. Has greatly enjoyed her California visit. My friend Lord escorted her to many places, among them the great panorama of Waterloo in which he felt that as a Napoleon she might have a hereditary interest.

American papers have a good deal to say about the Hawaiian revolution. I also send you an *Advertiser* containing my address at the graduating exercises of Oahu College. You will be interested in the regulations on the coming election issued in the *Gazette* by the Cabinet. They represent an immense amount of careful work. The *League* is still the government. Have you had an opportunity of joining it?

1st August, 1887. The girls arrived in good condition after a rather uncomfortable night.

As representative for the special session it might be well to nominate some native from Kauai, say Gandell or Kaiu or Alapai or Mika.

If you get elected as noble, it will be a matter of great regret if we have given up house keeping and so are unable to entertain you.

I should think that you could not be an inspector of election and a candidate at the same time.

Grove Ranch pays another dividend, $10 a share.

22 Aug. 1887. There has been an unfortunate split in the Cabinet, temporarily patched up. It relates to an appointment to commander-in-chief claimed by Col. V. V. Ashford, promised to him by a part of the Cabinet and refused by another part. It is much to be regretted. It is difficult for me to entertain feelings of respect toward office-seekers. If a man nominates himself to an office, it is *prima facie* evidence of his unfitness.

George Wilcox will take down ballots for tickets for nobles for the whole Island of Kauai.

6 Sept. 1887. I am still coquetting with the *Advertiser,* may take it— may not; wish I had some one to decide for me.

A letter from Cousin Charlie Dole enquiring after Walter and Herbert, had not heard they were going to Cornell.

13 Sept. The reform ticket has been entirely successful on Oahu, showing that a great many natives are in full sympathy with the new movement, but that the balance of power has departed from the Hawaiian race. The opposition is evidently inspired by Kalakaua and is his last struggle for despotic power. He will now submit to toe the mark, but will always watch for a chance to make a break from the trammels of law.

Rosa says we owe our success to gin and money. His crowd have so generally relied on those potent influences that they cannot understand how any election can be carried without them.

Castle, Smith, Luther Wilcox *et al.* propose to go to Pearl River Lagoon next Friday in a sloop yacht, camp out on Ford's island and return on Saturday.

19 Sept. Hawaii and Maui and Molokai show a clean sweep for reform, with two exceptions. I think this election will solidify the new state of things and put us all right abroad; it is a nearly unanimous verdict of *guilty* against the late government.

We took our boating trip to Puuloa lagoon, had a splendid time, twelve of us distributed in two boats. The lagoon is a ground yachting place, miles and miles of sailing room in deep water and generally a good breeze.

The rise of ⅛ of a cent in sugar helps the last part of Grove Ranch crop to another dividend.

27th Sept. 1887. I do not believe I shall go into law practice after I close up here, so you had better not depend on me in your litigation. Thanks all the same.

Maybelle Ward wrote to Lizzie about Walter and Herbert visiting the Wards at Alameda. Maybelle was glad to know the boys and went with them when they started overland at Oakland.

Thurston, Emerson and others go down tonight to take the *Waialeale* at Kapaa tomorrow and go around the pali to look up a suitable spot for a local leper settlement.

11th Oct. 1887. Lizzie's wedding to Eben Low came off yesterday in Kawaiahao Church, Henry Parker officiating; an account of it in the *Advertiser* by Wray Taylor who played the wedding march. The bride looked very pretty in a cream colored cashmere and moire antique with white iridescent beads covering the front of the basque. Many attended the reception; the presents were numerous and useful. They started on their wedding tour by the *Kinau* for Puuhue, Waimea and Mana. Wilder gave them the stateroom.

We have about concluded to remain in Honolulu until the special session is over and have the unaccustomed pleasure of entertaining you at our house for a season longer than a week.

18th Oct. 1887. The *Australia* arrived this noon. Sugar has riz 1/10 cent. Hartwells did not come.

As an elected noble don't commit yourself to anyone as to whom you will vote for as officers of the assembly. Wilder wants to be President, but Castle is probably the best man, as Wilder has immense interests to injure his impartiality; Castle has no axes to grind and is a good parliamentarian.

My love to *all hands*.

SANFORD

The special session of the Legislature convened on November 3, 1887, with all proper ceremony. Kalakaua's opening speech seemed all that reason could desire. He recommended revision and amendment of any previous Acts, such as the opium bill, found to be unconstitutional or conflicting; also of the appropriation bill of 1886 "which seems to have been drawn up without due regard to the probable revenue." The king took pleasure in informing legislators that the Reciprocity Treaty with the United States had been extended for seven years, with a clause granting to national vessels of the United States the exclusive privilege of using Pearl River Harbor as a coaling and repair station; with moreover explicit mutual agreement that by this clause the Hawaiian kingdom ceded no territory and parted with no right of sovereignty or jurisdiction, and that such exclusive privilege was to be co-terminous with the treaty.

The so-called "Bayonet Constitution" signed by the king on July 6, 1887, was a revision of the Constitution of 1864, and prescribed changes long contemplated by men of the Hawaiian League. The right of suffrage was broadened to include American and European residents taking the oath to support the Constitution; no member of the Legislature might hold another public office; Nobles, instead of receiving appointment from the king, must show certain property qualifications and must be elected to seats in the Upper House; the king's veto of any bill might be annulled by a two-thirds vote of the Legislature; the Cabinet must approve of official acts of the king; and Cabinet Ministers might be dismissed only by vote of the Legislature.

The Reform Cabinet appointed by the king in 1887 included W. L. Green as Premier and Minister of Finance; Godfrey Brown for Foreign Affairs; Clarence W. Ashford as Attorney General; and, after some protest by the king, Lorrin A. Thurston as Minister of the Interior. It was an able group, Ashford and Thurston younger, more aggressive than the others, less interested, remarked R. S. Kuykendall, in making an effort to win the king over to their policies.

Notwithstanding widespread and intensive corruption during the six years preceding 1887, one administrative function had maintained its integrity. Or as W. D. Alexander phrased it: "Fortunately, one branch of the government, the Supreme Court, still remained independent and outlived the Gibson regime." Judge Fornander's death on November 1, 1887, left vacant the office of Fourth Associate Justice of the Supreme Court. On

December 29 of that year, when nominated to this post by the Reform Cabinet, S. B. Dole was advised to call personally on the king. "I met him," related the candidate, "in the wooden building in the palace grounds known as the bungalow, and had a pleasant interview with him, it being a quality of his disposition to greet both friends and foes courteously and with kindliness of demeanor, whatever the feelings in his own heart. Apparently complacent, he chafed under the surface at the limitations created by the new Constitution."

A counter limitation may well have been in the mind of King Kalakaua, when he finally granted this life appointment to the Supreme Bench. Disliking Dole, perhaps even fearing him, the king could not have been blind to the advantage that such a move would bring to himself, automatically excluding from active politics, as it did, a far too practiced and persistent opponent.

Although the Reform victory in the election of 1887 had resulted in a virtual ratification of the new Constitution, it was not to be expected that the king would continue to be entirely submissive. Hardly had the Legislature entered the second month of its special session when the king began to assert his unconfirmed veto. The Legislature, considering this illegal, so informed the king. At the special term, February, 1888, after the appointment of S. B. Dole as Fourth Associate Justice, the Supreme Court in one instance upheld the king's veto, Judge Dole dissenting. This being a test case, the decision applied to all vetoed bills.

For some time Sanford Dole had felt it unwise to continue the pressure of an active private practice added to the stress of political uncertainty, and had looked forward to long visits in the United States and possibly Europe before taking over the editorship of the *Advertiser*. Appointment to the Supreme Bench now radically altered these plans. Although he often found himself working Sundays too on Supreme Court cases, he could at least hope now and then for a free Saturday. And with F. M. Hatch, a young lawyer and nephew of the late Judge Harris, he bought a sloop yacht which seemed to sail as well without a name. By May 15, 1888, Dole told his brother:

We had a fine trip to Pearl River, Thurston, Smith, Austin and H. Waterhouse by Williams' boat, the *Pokii*. Camped on Ford's island, caught eels by torch light, sailed next day, Saturday, and raced home, arriving at

3:00 P.M. The *Pokii* beat us by a minute, but with fair time allowance for difference in tonnage, we beat them.

June 12. Yesterday 8 yachts and the wheelbarrow steamer went to Pearl River; splendid sailing, and finally concentrated at Mark Robinson's at a very nice feast. Luther Wilcox and I went down in my sloop and George Wilcox returned with us. An exciting sail coming home.

In August when George Dole occupied his brother's Emma Street home during the regular legislative session of 1888, Sanford exchanged houses, taking Anna and visiting with the rest of the George Doles at Kapaa, while himself presiding as Supreme Court Justice at Lihue Court Week. Letters to George carry weekly bulletins:

Kapaa 18 Aug. 1888. On Wednesday with Spencer, Chapman, Charley Dole and two Hawaiians, hunted goats on the range south of the Huleia river. Went up the ridge at the mouth of the river and worked along toward Haupu, then down to Kipukai from the highest part. Bagged four goats and one kid, taking the latter along to Wilcoxes for a roast. Had three guns along, took a sea bath at Kipukai; and reached Grove Farm by dark after a thoroughly good time. As I write, my namesake Sanballat has been assisting me with such intimate attentions that I had to send him off to examine works of art under Anna's direction. Here he is again.

Yesterday I took some unusually cross bees out of the hive—stung three times. The hives with boxes instead of frames are much more convenient for removing comb.

Henry Dimond encourages me with the prospect of a bullock hunt, camping in the woods for one night. Except to return by Saturday's steamer. Please have Ah Nam get Ah Kim, the cook, to have breakfast ready Sunday morning.

Honolulu 12 Sept. 1888. I send by *"Makee"* the horse, brake, trunk, valise, water-wheel and bag containing saddle, saddle cloth, headstall and a pair of your shoes.

The legislature adjourned subject to the call of the President.

Honolulu 25 Sept. 1888. You are rarely blessed in the heroic cheerfulness and sweetness of your wife to inspire you, but lean not too heavily, she needs the support of your courageous spirit.

Brigham came by the *Australia* and is in good spirits; stays with us and goes on to the Colonies by the Mariposa. After returning from Melbourne he will stay for a year or so, working up his history of the Islands.

I ride Duke every day or two, gradually teaching him to gallop with his right foot forward to improve his gait.

Shall I sell any of my Grove Ranch stock at par? Reduction in sugar duties in America will act unfavorably upon our net profits.

9 Oct. Unsettled weather, wind in all directions, but fortunately very little rain, as our housebuilding is not yet closed in; new bedroom, dressing room and bath, frieze all around bedroom to be painted by the well known artist, A. C. D., who has recently studied with Tavernier. Fireplace in the corner of new back parlor.

Rowell, Eben Low and I took a sail around the bell buoy Saturday afternoon.

I think I can sell my Grove Ranch stock for $260, par $250.

What kind of a time did the children have going to Niihau by boat? We miss you here in town ever so much.

23 Oct. 1888. The minstrel performance Sat. eve must have been quite a success from what I hear. Rowell's mule was one of the performers and was ridden around the stage by Halstead who took off Rowell with great success. When he rode up to the milk-shake machine and ordered a milk-shake and told the proprietor to charge it to "roads and bridges," it brought down the house.

Relief from political tension was still found in satires and minstrel shows, players taking off men in their own party and mimicking with zest. These skits by the amateur minstrel company were presented in the opera house opposite the palace. The *Hawaiian Gazette* pictured Rowell's "government-fed" mule hoofing it onto the stage from the wings with a startled look at its suddenly palatial surroundings. The house was crowded even to extra chairs in the corners. Watching with interest from the royal box was a large party from the palace, led by the king and young Prince David Kawananakoa.

Much public activity, now under separate county control, was directed at that time from the ministry of the interior in Honolulu. It was a familiar sight to see civil engineer W. E. Rowell as Superintendent of Public Works jogging about on his sure-footed mule, keeping an expert eye on government construction of various sorts from school buildings and a safe kerosene warehouse to the insane asylum and, at last, a lighthouse on Barber's Point. Additional projects on which Rowell reported to Minister Thurston in 1888 were the Oceanic Steamship Wharf with space for the California mail steamer, or two sailing vessels, and the new Inter-Island Wharf on the Esplanade at the foot of Keku-anaoa Street. A survey of the bar of the harbor had been begun, looking toward dredging a deeper channel entrance; also official maps made for necessary grading of some streets. And it was remarked that an addition to the Post Office would be necessary, if a parcel post treaty should be concluded with the United States.

Telephones had been known on Maui ten years before, having been brought by C. H. Dickey. In the palace at Honolulu the king could talk by telephone from his apartments to those of the queen. S. G. Wilder, then a Cabinet Minister, had a telephone installed between his office at the capitol and his lumber yard. Mr. Dickey also put in a telephone at Judge Dole's Emma Street house to communicate "with the home of his sister nearby," actually the home of Mrs. George Dole's sister, Mrs. Ellen Riemenschneider, across the way on Emma Street. On Kauai the only physician, Dr. Smith of Koloa, had soon been connected by telephone with growing families in Wilcox, Rice, and Dole homes at Lihue and Kapaa.

In Honolulu a system of small tramcars hauled by mules was gradually laying twelve miles of tracks out to Punahou, Kalihi and Waikiki, and up Nuuanu as far as the foot of Judd hill, where the plodding mules must perforce be unhitched and transferred to the other end of the swaying bus to start the return journey. A more spectacular change put an end to dark nights in Honolulu. On March 23, 1888, little Princess Kaiulani, by turning a master switch, first lighted the streets of the city from the government electric system. The king's small dynamo, installed for the coronation and to defend the palace, had been removed, and a large waterwheel set up for the new power plant on the stream in upper Nuuanu opposite the Wood estate. Even with all this preparation, the city was startled into wonder at sudden lights eclipsing the soft rays of the moon just past the full. "Printers, policemen and all other nocturnal fry rushed out to see the flaming arcs at the street corners. Policeman Holoua was distinctly recognized in front of the Police Station from the door of the *Gazette* office."

As Minister, L. A. Thurston directed such varied activities as the initiation of a new homestead law formulated by S. B. Dole in 1884, but neglected for three years by the administration; the Post Office and postal savings; immigration of laborers from the Azores, China, and Japan; Honolulu Waterworks and extension of such systems outside of the capital city; public health, including the Molokai Settlement.

Lorrin Andrews Thurston was a true native son of Hawaii, perhaps even more intensely so than some, since his Mission

Above: Executive Council of the Provisional Government

Below: Cabinet and Executive Council of the Republic of Hawaii

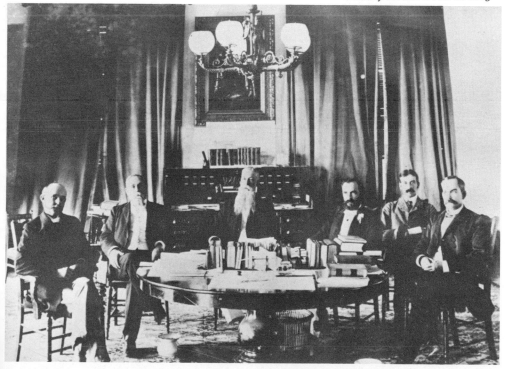

The Constitutional Convention of 1894

grandfathers were pioneer Reverend Asa Thurston and Judge Lorrin Andrews. All his life he was known as Kakina, the Hawaiian transliteration of Thurston, and often signed himself Kakina. As a boy on Maui everything in the outdoor world called so imperatively to his impetuous spirit that engineering was his early choice as a profession. With Hawaiian, however, as natural to him as English, he was soon interpreting in Judge Hartwell's Honolulu office, where also he read law while earning his way to and through Columbia Law School. Then he returned to a very full and active life for his native land. Friendly, yet impulsive to the point of seeming a political firebrand in his zeal for honest government, Thurston's legal training acted as a balance wheel in the many-sided interests of this present job as Minister of the Interior.

In his own *Memoirs of the Hawaiian Revolution* Thurston outlined the hitherto almost roadless condition of all the islands in 1887, and paid loyal tribute to excellent work by one of his schoolmates at the Haleakala Boys' Boarding School. This was Robert Kalanipoo, who served in charge of laying out and constructing highways in Kona. Much of Olaa district, long supposed to lie on a rocky bed of *a-a,* was revolutionized into an agricultural homestead area by the discovery of Surveyor J. M. Lydgate that apparently only deep, rich soil covered much of the Crown lands south of Hilo toward Kilauea Volcano. Old horse trails on Hawaii, Maui, Oahu, and Kauai were resurveyed and macadamized where possible. The Honolulu water system was expanded to draw from higher springs and streams about Hillebrand Glen in Nuuanu. Charles B. Wilson, another Maui schoolmate of Thurston and father of former Mayor Wilson of Honolulu, became the very efficient superintendent of the Honolulu Waterworks. For Kalaupapa Settlement on Molokai, Wilson piped a permanent water supply from Waikolu Valley, a boon long dreamed of and partly begun by Damien, the heroic priest.

Honolulu harbor soundings and borings of the narrow, shallow entrance led to dredging and new wharves both for the government and for B. F. Dillingham, whose persevering development of the Oahu Railway and Land Company had brought "Pearl Harbor and the new settlement, Pearl City, within less than an hour's ride of the capital." The west side of the harbor covered a fishpond or shallow tideland area. Dillingham proposed dredging for wharf slips through this shoal water outside his property into deep water beyond. To wharves on Oahu Railway and Land Company holdings Minister Thurston voiced no objection, yet from conviction he maintained the policy that control of the entire water front should rest with the government.

A question naturally arose. Had the shoal water originally existed there when Dillingham's predecessors obtained title to the area? Or had a partial filling-in process gradually been brought about by accretion of silt from freshets in the Nuuanu stream? The question brought up a nice point in law. With the approval of the Cabinet, Minister Thurston proposed that Mr. Dillingham admit government ownership of the shoal water and accept a lease permitting him to dredge through to give the railroad access to deep-water wharves. Ultimately this suggestion was accepted and a lease granted, vesting control of the water front in the government.

Honolulu was becoming thickset with memories, none, to Sanford Dole, more gracious or more poignant than those of Bernice Pauahi Bishop in her beautiful, hospitable home at the very center of the city. Pauahi followed, he often said, the dictates of her own heart, simply and modestly declining from Kamehameha V the sovereignty of Hawaii *nei*. "How greatly different," added Dole, "would have been the subsequent course of Hawaiian history under her intelligence, her patriotism and her integrity!"

As early as 1875 Sanford Dole's weekly journal, *The Islander,* included notices of the Natural History Museum in one room of Aliiolani Hale. With King Kalakaua as chairman, C. R. Bishop became one of the executive officers for the care of such collections as had already begun to accumulate. After the death of his wife in 1884, Mr. Bishop consulted with friends like S. B. Dole and Dr. C. M. Hyde as to a building which should house the priceless Hawaiian relics which in her lifetime Mrs. Bishop had used and treasured. Her own living memorial she herself, as the last of the Kamehamehas, had created in the hearts of Hawaii's youth by her legacy endowing the Kamehameha Schools.

To Mrs. Bishop's personal memorabilia her husband had added

by purchase scientific collections and ethnological manuscripts such as Judge Fornander's "Hawaiian Folklore." The collections were growing, and a building of lava rock at Kalihi on the grounds of the young Kamehameha School was by 1888 in process of construction. As to a curator for the museum both Bishop and Sanford Dole recalled W. T. Brigham's interest and training in the arrangement of such collections. Queries by letter found Brigham lecturing in Boston and California, and considering an offer of appointment by Senator Stanford as librarian of the new Leland Stanford Junior University. Enthusiasm for the Islands however was always present with Brigham, who rejoiced in Dole's appointment to the Supreme Bench as most eminently fit. In regard to C. R. Bishop's plans Brigham declared characteristically that a more widely known memorial to Mrs. Bishop than any local building would be a history of her Islands such as had never yet even been projected, such a history as should set forth not only the life of her people in those isles of the blest, but should present a fully illustrated account of all its natural history, its volcanoes, plants, birds, and fishes. After Brigham arrived in October 1888 this ambitious project was abandoned, when it was learned that Professor W. D. Alexander had already done considerable work on a history of the Islands to be published by private subscription. Mr. Brigham therefore applied himself to arranging collections for the Bernice Pauahi Bishop Museum.

The month of June 1889 saw the moving of George Dole's family. With his two oldest boys at Cornell and seven more close on their heels, as well as the three girls, it seemed the wisest course to move the entire family and settle nearer to colleges and universities. Sanford had suggested more than one alternative, looking toward ranching on Maui or sugar cultivation at Makaweli, Kauai, but George finally made the decision to sell out his Makee plantation stock and establish himself in the good fruit-growing region of southern California. In partnership with Sam Hundley and Adam Lindsay of Kauai he already owned a good orange and grape orchard at Riverside, and so the die was cast. To the delight of other families Charlie Dole often told in later years of the family excitement on reaching San Francisco; of crossing to Alameda on a big ferry boat; losing their way and stringing out for two or three miles along the railroad track to the right station. And to this day it is Cousin Maybelle Ward Walker who describes her mother's disappointment that not one of the nine children would leave Father and Mother and baby Kenneth—with a Japanese nurse in a *kimono!*—to go over to stay with the Wards in Alameda.

Sunday dinner at two o'clock was then agreed upon for everybody, father Ward giving cousin George explicit directions as to tickets and stations. At home mother Ward and the Chinese cook stretched out the table and made all ready with the best dishes. Father Ward went to meet the train. Not a single Dole got off. So he hastened over to the Broad-Gauge station. Still no Doles. Back and forth every half-hour he hurried the six blocks between Broad- and Narrow-Gauge stations to meet every train. At half-past four the three Wards finally gave up, sat down at one end of their long table, and were beginning to eat when the Doles came staggering up the front steps. By mistake they had taken tickets on the wrong railway, and had gotten off one station too soon, but they set out to walk, although three-year-old Sanford kept asking, "When do we get to a dinner?"

At last everybody was happy with the big roast beef, mashed potatoes, vegetables, piles of bread and bowls of jelly. Next day the cook announced, "That childen plenty like jelly."

To Sanford at Honolulu, as well as to Brother George, there seemed only dim prospect of continued income from sugar stocks. A merger of Grove Ranch with Paia Plantation was under consideration, and at a corporation meeting in 1888 A. S. Hartwell was voted in as president of Grove Ranch. Possibly Sanford Dole contemplated putting more funds into a small cattle ranch which he had started on land bought of W. E. Rowell at Kapahulu on the western slope of Diamond Head. Certainly he took keen personal as well as often financial interest in the education of his brother's children. Whatever the ultimate cause, Sanford sold his Grove Ranch holding in October of 1888. Later George wrote in glowing terms of possibilities in California orchards, hoping that in time Sanford would come to make his home there. He did invest in a California fruit farm, and later whenever feasible enjoyed visits at Riverside with his brother's family, but Sanford Dole's long life remained indissolubly bound up with the life of Hawaii *nei*.

A change was dawning in Honolulu. Partly because of the interest taken by King Kalakaua in their work, the artists Joseph and Isobel Strong had remained. The port city had been well known to his parents as missionaries to Micronesia. Charles Furneaux, a landscape painter from Boston, had come to the Islands with Will Brigham for the great lava flow of 1881. And in 1884 Jules Tavernier had followed his friends the Strongs from their joint studio in San Francisco. People, "even missionaries," wanted pictures. Anna Dole studied with both Furneaux and Tavernier, nor was she by any means their only pupil, for quite a miniature art renaissance was emerging on the Hawaiian scene. This was described by H. M. Luquiens, then of the University of Hawaii, in his admirable account of Jules Tavernier printed in 1940 by the Honolulu Academy of Arts.

And in January of 1889, when Robert Louis Stevenson's yacht, the *Casco,* rounded Diamond Head, it was met offshore by Joe and Isobel Strong. Visited very soon on the yacht by the king, the Stevensons were indeed welcomed, yet by some at first considered almost as Bohemian as the Strongs. It is to Stevenson's step-son, Louis Osbourne, brother of Isobel Strong, that we owe an interesting portrait of Kalakaua.

Waikiki in 1889, Osbourne wrote, consisted of twenty or thirty houses, set in large shady gardens, and bordering on the most incomparably lovely beach in the world. At one end of the vast curve the majestic outline of the extinct volcano, Diamond Head. At the other, far distant, the lofty range of the Waianae Mountains. Here at Waikiki R. L. S. rented a house, his own room a dilapidated, cobwebby little shack where he worked happily and whence the purple sunsets over Waianae were his daily delight.

Here King Kalakaua would drop in for a talk, while the horses of the royal equipage flicked their tails under a neighboring tree, and the imposing coachman and footman dozed on their box. The king was a man of extreme distinction, with a most winning graciousness and charm. "He would have been at ease in any court in Europe,—a grave, earnest, rather careworn man, who seldom came to see us without his chamberlain carrying books."

Stevenson too enjoyed these visits, and had the Islands not been already "far too given over to the evils of civilization," he might have been more than half inclined to accept the king's repeated invitation to make Hawaii his home and champion the Royalist cause. Arthur Johnstone's able study, *Stevenson in the Pacific,* stresses the novelist's predisposition toward everything Polynesian, even to accepting Samoan views recently brought north by Mrs. Stevenson's son-in-law, Joseph Strong, artist on "the 'amazing' Hawaiian Embassy, Kalakaua's most notorious political caper." So vivid was the talk of an evening as to kindle the flame of Stevenson's knight-errantry to writing his first Samoan letter, then and there to be sent off for publication in London before he had ever set foot in Samoa.

This first Honolulu visit, when April brought warmer days and actually swimming in the sea, delighted Stevenson in improved health and often long walks across the Waikiki bridge to call at the *hau*-tree *lanai* of the Jake Browns, or just beyond at the beautiful grass house where the Frank Damons lived; best of all perhaps to stop half-way where the scream of peacocks announced Princess Kaiulani's banyan tree and under it the little maid, "daughter of a double race." There in May Stevenson bade her farewell, her father, another Edinburgh Scot, "rugged and austere, but kindly and regardful," escorting her as far as San Francisco on the long journey for her education in the British Isles. Accompanied thither she was by Mrs. Thomas Rain Walker, wife of Dole's long-time friend who had become the British Vice-Consul for Hawaii.

Now that a great hotel does modern honor to Princess Kaiulani, Stevenson's farewell poem has become a part of it. Equally fine, though less familiar are his accompanying prose lines: "When she comes to my land and her father's, she will remember her own islands, and the shadow of the mighty tree; and she will hear the peacocks screaming in the dusk,—and think of her father sitting there alone."

Hardly had the Stevensons sailed for the South Seas in June of 1889, when political undercurrents began to swell to the surface. In 1887 when Queen Kapiolani and her party returned from London, Princess Liliuokalani, heir-apparent, had been at no pains to conceal her dissatisfaction with the liberal Constitution granted at the point of bayonets, as it were, by her royal brother. Her diary entry for September 26 stated succinctly that the king should not that day have signed a lease of Pearl Harbor to the United States, limited though that lease was to the duration of the Reciprocity Treaty, and specifically guarded though Hawaii was against loss of sovereignty in the Pearl River region. His Hawaiian Majesty had indeed made a point of publicly and officially stating these specific terms at the opening of the special legislative session of 1887. Nevertheless, to the princess and to many other Hawaiian nationalists Pearl Harbor became a symbol of domination by foreigners—a red flag of threat and fear.

Living at Liliuokalani's large country home in Kapalama, some two miles north of Honolulu, was young Robert Wilcox, one of the king's educational protégés, and very handsome in his Italian uniform. Nightly assemblies of malcontents at Kapalama were spurred on by several of these wards of the government, eager to demonstrate their proficiency in foreign military tactics.

Parts of the following account, written later by Judge Dole, were published in Volume II of Lorrin A. Thurston's *Memoirs of the Hawaiian Revolution*. Rumors of these Royalist meetings came to the public ear, but little was actually known and no apprehension felt by the authorities. Early on the morning of July 30, 1889, however, Honolulu woke with a start to learn that an armed force of several hundred men under Robert Wilcox had quietly taken possession of the palace grounds. Then as now these covered several acres in the heart of the city, but at that time were still enclosed by a massive wall of masonry from seven to more than eight feet high, according to the grade of the land. On the four sides were heavy wooden gates, in which were inserted small entrance doors of boiler iron.

On receipt of the intelligence of the armed force, government military companies were immediately called out by the Cabinet and stationed in the Royal Hawaiian Hotel at Richards and Hotel streets. Other volunteer citizens took positions in a house on Richards Street opposite the palace gate there, in the tower of Kawaiahao Church, and in the opera house opposite the main palace gate. According to the *Hawaiian Gazette* of August 6: "All able-bodied Government officials were summoned for armed duty, and many of these were furnished with fire arms. Mr.

Justice Dole shouldered a rifle among the others." After conducting some of the volunteers, like W. T. Brigham and Ned Damon, to the church tower, Mr. Dole took his rifle, reported to headquarters, and was sent with a few men to occupy the opera house, which was across King Street *makai* of the palace grounds.

The king, on hearing of the approach of the Wilcox party, had retreated with a small detachment of palace troops to his boathouse in the harbor, leaving the palace in charge of Robert Waipa Parker, captain of the Royal Household Guards, with instructions to permit Wilcox to take possession of the grounds only. Without opposition, the insurgents took breech-loading field pieces and ammunition from the royal barracks. Two of these guns were placed in front of the palace, one on the east, the other on the west side.

The streets were quickly thronged by excited men. Somewhere on King Street a musket went off—for what reason no one seemed to know; general firing began immediately. The two field pieces opened with a broadside, scarring the façade of the opera house from top to bottom with shrapnel. The crews of this insurgent battery were promptly picked off by rifle fire, two of them wounded, one killed. Brisk musket fire ensued. Sharpshooters in the higher buildings outside the palace wall drove the insurgents from one part of the grounds to another, some to the bungalow, others to the dry moat around the palace basement where they surrendered to Robert Parker. He telephoned for instructions from the active headquarters of the government, temporarily at the police station, and was told to send his prisoners one by one through the front gateway where they should surrender. Out they came on a dead run.

Early in the morning Wilcox had detailed twelve men to take possession of the government building, or courthouse. They let the janitors lock the doors, while the detachment remained outside. When one of these was killed, the others gave up the fight, escaping across Queen Street in the rear. During this skirmishing a daring rifleman of the enemy stood out in the open in front of the courthouse. Protected only by a palm tree, he fell when fired upon by someone in the opera house, and lay there in the sun all day. Late in the afternoon, on looking up the day's casualties, it was found that this body had mysteriously disappeared; and it was learned afterward that the supposed casualty had not been even wounded, but finding himself in danger, had dropped to the ground and simulated death the rest of the day in perfect safety.

About noon, during this interchange of hostilities, government defenders in the opera house saw a man in white leave the palace and walk slowly toward the Likelike Street gate, paying no attention to the fusillade that opened up on him. He was carrying something in his hands apparently not a weapon. Orders came to cease fire on a non-combatant. But before that could be effected, he turned about, and deliberately retraced his steps to the palace, which he reached unscathed. Later he was found to be the king's steward, who had started to take a noon lunch to the boathouse in the harbor where Kalakaua was spending the time.

Against the palace itself and the sixteen Royal Guards holding it, no attempt was made by the insurgents. At nightfall, however, they might resume possession of the field guns with serious results to life and property. A plan of attack was therefore devised by Lt. W. E. Rowell of the company stationed in the Royal Hawaiian Hotel. A few bombs were made, two from one stick of dynamite, each weighted with an iron spike, and a fuse adjusted. Assigned to hurl these from Palace Walk over the high wall, was Hay Wodehouse, son of the British Commissioner, and also efficient catcher of the Honolulu Baseball Club, with a good throw to second base. When three or four of these bombs had exploded on top of the bungalow, tearing open the iron roofing with the roar of a cannonade, the insurgents rushed out, one wrapped in a sheet and waving part of it as a white flag. Thereupon the detachment in the hotel grounds marched over, received their surrender, and marshaled them to the police station.

After such an insurrection, the community considered the high palace wall a menace to the public peace. At Kalakaua's prompt objection to its removal, the Cabinet prepared, if necessary, to march upon the palace with an armed force. The king's final acquiescence, however, averted a crisis. Later, under a new Cabinet, the king obtained a large appropriation for the heavy iron fence which to this day surmounts the lowered wall.

According to Hawaiian testimony, as stated by L. A. Thurston, the interplay of motive in the counter-revolt of 1889 is not easily unraveled. Wilcox was ready for action. Kalakaua believed that the young revolutionist was proceeding in the interest of king versus Cabinet and Constitution, whereas actually his object was the abdication of Kalakaua in favor of Liliuokalani. When this intelligence came to the king's ears, he instructed Captain Parker to admit the insurgents to the palace grounds only, he himself retreating quietly to his boathouse.

The insurrection was quickly over. Robert Wilcox, charged first with treason and later with conspiracy, claimed that Kalakaua was cognizant of all the plans. "The King could do no wrong." Promptly the Hawaiian jury acquitted the defendant of any wrongdoing.

LULL BEFORE THE STORM
1890–1892

WORD from the George Doles at Riverside, California, was eagerly looked for on Emma Street in Honolulu. By October 1, 1889, George had dried and delivered his crop of raisins, eight and three-quarters tons, and was ordering ten tons of bonemeal for next year's grapes and oranges. Looking forward to a visit from Sanford and Anna, George begged his brother to bring him the best seeds he could get: of palm, guava, mango, alligator pear, and lime.

News from Walter Sanford Dole at Cornell highlighted the thrills of having rowed with the winning crew, and their ovation next day on returning from Philadelphia to Ithaca where the crew was noisily conveyed uptown in two carriages, each drawn by "about a hundred fellows," houses along the route festive with lanterns and brooms for a "clean sweep," all topped off by fireworks.

Inevitably memory brought pictures of the boy Walter Sanford, who, having once made himself a small canoe at Kapaa, had at last won permission to paddle alone southward along the coast to the Wailua River. In quiet weather this was feasible, but on the windward side of the island a stiff breeze might suddenly spring up. By carriage and horseback the rest of the family followed the three miles along the old shore road. Tall father drove slowly, little mother watching with unspoken anxiety when the canoe disappeared on a turn of the road around a headland. At the mouth of the river rough water seemed about to swamp boat and paddler, but in due course both made the turn and arrived right side up to join the family for a river picnic in celebration.

"George Dole's tribe" this interesting family was sometimes called. Commiserated with by strangers, little mother Clara smiled with a joy known to mothers, and said, "But we need each other as much here as when we lived so far out of the world on the hill at Kapaa." She was smaller than her slight oldest daughter Marion, who to this day recalls her mother's habit of quietly reading German or French books while nursing her babies, and so being furnished with inspiration for some interesting paper for the local women's group, to which members with smaller families often found it difficult to contribute.

To put off the evil day when his nieces and nephews might forget their Hawaiian home, Uncle Sanford soon formed the habit of writing to young Clara of yachting parties and races in the harbor; of Anna's pleasure with her new Boston camera; or of driving with Anna up to their Pauoa Valley orchard and walking home to Emma Street, leaving the carriage to be driven back with alligator pears and figs which they longed to share with the Riverside family.

Punahou was described as pleasanter for the pupils than when Clara and Emily had attended there, several lawn tennis clubs making quite an innovation. And Clara was urged to make a practice of exercising with her dumbbells and Indian clubs, her uncle confessing that he could not get along without regular use of his own very long ones.

"Having no nieces or nephews around, I must fall back on pets," admitted Sanford.

Sheila, the carriage horse, has a new colt, Bravo, that follows me around and noses the halter and saddle when I put them on him just for practice. There is a well behaved kitten, also eleven tame chicks that I must feed often, or their mother threatens me. Sheila and Bravo go out to pasture at Kapahulu when I leave for Court circuit on Hawaii. Our orange tree on the terrace near the henyard is full of good ripe fruit. Perhaps it beats a Riverside orange tree for the first crop. One of the young trees at Pauoa has begun to bear highly flavored fruit like Kona oranges.

On Saturday Anna and I went out for a pleasant ride on the new rail-road to Pearl River as far as the road is finished, going part of the way at a speed of thirty miles an hour. We are disappointed not to be with you at Christmas.

Profiting by a leave of absence granted him from the Supreme Court, Judge Dole was able to get away in 1890 to the United

States. *The Friend* listed Mr. Justice Dole and wife as sailing for San Francisco on the S.S. *Zealandia,* on the 9th of February. After seeing friends in the region about the Golden Gate, the Doles spent some time at Riverside. With the old Cate home in Castine, Maine, as their objective, Sanford and Anna stayed over with her sister in Boulder, Colorado. After enjoying theaters and art galleries in Chicago, Washington, New York, and Boston, there came a real vacation for Sanford, the open-air pleasure of yachting up and down the Maine coast. Then he started for home, leaving Anna for a satisfying visit with her mother's family in Castine.

By letters from Honolulu, Sanford told his niece Clara of sailing in an exciting Fourth of July yacht race, not winning, but getting wet and having a good time generally; told too of going into the paddock to see immense birds, eight or nine feet high, in Dr. Trousseau's ostrich farm near Kapiolani Park, where the doctor's nephew shouted to him, "Don't go there, they will kick you!"

Among occasional messages for her father in Clara's letters Sanford included on September 23, 1890: "Tell George that the Committee on the Constitutional Convention reported against it today by a majority of six to three. There is a motion to discuss the report today, another motion to set it for Thursday." The election of 1890 had seated in the Assembly a minority of Reform members, but by good fortune this delay occurred in discussion of a convention to restore the Constitution of 1864, a project encouraged by the king and actively fostered by Hawaiians in their *Hui Kalaiaina* or Political Economy Party.

News items of graduating exercises at Oahu College interested Clara, also the fact that Lizzie Low's baby girl was a week old, but as yet having no name, was called the Rose of Paradise. And a later letter to Anna told of the baby being christened Anna Dole Low at St. Andrew's Cathedral just before Lizzie took her home to Puuhue Ranch on Hawaii, where Eben Low was an intelligent, energetic manager, and at the same time tax collector for Kohala.

Always eager for the fun and relaxation of yachting, Sanford described to Anna in October 1890 a delightful jaunt of his own planning in the yacht *Spray* with a good breeze and no one ill. Ellen Riemenschneider, Hessie Dickson, Clara Fuller, Will

Brigham, Alfred Carter, and himself made up the party, with Kapu, the pilot. After sailing into Pearl River and about the lagoon, they landed on Ford's Island and appreciated their lunch of poi, dried fish, smoked salmon, cold chicken, with watermelon and ginger beer. With the tide over the landing rocks the ladies had to be carried ashore and on board again. Brigham too was transported in like manner, only it took two to carry him. Afterward the ladies were set ashore at Aki's Landing and went home by land on the railroad cars to avoid the long sail back which to the men of the party brought keen joy.

After the November term of Court at Waimea, Hawaii is over, I may get away by the December steamer to meet you at Riverside. This would give me about a fortnight on shore. I wish I could do your packing for you and escort duty across the continent, and I would if I could. The George Gays are going up by this *Australia* so that you will see them at Riverside.

I rode over to the Tom Walkers' last evening before dark and found them with a number of young people having lawn tennis with tea and cakes. My new mare is improving as a saddle horse; I think I shall call her Belladonna after Don and Bel. Ah Soon has had a letter from China saying that Ah Nam has a new wife and has started back to the Islands in a sailing vessel. I should be glad to have him here on the place while I am away.

Mr. C. R. Bishop says the Allens are having a beautiful time in England and Paris. Free sugar in the United States is going to have an injurious effect here.

Good bye, Dear. I hope you will have an enjoyable trip across the continent. I sent your draft to the care of Lucy Adams and the duplicate to the Tremont National Bank of Boston.

As planned, Sanford went up by the December boat and was at Riverside in time for Christmas. On the way he met King Kalakaua, who was trying the benefit of the climate for a serious illness. Going back by the return *Mariposa,* Sanford and Anna took as their guest his young cousin, Maybelle, daughter of Cousin Annie Titcomb Ward of Alameda. Maybelle's letters home, treasured to this day, paint vivid pictures of her first visit to the Islands and much of her fresh delight in the Emma Street home. Enjoying the sea and the ship's company fully as much as did her cousin Sanford, she joined him early on deck as the steamer passed between Molokai and Koko Head. When they landed Maybelle found, not an ordinary hack, but a fine rockaway carriage to convey them to Emma Street. And what a perfect paradise the lovely home appeared, as they drove up the avenue of tall royal palms, in a garden of trees and flowers, with tall ferns in huge pots along the porch. An old Chinaman, Ah Nam, the cook, who was raking the long grass, came running eagerly to meet them, then up the steep steps to fling open all the doors and windows of the pretty house.

While waiting for lunch all three walked around the great yard, finding many green bunches of fruit in the banana patch. When her cousin Sanford said he would give Maybelle a whole bunch to take home with her later, she secretly prayed he might not forget. Ripe guavas were delicious and ripe pomegranates, as they wandered on the grass in an orchard of tamarind and mango, orange, lime, and lemon; lots of lovely roses too, and oh, the oleanders, perfectly exquisite and all fragrant, white, deep and light pink.

After lunch two ladies came to call, Mrs. and Miss Judd, then another carriage with Mrs. Wilder and her daughter Helen, very pleasant. Later the Doles and their guest on the porch, enjoying it so much, also later in the moonlight, when they strolled down to the gate and met two young men, one of whom talked so well of having lived in China.

Next day Anna and Maybelle made the beds after breakfast. Then Lizzie Low's sister Emma came to call with her bright little boy and cunning little girl. Emma was so pleasant. Later came Mr. Mackintosh, Episcopal minister and principal of the school across the street, very English, "Oh I say," and "You don't tell!"

Next day Ah Soon came in from the pasture near Diamond Head, to stay and make the beds, keep the rooms in elegant order and care for the garden too. Both Ah Nam and Ah Soon took off their shoes and moved silently about the house on stocking feet. More callers, first Mrs. Severance; then Mother Rowell to inquire for the George Doles; then three lovely ladies from Waikiki, Mrs. James Castle, a fascinating little woman with fair hair and rosy cheeks, in a rich grey silk and an enchanting grey bonnet and gloves, with her sister, Miss Nellie White, and their sister-in-law, Mrs. Zadoc White.

Cousin Sanford walked up the drive later with Mr. Hutchinson, an interesting English sculptor, who stayed to dinner and most all evening. Next morning, in a carriage, came a lovely little old lady, Mrs. Rice, and her handsome daughter, Mrs. Cooke, both very charming. After lunch the sculptor came back to doctor some of Anna's statues, a good many ever so white gods and goddesses, which seemed to be all the rage in Honolulu. Cousin Sanford coming home to lunch, brought Maybelle a big square envelope addressed to her, with a crown on the back and an invitation to a ball at Iolani Palace the evening of the arrival of His Majesty the King from California. "Of course we are going! And I shall wear my lovely pink dress." Many more callers later, quite a reception.

On a shopping expedition ever so many native women on one corner of Nuuanu Street were selling leis, perfectly exquisite tuberoses, and heliotrope. "Please be sure to keep my letters, Mother," begged Maybelle, "I want to have them always with the invitation to the Royal Ball from H.R.H. Princess Liliuo-kalani-Regent."

Cousin Sanford and Maybelle one day walked up to his orchard, quite near, only half an hour, in Pauoa Valley. His stock ranch at Kapahulu was way off toward Diamond Head. At Pauoa, Ah Fong looked after the alligator pears, bananas, oranges, and lemons, and was to bring down a ripening bunch of bananas next day. "Then I chewed sugar cane which Cousin Sanford cut up for me, and we walked back to Emma Street."

On Sunday all three cousins went to Kawaiahao Church and Sunday School, where Sanford's class was. Afterward they met Lizzie Low's mother, Mrs. Napoleon, very Hawaiian, with lovely hair and a rare sweet smile, and a very graceful way of moving about. She took Maybelle to the churchyard to the grave of Lizzie's first child, the dear little boy whom the whole Ward family had loved, when Lizzie had come to California with him. There was a neat little gravestone amid many hibiscus in full bloom.

At Mrs. McCully's tea next day Maybelle was excited to meet not only Mrs. Severance again, but even Mrs. Dominis, the regent, and Queen Kapiolani herself, and to watch them depart in an open barouche with coachman and footman in green and gold livery and tall green silk hats. A letter came from Lizzie begging Maybelle to give her at least two months and to come at once, but Anna thought it best for Maybelle to continue her Honolulu visit and return some of the calls, then go up to Lizzie's later.

On the 29th of January the whole town was in the wildest excitement. After breakfast Mr. Brigham drove up in his brake and without even waiting to get out, shouted, "Mr. Dole! The *Charleston* is just off the harbor with her yards aslant and both Hawaiian and American flags at half mast!! Can't mean anything but that the King is dead!" It was a shock to find that he had died over a week before and only yesterday Mrs. Dominis and the queen, both smiling and happy at Mrs. McCully's tea, were looking forward to the king's return on Saturday.

Cousin Sanford went off to town at once with Mr. Brigham. Cousin Anna and Maybelle hurried into street clothes, and umbrellas in hand, walked down town. Everybody was out. Natives rushing hither and thither in bright *holokus* and big hats. Carriages and saddle horses and people on foot. The wharf was packed, the *Charleston* at anchor in the harbor, draped in black, the two flags at half mast and her yards aslant. There stood the grand arch of triumph in gilt with stripes of red and black, under which the king was to have passed in a coach drawn by four snow-white horses. Cousin Sanford met them on his way home and to Maybelle's surprise gave her home letters which had come by the *Charleston* and which she began to read over and over.

Cousin Sanford in a beautiful black suit then walked down to the palace to help swear in Mrs. Dominis as queen before Cabinet Ministers, Supreme Court Judges, and Privy Council. Poor Queen Kapiolani was thus set in the background, and she was a very good woman, said Cousin Anna. Cousin Sanford said that Mrs. Dominis came in a black *holoku* and very calmly took the oath to support the Constitution of 1887.

Then for the last time proclamation of the accession of a new sovereign was made through the streets by the king's heralds, successors to the *kuahaua* (ancient town crier). This had been an early custom, the *kuahaua* of 1853 being a little old man with seven-cylinder lung power who would shout at the corners and along the streets: "*E Hoolohe* (Hark Ye! Take Notice!)" and

then pour forth his announcement of government measures to
control the smallpox epidemic of that year.

During the evening of January 29, 1891, Mr. Brigham came
again to tell the Doles of having been on board the *Charleston*
with Lt. Stoney. He met Admiral Brown and everyone was very
sad, for they had found the king so jolly and pleasant on the
voyage to San Francisco. The Admiral's quarters were filled
with floral emblems from the San Francisco funeral. Mr.
Brigham heard all the orders given for the afternoon; at 5 o'clock
a boat to leave first, then the launch with the casket; then the
Admiral and officers with the band; to be met at the wharf by
the cabinet and escorted to the palace where the Supreme Court
judges were to meet them.

At 4:30 Mr. Brigham escorted Mrs. Dole and her young cousin
to the palace on the front lawn to the left. At five, minute guns
began to fire until the procession started from the wharf, the
casket on a gun carriage passing under the big arch now draped
in black, as were the palace gates and arch. Native policemen in
white suits and helmets with crepe arm bands lined the driveway. Burning torches formed a half-circle in front of the palace,
at the left the Royal Hawaiian Band in blue, red and gold,
at the right the Household Guard in matching uniform; at
each side of the steps the chamberlain and aides in blue suits and
shoulder capes of brilliant feathers. On the porch and at the front
door were guards holding immense *kahilis,* beautiful and truly
regal.

At the entrance stood the Supreme Court judges in black cloth
suits with crepe arm bands. And the whole veranda was filled
with black-robed women "very energetic in their wailing. Suddenly we heard the *Charleston* band playing the Dead March
which caused an even louder wail of woe from all sides."

Back of the palace, as if at command, the whole sky grew
darker and darker, until completely black. And just as the procession arrived at the palace gate an intensely brilliant double rainbow arched against the black sky, touching the ground at both
ends. Never had even the California guest seen such exquisite,
vivid colors, which shone until the procession had passed in out
of sight.

As the procession approached the palace, the band suddenly

joined in the stately anthem, and out on the upper balcony came poor Queen Kapiolani, a solitary figure in black, kneeling and leaning out over the railing, tears streaming down her face, while the bluejackets bore the casket through the door beneath her. Then she staggered back into the palace which resounded with wailing. As the sailors and Marines reappeared at the door, rain poured down in a heavy shower, the band playing exquisitely the hymn, "Nearer My God to Thee." It was all very strangely sad and solemn.

Next day, Friday, Judge Dole came home early to take Mrs. Dole and their guest to the palace for the official lying in state. Both Judge and Mrs. Dole must go into mourning for two months. The throne room was draped in red and gold, like the two great chairs. In the center of the long room stood the black casket with gold handles, six on a side; this was on a black pedestal over which an immense cloak of yellow feathers had been laid. Over the casket was thrown a smaller, much handsomer cape, on which lay a square cushion of dark red velvet and on that the golden crown, scepter, and sword of the late king. At the four corners stood his guard in bright uniforms and white-plumed helmets. At each side twelve men and two at the head, holding magnificent *kahilis*.

At the head of the casket sat Queen Kapiolani wailing and sobbing, the new queen on her right, Mr. Dominis on her left. At the foot were relatives in black dresses, and behind them the representatives of foreign countries. Four chairs near the wall next to the doorway were assigned to the judges' wives. Here Mrs. Dole was seated, with her young guest behind her, and back of her stood the four judges. Everywhere were flowers, and the emblems brought from San Francisco. In the corner by the empty throne on the floor sat native women, wailing continuously. More filled the hall, the whole palace draped in black inside and out. After two hours the Doles left with their cousin, who never forgot the experience.

Sunday morning, after breakfast of Boston brown bread and baked beans, Sanford went to his class at the native church, the two ladies to Fort Street Church where the auditorium was draped in black and Dr. Beckwith preached a funeral sermon.

Many callers continued to arrive at the Emma Street home,

with Mr. Brigham often at odd moments running in through the gate of his place next door. He was like a refreshing breeze, rattling away as fast as his tongue could go and brightening the ladies up, if they were too quiet. He even invited Maybelle to go up Punchbowl with him when the roads dried off. Cousin Anna later said that was a great concession, for Mr. Brigham detested women and would never put himself out for one. Meanwhile it would rain in torrents every two minutes, alternating with sunshine.

One day Mr. Haight called and took Maybelle down to the fish market, a long low shed by the water's edge, with stalls very close together and covered with fish of every kind, or poi and various meats for sale by Chinamen. All was a perfect Babel of chatter, shouting, and laughing. The native women in brand span clean *holokus* of every color, one even of purple silk, all carrying their fish tied up in green leaves with head and tail sticking out. Cousin Sanford had said that it was a sort of dress occasion, especially on Saturdays. And what a variety of faces, some toothless, old folks and gay young ones, all sorts of temper showing through their expressive eyes. Walking back through Chinatown, it seemed as large as the one in San Francisco.

One day when it was late and raining hard Sanford came home pretty wet and invited Maybelle to come out on the grass and have a rain bath. So she quickly slipped into her oldest clothes covered with a *holoku* lent by Cousin Anna, and ran out barefoot with Cousin Sanford. It was such fun that when the rain stopped, they played the hose on each other. Cousin Anna feared that the California family might be shocked, but Maybelle came out to supper radiant, feeling like another person, so cool and refreshed. All three spent the evening reading and listening to the rain.

During Chinese New Year's the cook and house-boy had two days' holiday. Anna and Maybelle then made the beds and breakfast which was very easy on Sunday, since Ah Nam had made the Boston-baked beans and brown bread before he left. At dinner in the Hawaiian Hotel fried bananas were so good, and different from any in California, that the two ladies walked over to Nuuanu and were delighted to find some of the big cooking bananas, a hand of fifteen for ten cents.

On Monday the ten-o'clock tram car took them from town out to Waikiki to return Mrs. James Castle's call; crossing her immense front lawn to the *lanai* overlooking the sea, they found a huge room comfortably, not elaborately, furnished. The following week they were invited to come out for a sea bath and dinner. One day they returned calls in Nuuanu, arriving back at Emma Street just in time to find Mrs. T. Rain Walker calling, with an invitation for lawn tennis which they always had on Wednesdays. That too proved a real pleasure, the lawn tennis court being cool and green and partly shaded.

One evening Maybelle helped Anna arrange the tables for twelve guests coming to play whist. Among them Maybelle especially liked Mrs. Charles Carter and had such a good talk with her husband about a sweetheart of his when he was fourteen; if she had only been fond of him, he said, they might both have been very unhappy today! And after every one had gone, Sanford and Maybelle cleaned out the ice cream freezer, Anna standing by laughing and holding the cake plate for them.

One of the afternoon walks taken by Anna and Maybelle was down town to the undertaker's to see the king's new coffin. Earlier kings had been buried in coffins of native *koa* wood; accordingly, although the San Francisco one was handsomely appointed at a cost of five hundred dollars, Queen Kapiolani had insisted on a *koa* one of fine grain and highly polished. On it was a silver crown and shield with the inscription and a wreath of flowers in silver.

After the empty California casket had been removed, men returned to the throne room to find for it a sacrifice from among the king's people. For this coffin which had held the king's body had become *kapu* (sacred); it must never be used again, but must be filled with a sacrifice and buried at once in the churchyard. Lahilahi, one of the new queen's little serving maids, having watched many hours, had broken the strict *kapu* of the watch by falling asleep among the flowers. She must be the one. But as the men stooped to take her up, Queen Liliuokalani, watching at the head of the bier, raised her hand and said quietly, "She is mine. Leave her here. You know and I know our ancient *meles* telling of the banana tree which grows as a man, produces fruit and then dies. Even so let it be here for my brother. Take a young banana tree as symbol of sacrifice."

"And so," Mrs. Lahilahi Webb of the Bishop Museum told clearly more than half a century later, "according to our ancient sayings and at the Queen's behest, the stalk of a young banana tree was laid as a symbol within the King's casket of *laau haole* [foreign wood], and buried that night in the old church yard at Kawaiahao."

Sunday, the 15th of February, witnessed the barbaric splendor of a Hawaiian royal funeral. Cousins Anna and Sanford attended the formalities at the palace, while Maybelle watched at home for Anna to come back and go over to Nuuanu to see the procession from Chief Justice Judd's house. Cousin Sanford marched of course with the other Supreme Court justices. At Emma Street, the booming of the minute guns from Punchbowl shook the whole house. Otherwise the air was so still that Maybelle could faintly hear the band playing at the palace. "Strange," she thought, "it seems more like the Fourth of July than Sunday."

Nuuanu sidewalks were crowded with all sorts of people. One of the gentlemen at the Judds' counted 3,263 persons in the procession. Holding by a long rope wound with black and white, those drawing the hearse were not horses, but two hundred Hawaiian men in black trousers, white shirts, black hats and crepe armbands.

The hearse itself was solid black, a platform with four pillars supporting a black canopy over the *koa* casket, partly covered by the magnificent robe of yellow feathers. Before and behind and on both sides marched men, carrying the many-hued, magnificent *kahilis;* then the pall-bearers, and girls with ever so many beautiful leis of flowers. Queen Kapiolani's royal coach, draped in black, was preceded by two black *kahilis* and followed by two white ones. Then came the state coach, bearing the new queen and her husband, the prince consort, two footmen at the horses' heads, two on the driver's seat, all in scarlet suits, knee breeches, and black hats; two scarlet *kahilis* before and two white ones behind. It was magnificent. All the sailors and Marines from the three warships in port marched in uniform, minute guns booming from Punchbowl, receiving regular and equally thundering reply from the *Charleston* in the harbor. It was something never, never to be forgotten.

Yet next day proved just another day with social visits paid and returned, and ears listening, above all the numerous whistles, for the special one telling that a California steamer had arrived. One evening a tin horn blew and that meant there would be home letters in two hours. To fill the time Anna and Maybelle walked over to Nuuanu to call on the P. C. Jones family, while Sanford walked down to the post office for those long-looked-for letters from home.

One afternoon a friend of Lizzie Low's came to take Maybelle down to the natives' *hookupu* to Admiral Brown, thanking him for taking care of their king. Brewer's Wharf was crowded and the band was playing. Bags of sugar were piled high on two sides, native and Chinese boys sitting on them shouting their delight at the festival. Two gentlemen seized Anna and Maybelle by the arm and worked through the crowd to the Admiral, a large round man almost smothered in leis. A never-ending stream of native women and children brought each a lei with a cocoanut, a few eggs in a bundle, a chicken, a bunch of bananas, a fan, a basket, even a live pig or a turkey, and always flowers, with live sheep even, and squawking hens. Eight boatloads could not get them all out to the ship. It was lively enough, and a happy change from the recent scenes of mourning.

After a gay lunch party given by Anna on her hospitable verandas for fifteen young girls, Maybelle packed her trunk for her visit on Hawaii with the Lows. She enjoyed every moment from the lovely crossed leis of fragrant green *maile* and fresh rosebuds brought by Lizzie's sister Hattie, to the interisland voyage to Mahukona, a cattle drive at the ranch, and a visit to the volcano. Most of all perhaps talks with Lizzie and her baby at the ranch, especially when Baby Anna was often called Annabelle, including part of Maybelle's name. Maybelle's own mother had coined her daughter's name and Sanford himself had later written in Maybelle's autograph album: "Remember that you are named for the flowers, and that flowers are the smiles of angels."

The two scant years of Liliuokalani's reign echoed much of the political unrest characterizing the seventeen disturbed years of her late brother's sovereignty. Economically, the McKinley Tariff of 1890, by which the United States Congress removed duties on all imported sugars and paid a two-cent bounty on every pound of domestic sugar, destroyed at a blow the advantage previously granted to Hawaiian planters by virtue of the Reciprocity Treaty. Attempts to negotiate a free-trade agreement between Hawaii and the United States failed to arrive at terms mutually acceptable. Island sugar production slowed down. Depression set in.

Many discussed annexation, not in order to abolish the Hawaiian monarchy, but in the sincere belief that only a stable, constitutional government and political alliance with the United States could save life, liberty, and property in the Islands. To Royalists the very thought of annexation aroused bitter resentment, and they had every right to such feelings. As keen if not keener interest in the possibility of annexation stirred among Hawaiian women, while they sat at their quilting frames and talked, as women will. Older ones among them had not forgotten when, after Hawaiian flags had been destroyed, by British order, Admiral Thomas had had the first new one made on his flagship for Restoration Day at Thomas Square.

"*Au-wé, au-wé,*" sighed the women of 1891, "maybe soon only Stars and Stripes will fly over our Palace. But this time, we, Hawaiian women, we do not wait for anybody to bring back our flag. We will make our own flags. We will keep them in our own way." And even today the emblem of Hawaii continues this loyal expression in accurate needlework design at women's hands, four flags centered about the coat of arms in the design of many a large homemade quilt.

Nor were those of Hawaiian blood the only ones to deplore possible loss of the Hawaiian flag. For more than a few conservative citizens and residents by birth or adoption, yet of European and American parentage, shared this preference of monarchical government; and rejoiced when on March 9, 1891, Princess Victoria Kaiulani, daughter of the queen's sister, the late Princess Likelike, was duly appointed and proclaimed heir-apparent.

Wrote Sanford Dole many years later:

Few business and professional men, however, could subscribe to the avowed policies of Queen Liliuokalani. Almost at once, a question arose between the new Queen and the ministers under Kalakaua, who insisted that they held over under the laws; but the Supreme Court, to which the point was submitted for settlement, decided in favor of the Queen's right to select a new Cabinet. Its members were: Samuel Parker, for foreign affairs; Charles N. Spencer, for the interior; Hermann A. Widemann, for finance; William A. Whiting, attorney general. In the course of that year, John O. Dominis, the husband of the Queen, died, whereby she lost a level-headed adviser.

Not long after the advancement of Liliuokalani, Robert Wilcox, supposed to have been in sympathy with her in the uprising of 1889, was engaged in a movement to enlist Hawaiians in a revolution to supplant the Queen and establish a republic, of which Wilcox was not slow in announcing himself as a candidate for president. The plans and hopes of these revolutionists were publicly discussed. The government eventually arrested Wilcox and over a dozen of his associates on the charge of treason. Committed for trial by jury before a justice of the Supreme Court, Mr. Wilcox was acquitted.

Meanwhile in the Dole family one year to a certain extent repeated another. Anna, agitated by receiving news of her mother's illness, sailed with Maybelle Ward for California in April, Anna going on at once to Maine. Leaving Ah Nam and his wife in charge of the Emma Street home, Sanford wrote to Anna on May 10, 1891, from Hilo where he was holding court, living with the Severances near the courthouse. Many asked for Anna whom they had expected to see with him. His word picture of the town is filled with serenity: "It is a beautiful Sunday morning with the sun shining, a gentle wind stirring the tree tops, flowers in every direction and the music of Sunday School children singing near by. We arrived Thursday afternoon and the time has been pretty much occupied with festivities for the Queen who came up by the steamer with us."

Touching at Mahukona on the way, the queen and her party had taken the little plantation train for Kohala and the *luau* prepared there. Lizzie and Eben Low were both busy with official duties of entertainment. Even the little wharf at Mahukona had been gay with ferns and a royal salute of Chinese bombs fired as the *Kinau* came to anchor.

Sanford rode up to Puuhue and saw red-cheeked Baby Anna Dole Low. Back to Mahukona after dark, and with the royal party he boarded the steamer to spend the night at anchor off Kawaihae, leaving at dawn with smooth weather and fine views of the Hamakua coast, numerous waterfalls, precipitous shores, and beautiful *kula* lands rising to the mountains.

At Hilo anchorage a double canoe with a green bower over

it conveyed the queen to the waiting crowd. Next day came a big *luau* in the courthouse yard and a ball in the evening in the court room. At the *luau* Judge Dole was placed on the queen's left, with Miss Whiting on his left and Attorney General Whiting on the queen's right. Next day a large party accompanied the royal carriage to the end of the new volcano road for a picnic, while Judge Dole held court all day. In the evening some were invited to the palace, as they called John Baker's house where the queen stayed, and where they enjoyed the band and ice cream. Next day the royal party was to leave by the steamer for Ka-u.

In Honolulu, after the jubilee of Punahou School in June, Sanford described his pleasure in seeing many old friends, including the Gulicks from Spain, the Alexanders, and Sam Armstrong with his two daughters. Hearing from Anna of Uncle Ned Adams' poor health, Sanford extended his commiseration, although actually it did seem to him as if, with the three oldest children, Ned, Lucy, and Nina, all self-supporting, and with good provision made for the rest, Uncle Ned might cheerfully face the Lord's arrangements. To brood over misfortunes seemed to Sanford simply adding another element of misfortune, by refusing to cultivate an abiding sense of harmony through God's pervading presence and active influence in every line of movement. "No one can afford to be without this confidence at any time, much less in time of trouble," concluded Sanford with the philosophy which companioned him always and created the peace and balance of mind characterizing his entire outlook. This serenity was saved however from being coldly remote, for it was coupled with a very human warmth of understanding which in this instance prompted the forwarding of a bank draft sufficient to cover Uncle Ned's expenses for a winter's sanitarium recuperation.

A June steamer brought freight sent by Anna from Boston, everything in good order, reported Sanford, except a broken rocker on the comfortable chair. The carriage looked just right, the little rug lovely, the water color was an acquisition, and all the preserves very tempting. Since no invoices were found, Sanford and Mr. Allen had opened everything to appraise the customs duties. Sanford wrote:

On June 3rd the corner stone of Central Union Church was laid with elaborate exercises including twelve addresses, that ought to put it pretty thoroughly to sleep.

Your nice long letter came Tuesday. I am so glad that you have the satisfaction of being with your mother in her *pilikia;* it will be a great comfort to you always.

The forenoon of the June 11th holiday Sanford enjoyed working over his treatise on Hawaiian water rights, which he hoped soon to finish and publish. In the afternoon he traveled in the cars to Dr. McGrew's place at Ewa, where were also Joe Carter with Mary, Saidie, and young Mrs. Cartwright with her little girl. Dr. McGrew, Kate, and Saidie took a little boat sail with Sanford, who had to come home bareheaded after his hat blew out of the train. Pleasant dinner at Brigham's place in Liliha, with young Ned Adams who was occupying the Emma Street guest room, making the house less forlorn. Lizzie and Baby Anna were visiting Lizzie's sister Emma Mahelona's family, Eben Low to come later.

Of Sanford's solitary evenings at home more than one was spent on expanding a paper on "The Political Importance of Small Land Holdings for the Hawaiian Islands." Increase in roads during the recent vigorous administration and the settling of 213 homesteaders had made a start at building up a rural population with individual stakes in the land. Further development of this policy must go far toward producing a class of conservative voters in place of those driven to unhealthy political extremes by aimlessly crowding into more congested areas. The rural policy and population of New Zealand was tellingly cited as illustration. Presented before the Honolulu Social Science Association this paper called forth an able review in the *Hawaiian Gazette* of August 1891.

In far Castine Anna Dole eagerly received her husband's reflection of those long summer days of 1891:

I had my dinner with the Swanzy's last week. Only one other guest, Mr. Morong of the Iroquois. Swanzy and I were badly beaten at whist. Mrs. Swanzy wore a Directoire gown; they are getting quite common here and are very pretty for most women. Yesterday noon I went up to Hartwell's and had dinner with them. Mrs. Hartwell and half of the children were at Koloa.

I dined with the Mackintoshes last evening and sat out on the veranda with the parson smoking and talking theology till 9 o'clock. His attitude toward heretics has been visibly affected in the direction of toleration.

The July term of court is always held here. Since Judd went to Maui I have been the only member of the Supreme Court in Honolulu. I expect to work pretty hard for four weeks; intend to open court every morning at 9 o'clock.

I am to hold the September term in Ka-u. I have got your paintings back into my room at the Court House, and enjoy having them. Judge McCully's room has been joined to the small courtroom next to it, the partition having been removed, and making a fine large courtroom as large as the one below. McCully will take Preston's old room.

The golden shower trees in our yard are in their glory.

Faxon Bishop and Annie Walker are to be married July 21st. We have received an invitation.

For July 4th, I consented to be an officer of the day at the Rifle Range for competitive shooting all day. I was rather sorry I did not decline and go on one of the yachts in the race instead.

The Doles at Riverside seem to be well. Charlie competed in five high school athletic contests, winning 3 first and 2 second prizes. For boys under 14 Alfred won first prize in a 100-yard race. Herbert was in the Cornell Freshman crew which beat Columbia Freshmen at New London. Walter did not row this year, has been on a surveying party in vacation and is now in Chicago writing up his thesis on the drainage works of that city. Herbert finishes his vacation in an architect's office in New York.

July 31, restoration day, saw three yachts sailing to Pearl River with five ladies: Mary Burbank, Nellie Lowrey, Carrie Castle, two Misses Armstrong. These all returned to town by rail. We had a good cruise, landing for lunch, after which W. O. Smith and I had an exciting combat with chunks of watermelon. We both survived, but Smith did not get the pulp out of his hair until he got home.

The British Club has suspended its boarding department until the new building is in running order. The Allens kindly took me in for the time.

I am sorry to learn that your side is hurting you again; you must let the nurse do the lifting. If you keep yourself in good physical condition, of course you can be of much greater service. I am glad that Nina Adams was of such help to your mother. Don't trouble yourself in the least about staying on. I think that everybody would most fully approve of it. Many still enquire after you and your mother. For me to join you at Castine and stay on seems out of the question.

Good bye, Dear, with a great deal of love.

Summer letters from young Clara at Riverside helped to make Sanford's empty house a home. From one of these he concluded that she had found the secret of success in journalism, namely, to write down only the interesting things. He despaired of making as successful a return in his answer—

but then Honolulu, unlike Riverside, has not had a visit from President Harrison and the chance of giving him a black eye with a well aimed bunch of roses.

I wish I could share some of my mangoes and pears with you, also quantities of white guavas with sugar and cream for breakfast.

16 Oct. 1891. Anna returned on Tuesday and was glad to get home. The house is quite a different place with her there from what it has been. She has told me about her short visit in Riverside, and with your sister Marion at Stanford University.

In September Judge Dole held court four days on Hawaii, staying with the manager of Hutchinson Sugar Company. Then he rode on a mule to the volcano with Edward Hitchcock and Judge Lyman, forty miles, and was glad to get off that mule. The new Volcano House was a large, pretty building, having several fire places, a billiard room, a veranda closed in with glass, sulphur steam baths, and a bridal chamber! At a clearing in the woods on the way down to Hilo the air was full of fragrance from an open space, acres perhaps, of yellow ginger in luxuriant bloom.

After two days in beautiful Hilo, Lizzie and Eben Low summoned Mr. Dole to Puuhue Ranch for the first birthday of Anna Dole Low, with a luau and dance for some seventy guests from Kohala and Mana. Baby Nan was a most attractive baby, almost never cried, had four teeth, and ate with a fork. Such items of news were gauged for the Riverside young people who still had the joy of a baby among them. They called themselves "the lucky thirteen," when Elwyn Hathaway topped off the family in April of 1890 by adding a Californian to the happy group. Oldest brother Walter's terse reaction in writing Cousin Maybelle Ward was: "Have you heard of the thirteenth?—a boy as usual."

On more than one of these court tours to Hawaii Sanford Dole stayed in Kohala with old friends, the family of Cornelius Bond, who had been one of Father Dole's pupils on Kauai. Once when he was leaving Kohala, the tall Judge asked small Edith Bond whether she would prefer to have him send her a Bible or a fairy book. Never at a loss for an answer, Edith replied promptly, yet with a shade of wistfulness, "We *have* a Bible,

Mr. Dole." The *Blue Fairy Book* which came is still cherished unto the third generation.

During the obsequies of King Kalakaua in 1891, the Bonds were in Honolulu with Grandmother Moyle from California. Invited to dinner at the Doles', they brought also Renée, a child in the family whose mother had died at her birth. Renée had glorious dark red hair and an insatiable desire to learn why the King need not be buried at once like common folk. Both Anna Dole and the Judge fell promptly in love with small Renée and seriously begged Mrs. Moyle to let them adopt her. This could not be, but how the Doles would have adored such a child for their own!

Pursuing the apparently even tenor of his ways, Sanford Dole walked quietly through the almost ominous days of the year 1892. A small group interested in political annexation to the United States, if no other measure served, held its meetings secretly in the law office of L. A. Thurston. The thought of such a club had originated with Henry E. Cooper, an experienced young Boston lawyer who had come, it was said on the Honolulu waterfront, "to fish in troubled waters." As a matter of fact, while in California Cooper had been attracted to Hawaii by legal intricacies of land title and tenure. Thurston, back in law work himself, and long an ardent supporter of independence for Hawaii, had been forced to agree with Cooper that it was wise, not to promote annexation, but to be ready to act, should the queen's policy revert to that of an absolute monarch. The Annexation Club even sent Thurston to Washington, whence he brought back word that the Administration would be exceedingly sympathetic to a proposition of annexation from responsible men in the Hawaiian Islands.

But this seems not to have particularly affected Sanford Dole, work on the Supreme Bench filling his time and attention. In accordance with a law of 1888 that no new appointments to the Supreme Court would be made, Dole was twice promoted; first in 1890 from fourth to third Associate Justice, due to the death of Judge Preston; and again from third to second Associate, due to the death of Judge McCully in 1892. This left the prescribed three: Chief Justice Judd, First Associate Justice Bickerton, and Second Associate Justice Dole. Also in all probability it left on the shoulders of these three even greater burdens of judicial work than in earlier years. Occasional reference to this appears in Judge Dole's letters with a corresponding inability to keep his mind clear for work under required pressure.

To a certain extent there was benefit from a change of scene in conjunction with court sessions, especially at the altitudes on the Kohala Mountains and Mauna Kea. In September 1892 Sanford and Anna Dole were rusticating for a few weeks at Paul Isenberg's ranch at Waialae, now the Waialae Golf Club. With Paul as their guest, his wife on Kauai, the Doles were delighted to spend a few weeks there, bringing their cook and provisions including spring chickens and plump ducks. With the sea at their front door they lazed to their hearts' content.

Wishing that young Clara Dole were with them, her uncle hoped to lure her away from California with tales of how they might take a net out into the shallow water of the bay, wading up to their waists and hauling in a few mullet, *weke, moe,* and *papio* with a crab or two. Or perhaps row farther out in the boat, get onto some decorous breaker and ride him in for a hundred yards, not a great deal of work except possibly for the breaker. Or ride *mauka* into the valleys to shoot goats and hunt tree-shells. Or just sit under the tall cocoanut trees, far more luxuriant at Waialae than those at Waikiki, and let a native boy drop down a few nuts for Paul's pet monkey to peel. This was Bob, a very interesting relative, who peeled cocoanuts very well, "then we could eat and drink, giving Bob a whole nut for his pay. If it is heavy, he holds it to his mouth with his two front hands and one hind hand; and when drinking, his eyes wink with an expression of sincere enjoyment. Then he holds the nut up and tries to look into the hole to see if there is any more milk."

On the second day at Waialae Judge Dole had been called back to Honolulu to consider a question from the Legislature as to what constituted a majority when there were vacancies. With Judge Bickerton at Waikane, near Kualoa, for his health, Judd and Dole drove the seventeen miles, and worked on the case a whole day, driving back to Kualoa to sleep. "Reached Honolulu at dark Sunday night, and Waialae not till late on Monday. Three days of my vacation gone.—Tell Ethelbert the grey cat climbs to my shoulder and when I eat, sticks out his paw to turn every fork load of food in his own direction. His name is Catiline, but Catamaran for short. Bravo, the colt, is over three years old, may be ready for you when you come. So far I have had Ah Soon ride him around the yard while I lead him. Shall soon begin seriously to train him to the saddle," wrote Dole to his niece.

At times an evening at home would be available for carrying forward a point or two in Dole's thesis, "Evolution of Hawaiian Land Tenures." This may have been a primary consideration led up to by his studies the year before in Hawaiian water rights and individual land holdings. Without doubt too W. D. Alexander's *A Brief History of the Hawaiian People,* recently appearing from the American Book Company press and published by order of the Hawaiian Board of Education, held much of stimulus toward building up from findings in his law cases the effective nucleus of local references which Sanford Dole had long had in mind.

Added incentive, were any needed, must certainly have been supplied by Alexander's discovery in the palace attic of 132 old trunks filled with foreign office and legislative documents. As Surveyor General of the kingdom and organizer of the complicated system of Hawaiian land surveys, Mr. Alexander's duties included likewise exploration of the palace basement where camphor and *koa* wood boxes were loosely stored, these containing records of the Department of the Interior, Post Office, Customs House and Chinese Immigration. A subsequent legislative appropriation of $2,500 was thus the first step toward establishing the care due to Hawaii's public archives. Chaplain R. R. Hoes of the U.S.S. *Pensacola* was engaged to make a start on sorting part of these invaluable documents.

One can feel Sanford Dole's absorbed concern in these proceedings, and one can even touch it concretely in the wave of public interest which culminated during this year. In December 1891 there gathered for preliminary discussion at the rooms of the Hawaiian Board of Missions on Beretania Street a group of men who were themselves making history and were convinced that, even with Alexander's new *Brief History* in hand, much was passing unrecorded.

In January 1892 at the Honolulu Library and Reading Rooms formal organization of the Hawaiian Historical Society took place. The first roster of members is impressive. Professor W. D.

Alexander, Dr. G. P. Andrews, Hon. C. R. Bishop, B. F. Dillingham, Hon. S. B. Dole, three brothers Emerson, W. F. Frear, Chaplain Hoes, Rev. Dr. C. M. Hyde, two brothers Lyons, Rev. A. Mackintosh, Dr. A. Nichols, Rev. J. Okabe, W. C. Parke, Dr. C. T. Rogers, Professor M. M. Scott, F. J. Testa, and last, but by no means least, T. G. Thrum. An outstanding group of twenty-one men to whose number were added before the end of that year over two hundred more, of many racial, religious, and political leanings. The queen was asked to be patron, and more than twenty distinguished men in other parts of the world were interested and proud to be recorded as corresponding members.

It was local members of the Hawaiian Historical Society, who on December 5, 1892, listened to and later printed as their third official paper Judge Dole's *Evolution of Hawaiian Land Tenures.* Not, it may be argued, a brilliant treatise, but a very readable and careful account picturing "the golden age of Hawaii when there was no need for fighting, because there was land and water enough for all, and all were busily employed"; the development of the chiefly class under the highest chief, or king; Kamehameha's long and vigorous reign when he began to establish the hereditary transmission of estates and security of tenure; the Bill of Rights in 1839 by Kamehameha III, the Hawaiian Magna Charta; the establishment of a responsible government detached from the king; the Land Commission of 1846; and finally the Great Mahele, or Division of Lands by king and chiefs.

It was the founders of this Hawaiian Historical Society who looked back into the years before the present of that day, and beyond into the unknown future of Hawaii *nei.* Everywhere ambition and unrest might be seething and threatening at any moment to erupt, but for these scholars and scientists, business men, planters, surveyors, lawyers, preachers, bankers, and teachers, there was a dignity and a permanence about the life of these Hawaiian Islands which they were convinced the world itself could not but recognize.

REVOLUTION
1893

INCREASING political tension presaged storm. Judge Dole's reminiscences describe the prolonged Legislature of 1892 as an Assembly almost equally divided between supporters of the administration and the opposition, the latter slightly in the lead. The session was rather a stormy one in which one Cabinet after another was voted out, some remaining in office only a few days. He wrote:

In November the Queen seemed willing to take the obvious course, and appointed ministers from the opposition, but only the first of them was a member of the Legislature: G. N. Wilcox, minister of the interior; Mark P. Robinson, of foreign affairs; P. C. Jones, of finance; Cecil Brown, attorney-general.

The administration of public affairs took on a more businesslike character under the conservative cabinet, but this did not wholly please the Queen. She favored the lottery, whose promoters promised the government a princely annual tax for the license; she wanted to have personal control of the government; and the loss of royal prerogative resulting from the constitution of 1887, was a grief to her.

As the year drew to its close, there was much intrigue between the Palace and the Legislature, which had continued in session beyond all precedent. Some of the members needed to return home for attention to their own affairs. The Queen promoted delay until, in the absence of several opposition members, an opium license and a lottery bill were passed.

Perhaps more than at any other point Liliuokalani's plan to license a lottery augured trouble for her realm. A committee had waited upon her to beg her not to sign the bill whose results would mean destruction for Hawaiians only too ready to wager all they had, even to life itself, at the drop of a hat. As a girl,

Lydia Paki had dearly loved and in turn been loved by her Royal School teacher, Mrs. Juliette Montague Cooke, on whom she still often called. At Christmas time in 1892 the queen had sent her a welcome gift of all the music which she herself had arranged or composed.

Now, during the crisis of 1893, even at the age of eighty, Mother Cooke had climbed the steps of the palace with the committee to implore her former pupil to reconsider her decision sanctioning a lottery. The queen, wrote Mrs. Cooke to her sister, "made me sit by her and referred pleasantly to what she had been taught in school. She said she could not promise not to sign the bill. She meant to do what seemed best for the natives."

The story of those eventful days in January 1893 moves forward in Sanford Dole's own account taken from both printed and manuscript sources:

On the 13th of January, 1893, with one defection from the opposition, a vote of want of confidence in the G. N. Wilcox ministry was introduced and carried; and Liliuokalani, after the appointment of a new Cabinet, was ready to prorogue the legislature the following day. The new ministers were: Samuel Parker, foreign affairs; J. F. Colburn, interior; W. H. Cornwall, finance; A. P. Peterson, attorney-general.

The public was much disturbed, particularly at the lottery franchise law and the change of ministry. During the next forenoon rumors filled the air, to the effect that the Queen was bent on some radical step, perhaps even with reference to the constitution. At noon the legislature was prorogued with the usual ceremony: a royal salute from the Punchbowl battery, as the Queen left the Palace for the Legislative hall, where the Household Guards were drawn up for an honorary welcome. She entered the hall attended by her ministers, the court chamberlain, court ladies, and *kahili* bearers; she was elaborately dressed, with a coronet of diamonds on her head. The royal feather cloak covering her chair made a regal throne. With great dignity she read the address of prorogation. It was an impressive function. There was however only a slim attendance of legislators, members of the opposition being notably absent.

This was Saturday, January 14th. As the ceremony ended, the Queen's chamberlain announced to many present, local officials and foreign representatives included, that a meeting would be held in the Palace that afternoon, to which they were invited.

I did not attend the afternoon meeting, feeling that events were likely to occur which I could not countenance, and that I probably should not have an opportunity to oppose them by protest or otherwise. So I spent this Saturday afternoon in giving a boat trip off the harbor to a party of school boys, to whom I had promised the treat. Upon returning late in the afternoon, I was informed that exciting events were occurring at the Palace.

When the gathering there became general, a procession mainly of Hawaiians, dressed in their best apparel for the occasion, the leader carrying on his breast a document purporting to be the proposed Constitution, marched into the palace yard. In a room adjoining the throne room the Queen met her ministers with the draft of the new constitution and requested them to sign it with her. The whole Cabinet demurred, much to the Queen's displeasure. Inasmuch as they were officials of but a day or two and had hardly had time to take in the Queen's very revolutionary program, their action was not surprising, even had they been willing to promote her policy. Her indignation was such that all the Cabinet except Samuel Parker hastily abandoned the Palace.

As I went up Fort Street from the wharf, I found the office of W. O. Smith thronged with business and professional men and others, Hawaiians among them, all apprehensive of trouble, looking for information and an opportunity to protest against the Queen's action. Thither came also the three Cabinet members who had fled from the Palace. They informed the office gathering of the Queen's demand and their own hesitation in regard to it.

A Committee of Thirteen was chosen to act in the emergency. The feeling was earnest and tense, showing no disposition to brook any effort by the Queen to tamper with the constitution, or in any wise to impair its recognition of equal rights and the sovereignty of the people. There was free expression of impatience at the Queen's rule and some manifestation of an inclination to have done with it.

In the meantime Her Majesty, disappointed at failing to obtain the support of her Cabinet in the proposed measures, entered the throne room where many had assembled, and announced that owing to the hesitation of her ministers, she was unable that day to carry out her plan. Then she went out on to the palace balcony and harangued the crowd, including the Hui Kalaiaina, the delegation which had brought a draft of the proposed constitution. Briefly, and with much vigor she informed them that she was unable to carry out their wishes, but would do so in a few days. She was regal in her excitement; richly dressed and wearing a tiara of diamonds, and yet keeping herself in control. Her Majesty was for the moment still in the ascendancy in the affairs of the realm.

During the evening of that day, Saturday, January 14th, I attended a small meeting at the home of Mr. Thurston on Judd Street. The others present were L. A. Thurston, W. O. Smith, F. W. Wundenberg, W. R. Castle, C. L. Carter, and A. S. Hartwell. Some difference of opinion as to radical action developed. We knew that United States Minister Stevens was in sympathy with us.

Next morning the Committee of Safety met, and decided to call a mass meeting on Monday the 16th, to ask it to confirm the appointment of the

Committee of Safety, and authorize it to take whatever measures it might consider necessary to protect the public interests.

The mass meeting held at the Armory on Monday was very large, enthusiastic and harmonious. William C. Wilder, of the Committee, was chairman. A few brief and vigorous addresses were made. The Committee of Safety, selected on Saturday from members of the Annexation Club, was confirmed and given power to "further devise such ways and means as might be necessary to secure the permanent maintenance of law and order and the protection of life, liberty and property in Hawaii." This committee was made up of the following men: Henry E. Cooper, chairman; Andrew Brown, John Emmeluth, Edward Suhr, W. C. Wilder, W. O. Smith, W. R. Castle, T. F. Lansing, C. Bolte, Henry Waterhouse, F. W. McChesney, L. A. Thurston and J. A. McCandless. In the afternoon the committee, realizing that the community was in a state of unrest, requested the United States Minister, Mr. Stevens, to land a force from the U.S.S. *Boston* then in the harbor. This was acceded to, and a body of sailors and marines came ashore late in the afternoon. This force sent a guard to the United States legation and found camping ground at W. M. Gibson's former home *makai* of the Opera House, about the locality of the present Federal Building.

Alarmed at the fever heat of excitement which had already reached the high temperature of political rebellion in 1880 and 1887, the queen and her advisors issued on Monday morning a signed statement that in future no changes in the Constitution would be sought except by the method prescribed in the Constitution itself. To men who in good faith had twice accepted Kalakaua's frail promises, royal edicts had lost their savor. Wherewith could they be salted, save by counter-revolution? The tide of destiny none might withstand.

The next meeting of the Committee of Safety was held that very evening, Monday the 16th, at the home of Henry Waterhouse on Nuuanu Street, to consider organization of a new government. Some sixty citizens were present. A call was sent out for J. H. Soper, who had been marshal under Kalakaua and for a short time under Liliuokalani. At the Saturday meeting of the Committee Soper had walked out, unwilling to have anything to do with the queen's ministers who had come to the Committee for help. Mr. Soper's recollections, as told to his son, W. H. Soper, are here very much to the point:

Chairman Cooper said to Mr. Soper: "The sense of this meeting is that we must have a change of government which may require force. Your name has been unanimously accepted as that of the logical man to head the military. Will you accept the appointment as Commander-in-chief?"

Soper replied, "You men are making a desperate move. Until you can explain your proposed plan of action I cannot give you a reply. Furthermore, who is your leader?"

On being told that no plan of action had been agreed upon, nor leader suggested, Soper replied, "This is extremely dangerous. Then count me out, for without a leader you are bound to meet disaster."

When asked for suggestions, Soper's reply was: "There is just one man in this community who can head this thing successfully. If he will accept the position, I will serve with him and under him to the end."

At that point T. F. Lansing stood up at the back of the room and called out: "Well, Soper, name your man."

Soper replied: "My man is Sanford B. Dole."

This name met with the immediate approval of the entire group, and Mr. Dole was advised by telephone that Mr. C. Bolte was coming over to escort him to the meeting.

When Dole arrived, he and Soper had a conference in the front yard of the Waterhouse home. Soper explained that while he had perhaps exceeded his authority in placing Dole's name before the meeting, it had been received with unanimous acclaim by those present.

After entering and hearing from several speakers, Dole said, "Why abrogate this little monarchy in the center of the Pacific? I believe it would be wiser and a more diplomatic move to hold the sympathy of the Hawaiians by retaining the monarchy and thus keeping the situation under control. My advice is to prevail upon Liliuokalani to retire in favor of her niece Kaiulani, of her own choice to appoint the Princess as Regent with a well-selected Commission of four or five prominent citizens, both Haoles and Hawaiians, to advise and direct her during her minority. Her little realm would have the full support of the United States and Great Britain; Hawaiians would know that they had not lost their kingdom; and all the various island communities would be welded into an ideal whole."

On Mr. Bolte's arrival at Emma Street Judge Dole, taken entirely by surprise, had expressed unwillingness to accept the honor and responsibility placed upon him. But he himself found the large gathering "unanimously in favor of setting aside the monarchy and establishing a republican form of government with the view of eventual annexation to the United States." Judge Dole's own proposition for a regency during Kaiulani's minority, he was assured by the committee, "would not receive the slightest support from the personnel of the movement." Finally he told them that he would consider their proposal and give them his answer next day.

That night was not devoted to sleep in the home on Emma Street. It marked rather a crucial decision whether to abide by a rooted conviction that in a democracy the majority must rule. His own minority report for a regency had been turned in, honestly and frankly. Instantly outvoted, he had then suggested L. A. Thurston as the logical leader of the proposed government, but had been met by Thurston's belief that it would be wiser to have a less radical, more conservative leader.

On Tuesday morning therefore, when Judge Dole's suspense had in a measure cleared, he "looked forward, if a new government should be established, to annexation to the United States in a few months, and so to an end to Hawaiian difficulties."

Driving out early to the residences of Professor W. T. Brigham, Judge Hartwell, and Attorney L. A. Thurston, he found five gentlemen in favor of his accepting the proposal of the Committee of Safety. At Judge Hartwell's he met also Judge Whiting; and while at Mr. Thurston's Mr. H. F. Glade came in. Mr. Hartwell referred to the Lord George Paulet episode of 1843, wherein the Hawaiian *status quo* was restored after several months; and tentatively discussed a similar outcome in 1893, possibly weighing in his mind the seriousness of a permanent effacement of the Hawaiian monarchy. Judge Dole returned home to breakfast, with his mind fairly well made up to accept the position.

After a clear decision as to his profession in 1867, the next twenty-five years of Sanford Dole's life had gradually led on to this second milestone. Yet he himself admitted that the proposal to accept the presidency of Hawaii's new government utterly amazed him. To others, like Colonel Soper, the situation seems to have held more of logic than surprise. Significant too is Dole's outspoken preference even then for a continuance of the monarchy under a regency for Princess Kaiulani. Of no less significance perhaps is it to find in Judge Hartwell's autobiographical account, printed by the Hawaiian Historical Society in 1945, that because of his own complete agreement with Dole's farsighted policy as to a regency, Hartwell himself took no part in the revolution of 1893. Once the new government had become established, however, Hartwell supported annexation as the only logical move.

Judge Dole's own accounts take up the thread of the story:

In the forenoon of January 17th I completed official duties at the court house, wrote my resignation as Associate Justice of the Supreme Court and sent it to the Cabinet; and then went to W. O. Smith's office, headquarters of the Committee of Safety, and accepted their appointment.

After lunch I went to Mr. Thurston for the draft of the intended proclamation, which he and others had been preparing, although he had been sick abed for several days. On my way down town, I called on Mr. Stevens, the American minister, and gave him a duplicate draft of a letter I hoped to send him during the afternoon. As I left him, he said: "I think you have a great opportunity."

Upon reaching Mr. Smith's office, I found the committee assembled, with several others who had accepted positions in the proposed executive and advisory councils. Volunteers from the Armory were to arrive at the Government Building at about two o'clock to meet the Committee of Thirteen and the proposed Executive of the new government, and take possession of the building and hold it against any and all opposition. The signing of some commissions was quickly attended to, including one making Mr. John H. Soper commander of our forces. Upon receiving it, he hurried off to hasten the Volunteers. Then arrived the time for action.

I asked Mr. Albert S. Wilcox to reconnoiter the Government Building. He reported all quiet, the steps of the Opera House occupied by a number of Hawaiians. I stepped to the door of Smith's office; across the street stood half a dozen big Hawaiian policemen who had watched our headquarters a good part of the day. We had no inkling of their instructions. We were for the most part unarmed. Our pockets were filled with documents of a seditious nature. Those were critical moments for both sides. Success or failure in the initiation of our movement seemed equally balanced.

As I stood at the door, a pistol shot was heard a block *mauka,* above our position. The report acted like a magnet, drawing all within its sound to the locality. The big policemen opposite us disappeared. Taking advantage of this, we immediately started on foot for the Government Building, about twenty of us in all. Merchant Street we found almost deserted. The gathering in front of the Opera House had vanished, all flocking to E. O. Hall & Son's store, corner Fort and King Streets, where a wagon loaded with ammunition for our forces had been stopped by policemen, one of whom seized the reins at the horses' heads. Captain Good, the guard on the wagon, drew his revolver and shot this man in the shoulder. The policemen drew back, and Ed Benner of Castle & Cooke's drove the wagon on toward the Armory. James W. Pratt, with two revolvers, had been ordered by Marshal Wilson to prevent departure of this ammunition, but the single shot, which started the revolution, had been fired when Pratt arrived. Much of the success of our movement was undoubtedly due to the quick decision and courage of Captain Good in this incident.

Upon our arrival at the Government Building, we found but one armed volunteer present, Mr. Oscar E. White. We also found Mr. J. C. McCarthy, a determined royalist, detailed by the government to command armed forces from the police station. Fortunately for us—and perhaps also for them—this force did not arrive, the Cabinet being unwilling at the last moment, said Marshal Wilson later. Our own volunteer supporters soon began to arrive, an important and conspicuous feature of the force being the well-known Drei Hundert, a body of German residents organized for some time in military formation.

None of the Queen's Cabinet was found in the Government Building, all of them being at the temporary headquarters of the Royal Government in the police station. Mr. Hassinger, clerk of the interior department, Mr. Hastings, of the foreign office, and subordinate clerks, were called together at the entrance, informed of our mission, and requested to surrender the building. They acceded without protest, and were requested to continue their official duties as usual. To this they assented. Mr. Henry E. Cooper, chairman of the Committee of Safety, then read a proclamation abrogating the monarchy, and establishing the Provisional Government, to exist until annexation to the United States was consummated. There was no audience present to listen to the proclamation except the clerks, some of our volunteers and Colonel McCarthy waiting for the armed force from the Police Station with whom he was to interfere with our plans. As the reading neared its end, Mr. Charles L. Carter was sent with my letter, announcing our action, to United States Minister Stevens, who responded with a letter of recognition of the Provisional Government.

The proclamation appointed an executive body for the Provisional Government: S. B. Dole, president and minister of foreign affairs; J. A. King, minister of the interior; P. C. Jones, minister of finance; and W. O. Smith, attorney-general. It further appointed an advisory council of fourteen with legislative authority. These men were: S. M. Damon, A. Brown, L. A. Thurston, J. F. Morgan, J. Emmeluth, H. Waterhouse, J. A. McCandless, E. D. Tenney, F. W. McChesney, F. Wilhelm, W. R. Castle, W. G. Ashley, W. C. Wilder, and C. Bolte.

All officers of the Royal government were requested to remain in office, except: Queen Liliuokalani; Marshal Wilson; and the Queen's Cabinet. All Hawaiian laws and constitutional principles not inconsistent with the proclamation were retained in force, subject to action by the Executive and Advisory Councils.

Other foreign representatives, beside the United States Minister, were notified of our action. Mr. Hastings, of the foreign office, was of great assistance in this duty, because of his familiarity with diplomatic forms of usage; and soon, with the ready assistance of Prince David Kawananakoa, the notes were ready, and the remaining diplomats and all consuls received notification during the evening. We had replies from almost all of them before midnight, recognizing the Provisional Government.

The office of the interior department, on the left of the entrance hall, was first used as the executive office of the new government. When we moved into this room, we found Miss Vida, stenographer of the late government, sitting there in tears. Deserted by her employers, she had apparently been forgotten, but had pluckily remained at her post, awaiting orders. We promptly released her from her vigil and, I am happy to say, continued her in our employ. Later in the evening, the executive and advisory councils occupied a large room in the rear, formerly the office of the minister of finance.

Governor Cleghorn called and promised the withdrawal of the Household Guards from the barracks early next morning. The Governor was not in sympathy with the Queen's plan for a new constitution, since the prospects of his daughter, Princess Kaiulani, as heir-presumptive to the Hawaiian throne, were endangered by her aunt's ambitions. Commander Soper, occupying the room that the councils had abandoned, was busy in the afternoon organizing our somewhat miscellaneous forces, and as darkness came on he arranged for squads of armed men to patrol the streets. There was apprehension lest lawlessness in some form might break out, and an invitation was sent over to the United States camp nearby that a squad of American troops might join our hastily equipped men in this patrol service. This invitation received a curt refusal.

The personnel of the Royal government, keenly stirred by the progress of the revolution, were busy with advisers and sympathizers, who at one time invited the executives of the new government to meet them in conference. This invitation was declined. Negotiations were pending with the Cabinet and the Queen. Members of her ministry called on us, and Mr. S. M. Damon, one of the Advisory Council, called on the Queen who was considering the situation with some of her ministers and friends.

Shortly after dark, the Honorable W. H. Cornwell, minister of finance in the Queen's Cabinet, called at the Government Building to bring the Queen's written surrender, signed by the Queen and all the members of her Cabinet. This document contained a protest against the presence of American forces on shore and professed to yield the Queen's authority to these forces until, upon investigation, the United States should reinstate her as monarch. In conformity with this action of the Queen, the force in the police station surrendered the building and war material to the Provisional Government.

Two orders were issued by the new government that evening. One called upon those favorably inclined toward its authority to furnish the government with arms and ammunition in their possession. The other proclaimed martial law and suspension of the writ of *habeas corpus* on the island of Oahu. About ten o'clock, leaving Captain King, minister of the interior, in command at headquarters, the executive and advisory councils adjourned till next day.

In addition to executive offices at the *Ewa* end of the government building, Captain King commanded volunteer troops quietly assembling and quartered in the legislative hall which occupied the whole *Waikiki* end of the ground floor. Albert

Judd, then a lad of eighteen, oldest son of the Chief Justice, afterward told his children and later recorded for the Social Science Association that, during the afternoon of January 17, he brought his goat gun, a Winchester 44–40, bought with proceeds from the sale of his pig Lucy, to the side gate of the wooden fence around the government building, and announced to the sentry, W. E. Rowell, that he wanted to volunteer in Company B, the crack company of the Honolulu Rifles. "Then come in," said Rowell, admitting him, "and shoulder your gun as a sign that you have enlisted." The halls and lanais were filled with men mostly in the regulation dark blue uniform. Other Punahou boys had likewise enlisted, Clarence Cooke among them, and J. Q. Wood, one of the teachers.

A handsome officer, Captain Hugh Gunn, assembled the company in front of the building to put it through the manual of arms, with which young Judd was easily familiar, having served not so long since with other so-called "*haole* blue bloods" in the Kaiulani Guards. Trained under J. A. Hassinger, chief clerk in Kalakaua's ministry of the interior, this group paraded in incredible zouave uniforms of red bloomers with black side stripes, white stockings, blue blouses with red cross-bars and dinky caps, their chief function being to line up behind the king and royal party on his big reviews. Drilling now in front of the government building, recruits could look through the palace gates and see the Household Guards drawn up, also the Austrian field pieces readying for action, to be aimed, probably, straight across the street at Company B.

Volunteers for sentry duty at the gates at headquarters took their stations. As it grew dark, boxes of horse blankets arrived, with cases of corned beef and hard tack, and a large hot coffee urn from Nolte's coffee saloon. Some of the boys were too excited to eat. Most of the talk was of what the queen's troops would do, of the safety of the government building of solid concrete; no one thought or spoke of the American troops stepping in to help when the fight came. Waiting was not easy. J. Q. Wood started the Punahou boys singing. Men gathered around, all joining in "Solomon Levi," the "Battle Hymn of the Republic," then on their feet and hats off, "My Country 'tis of Thee." Some choked. None sang beyond the first stanza, for an orderly from headquarters rushed in shouting, "Stop your damn noise. The queen has surrendered. Orders are to keep quiet."

The strain eased, but excitement held. None knew what the future might be. The rank and file had but one thought: "The Queen has surrendered and Dole is our leader. The Revolution is over."

Actually, the organization of the Revolution was but begun, and during that night Captain King was in command. Who better fitted to pilot the new ship of state through the alarms of her first night? The people were on an island, beset by the gathering storm of revolution. Sea-farers had always come to Hawaiian shores, bringing salty phrases to the language. Early plantation workers had not been hired, but shipped by contracts like seamen before the mast. From Honolulu ships went up, against the wind, never down, to Maui or Hawaii; and down, never up, to Kauai, the prevailing trades carrying down the wind to that isle of the blest.

On his daily walks along Emma Street, Sanford Dole had a habit of turning north for a chat in the roomy, old-fashioned house just *mauka* of Princess Ruth's palace, a house later moved to allow extension of Vineyard Street; a house built and presided over by its practical, part-Hawaiian owner, granddaughter of Trader William Heath Davis, and mother of lively boys who at times climbed Princess Ruth's wall close to her fruit trees. Husband and father in this home was the seafaring Scot, James Anderson King, who had commanded many an interisland vessel of the Wilder Steamship Company, was also its general superintendent and had naturally named one of his boys Samuel Wilder King. Another of his boys was William Heath Davis King who gave these pictures from his family memories. Not without reason did Sanford Dole close private letters with Aloha to *olohana* (all hands). Not without reason did he love to sail choppy seas to and from Pearl River lagoon. Hawaii was part and parcel of the sea and things of the sea. Not without reason were Financier P. C. Jones and Attorney W. O. Smith members of Dole's first Cabinet, dependable, experienced men. Quite as naturally Captain J. A. King, who knew not only men and the ways of men, but the sea and the ways of the sea, commanded alone on that first night at the new government headquarters.

Wednesday, January 18, was pictured by the weekly *Hawaiian Gazette* as an eventful day in Hawaiian politics, when the palace and barracks were both turned over to the Provisional Government; the queen withdrew to her private residence at the old Dominis home, Washington Place, under an honorary guard of sixteen men granted her by the new government; the Household Guards at the palace were paid up to the 1st of February and disbanded; and although no special effort had been made to recruit troops, volunteers poured in steadily from all quarters. Government clerks were admitted without passes at headquarters in Aliiolani Hale, and the necessary work of the departments was carried on.

Judge Dole's own words from printed and unprinted sources continue to weave the pattern of the historical picture:

When the barracks were given up, we installed a garrison there under command of Captain Good. Early in the forenoon, the Royal standard was seen floating from the Palace flagstaff, probably the routine work of the Palace janitor. A messenger boy was sent over to have it lowered. For some time, pressure of affairs required all-day sessions of the councils daily. In a few weeks, this rule was relaxed to afternoon sessions every day; and later to meetings once or twice a week, members of the advisory council serving without pay.

On January 18th a commission of five had been appointed to proceed to Washington. This included L. A. Thurston, W. C. Wilder, W. R. Castle, Joseph Marsden and C. L. Carter. The small steamship *Claudine* was chartered, provisioned for the voyage to San Francisco, and dispatched on January 19th. This commission agreed with President Harrison on a treaty of annexation, which on February 14th was sent to the Senate for ratification. Since the term of the President-elect, Mr. Cleveland, was however to begin on March 4th, the Senate awaited expression of policy by the incoming President. On March 7, 1893, Mr. Cleveland requested that the Senate surrender the draft of the treaty.

In the meantime the military force of the Provisional Government was more fully organized. Necessary legislation was enacted, embracing the powers of the government, laws against sedition and treason, for the creation of a National Guard made up of four companies, one a permanent force under pay, and three volunteer companies; and laws for the control of the importation of firearms and explosives. The lottery and opium acts were promptly repealed. The position of vice-president of the Provisional Government was created, its holder to be selected from members of the advisory council. Appropriation bills were passed; a national loan was authorized. The old statute providing governors for the larger islands was repealed.

Legislation as to public health, land matters and miscellaneous subjects occupied much attention.

Rumors were frequent of threatening action against the public order; inflammatory newspaper articles appeared. Business of the town however moved as usual. Yet a feeling existed in the councils that conditions were unsatisfactory. A motion was therefore adopted favoring a request to the American Minister that he assume a quasi protectorate of the Hawaiian Islands, pending settlement of negotiations at Washington. Mr. Stevens assented, and on February 1st raised the United States flag over the Government Building, while the guns of the *Boston* fired a salute. A company of United States marines was stationed in the Government Building, and a force of sailors was given the C. R. Bishop residence and grounds, an area now partly occupied by the Kauikeolani building on King near Bishop Street. Matters quieted down. Volunteer soldiers were allowed to return to their regular occupations. On the 5th of February the order for martial law was rescinded, and the right of the writ of *habeas corpus* was restored.

In a thesis, on "Diplomatic Relations Between the Hawaiian Kingdom and Japan," written recently by Shinichi Watanabe at the University of Hawaii, the statement is made that Minister Stevens' decision to raise the flag on February 1, 1893, had been motivated by Consul General Fujii's demanding the suffrage for the thousands of Japanese in Hawaii, coupled with the rumor that the queen might promise them the right to vote in return for their political support. That this raising of the American flag relieved acute tension in the Islands there can be no doubt.

On February 7 the *Hawaiian Gazette* remarked an official call paid aboard the U.S.S. *Boston* by President Dole and Attorney General W. O. Smith with members of the Advisory Council, local military forces, and the Foreign Office. Leaving Brewer's Wharf in the *Boston's* launch flying the Hawaiian flag at its bow, the party was met, as it drew alongside the man-of-war, by a salute of 21 guns and the Hawaiian flag at the masthead. Did Sanford Dole recall his boyhood voyage to Maui forty years before aboard the United States sloop-of-war *Portsmouth?* In 1893 the official visit allowed time for little more than drinking President Dole's health and his return compliment for the health of President Harrison. A final salute of 21 guns ushered the Hawaiian party ashore.

Meanwhile, unaware of political changes in her home land, the young Hawaiian Princess Kaiulani, was pursuing her further education among "conscientious Christian ladies" at Harrowden Hall, sixty miles from London. Vacations were spent happily in the hospitable home of her guardian, Mr. Theophilus H. Davies, formerly of Honolulu.

When, late in January 1893, Mr. Davies received the first incomplete news of the Hawaiian Revolution, he considered it very grave indeed. Writing on the 31st to Hawaiian Minister Mott-Smith at Washington, Mr. Davies stated that he "had had a great deal of sympathy for the Queen and for the G. N. Wilcox Cabinet. The Queen hardly knew whom to trust, and fell back on her own bad judgment." On February 1, in letters published three years later in the *Advertiser* at Honolulu, Mr. Davies strongly urged "that Princess Kaiulani be proclaimed Queen with a Council of Regency, of which Mr. Dole might be head."

Realizing, however, by March that there was no time to lose, Mr. Davies wrote the princess, advising her to go with him to Washington. This was a state mission from which a seventeen-year-old girl might well shrink, but bravely she made reply: "Perhaps some day the Hawaiians will say, 'Kaiulani, you could have saved us, and you did not try.' I will go with you to Washington." That statement, said her guardian, was the only political action the princess took after the Revolution.

These facts have been brought to public attention by Editor Harriet Ray, formerly of the Paradise of the Pacific in her timely article of June, 1955, "The Princess of the Peacocks." And with this account is printed for the first time one of the many jubilant *mele* composed for the princess by Hawaiian friends in the expectation that she would soon be coming home. As reported later by *The Friend* at Honolulu, Kaiulani made a most favorable impression on Mrs. Cleveland, and doubtless served to influence her husband's efforts toward a restoration of the Hawaiian monarchy. A Washington dispatch of the 16th of March pictured a public reception at which Princess Kaiulani was noted in pleasant conversation with an old Honolulu acquaintance, Commissioner Charles L. Carter. However, it reported: "Guardian Davies observed the encounter and hastily steered another man up to supplant Carter. Mr. Davies does not allow the Princess to see the Annexation Commissioners, or have any communication with them. He is afraid they might undertake to show her that she is not promoting her own interests in coming here."

Sanford Dole's account of events presents the sudden collapse of hopes for a swift solution to official problems:

Owing to President Cleveland's opposition to the annexation of Hawaii, a measure welcomed earlier by President Harrison's Republican administration, the failure of our Annexation Commission to Washington became a matter of history.

This action by President Cleveland inaugurated months of uncertainty and anxiety for the Provisional Government of Hawaii, which did not end until the close of the year. Mr. Thurston remained in Washington as our representative to the Government of the United States, but he was unable during this long period to obtain definite word from the United States Government as to their interest in the problem of annexation. Toward the end of the year full information came to us around the world through the ports of Australia as to the plans of the President of the United States to restore Queen Liliuokalani to the throne. Great interest and excitement ensued in the Hawaiian Islands.

Very promptly after President Cleveland had called a halt to negotiations for annexation, he sent to Hawaii Commissioner James H. Blount with full powers over all other government officials and naval forces of the United States in Hawaii. This Commissioner was otherwise known as "Paramount Blount." His action was quite independent of the Provisional Government. He took evidence from a number of people, more especially Royalists, stopping enquiries when he had the information he wanted. He was treated well by the Provisional Government, but his demeanor and proceedings were such as to encourage the hopes of the Royalists. He called on me on March 30th, and again next day to introduce the subject of the United States protectorate over Hawaii. His proposal was at once to lower the United States flag on the Government Building, and return the sailors and marines, stationed on shore, to the *Boston*. I made no objection to his plan, except to ask him to defer it one day. He readily consented, and the movement was carried out on the first of April.

In quietly acquiescing to Commissioner Blount's plan to withdraw the protection of the Stars and Stripes, President Dole gave no hint of the tension created by this demand. No such official restraint however affected the special correspondent of the *San Francisco Chronicle* for its issue of the 14th of April. For three hours, this reporter told the world, President Dole kept the news to himself. Then he summoned the Cabinet for anxious consultation. It was resolved to meet the crisis firmly. Colonel Soper ordered the whole force of the Hawaiian troops under arms next morning. That night was a busy one at the barracks and palace. Alarm drills were held and President Dole himself inspected the soldiers at a late hour.

Floating rumors of a possible uprising by Royalists, aided by Captain Togo's Japanese troops from the battleship *Naniwa,* had no dispiriting effect on the government troops. Five hundred men were under arms and the Annexation Club promised to parade as many more. Indeed, a hundred American flags were raised over the town, and men went about their work with badges and buttons of red, white, and blue. Stated the *Chronicle:*

When Colonel Blount walked out for his breakfast, Honolulu looked like a New England county seat on the Fourth of July, and he could not gaze in any direction without seeing evidence of the prevailing sentiment. By 9 o'clock the street leading to Palace Square was picturesque with some 3,000 natives and orientals, on their way to see the bluejackets march out. True children of the tropics, most of [these spectators] were barefoot and had feather leis on their hats.

Between ten and eleven a great deal of stir and bustle was to be noted in the Government Building. Marines hurried about, making ready for departure. The Supreme Court adjourned, and Chief Justice Judd and his associates made a knot and talked over the crisis in low tones. Colonel Soper passed rapidly out of the building, with a service sword at his side and a revolver at his belt. The Cabinet ministers were restless. The coolest man of all was President Dole, who had left a life position to lead a movement which the United States had promised to support.

As the hands of the big clock in the tower neared the mark of 11, the outside crowd of half a dozen races pressed in and grouped themselves about the Kamehameha statute. Royalist leaders stood in the center of small groups, talking excitedly in the Kanaka jargon. The unknown might happen at any moment. The strain was relieved by the appearance of Captain Good, a scarred American veteran [heading] the regulars from the barracks. The troops had just been uniformed, and as they took their positions facing the crowd, their ranks compact and steady and tipped with the steel of a hundred bayonets, it was difficult for the annexationists, in spite of their low spirits, to suppress a cheer.

Behind Captain Good's command came the National Guard, its flanks and rear guarded by an artillery squad with a Gatling and two Hotchkiss guns. This militia was motley in its garb, made up of business and professional men who, it was plain, would not be afraid to use their muskets. The Provisional Government was fully able to hold every present element of danger in check.

Colonel Soper, Lieutenant Colonel Fisher and Major McLeod took their posts near the big gate to the Government grounds. President Dole walked out of the Capitol and joined the crowd that stood with uplifted faces watching the flagstaff, where a marine, with the halyards in his grasp, waited the signal to lower the colors. Commissioner Blount watched with the rest from the midst of a throng of Kanakas that closed admiringly around him. A trim bandsman in white stepped forward, glanced at the clock and raised the bugle to his lips. There was a long, ringing note or two, and then the flag, emblem of all Hawaii's new-born hopes, fell from its place. All over the throng came perfect silence. One heard the rustle of palm leaves in the wind.

"Present arms!" Colonel Soper gave the order, and then one realized that the Hawaiian flag had been raised. The military salute was its only recognition. The ensign had not gone up for Royalty and the Provisional people were using it only because they were denied a better one.

Various expressions were heard among the people in the crowd: Royalists, chagrined at the display of Provisional troops, but confident that the queen would come into "her own" again; British enthusiastic, one lady rejoicing in the United States' refusal to annex the islands to please "a parcel of nobodies."

Granted an interview with President Dole on the 5th of April, the *San Francisco Chronicle* correspondent found him comfortably dressed in immaculate white duck, and seated at his office desk as calmly as if he were in the presidential chair in Washington. "Hauling down the United States flag," he said, "had caused a ripple of excitement, but was not unexpected and opened the way for negotiations without restraint. A treaty of annexation might be signed by Christmas, but we are in no hurry; Mr. Blount is perfectly fair and square, and although some of us might like to talk things over with him [this with a twinkle in the Presidential eye] he is getting at facts in his own way."

Through the Minister of Finance, the *Chronicle* learned that the Provisional Government had ample funds, and was glad to pay the ex-queen her monthly stipend of $1,250; also that a more systematic handling of the Crown lands might produce increased revenue.

As to contract labor, President Dole and his finance minister agreed that several large plantations were already successfully paying their workmen without contracts, and that no difficulty would be experienced after annexation in conforming to United States regulations as to wages and immigration.

Nor were San Francisco papers alone in publishing such reports, for newspapers from California to Maine eagerly discussed every phase and item of the Hawaiian question. Republican journals were usually in favor of, Democratic sheets usually against, annexation. Outspoken in its favor came Boston comments, in particular from Gorham D. Gilman, formerly for many years a resident of Hawaii, and recently appointed Consul General for the Provisional Government.

Sanford Dole's own later accounts of Commissioner Blount explain in part why in Honolulu that official was sometimes referred to as "Minister Reticent":

During the stay of Mr. Blount in Honolulu, he was particular not to express opinions of his own about the issues he came to investigate. These were, especially, whether Minister Stevens had assisted the revolutionists in overthrowing the monarchy and establishing the revolutionary government; and also, if any assistance had been given, what influence it had in the success of the revolutionists. Mr. Blount's relations with the Provisional Government were uniformly pleasant, and his attitude toward me was always one of courtesy. His residence was thronged with callers from both sides. Mrs. Blount, who accompanied her husband, was entertained socially; but Mr. Blount's close attention to the business of his mission was something of a bar to his acceptance of social invitations.

Mr. Blount's report included considerable correspondence between himself and Secretary of State Gresham at Washington; in these letters Mr. Blount did not hesitate to express his opinions on local questions. No official copy of his report was furnished the Provisional Government before November, 1893.

United States Minister Stevens, who had raised the American flag over Hawaii in a temporary protectorate, viewed the lowering of it with deep chagrin. But Blount's authority was paramount even over that of the United States Minister Resident. Stevens had tendered his resignation on the 7th of March; and on the 4th of April he announced that he would leave the Islands in May. On the 9th of May Blount was appointed to succeed him.

As a Maine Republican, journalist, and diplomat of long experience, Stevens, in his reports to Washington, had repeatedly urged the value to the United States of annexing Hawaii. This and much more is ably demonstrated by Professor Julius W. Pratt in his published lectures at Johns Hopkins University, *Expansionists of 1898*. These give, however, no hint of the deep personal regard won by Minister Stevens during his four years' residence in Hawaii, although some of his earlier acts had aroused deep resentment throughout the community.

Relying on the steadying influence of the conservative Wilcox-Jones cabinet at the head of affairs, and in the belief that this group of four men was competent to carry Hawaii through to the next election of the Legislature, Minister Stevens felt free to leave Honolulu with Commander Wiltse on the U.S.S. *Boston* for a ten days' cruise to Hilo and the volcano. Imagine their astonishment to find on their return that the queen had just set fire to the nation by forswearing her allegiance to the Constitution. Diplomatic calls of remonstrance from the British and American legations were no longer feasible.

What followed has already been related. Stevens pursued his conscientious course, even the tragedy of his daughter's sudden death on Hawaii making no interruption in his all-night work on official dispatches. When he left the Islands on the 24th of May the farewell tendered him by the Annexation Club and all classes of people demonstrated something of the place he had made in Hawaii. Retiring to Maine, he lived long enough to make public justification of his acts while Minister to Hawaii, and as he died, he said to his only surviving daughter, "Tell them that I did not take down the flag in Honolulu."

How the American flag made its place in the Islands! At the departure of Lieutenant-Commander Swinburne, who had commanded the *Boston's* troops ashore, he called on President and Mrs. Dole, as announced by the *Hawaiian Gazette* of May 16, 1893, and delivered to their keeping until annexation the beautiful silk battle flag carried by the troops, from their landing for shore duty until the withdrawal of the protectorate by Commissioner Blount. One of the regulation silk battle flags of the United States Navy, this one was very finely made, all its stars embroidered in white silk.

Since rumors of hostility from the Royalist party continued, the Provisional Government decided to move its executive headquarters to the palace across the street, situated as this was near the center of a large lot which isolated the building at quite a distance from any of the streets surrounding its four sides. This allowed of better defense than the government building, which had remained headquarters, but was in a very exposed place, a public street passing within a few rods of it.

On June 2, 1893, by a unanimous vote of the Executive and Advisory Councils, the resolution was adopted that the offices of the Executive Council should be Iolani Palace, which as the seat of government should hereafter be known as the Executive Building (later the Capitol); Aliiolani Hale, the Government Building, to be known as the Court House (later the Judiciary Building).

Next day the *Pacific Commercial Advertiser* printed a lively description of activities at the new headquarters: troops of the permanent garrison had moved from the barracks to the palace basement the day before; books and tables arrived for the offices of the President and Minister of Foreign Affairs in the two rooms at the *ewa* corner, formerly the bedroom and library of the last king of Hawaii; the Attorney General's department in the large bedroom in front of the Foreign Office; but the business and law office of the Attorney General to remain in the Court House. The throne room would be used for public receptions and regularly as council chamber for joint sessions of the Executive and Advisory Councils.

Even without cable communication, Hawaii was not so far out of the world. From halfway around it dispatches, relayed often through California papers, had begun coming as early as February. From London there were hints that England, France, and Germany would not be likely to consent to the annexation of the Hawaiian Islands by the United States; that American aggression in the Pacific would occasion Australian remonstrance to which the British Government must perforce listen; that the heiress to the Hawaiian throne, then on her way home from Scotland, had received a dispatch from her aunt, the queen, containing an account of recent events at Honolulu.

Gratifying it must have been to read, also from London, that Mr. T. H. Davies, formerly British Consul at Honolulu, had written to the *London Times,* "assuring all having property in Hawaii that S. B. Dole is a man of refinement, culture and unimpeachable honesty, and that his present position is a guarantee of the gravity of the crisis and the integrity with which it will be met."

Private letters from friends and often from strangers in the United States, inquiring and often congratulating, were so frequent that Mr. Dole found answers almost impossible. His Unitarian cousin, Charles F. Dole, in Massachusetts wrote that he was not much moved by all the talk of annexation, nor belligerent enough to see any good reason for taking the Islands to obtain a new naval station which could hardly tend toward an era of peace and good will. Yet he hoped that Commissioner Blount would prove as fair and wise and patriotic as he was said to be.

Even the *Boston Transcript* printed a long article on the Hawaiian situation, and its correspondent C.F.N. wrote June 16, 1893, from Honolulu: "Chief Justice Elisha H. Allen early discovered Sanford Dole's unusual ability and anticipated for him a useful career. . . . In the community Mr. Dole is esteemed for clear sense, moderation and rectitude. In his profession as in politics he seems ever to have maintained the 'legal mind,' not prone to partisanship, most gentle, fair and just, yet showing at this juncture his stern Puritan make-up. A better man would be hard to find—without prejudice or suspicion in his nature— yet perfectly fearless in following his convictions."

From the Ward household in Alameda, California, his cousin, Annie, wrote as early as February 2 that they had been able to discuss little else but the Hawaiian excitement, since the arrival of a Honolulu paper from Sanford and Anna. They hoped fervently that the death of Secretary of State Blaine had not halted annexation proceedings in Washington. And all these sixty years Sanford Dole's reply has been treasured by Maybelle who had visited the Doles in 1891. Expressing his sense of misfortune in seeing Annie so seldom, the new president replied July 25, 1893, from "a little tower room off from the Foreign Office in the Executive Building, the band playing in the former Palace grounds as usual every Tuesday morning. My office was Kalakaua's sleeping room. For my address most anything will do on a private letter—Mr. S. B. Dole will do perfectly."

Of the fact that, owing to threats on his life, Sanford slept at times in this little tower room, or at the Allens' or Walkers', seldom at home and never two nights in succession in the same place, no mention is made, and only a word or two appears in regard to serious inroads being made, even on his superb health, by constant pressure and anxiety. Neither time nor opportunity offered for a quiet sail to Pearl River or a stroll up Punchbowl with Tom Walker of the firm of Theo. H. Davies & Co. In August the strain became so marked that reading and presiding at meetings became impossible. Leaving Acting-President Hatch on duty, Dole on the 1st of September took the steamer *Kinau* for Hawaii, his ship drawing a salute of twenty-one guns as she passed the U.S.S. *Boston* at anchor in Honolulu harbor. One can see his tall figure on deck, standing gravely at attention to acknowledge this unexpected courtesy from Admiral Skerrett, whose flag and the Hawaiian ensign dipped, while crowds cheered and a shore battery of twenty-one guns resounded in reply.

As often before, his refuge was at Puuhue in the Kohala Mountains where Lizzie and Eben Low were more than ready to welcome him. Always a special room in their home was kept swept and garnished for Mr. and Mrs. Dole. Daughters of the family recall that guest room as their first household duty. Every morning windows and beds were opened, though the Doles might not come for months at a time. And that room was strictly *kapu*. No one else, no matter what the emergency, ever occupied that room.

While Mr. Dole during September, 1893, gladly rested in the quiet of this prophet's chamber, a letter followed him there from Tom Walker, who was about to leave with his family for his old home in England:

HONOLULU
September 22nd 1893

My dear Dole,

My wife and I were exceedingly glad to learn that at last you are a little better, and should be very glad to learn that you would occupy a few weeks more in the beneficial mountain air of Kohala. Not so however, my daughter Beatrice, who is to see Mrs. Dole next Saturday, when she hopes to meet "the government," as she called you.

Your allusions to a friendship which I know must last into a future life, I can heartily reciprocate. I am always thankful for the providence which introduced me to my old chum of the days of empty pockets and swivel-eyed landlords.

We hope to have a few days with Mr. Davies in Victoria. Poor Davies will be awfully irritated by the *Hawaiian Star's* suggestion of personal motives with regard to Kaiulani [that she become the wife of Mr. Davies' oldest son]. I firmly believe that Davies' only interest in her return to Honolulu is that she may come back strong enough in character, and independent enough in means, to be a woman of great good influence, and to be removed from any dependence upon friends who might affect her in a retrogressive manner. When the ultimate settlement of Hawaiian affairs is arrived at, I can tell you more than I now dare say upon this topic.

My wife and I join in warmest regards; and I remain, my dear Dole,

Yours sincerely
THOMAS RAIN WALKER

Mindful of his longer Honolulu sojourn in 1889, Robert Louis Stevenson made a return visit of five weeks in September and October of 1893. His friend, Kalakaua, was gone. Kaiulani was still in England. On the queen he called formally. Of the Provisional Government he took no notice. Invited on some social occasion to President Dole's home, Stevenson wrote declining because of pressure of time.

Long conversations were held in French with Dr. Trousseau, his physician, and an ardent Royalist. Although deploring possible annexation to the United States, Stevenson refrained from whipping out his rapier in Polynesian defense, as he had done in Samoa. When able to have visitors, he received them with distinct grace. And he apparently enjoyed entertaining them while sitting for his portrait bust by the young English sculptor, Allen Hutchinson, a friend of Joe and Isobel Strong.

In December of 1889, in line with Hawaii's little Renaissance, Hutchinson had executed a portrait bust of King Kalakaua. At Kawaiahao Church bas-reliefs of Bernice Pauahi Bishop and her husband, the Honorable C. R. Bishop, remain some of the best of Hutchinson's excellent work. A number of his casts of Hawaiian types are in Bishop Museum collections. In 1894 he modeled a bust of President Dole which was left by the latter's will to the Hawaiian Historical Society. So far as is known, of the busts only that of Stevenson was cast in bronze, in England, where it was exhibited at the Royal Academy.

Of Stevenson's many callers in Honolulu during October, 1893 perhaps the most welcome one, in his stateroom when he left Honolulu for the last time, was Princess Kaiulani's father, A. S. Cleghorn, whose memory held forever Stevenson's serious offer to come right back, if his writing could be of any avail in Royalist service. Many there were who, like these two, longed that Princess Kaiulani might carry out the best traditions of Hawaii's monarchy. That possibility however had passed.

President Dole was still recuperating in the mountains of Hawaii, and it was still September of 1893, when Anna Dole wrote to assure her husband that Marshal Hitchcock reported all quiet on the Honolulu front; also that he would keep a strict watch at Emma Street even when Mrs. Dole was not at home and all the more when she was. This, she admitted, was a great comfort. Cousin Nina Adams, visiting for the summer vacation, went out almost constantly, and with very apparent pleasure. "Get strong and well, Sanford," begged Anna, "keep out of doors all the time and do not use your head at all." The proposed vacation of two weeks lengthened of necessity to more than six. By mid-October, however, Sanford was back, and almost himself again. Perhaps the greatest boon was to feel like writing letters during quiet evenings at home, especially to the family at Riverside who were eagerly on the watch for news:

HONOLULU. Tues. 31 Oct. 1893

I have a letter from you, dear Clara, but I don't know exactly where it is. I think you showed the usual Dole independence in wearing blue at your graduation. Perhaps your action will break up the monotonous white of such occasions, and make them more emblematic of the rainbow of hope as they ought to be.

We have to dine this evening on the U.S.S. *Philadelphia* by invitation of Captain Barker, and shall meet Admiral and Mrs. Skerrett. We went to the afternoon party on the *Philadelphia* on Saturday. She is a big ship, perhaps the largest man-of-war ever inside of the harbor.

Last Friday we gave a garden party, quite a large one and a pleasant success. Over 300 invitations were given and 200 or more came. There was a tent covered with French and German flags *mauka* near the tamarind tree where ice-cream and sherbet were served; near the house, *mauka* of the golden shower tree, was a long table and several smaller ones where coffee, tea and cake were dispensed. The grounds were shady and people seemed to enjoy themselves. A lot of girls acted as waiters and distinguished themselves; it is whispered among them that one lady, whose name they will not divulge, was prevailed upon to eat five plates of ice-cream. It was so good however, that I don't see how it necessarily required much other inducement.

Nina Adams leaves tomorrow by the *Warimoo* for Portland via Victoria. We have enjoyed her visit very much and she has had a good, and of late a rather gay time.

Admiral Skerret of the Pacific Squadron, but now transferred to command the Asiatic Squadron, is to come to the Executive Building tomorrow to say good bye to the Government; the troops will be drawn up, the band will play the "Star Spangled Banner" and "Yankee Doodle"; the Admiral and his staff will shake hands with the Government, and when he goes, the band will play again, the troops will present arms and every body will feel better. We are sorry to have him go. He came just after the Provisional Government was organized and has been here ever since. We enjoy Captain Barker of the *Philadelphia*. He is an attractive man and is moreover a devoted friend of the Government and I believe him to be strongly in favor of annexation.

I have had a lovely visit on Hawaii, which included a trip to Mr. Hitchcock's mountain house between 6,000 and 7,000 feet elevation on the east slope of Mauna Kea. The house is just on the edge of the dense woods, and above is an open rolling country with scattered groves of great koa and mamani trees, the latter full of their yellow blossoms and frequented by the lovely red birds, iiwi and iwapolena. We were there nearly a week and it was so cold that we had a fire in the big fire-place night and day. Lizzie and Mary Low accompanied me, and Edw. Hitchcock, Jr. came up from Hilo. Some mornings there was frost around the house. All our cooking was done at the fire-place and we had good appetites for the good food. An important item was wild beef procured from our native guides. I went on one cattle hunt—unsuccessfully, but shot a number of wild hogs and some plover.

The house was surrounded by quantities of Akala, wild raspberries, one of the most beautiful fruit in the world, dark red and so juicy in appearance and so large, some as large as a medium sized fig; they are however not near so good to eat as the American raspberry. On our way back, the Horners got up a trip to the top of Mauna Kea from Umikoa, their ranch house. As I had been once to the top I went down into Hamakua instead; but Lizzie and Mary Low joined them and lots of Horners besides.

Tell George I will write him by the *China* next week. He says you are keeping house during your mother's absence. I wish we might see you here some time. Bravo is pretty well grown, but not broken yet. He ought to be ridden. Sheila and Betty both have colts.

I am saving up stamps for Norman. Good by, dear, with a great deal of love for you and all the rest.

SANFORD

Stamps! A fever of excitement over Hawaiian postage stamps had been aroused among amateur as well as professional collectors, both in the Islands and in the United States. Earlier issues of the monarchy had promptly been surcharged "Provisional Government 1893," and official announcement from Postmaster General J. M. Oat assured the public that after these newly surcharged stamps went on sale May 20, 1893, none of the old issue would be sold for postal purposes. Whether the Provisional Government itself would continue long to exist, none could say. No wonder young Norman Dole and thousands like him were on tiptoe with the zeal of acquisition.

Heart-warming to Mrs. Dole must have been letters of sympathy as to her husband's health. The whole state of Maine, it seemed, was roused in her behalf. One letter from a complete stranger brought this assurance from his brother who knew President Cleveland personally: "We need not fear the results of his delay. The democratic as well as the republican party will not consent to let you alone; people do fear a future demand for statehood, but this is not now the question and should not embarrass us in reaching a speedy decision."

Later in the year, when President Cleveland named Albert S. Willis of Kentucky to succeed Blount as Minister to Hawaii, with instructions to reinstate the queen, Anna Dole's sister, Jennie Witherle, of Castine took up the cudgels in defense of former Minister Stevens, predicting a violent reaction against President Cleveland. One flare-up of Northern suspicion was that Blount, a Southerner, might have been working in the interests of establishing the Louisiana lottery in Hawaii. Anna's brother assured her that the press of the Republicans throughout the country was united in condemning Cleveland's action and demanding that the Provisional Government be treated fairly. Edmund P. Dole found that even many Democrats opposed their Democratic President, and he longed to get out to Honolulu to aid "in any possible scrimmage." Brother-in-law William Witherle wrote Anna: "We are for the Provisional Government every time and all the time."

Fearing that the wrong might already have been done, Jennie Witherle asserted that the country would not have Cleveland reinstate the queen. Nellie Adams, sitting beside her sick husband, Uncle Ned, in Cambridge reported that he "devours the papers every day." A Michigan paper quoted the new Minister Willis as surprised to find the Provisional Government headed by respectable gentlemen instead of low-class whites and beachcombers, as he had been led to believe. From Washington, Orramel Gulick of Honolulu went far in asserting that Cleveland, Graham, Blount, and Nordhoff, also the *New York Tribune,* had struck against the Hawaiian rocks and were going to pieces. Senator Hawley of Connecticut thought that President Cleveland ought to be impeached for his secret, underhand instructions to Willis.

Meanwhile, five thousand miles to the westward, Captain Barker of the U.S.S. *Philadelphia* had called formally on President Dole in October. The naval party was received in the Gold Room by the President, his staff and councilors. To Captain Barker, Dole appeared

a tall, fine-looking man with a full beard, having eyes which I imagine martyrs might have—steady but compassionate. I spoke to the President in relation to visiting the *Philadelphia*. I said I was well aware that the head of a government was not obliged to return a call made by a captain; but that considering the rumors afloat that the *Philadelphia* had come for the purpose of restoring the Queen, it might have a good effect on the people if he should come on board and be received with proper honors.

Upon leaving, the government troops again presented arms, and the band struck up the "Star Spangled Banner," as we returned to the ship. I was accompanied by Fleet Surgeon Winslow, Fleet Paymaster Hendee, Assistant Engineer Little, Lieutenant Wood, Lieutenant Little, Lieutenant Seabury, Lieutenant Sharp, Lieutenant Wehrlich, Lieutenant Sims, Ensign Ziegemier, Ensign Willard and Assistant Engineer Holmes; also by Consul General Severance. That so many of us went in full uniform, was very pleasing to the President and to the government.

During the afternoon, the President sent off word that he would visit the *Philadelphia* the following day with his staff and several members of his Cabinet.

The rail of the *Philadelphia* and the yards of the *Adams* were manned and the officers in special full dress drawn up to receive the President, who came officially, while a salute of twenty-one guns was fired upon his arrival and his departure.

Captain Barker's autobiography, *Everyday Life in the Navy,* pictures too the hospitality of the people of Honolulu, and, a feature not common in other ports, the fact that every vessel, snugly moored to the reef, was soon connected with the central telephone office by wires easily run on board with little danger of their parting even in a very strong wind. In a series of afternoon receptions aboard the *Philadelphia,* to which hundreds of both Royalists and Annexationists were invited, it was rather surprising to see the apparently pleasant personal relations between members of differing political parties.

Rigid rules of discipline, however, were established by Captain Barker on his battleship and lived up to by those who gave orders as well as by those who carried out orders. "This was the more necessary as we knew not when our services might be required to protect American lives and property, and it behooved us to be always ready."

Early in November 1893 United States Minister Willis arrived in Honolulu under sealed orders. He made his official call on President Dole of the Provisional Government with expressions of friendship from President Cleveland. Rumors persisted however as to possible restoration of the ex-queen. On the 24th of

November an Australian-bound steamer brought United States newspapers with Secretary of State Gresham's recommendation that the monarchy be restored as an official duty of President Cleveland. This had been given out on the supposition that in Honolulu United States resident Minister Willis had already carried out his instructions to do just that.

This news shot through Honolulu with a fever of excitement. Daily papers issued extras. To Royalists it was confirmation of hopes. At the barracks next day Vice-President Hatch of the Provisional Government was made chairman of "another of the mass-meetings characteristic of the supporters of the Provisional Government." Later he described it as "purely spontaneous, a town meeting in the best New England sense; of the kind common at the time of the [American] revolution; a meeting of the business men of the town and of its mechanics and workmen without distinction of race. Speeches were extemporaneous, with no noisy enthusiasm, the whole tone one of consultation rather than denunciation. As the meeting progressed a wave of indignation took possession of it, . . . [at] the assumption by the President of the United States that the matter had been submitted to him as an arbitrator."

President Dole's personal recollections detail subsequent events:

When information reached the Government that Willis was engaged in interviews with Queen Liliuokalani, a letter was sent to him by President Dole asking him if this information was correct. The next day a letter came from Mr. Willis asking for an interview. This was promptly granted. On the 20th of December Mr. Willis came with his secretary at the time appointed and read to the President and the Cabinet at the Capitol demands, accompanied with considerable reasoning and argument, for the immediate surrender by the Provisional Government of their powers and authority to Queen Liliuokalani.

As he finished reading the paper, President Dole said to him: "The Government will take the matter under consideration and answer you as soon as they are ready."

A reply to Mr. Willis' demand was drafted, on the 23rd of December was submitted to the councils for their action thereon, and was approved by them with some brief modifications. At midnight of the same day, the reply was delivered to Mr. Willis; he immediately forwarded it to San Francisco by the United States revenue cutter *Corwin,* which had been waiting for it.

Then followed Black Week, as it was termed by local newspapers. The ships of the United States under orders from Mr. Willis were required to have their boats in the water and in readiness to land; guns of the sailors and marines stacked on deck in readiness; and visitors from shore freely allowed to visit the ships and witness these preparations. In view of the hostile character of this action of the navy, the Provisional Government fortified the Capitol by sand-bagging all the verandah which runs on all four sides of the two stories of the building, and also the edge of the roof. A platform, placed along the wall of the dry moat which runs around the building, made a banquette upon which riflemen could stand to fire, protected by sandbags piled over the raised edge of the moat.

Rumors of intended landings by the American forces were numerous and definite. Since the Executive Building could be shelled by cannon from a warship stationed at a certain place in the harbor channel, arrangements were made for quickly evacuating the building with state papers, archives, treasury and the like, if occasion required. The plan in such a case, was to move across to the Royal Hawaiian Hotel and make that government headquarters. The hotel building and grounds were too well surrounded by buildings to leave an opening for possible attack from the harbor, while the position of the British consulate in their rear, and the Queen's residence farther back and almost in line, rendered an attack with small arms and machine guns from the front most unlikely.

During these days of uncertainty the citizens felt so much unwillingness to be on fighting terms with the United States that they decided, in case forces were landed from the men-of-war and marched to the Capitol, that they would receive them in hostile array until military activities should be begun on the part of these United States forces, at which time the President of the Provisional Government would offer to surrender to the forces of the United States. Plans were tentatively adopted for resisting the United States troops in case they landed, by sharp-shooters along the streets which the troops must take in passing to the Capitol.

Finally however a committee of citizens called on the President of the Provisional Government to enter a protest against submitting or surrendering to the United States forces; urging instead armed resistance, stating that they represented the feelings of the Volunteers and the regular troops. The Government was pleased with this announcement, and readily decided, in case of attack, to resist to the last. I think this sentiment was quite unanimous in the Provisional Government through the ranks.

The threatening attitude of the warships continued, creating great disquiet in the community. The Japanese minister offered his legation to wives and families of members of the Government and others, in case of hostilities. The British legation was permitted to have a guard from a British man-of-war in the harbor. Minister Willis' most serious consideration was called to the dangerous and critical condition of the community. Threats of assassination of the officers of the Government were made. Persons began to pack their valuables with a view to immediate departure; large quantities of bandages were prepared. The situation was one of warfare, without the incident of actual combat. Even the Queen called upon the Provisional Government for protection, which was awarded her. At great expense the Government was compelled by public apprehension to largely increase its military forces. Its offices continued in a condition of defense and preparation for siege; and the community was put into a state of mind bordering on terrorism.

In the midst of this excited situation United States mail arrived stating that the President of the United States, upon receiving the answer, dated December 23rd, of the Provisional Government to Minister Willis' demand for surrender to the Queen, had passed it over to Congress with the exclamation that it was an extraordinary document.

As the prevailing feeling in Congress was sympathy with the Hawaiian Government, our tense situation in Honolulu was immensely relieved, and affairs at once assumed a more serene condition.

MR. DOLE TO MR. WILLIS

P RESIDENT CLEVELAND'S words spoke truth in more senses than he realized when he characterized President Dole's reply of December 23rd to Mr. Willis as an extraordinary document. By many it has been adjudged a state paper of such dignity and importance that from the covers of the United States Senate Reports it has been transferred in full to form this chapter.

DEPARTMENT OF FOREIGN AFFAIRS
Honolulu, December 23, 1893

SIR: Your excellency's communication of December 19, announcing the conclusion which the President of the United States of America has finally arrived at respecting the application of this Government for a treaty of political union with that country, and referring also to the domestic affairs of these islands, has had the consideration of the Government.

While it is with deep disappointment that we learn that the important proposition which we have submitted to the Government of the United States, and which was at first favorably considered by it, has at length been rejected, we have experienced a sense of relief that we are now favored with the first official information upon the subject that has been received through a period of over nine months.

While we accept the decision of the President of the United States declining further to consider the annexation proposition, as the final conclusion of the present administration, we do not feel inclined to regard it as the last word of the American Government upon this subject, for the history of the mutual relations of the two countries, of American effort and influence in building

274

THE WORLD'S
Average Circulation in 1882
22,331
PER DAY.

The World.

THE WORLD'S
Average Circulation in 1893.
400,881
PER DAY.

PRICE **FIVE** CENTS.

NEW YORK, SUNDAY, JANUARY, 21, 1894.

PRICE **FIVE** CENTS.

HE CAN'T LET GO.

A mainland version of President Cleveland's dilemma. Apropos of this cartoon is a letter from F. O. Lyman to S. B. Dole, dated January 4, 1894, in which he tells of Cleveland's having taken hold of "a live electric wire which cannot be dropped until he is compelled to admit that he is wrong or has been thoroughly shown up and discredited before the world."

Flag raising over Iolani Palace, 1898

up the Christian civilization which has so conspicuously aided in giving this country an honorable place among independent nations, the geographical position of these islands, and the important and, to both countries, profitable reciprocal commercial interests which have long existed, together with our weakness as a sovereign nation, all point with convincing force to political union between the two countries as the necessary logical result from the circumstances mentioned. This conviction is emphasized by the favorable expression of American statesmen over a long period in favor of annexation, conspicuous among whom are the names of W. L. Marcy, William H. Seward, Hamilton Fish, and James G. Blaine, all former Secretaries of State, and especially so by the action of your last administration in negotiating a treaty of annexation with this Government and sending it to the Senate with a view to its ratification.

We shall therefore continue the project of political union with the United States as a conspicuous feature of our foreign policy, confidently hoping that sooner or later it will be crowned with success, to the lasting benefit of both countries.

The additional portion of your communication referring to our domestic affairs with a view of interfering therein, is a new departure in the relations of the two governments. Your information that the President of the United States expects this Government "to promptly relinquish to her (meaning the ex-Queen) her constitutional authority," with the question "are you willing to abide by the decision of the President?" might well be dismissed in a single word, but for the circumstance that your commission contains, as it appears to me, misstatements and erroneous conclusions based thereon, that are so prejudicial to this Government that I cannot permit them to pass unchallenged; moreover, the importance and menacing character of this proposition make it appropriate for me to discuss somewhat fully the questions raised by it.

We do not recognize the right of the President of the United States to interfere in our domestic affairs. Such right could be conferred upon him by the act of this Government, and by that alone, or it could be acquired by conquest. This I understand to be the American doctrine, conspicuously announced from time to time by the authorization of your Government.

President Jackson said in his message to Congress in 1836: "The uniform policy and practice of the United States is to avoid all interference in disputes which merely relate to the internal government of other nations, and eventually to recognize the authority of the prevailing party, without reference to the merits of the original controversy."

This principle of international law has been consistently recognized during the whole past intercourse of the two countries, and was recently reaffirmed in the instructions given by Secretary Gresham to Commissioner Blount on March 11, 1893, and by the latter published in the newspapers in Honolulu in a letter of his own to the Hawaiian public. The words of these instructions which I refer to are as follows: "The United States claim no right to interfere in the political or domestic affairs or in the internal conflicts of the Hawaiian Islands other than as herein stated (referring to the protection of American citizens) or for the purpose of maintaining any treaty or other rights which they possess." The treaties between the two countries confer no right of interference.

Upon what, then, Mr. Minister, does the President of the United States base his right of interference? Your communication is without information upon this point, excepting such as may be contained in the following brief and vague sentences: "She (the ex-Queen) was advised and assured by her ministers and leaders of the movement for the overthrow of her government that if she surrendered under protest her case would afterward be fairly considered by the President of the United States. The Queen finally yielded to the armed forces of the United States, then quartered in Honolulu, relying on the good faith and honor of the President, when informed of what had occurred, to undo the action of the minister and reinstate her and the authority which she claimed as the constitutional sovereign of the Hawaiian Islands." Also, "it becomes my further duty to advise you, sir, the Executive of the Provisional Government, and your ministers, of the President's determination of the question which your action and that of the Queen devolved upon him, and that you are expected to promptly relinquish to her her constitutional authority."

I understand that the first quotation is referred to in the following words of the second, "which your action and that of the Queen devolved upon him" (the President of the United States), and that the President has arrived at his conclusions from Commissioner Blount's report. We have had as yet no opportunity of examining this document, but from extracts published in the papers and for reasons set forth hereafter, we are not disposed to submit the fate of Hawaii to its statements and conclusions. As a matter of fact no member of the executive of the Provisional Government has conferred with the ex-Queen, either verbally or otherwise, from the time the new Government was proclaimed till now, with the exception of one or two notices which were sent to her by myself in regard to her removal from the palace and relating to the guards which the Government first allowed her and perhaps others of a like nature. I infer that a conversation which Mr. Damon, then a member of the advisory council, is reported by Mr. Blount to have had with the ex-Queen on January 17, and which has been quoted in the newspapers, is the basis of this astounding claim of the President of the United States of his authority to adjudicate upon our right as a government to exist.

Mr. Damon, on the occasion mentioned, was allowed to accompany the cabinet of the former Government, who had been in conference with me and my associates, to meet the ex-Queen. He went informally, without instructions and without authority to represent the Government or to assure the ex-Queen "that if she surrendered under protest her case would afterwards be fairly considered by the President of the United States." Our ultimatum had already been given to the members of the ex-cabinet who had been in conference with us. What Mr. Damon said to the ex-Queen he said on his individual responsibility and did not report it to us. Mr. Blount's report of his remarks on that occasion furnish to the Government its first information of the nature of those remarks. Admitting for argument's sake that the Government had authorized such assurances, what was "her case" that was afterwards to "be fairly considered by the President of the United States?"

Was it the question of her right to subvert the Hawaiian constitution and to proclaim a new one to suit herself, or was it her claim to be restored to the sovereignty, or was it her claim against the United States for the alleged unwarrantable acts of Minister Stevens, or was it all of these in the alternative; who can say? But if it had been all of these, or any of them, it could not have been more clearly and finally decided by the President of the United States in favor of the Provisional Government than when he recognized it without qualification and received its accredited commissioners, negotiated a treaty of annexation with them, received its accredited envoy extraordinary and minister plenipotentiary, and accredited successively two envoys extraordinary and ministers plenipotentiary to it; the ex-Queen in the meantime being represented in Washington by her agent who had full access to the Department of State.

The whole business of the Government with the President of the United States is set forth in the correspondence between the two governments and the acts and statements of the minister of this Government at Washington and the annexation commissioners accredited to it. If we have submitted our right to exist to the United States, the fact will appear in that correspondence and the acts of our minister and commissioners. Such agreement must be shown as the foundation of the right of your Government to interfere, for an arbitrator can be created only by the act of two parties.

The ex-Queen sent her attorney to Washington to plead her claim for a reinstatement in power, or failing that for a money allowance or damages. This attorney was refused passage on the Government dispatch boat which was sent to San Francisco with the annexation commissioners and their message. The departure of this vessel was less than two days after the new Government was declared, and the refusal was made promptly upon receiving the request therefor either on the day the Government was declared or on the next day. If an intention to submit the question of the reinstatement of the ex-Queen had existed, why should her attorney have been refused passage on this boat? The ex-Queen's letter to President Harrison dated January 18, the day after the new Government was proclaimed, makes no allusion to any understanding between her and the Government for arbitration. Her letter is as follows:

His Excellency BENJAMIN HARRISON
President of the United States:

MY GREAT AND GOOD FRIEND: It is with deep regret that I address you on this occasion. Some of my subjects aided by aliens, have renounced their loyalty and revolted against the constitutional Government of my Kingdom. They have attempted to depose me and to establish a provisional government in direct conflict with the organic law of this kingdom. Upon receiving incontestable proof that his excellency the minister plenipotentiary of the United States aided and abetted their unlawful movements and caused United States troops to be landed for that purpose, I submitted to force, believing that he would not have acted in that manner unless by the authority of the Government which he represents.

This action on my part was prompted by three reasons: The futility of a conflict with the United States; the desire to avoid violence, bloodshed and the destruction of life and property, and the certainty which I feel that you and your Government will right whatever wrongs have been inflicted upon us in the premises.

In due time a statement of the true facts relating to this matter will be laid before you, and I live in the hope that you will judge uprightly and justly between myself and my enemies. This appeal is not made for myself personally, but for my people, who have hitherto always enjoyed the friendship and protection of the United States.

My opponents have taken the only vessel which could be obtained here for the purpose, and hearing of their intention to send a delegation of their number to present their side of this conflict before you, I requested the favor of sending by the same vessel an envoy to you, to lay before you my statement, as the facts appear to myself and my loyal subjects.

This request has been refused, and I now ask you that in justice to myself and to my people that no steps be taken by the Government of the United States until my cause can be heard by you.

I shall be able to dispatch an envoy about the 2d of February, as that will be the first available opportunity hence, and he will reach you by every possible haste that there may be no delay in the settlement of this matter.

I pray you, therefore, my good friend, that you will not allow any conclusion to be reached by you until my envoy arrives.

I beg to assure you of the continuance of my highest consideration.

LILIUOKALANI R.

HONOLULU, *January 18, 1893*

If any understanding had existed at that time between her and the Government to submit the question of her restoration to the United States, some reference to such an understanding would naturally have appeared in this letter, as every reason would have existed for calling the attention of the President to that fact, especially as she then knew that her attorney would be seriously delayed in reaching Washington. But there is not a word from which such an understanding can be predicated. The Government sent its commissioners to Washington for the sole object of procuring the confirmation of the recognition by Minister Stevens of the new Government and to enter into negotiations for political union with the United States. The protest of the ex-Queen, made on January 17 is equally with the letter devoid of evidence of any mutual understanding for a submission of her claim to the throne to the United States. It is very evidently a protest against the alleged action of Minister Stevens as well as the new Government, and contains a notice of her appeal to the United States.

The document was received exactly as it would have been received if it had come through the mail. The indorsement of its receipt upon the paper was made at the request of the individual who brought it as evidence of its safe delivery. As to the ex-Queen's notice of her appeal to the United States, it was a matter of indifference to us. Such an appeal could not have been prevented, as the mail service was in operation as usual. That such a notice, and our receipt of it without comment, should be made a foundation of a claim that we had submitted our right to exist as a government to the United States had never occurred to us until suggested to us by your Government. The protest is as follows:

I, Liliuokalani, by the grace of God and under the constitution of the Hawaiian Kingdom, Queen, do hereby solemnly protest against any and all acts done against myself and the constitutional Government of the Hawaiian Kingdom by certain persons claiming to have established a provisional government of and for this Kingdom.

That I yield to the superior force of the United States of America, whose minister plenipotentiary, his excellency John L. Stevens, has caused United States troops to be landed at Honolulu, and declared that he would support the said Provisional Government.

Now, to avoid any collision of armed forces, and perhaps the loss of life, I do, under this protest, and impelled by said force, yield my authority until such time as the Government of the United States shall, upon the facts being presented to it, undo the action of its representative and reinstate me in the authority which I claim as the constitutional sovereign of the Hawaiian Islands.

Done at Honolulu the 17th day of January, A.D. 1893.

LILIUOKALANI, R.
SAMUEL PARKER
Minister of Foreign Affairs.
WILLIAM H. CORNWELL,
Minister of Finance.
JOHN F. COLBURN,
Minister of the Interior.
A. P. PETERSON,
Attorney-General.

S. B. DOLE, ESQ., and others,
Composing the Provisional Government of the Hawaiian Islands.

[Indorsed:] Received by the hands of the late cabinet this 17th day of January, A.D. 1893.

SANFORD B. DOLE,
Chairman of the Executive Council
of the Provisional Government.

You may not be aware, but such is the fact, that at no time until the presentation of the claim of the President of the United States to his right to interfere in the internal affairs of this country, by you on December 19, has this Government been officially informed by the United States Government that any such course was contemplated. And not until the publication of Mr. Gresham's letter to the President of the United States on the Hawaiian question had we any reliable intimation of such a policy. The adherents of the ex-Queen have indeed claimed from time to time that such was the case, but we have never been able to attach serious importance to their rumors to that effect, feeling secure in our perfect diplomatic relations with your country, and relying upon the friendship and fairness of a government whose dealings with us had ever shown full recognition of our independence as a sovereign power, without any tendency to take advantage of the disparity of strength between the two countries.

If your contention that President Cleveland believes that this government and the ex-Queen have submitted their respective claims to the sovereignty of this country to the adjudication of the United States is correct, then, may I ask, when and where has the President held his court of arbitration? This Government has had no notice of the sitting of such a tribunal and no opportunity of presenting evidence of its claims. If Mr. Blount's investigations were a part of the proceedings of such a court, this Government did not know it and was never informed of it; indeed, as I have mentioned above, we never knew until the publication of Secretary Gresham's letter to President Cleveland a few weeks ago, that the American Executive had a policy of interference under contemplation. Even if we had known that Mr. Blount was authoritatively acting as a commissioner to take evidence upon the question of the restoration of the ex-Queen, the methods adopted by him in making his investigations were, I submit, unsuitable to such an examination or any examination upon which human interests were to be adjudicated.

As I am reliably informed, he selected his witnesses and examined them in secret, freely using leading questions, giving no opportunity for a cross examination, and often not permitting such explanations by witnesses themselves as they desired to make of evidence which he had drawn from them. It is hardly necessary for me to suggest that under such a mode of examination some witnesses would be almost helpless in the hands of an astute lawyer, and might be drawn into saying things which would be only half-truths, and standing alone would be misleading or even false in effect. Is it likely that an investigation conducted in this manner could result in a fair, full, and truthful statement of the case in point? Surely the destinies of a friendly government, admitting by way of argument that the right of arbitration exists, may not be disposed of upon an *ex parte* and secret investigation made without the knowledge of such Government or an opportunity by it to be heard or even to know who the witnesses were.

Mr. Blount came here as a stranger and at once entered upon his duties. He devoted himself to the work of collecting information, both by the examination of witnesses and the collection of statistics and other documentary matter, with great energy and industry, giving up, substantially, his whole time to its prosecution. He was here but a few months, and during that time was so occupied with this work that he had little opportunity left for receiving those impressions of the state of affairs which could

best have come to him, incidentally, through a wide social intercourse with the people of the country and a personal acquaintance
with its various communities and educational and industrial enterprises. He saw the country from his cottage in the center of
Honolulu mainly through the eyes of the witnesses whom he
examined. Under these circumstances is it probable that the most
earnest of men would be able to form a statement that could
be safely relied upon as the basis of a decision upon the question
of the standing of a government?

In view, therefore, of all the facts in relation to the question of
the President's authority to interfere and concerning which the
members of the executive were actors and eyewitnesses, I am
able to assure your excellency that by no action of this Government, on the 17th day of January last or since that time, has the
authority devolved upon the President of the United States to
interfere in the internal affairs of this country through any conscious act or expression of this Government with such an intention.

You state in your communication—

"After a patient examination of Mr. Blount's reports the President is satisfied that the movement against the Queen if not
instigated was encouraged and supported by the representatives
of this Government at Honolulu; that he promised in advance
to aid her enemies in an effort to overthrow the Hawaiian Government and set up by force a new government in its place; that
he kept his promise by causing a detachment of troops to be
landed from the *Boston* on the 16th of January, 1893, and by
recognizing the Provisional Government the next day when it
was too feeble to defend itself and the Constitutional Government
was able to successfully maintain its authority against any threatening force other than that of the United States already landed."

Without entering into a discussion of the facts, I beg to state
in reply that I am unable to judge of the correctness of Mr.
Blount's report from which the President's conclusions were
drawn, as I have had no opportunity of examining such report.
But I desire to specifically and emphatically deny the correctness
of each and every one of the allegations of fact contained in the
above-quoted statement; yet, as the President has arrived at a
positive opinion in his own mind in the matter, I will refer to
it from his standpoint.

My position, is briefly, this: If the American forces illegally assisted the revolutionists in the establishment of the Provisional Government that Government is not responsible for their wrong-doing. It was purely a private matter for discipline between the United States Government and its own officers. There is, I submit, no precedent in international law for the theory that such action of the American troops has conferred upon the United States authority over the internal affairs of this government. Should it be true, as you have suggested, that the American Government made itself responsible to the Queen, who, it is alleged lost her throne through such action, that is not a matter for me to discuss, except to submit that if such is the case, it is a matter for the American Government and her to settle between them. This Government, a recognized sovereign power, equal in authority with the United States Government and enjoying diplomatic relations with it, can not be destroyed by it for the sake of discharging its obligations to the ex-Queen.

Upon these grounds, Mr. Minister, in behalf of my Government I respectfully protest against the usurpation of its authority as suggested by the language of your communication.

It is difficult for a stranger like yourself, and much more for the President of the United States, with his pressing responsibilities, his crowding cares and his want of familiarity with the condition and history of this country and the inner life of its people, to obtain a clear insight into the real state of affairs and to understand the social currents, the race feelings and the customs and traditions which all contribute to the political outlook. We, who have grown up here or who have adopted this country as our home, are conscious of the difficulty of maintaining a stable government here. A community which is made up of five races, of which the larger part but dimly appreciate the significance and value of representative institutions, offers political problems which may well tax the wisdom of the most experienced statesman.

For long years a large and influential part of this community, including many foreigners and native Hawaiians, have observed with deep regret the retrogressive tendencies of the Hawaiian monarchy, and have honorably striven against them, and have sought through legislative work, the newspapers, and by per-

sonal appeal and individual influence to support and emphasize
the representative features of the monarchy and to create a public
sentiment favorable thereto, and thereby to avert the catastrophe
that seemed inevitable if such tendencies were not restrained.
These efforts have been met by the last two sovereigns in a
spirit of aggressive hostility. The struggle became at length a
well-defined issue between royal prerogative and the right of
representative government, and most bitterly and unscrupulously
has it been carried on in the interests of the former. The King's
privilege of importing goods for his own use without paying
duties thereon was abused to the extent of admitting large quantities of liquors, with which to debauch the electorate. He promoted the election of Government officers, both executive and
judicial, to the legislative assembly, and freely appointed to office
elected members thereof.

In the Legislature of 1886, of which I was a member, the party
supporting the Government was largely in the majority, and
nearly every member of such majority held some appointment
from the Government, and some of them as many as two or
three, thereby effectually placing the legislative branch of the
Government under the personal and absolute control of the
King. The constitutional encroachments, lawless extravagance,
and scandalous and open sales of patronage and privilege to the
highest bidder by Kalakaua brought on at length the Revolution
of 1887, which had the full sympathy and moral support of all
the diplomatic representatives in Honolulu, including Minister
Merrill, who was at that time President Cleveland's minister here.

This revolution was not an annexation movement in any sense,
but tended toward an independent republic, but, when it had
the monarchy in its power, conservative counsels prevailed, and
a new lease of life was allowed that institution on the condition
of royal fidelity to the new constitution, which was then promulgated and which greatly curtailed the powers of the sovereign.
Kalakaua was not faithful to this compact, and sought as far
as possible to evade its stipulations. The insurrection of 1889
was connived at by him, and the household guards under his
control were not allowed to take part in suppressing it. The
Princess Liluokalani was in full sympathy with this movement,
being a party to it, and furnished her suburban residence to the

insurgents for their meetings. The arrangements were there made, and the insurgents marched thence for their attack upon the Government. The affair was suppressed in a few hours of fighting, with some loss of life to the insurgents, by the party which carried through the Revolution of 1887.

The ex-Queen's rule was even more reckless and retrogressive than her brother's. Less politic than he, and with less knowledge of affairs, she had more determination and was equally unreliable and deficient in moral principle. She, to all appearance, unhesitatingly took the oath of office to govern according to the constitution, and evidently regarding it merely as a formal ceremony began, according to her own testimony to Mr. Blount, to lay her plans to destroy the constitution and replace it with one of her own creation. With a like disregard of its sanctions, she made the most determined efforts to control all of the appointments to office, both executive and judicial. The session of the Legislature of 1892 was the longest that had ever occurred in our history, and was characterized by a most obstinate struggle for personal control of the Government and the legislature on the part of the Queen. This was strenuously resisted by the opposition.

During this contest four ministerial cabinets were appointed and unseated, and the lottery-franchise bill, which had been withdrawn early in the session for want of sufficient support, was at the last moment, when the opposition was weakened by the absence of several of its members, again brought forward and passed through the exercise of improper and illegitimate influences upon the legislators, among which were personal appeals on the part of the Queen to them. The cabinet which represented the opposition and the majority of the legislature which the Queen had been compelled to appoint was unseated by similar means, and with a new cabinet of her own choice the legislature was prorogued. This lottery franchise was of a character corresponding with similar institutions which have been driven out of every State of the American Union by an indignant public sentiment. If it had been established here it would in a brief period have obtained full control of the Government patronage and corrupted the social and political life of the people.

Although the situation at the close of the session was deeply discouraging to the community, it was accepted without any intention of meeting it by other than legal means. The attempted *coup d'etat* of the Queen followed, and her ministers, threatened with violence, fled to the citizens for assistance and protection; then it was that the uprising against the Queen took place, and, gathering force from day to day, resulted in the proclamation of the Provisional Government and the abrogation of the monarchy on the third day thereafter.

No man can correctly say that the Queen owed her downfall to the interference of American forces. The Revolution was carried through by the representatives, now largely reinforced, of the same public sentiment which forced the monarchy to its knees in 1887, which suppressed the insurrection of 1889, and which for twenty years has been battling for representative government in this country. If the American forces had been absent the Revolution would have taken place, for sufficient causes for it had nothing to do with their presence.

I, therefore, in all friendship of the Government of the United States, which you represent, and desiring to cherish the good will of the great American people, submit the answer of my Government to your proposition, and ask that you will transmit the same to the President of the United States for his consideration.

Though the Provisional Government is far from being "a great power" and could not long resist the forces of the United States in a hostile attack, we deem our position to be impregnable under all legal precedents, under the principles of diplomatic intercourse, and in the forum of conscience. We have done your Government no wrong; no charge of discourtesy is or can be brought against us. Our only issue with your people has been that, because we revered its institutions of civil liberty, we have desired to have them extended to our own distracted country, and because we honor its flag and, deeming that its beneficent and authoritative presence would be for the best interests of all of our people, we have stood ready to add our country, a new star to its glory, and to consummate a union which we believe would be as much for the benefit of your country as ours. If this is an offense, we plead guilty to it.

I am instructed to inform you, Mr. Minister, that the Provisional Government of the Hawaiian Islands respectfully and unhesitatingly declines to entertain the proposition of the President of the United States that it should surrender its authority to the ex-Queen.

This answer is made not only upon the grounds hereinbefore set forth, but upon our sense of duty and loyalty to the brave men whose commissions we hold, who have faithfully stood by us in the hour of trial, and whose will is the only earthly authority we recognize. We cannot betray the sacred trust they have placed in our hands, a trust which represents the cause of Christian civilization in the interests of the whole people of these islands.

With assurances of the highest consideration,

I have the honor to be, Sir,

Your Excellency's obedient servant,

SANFORD B. DOLE,
Minister of Foreign Affairs

His Excellency ALBERT S. WILLIS,
U.S. Envoy Extraordinary and Minister Plenipotentiary

PROVISIONAL GOVERNMENT AND REPUBLIC
1893–1897

HEARTENING indeed to the Honolulu of Black Week would have been knowledge of the strong, steady words in the foregoing chapter, could restrictions as to official secrecy have been lifted in Hawaii at that time. Certainly press representatives in the United States fell avidly upon the document the moment it was released in Washington.

The tenor of the preceding first state paper, Dole to Willis, is carried forward by its own clear reasoning. The Provisional Government had been founded by men of steady determination, most of whom were well versed in history and in legal procedure.

1. *Mr. Dole, Mr. Willis, the Queen*

That this reply to Willis was drafted and written by Sanford Dole seems obvious. Its very phrases, its steadfast courage bespeak his hand, its quiet logic his temperament and experienced legal mind. It is Dole who speaks, as it is indeed Dole who signs. Others in the Executive and Advisory Councils had worked on it with him, for from the start these men, pledged to a constitutional government for Hawaii, were remarkably unanimous in thought as in action. This close agreement carried them through difficult days and months and finally years, steadying their aim from the very first and winning for them in this instance that unintentional accolade from, of all men, Grover Cleveland: "This is an extraordinary document."

Nor, once Willis' demand and Dole's reply were made public, was the press of the United States slow to distinguish between the documents and the presidents. The *New York Sun* of January 16, 1894, stated:

No greater contrast, and to Americans no more gratifying, can be found in the Hawaiian correspondence than that between Mr. Cleveland's special message in December and Mr. Dole's recent response to the demand made by Mr. Willis for the surrender of the Provisional Government. Mr. Dole's paper mingles merited contempt for Cleveland's notions with deep admiration for the American people. In intellectual power, in logic, in common sense, Mr. Dole's paper towers far above the other.

The note of Americanism, such as Jefferson and Monroe and Marcy struck, comes in these documents from Honolulu, not from Washington. It is humiliating to see that the Hawaiian President teaches the Chief Magistrate of the United States what American sentiment is, and sets him a copy of what in tone and principle an American state paper should be. Judged by these two documents merely, it is Hawaii that should annex the United States; it is Dole that shows up as the fitter man to lead our sixty-five millions in international policy.

Think not for a moment however that at this point official correspondence ceased between United States Minister Willis and the executives of the Provisional Government. In the growing tension of Black Week, President Dole wrote on December 27 asking to be informed with the least delay whether the United States minister held instructions to enforce his demands by the use of arms. In reply, Minister Willis stalled, requesting seven specific definitions of terms used in Dole's letter. On the 29th of December the third official note from Dole to Willis announced wide-spread relief occasioned by the arrival of United States newspapers, stating that President Cleveland had referred the Hawaiian question to the "broader authority and discretion of the Congress." Willis' reply, delivered to Dole's private residence late at night, suggested official withdrawal of all his correspondence. On New Year's Day 1894 Dole answered briefly that nothing could be further from his intentions than to withdraw any of his official letters; he had written merely to inform the American minister that President Cleveland's special message to Congress rendered it unnecessary for the Provisional Government to press Willis for further reply to its question as to the possible use of armed force.

Still perplexed however as to President Dole's statement that the undefined and ambiguous attitude of the American minister had occasioned the terrors of Black Week, Willis persisted in requesting at early convenience the desired specifications.

Nothing, as it proved, was more welcome to the Provisional Government than to furnish just such specifications, affording as this did an opportunity to place on record the relations of the Provisional Government to the American administration since Cleveland's recall of the annexation treaty from the United States Senate. President Dole therefore requested Minister Thurston, who happened to be in Honolulu, to draft the reply, which was adopted by the Executive Council, with but slight modifications. Representing Dole's considered opinions, this also is classed among his important state documents.

This paper of January 11, 1894, covered more ground than Dole's first reply of December 23, 1893. Good reading today, it proves equally valuable as a historical record. It is above all a plain-speaking "indictment of American diplomacy," and nowhere more ably characterized than by an editorial in the *Philadelphia Press* of February 17, 1894. Without date or superscription this isolated clipping has lain these sixty years among Judge Dole's private papers, until just recently, 1954, identified for us by a most extraordinary service on the part of the Serials Division of the Library of Congress. This reflects the American view:

President Dole's letter of specifications is calm, circumspect, and studiously polite. Nothing could have been more maladroit than Mr. Willis' call for specifications. He might easily have repelled President Dole's general charge, or better still have ignored what could not be answered. But when, in seeking to defend his chief and his mission from a stinging accusation, he demanded particulars, he gave President Dole the opportunity of writing a letter which will stand forever as an unanswerable indictment and an overwhelming condemnation of President Cleveland's action on this subject from beginning to end.

The Hawaiian President is adroit, self-poised, dexterous in fence and unerring in logic. He thoroughly knows his ground in law and in reason and he holds it with a coolness, courage and confidence which are altogether admirable. In comparison with his deft art both [Secretary of State] Gresham and Mr. Willis appear like woodchoppers in diplomacy.

In eloquent and earnest terms he pictures the ties of commerce and friendship and blood which bind the people of Hawaii to the United States, their reverence for our flag, and their sincere devotion to our principles of liberty. They are of our own kith and kin. It is a strange irony of fate which compels a people thus seeking our alliance to stand on their guard and to resist and unmask the Government whose friendship they seek. No wonder that when Mr. Willis saw too late the rebuke to which he had opened himself, he begged Mr. Dole to withdraw his preliminary letter, and no wonder that President Cleveland has withheld the present terrific arraignment from Congress and deepened his own shame by letting it come to the American people in an irregular way. But it remains a blistering condemnation of both for all time to come.

Had cable communication with Hawaii existed, Black Week might have clouded Honolulu even more intensely than it actually did. For not until January 26, 1894, did the steamship *Warrimoo* bring from Vancouver a newspaper copy of Minister Willis' official dispatch No. 3. This reported to Washington his startling private interview of November 13, 1893, with former Queen Liliuokalani, in which he informed her of President Cleveland's stipulation that, if reinstated as queen, she grant full pardons to those who had overthrown the Hawaiian monarchy. Asked by Mr. Willis whether she would comply with this demand, she answered slowly and calmly that she would abide by the law of her country, which carried for traitors the death penalty with confiscation of property. Distinctly Mr. Willis repeated her words: "It is your feeling that these people should be beheaded and their property confiscated?" She replied, "It is. These people were the cause of the revolution and constitution of 1887. There will never be any peace while they are here."

This record remains today in reports of the United States Senate Committee on Foreign Relations, of which Senator Morgan was chairman. Willis could do no more than write the long way to Washington for further instructions. Meanwhile he continued to reason with the queen, pointing out that her restoration depended solely on her own attitude. Finally she yielded, insofar as to suggest the alternative penalty of banishment. But in Honolulu no word of this was made public by Minister Willis, who in Captain Barker's account, *Everyday Life in the Navy,* is given credit for having handled a difficult situation bravely and wisely.

Whispers of suspicion inevitably filled the air not only in Honolulu, but even in Washington and London. Through British supporters the queen's followers became confident that she would be reinstated by President Cleveland. Captain Rooke of the British warship *Champion* told Honolulu ladies that they must be ready to depart at a moment's notice; both he and Captain Togo of the Japanese cruiser *Naniwa* were ready to land troops at any hour for patrol duty while men from the U.S.S. *Phila-*

delphia were driving the Provisional Government out of the palace grounds.

This too is clearly told by Captain, afterward Rear Admiral, Barker, in his careful record of those days of stress. He perhaps as much as any other person was aware of the strain under which his friend President Dole and other members of the Provisional Government maintained customary routine while preparing state papers in reply to Minister Willis' questions and demands. Feeling against Mr. Willis at one time ran high, but he continued in office at Honolulu as United States minister for the rest of his life. "To a large extent," stated Judge Dole later, "Mr. Willis lived down the prejudices against him and won a high degree of public regard as a wise and faithful American official." Full military honors were accorded him on his death in 1897, even to his lying in state in the throne room of the palace.

2. *Convention and Republic*

The Provisional Government was admittedly a temporary arrangement predicated on annexation to the United States. Although feeling in Congress and in many sections of the Union favored this political move, the Hawaiian government became convinced that the Cleveland administration was fixed in its opposition to the annexation project. Establishment of a permanent form of government became therefore the next logical step for Hawaii. To this end the Provisional Government passed an Act calling for an election of eighteen delegates to join the nineteen Council members in a Constitutional Convention, these delegates to swear allegiance to the Provisional Government and opposition to the monarchy. Numbers of Royalists at once protested this Act 69 of the Provisional Government, declining to take this oath or to vote at the election.

Minister of Foreign Affairs F. M. Hatch, pointed out that the Provisional Government by "its very form invited interference from abroad; that the convention was frankly a war measure in part, was cosmopolitan in membership and represented a wide field of views."

Unknown to each other, both President Dole and Minister Thurston, the latter on his way home from Washington, began

work on tentative drafts of a constitution for the proposed Republic of Hawaii. These notes were submitted at daily meetings
with the executive council augmented by a number of representative men who went over every sentence with great deliberation,
but made no material changes. The resulting draft, in the main,
stated W. D. Alexander, "modeled after that of the United States,"
was printed and formed the basis of consideration for a constitution of the new Hawaiian republic. A galley proof of this draft
remains to this day among Judge Dole's papers.

One valuable source of help in shaping this document was
found in a published treatise, *Political Science and Comparative
Constitutional Law* by Professor J. W. Burgess, at that time
dean of the faculty of political science in Columbia University,
New York. President Dole discussed difficult points with the
author by letter, received wise suggestions in reply, and later
sent him printed copies of the first draft and the Constitution
as finally adopted by the Convention. This correspondence is
still on file in the manuscript collection of the Columbia University library.

Wrote Sanford Dole in April 1894 to his young niece Clara
in California, "We feel, that the work of getting a good constitution through is perhaps the most difficult task we have had yet.
I ride on horseback a good deal, generally early in the morning.
I have not been out much in the evenings, but when you come
for a long visit to renew your love for Hawaiian skies and mountains and seas, I will brace up and you shall never be without
an escort. I have no doubt that when your mother was away,
you were just as busy as I am with government business."

Gratifying it must have been to Sanford Dole and his colleagues
to receive later that year the American edition of the *Review
of Reviews,* in which Editor Albert Shaw's detailed analysis
stated in brief:

The new constitution of the Republic of Hawaii, impressively proclaimed at Honolulu on July 4 as the organic law of the Islands, is a
document whose provisions evince statesmanship of a high order. The
difficulties to be overcome were many and serious.

A very important feature is a body entitled the Council of State, to
serve without pay. Any one reasonably familiar with conditions in the
Hawaiian Islands can understand the advantage of this council, ready

at any moment of emergency to support the president and cabinet with advice and with the nation's moral as well as legal authority.

Not often in the history of constitution-making has a document of this character been more firmly and judiciously adapted to the precise conditions under which it would have to go into effect. And its operation will be observed with no little interest by students of political and legislative science.

On occasional drives into the valleys or out on the plains one whose companionship Sanford Dole valued was Captain Barker of the U.S.S. *Philadelphia.* The pleasure was mutual, Barker telling afterward in his autobiography of Dole's attractive personality and sound judgment, his fluency in Hawaiian and the affectionate respect in which he was held, especially among the Hawaiians. At times Dole would relate instances of devotion and patriotism among Provisional Government supporters which greatly sustained him in emergency and had made him confident of ultimate success.

For Captain Barker, the event of April 4, 1894, was a yachting party to Pearl Harbor. Mr. P. C. Jones was host, his guests including President Dole; Mr. G. N. Wilcox, "Prime Minister in the celebrated Wilcox Cabinet; Robert Wilcox who acted as pilot; Governor Wells from the United States; Rev. A. S. Twombly of Newton, Mass., Attorney-General W. O. Smith; Chief Justice Judd, Mr. Waterhouse and myself. We were more than three hours sailing in the open sea and in the Lochs of Pearl Harbor, where we saw in the distance Admiral Irwin's surveying party at work to discover the character of the bar at the entrance to the harbor."

The election of delegates to the Constitutional Convention, wrote Judge Dole later, had taken place "in an orderly manner; and the convention held its first sitting on May 30, 1894, in the court room of the Supreme Court. There was no pomp or ceremony observed. At eleven o'clock this hall, formerly used as the meeting place of the legislature, was crowded even to the doors and corridors."

Among special guests were Admiral Walker and his staff with Captain Barker and officers of the U.S.S. *Philadelphia;* the captain and officers of the Japanese man-of-war *Takachiho;* the Chief Justice and Justices of the Supreme Court; L. A. Thurston,

Hawaiian Minister at Washington; R. W. Irwin, Hawaiian Minister Resident at Tokyo.

After a prayer by the Rev. H. H. Parker, President Dole addressed the councilors and delegates on the

difficult and delicate character of the duty which the Convention is called upon to perform, in the civil progress of the State; believing that we may achieve success, if there is secured to all a system of impartial justice and wise administration, and if there is established in the minds of those who may be, from the exigencies of the situation, excluded from participation in the government, a sentiment of confidence in the integrity of the rulers. The final test of the work will be measured by our success in holding power without abusing it.

Permit me in closing to quote words of Washington as a member of the Convention which framed the Constitution of the United States of America: "If, to please the people, we offer what we ourselves disapprove, how can we afterward defend our work? Let us raise a standard to which the wise and honest can repair; the event is in the hands of God."

Of many spectators at subsequent sessions one of the most interested was the Rev. A. S. Twombly, acting pastor of Central Union Church. At these open sessions he found President Dole officiating as chaplain, and observed that the public press received a weekly statement of government expenses and receipts.

After twenty-three working days the final draft of the Constitution was adopted unanimously and signed by thirty-five members in session. In his closing remarks President Dole referred to the fact that not even persistent rumors of attack had affected the quiet routine of convention sessions, and that progressive reports on the work appearing in the daily press had produced an unexpected wave of sympathy sweeping the United States.

Attorney General W. O. Smith drew attention to the fact that supporters and leaders of the government, stigmatized as aliens, adventurers and filibusters, had assembled a convention consisting of "six native Hawaiians, fourteen Hawaiians born of foreign parents, nine Americans, three British, three Portuguese and two Germans; that all had resided here a long time and were fully identified with the country. Not one of them could be called an alien and those who stated that the Convention did not represent the Islands stated that which was not true."

"At least," remarked Judge Hatch later to the Hawaiian Historical Society, "the Convention put an end to the accusation that the Provisional Government consisted of eighteen men representing nobody. The constitution which was the child of its deliberations has the distinction of being the only Hawaiian constitution considered in convention. Without protest from any quarter the Republic of Hawaii had taken its place in the world without disorder and without show of armed force. It was a government accepted by the community."

Of no slight significance is it to find that the first and last resolutions of the Convention were proposed by Hawaiians. On May 30, Delegate Kalua, "Circuit Judge for Maui, a good lawyer, a brilliant orator and one of the Reform Party in 1887 and 1893," moved for recess to observe the American tradition of Decoration Day. On the 3d of July Delegate Prince Albert Kukailimoku Kunuiakea, a descendant of the Kamehameha line, brought the Convention to its feet "to express appreciation of the President's modesty, courage and patience during session deliberations; hearty thanks for his courteous tact; and earnest wishes for his continued success in administering the government of the Hawaiian Republic."

Many still recall that sunny morning of the 4th of July, 1894, when, as the *Gazette* and Thrum's *Annual* reported, from the front steps of the Executive Building, the new Hawaiian Ship of State was launched on its voyage. Essentially a civil service, not a soldier was ordered out for it, the only uniforms in sight being those worn by staff and line officers.

Long before eight o'clock the crowd began to gather on the steps and balconies of the Capitol. When President Dole moved through the groups around the doors and went down the steps to the middle platform, he was greeted with cheers and applause. He stood for a minute, looking down on the people whose interests he had watched over so closely during the last eighteen months, and then began to read a short address ending in the proclamation which changed the government of the Islands from a temporary to a permanent one.

Reviewing rapidly the movement toward popular government begun as early as 1839, when Kamehameha III voluntarily surrendered his unlimited power, and not long afterward instituted the Great Mahele (Division) of Hawaiian lands, the speaker noted the Constitutions of 1852, 1864, 1887, 1893, and lastly 1894, expressing his hope "that freedom shall never come to mean license in the vocabulary of the Republic." Then he proclaimed the Republic of Hawaii the sovereign authority over the Hawaiian Islands, himself "by virtue of its constitution assuming office and authority as President thereof. God save the Republic!"

Hardly had this invocation died upon his lips, when a native Hawaiian, from the crowd in front, started "three cheers for President Dole," which was caught up heartily by the throng. The address and proclamation, read in Hawaiian by Delegate Kalua, were again greeted with cheers.

Chief Justice Judd, in his robe of office, thereupon administered the oath to the President, at which a new thirty-six-foot Hawaiian flag was flung to the breeze from the central flagstaff of the building, the signal for the cannon's boom of a national salute, with the familiar notes of *Hawaii Ponoi* from the band, proclaiming the birth of the new Republic.

3. *Necker Island and the British Cable*

More than one point posed a problem for the Hawaiian government in the matter of a trans-Pacific cable proposed by the British, Canadian, and Australian governments.

In 1857, when the Hawaiian monarchy had sent an expedition to take possession of the thousand-mile chain of islands and reefs from Hawaii northwest to Midway, no landing had been possible on Necker, a rocky islet about four hundred miles northwest of Kauai. In May 1894 Curtis J. Lyons, assistant in charge of the government survey office at Honolulu, became aware that British Navy men, coming into the office ostensibly for a routine time check with the Hawaiian government chronometer, appeared to be moved by a barely concealed, but very detailed interest in maps of this uninhabited island of Necker. Also, report had it that at this very time Her British Majesty Victoria's warship *Champion,* in port at Honolulu, was readying for target practice in Hawaiian waters.

Unable to get out of his mind the thought of a possible British cable landing at Necker, Curtis Lyons talked with his life-long friend, S. B. Dole. After consultation with Admiral Walker, commanding the Pacific Station of the United States Navy, a special Cabinet meeting of the Provisional Government authorized chartering the fast interisland steamer *Iwalani* and dispatching her without delay under command of Captain King, Minister of the Interior, to take formal possession of Necker. This was done on May 27, 1894, with a proclamation by the Hawaiian government. Much of this story was put together for the Hawaiian Historical Society by Surveyor General W. D. Alexander, supplemented in a later account, *American Polynesia and the Hawaiian Chain,* by E. H. Bryan, Jr., of the Bishop Museum.

Newspaper gossip of course proclaimed at once that the *Iwalani* and the cruiser *Champion* were racing neck and neck for this tiny rock in the Pacific. More than a few illuminating sidelights are thrown on the subject by Captain Barker of the U.S.S. *Philadelphia* which was moored near the British warship in Honolulu harbor. When on the 31st of May the *Champion* returned after a five-day practice cruise, her commander, Captain Rooke, happening to meet Captain Barker, at once voiced his annoyance over preposterous stories as to a race between a British warship and an interisland steamer. Rooke had had no intention, he asserted, of proceeding to Necker Island; furthermore, he considered the dispatching of the *Iwalani* an insult to England, and one which his government would resent, particularly since peaceful negotiations were under way at that very time between Great Britain and the Provisional Government, with a view toward the landing of a cable on that island. Captain Barker refrained from remarking that he himself was well aware of this fact.

Five months later, in October, 1894, the British Pacific-Cable Commission made formal application to the Hawaiian Cabinet for a long lease of Necker, but was informed that, according to the Hawaiian reciprocity treaty with the United States, no such action was possible without consent of the Congress of the United States. When the Hawaiian Cabinet, through Minister Willis, referred the matter to Washington, President Cleveland construed the referral as a request, and recommended it with the comment that Hawaii "has no fear of British aggression." Both Houses of Congress expressed disapproval, without taking definite action.

On September 24, 1894, Curtis Lyons had written urgently to President Dole:

We owe a deep and over-mastering duty to America in the matter of a cable route. It is not likely that England and America will ever go to war, but it *may* happen. And a *calling station* for orders to their naval forces, within striking distance of Pearl River, would be a most vital advantage which America should not allow to be in England's possession.

British power can make Necker Island habitable easily enough, although Admiral Walker seemed not to think so. Under whatever understanding they establish themselves there, they will never leave the island.

Please excuse my earnestness on this subject.

During the following summer, in July 1895, Captain King, dispatched officially as Minister of the Interior to the French Frigate Shoals, made a landing once more at Necker. He reported officially to the Hawaiian government that he had found the flag pole down, the Hawaiian flag gone, and inserted in its engraved copper cylinder a note stating that officers of H.B.M.S. *Champion* had surveyed Necker on September 24, 1894, the very day, as it happened, on which Curtis Lyons had written his anxious letter.

For thirty years this battered, oxidized copper cylinder was cherished by the late W. H. D. King of Honolulu. For in 1923 it was brought home as a relic by his younger brother, Hawaii's present governor, Samuel Wilder King, who as Lieutenant Commander in the United States Navy had that year conveyed to Necker a scientific company of Bishop Museum authorities.

Also to this day Curtis Lyons' daughter, Mrs. Emma Lyons Doyle, recalls the concern with which her father told in 1894 of the prolonged interest displayed among British Navy men in the Hawaiian chronometer at the Survey Office. Nor has she forgotten hearing months later a spirited street-car conversation between two elegant young English ladies obviously well acquainted with officers of H.B.M.S. *Champion*. "Why, of course [loudly] the *Champion* was off on target practice on May 27th 1894." But by whispered asides intended as Greek to the ears of a little American girl, the ladies implied that they were well informed as to the more serious state business pursued at Necker by British Navy men.

Passions ran high in Honolulu at that time. It is therefore but fair to add that contemporary official correspondence, recently acquired in microfilm by the University of Hawaii, discloses no actual controversy between the British government and

Hawaii as to the ownership of Necker; nor did the British dispute Hawaiian sovereignty. It was, moreover, authoritatively reported that the *Champion* was merely going out on routine target practice for a few days.

4. *Insurrection of 1895*

Notwithstanding the peaceful establishment of Hawaii's republic, rumors of Royalist opposition continued to indicate that an uprising on Oahu would follow arrival of a vessel freighted with arms and ammunition. Under Marshal Hitchcock, formerly of Hilo, the police force at Honolulu kept in close touch with the plot. It was learned that the schooner *Wahlberg* with a cargo of rifles and ammunition had cleared from San Francisco in November 1894, and some time later was seen standing off the windward coast of Oahu for a week. On the first Thursday afternoon of January, 1895, groups of Hawaiians began to gather without apparent cause at Kakaako, the entrance to Honolulu harbor at the foot of Alakea Street, near the old tow path for incoming vessels. Just as gradually however as they had appeared, these people, on the approach of a police detective, began to melt away.

Thwarted thus in their reported plan to land arms at the waterfront, take possession of the police station near by, and surprise the Honolulu garrisons, the insurgents beached their munitions at Kahala, two miles east of Diamond Head. On Saturday night, January 5, the rifles buried there in the sand were dug up and distributed to followers, who on Sunday evening began to move cautiously along the shore westward toward Honolulu.

It will be recalled that sixty years ago the Kahala and Kaalawai beaches on Diamond Head's eastern slope edged a distant and sparsely built, often dry and deserted country section, by no means the well-watered and populous residence suburb within fifteen minutes of town by car as we know it today.

About five o'clock that Sunday evening word was brought to the Attorney General and Marshal at headquarters that arms were concealed in the H. F. Bertelmann home at Waikiki. At once a number of government supporters near Kapiolani Park hastily armed themselves and joined Captain Robert Waipa Parker, a prominent Hawaiian leader of police detectives. From the Charlie Carter place near Bertelmann's came Carter himself with his cousin, Alfred Carter, also James Castle and A. L. C. Atkinson, with a policeman to serve the official search warrant for Bertelmann's house. Both Carters were young lawyers, Charles on President Dole's staff.

According to Alfred Carter's later account, armed Royalists in the canoe shed opened fire on them in a sharp skirmish. Charlie Carter dropped, conscious but mortally wounded. With the policeman, Alfred Carter kept on, whereupon all the insurgents, some seventy in number, started to run. Alfred Carter succeeded in getting his wounded cousin back to his house, where three physicians pronounced the wound not fatal. Calmly, Charlie Carter told them all that he would not live. At daybreak he was gone.

Bertelmann was taken into custody, and called out an order to cease fire. Many of the insurgents escaped up Diamond Head cliffs and scattered into the hills.

Hourly meetings of the Executive Council were held at the Capitol with frequent debate as to proclaiming martial law. About midnight, in the need for a secretary to the council, President Dole summoned from sentry duty a young attorney, Benjamin L. Marx, member of National Guard, Company B, who took up his abode at officers' quarters in the former royal bungalow close to the palace. Many years later Marx related for the Honolulu Social Science Association recollections from what he called his ringside seat at headquarters.

On Monday morning, January 7, martial law was declared. A disciplined government force under Captain Ziegler shelled the Diamond Head slope with a field piece, the gunner on shore aided by a second field piece operated by Captain J. W. Pratt from the deck of the tug *Eleu* dispatched from town. Major George Potter of the President's staff rode up and down the battle line, President Dole remonstrating with him for running the risk of being shot. Dispersed into the hills and valleys without food, some of the insurgents surrendered, and many were soon captured. Dole's subsequent reports pointed out that the insurgent forces had counted on taking Honolulu at the outset of hostilities and there commandeering ample food supplies without need of a previously organized commissariat.

In three days the insurrection was over. Yet for some time every precaution was taken, no one being allowed on the streets at night without a pass from military or police headquarters. With light touch of memory Marx sketched in his appointment during the excitement as bodyguard to President Dole, the commission issued by someone at headquarters without the formality of advising him. Setting out as usual to walk home from headquarters, President Dole chanced to look back to find young Marx following at a respectful distance, armed with cartridge belt and revolver.

"What do you think you are doing?" asked Dole. Marx informed him of his recent appointment as bodyguard to the President. Without comment, Dole returned to headquarters, and as commander in chief of Hawaii's army and navy, removed the onus of one superfluous military assignment.

"I was relieved," adds Marx, "in more ways than one, because, being the sort of pistol shot I am, the president was in real danger."

Appointed in 1896 as secretary of the Executive Council, and in 1898 as secretary to Sanford B. Dole, on the commission for framing the Organic Act, young Marx, as confidential secretary to all of the departments, was brought, he writes

into daily and intimate contact with members of the cabinet, and the better I knew them, the more I admired them.

Sanford Ballard Dole, was a noble character, trusted by everyone in the community, even by the Royalists. He was an idealist with clear vision of the future under the American flag, combined with great firmness and courage.

Francis March Hatch, Minister of Foreign Affairs, was one of the able leaders of the Hawaiian bar, and had one of the keenest, shrewdest minds I ever encountered. He had need of all his sagacity in meeting the needs of the infant republic.

James Anderson King, Minister of the Interior, was port captain for the Wilder Steamship Company. He had great strength of character and a fund of common sense that made him an extremely useful member of the Cabinet.

Samuel Mills Damon, Minister of Finance, was an experienced banker and head of the Bank of Bishop and Company. He was a man of great gentleness and charm of manner.

William Owen Smith, Attorney General, was a forceful and resourceful man, and a natural-born fighter. I shall never forget seeing him in action as president of the Board of Health, stamping out the cholera epidemic in September, 1895.

Foreseeing some such emergency as the insurrection, or the cholera epidemic of the same year, framers of the Constitution for the Hawaiian republic had provided for a special Council of State which could appropriate treasury funds without the necessity of calling a special session of the Legislature. Consisting of fifteen members, five appointed by the House, five by the Senate, and five by the executive, this council was subject to call at any time and served without pay. At its meetings members of the Executive Council might sit and take part in discussions without voting, as in legislative sessions. Strict account of emergency appropriations thus made was rendered to the next Legislature by the Minister of Finance.

One of Sanford Dole's first personal letters after the insurrection was written to a lifelong friend, Mrs. Sybil Augusta Carter, whose son had given his life for his country. As soon as she could, Mrs. Carter replied from the old Judd homestead in Nuuanu:

SWEET HOME
January 15, 1895

PRESIDENT DOLE,

My loved friend:

Your letter sustains me, because its thoughts are so noble.

My own sorrow is laid aside—I must send my aloha, and say, Be Strong. —I am calm, forgiving, but we must stop this state of things forever, after all the best natives have done in helping you. Our noble defenders must be thought of first.

I have faith in your justice, that you will not be faint-hearted.

Give my message to my dear friend, W. O. Smith. I want you to feel my strength attend you in your great responsibility. If you hesitate, you are lost. This is the message of a tender-hearted woman.

SYBIL AUGUSTA CARTER

Writing on the 11th of January, Dole told his brother's family in California:

We all feel Charlie Carter's death very much; it is a great loss. But the hostilities then begun brought on the rebellion before the insurgents were ready, disconcerted their plans and caused the fighting to be carried on out of town, instead of in town as they intended. We learn that the plan was to attack the city near midnight, several bodies moving in from different directions to inaugurate a reign of terror with fire and guns and bombs, hoping to overpower our forces at the Capitol and those outside before they could get together. The rebellion seems to be broken. We are searching for Robert Wilcox and Nowlein and their remaining followers in the mountains.

The spirit of our men, regulars, volunteers, sharpshooters, police and Citizens' Reserve, is all that could be desired. There is no skulking or holding back, the men cheerfully encountering any danger or hardship.

I have slept at home the last two nights, the previous three nights at the Executive Building, when I slept at all, and Anna at the Allens'.

Following repeated discussions in the Executive Council, two policemen were sent, on the 16th of January, to Washington Place to arrest the queen. Although she was protected there by thirty-five guards, no resistance was made, and the queen with one lady-in-waiting was taken to the former palace and placed under custody in two large rooms at the south corner of the second floor.

Detailed that night to accompany officers and men from headquarters, B. L. Marx proceeded with this squad to search the queen's residence. On her desk they found a fragment of a cement bomb, and in a pit in the garden arms, ammunition, and bombs sufficient to warrant charging the queen with misprision of treason, that is, omitting to report treason or felony of which she was cognizant.

To try the insurrectionists a military court was organized under Judge Whiting of the Supreme Court, with Judge W. A. Kinney as Judge Advocate, assisted by Deputy Attorney General A. G. M. Robertson and Attorney Alfred Carter. Paul Neumann, the queen's attorney, was counsel for the defense. The trials were held in the former throne room with morning and afternoon sessions, Attorneys Arthur Wilder and Benjamin Marx alternating as official court reporters. Years afterward Marx recalled vividly the dignity and poise of Queen Liliuokalani under trial; also that picturesque figure, her nephew, Prince Kuhio; with Robert Wilcox, trained in the military science of Italy; and Lot Lane, a magnificent specimen of manhood.

In thirty-five days one hundred and ninety cases were tried. The three death sentences required approval by President and Cabinet. Both United States Minister Willis and British Commissioner Hawes intervened earnestly for remission of the death penalty, supposing that all danger was over. Attorney General W. O. Smith replied that a large part of the arms, ammunition, and bombs were still in the hands of the insurgents.

The queen however was released after a few months of mild imprisonment, during which she signed and sent to President Dole her formal abdication and her oath of allegiance to the Republic of Hawaii. Mitigated to imprisonment and fines, the three death sentences were modified by the reviewing authority, a term more specifically phrased by historians Kuykendall and Day as "on the insistence of President Dole and a substantial body of public opinion." Before the end of the year all those under sentence of imprisonment were released.

Mr. Dole felt that the failure of this attempt by the Royalists had been due to its early discovery by the government and the orderly, resolute manner in which the suppression had been conducted, yet without animosity. Nor did anyone question its effectiveness in creating a feeling of intense relief in the community at large. Things Mr. Dole did not mention were the long days and nights he himself spent poring over evidence given before the Commissioners and their findings from every standpoint, as shown by Ed. Towse in his *The Rebellion of 1895*. At times the President called in Cabinet officers and brought up many points before the Advisory Council. Personal hearings were arranged for families, friends, and counsel of prisoners whose future lay in the keeping of this patient, calm, unpretending gentleman whom everyone knew, to whom anyone might turn, and whom all regarded with trust and respect.

For sixty years a worn half-sheet from the front page of the *Pacific Commercial Advertiser* has lain folded among Judge Dole's papers. This tells, exclusively by the issue of March 20, 1895, of President Dole attending with other friends and members of the Hawaiian Bar Association a joint session of the Supreme Court and Bar Association. B. L. Marx acted as court stenographer for this meeting which was out of respect to the memory of Charles L. Carter and Henry N. Castle. Both these young lawyers had believed that Hawaii was worth living for and worth dying for. As a forcible, fluent speaker Mr. Carter had been particularly gifted in his support of the deliberations

Mr. and Mrs. George H. Dole and family at Riverside in 1906

President and Mrs. Dole at Oakland Mole on their return
from Washington

Photograph presented to President Dole by Dr. T. A. Hassler, U.S.S. Baltimore

Manning the yards for President Dole in Honolulu harbor

of the recent Constitutional Convention, and in the springtime of life had met sudden death unflinchingly. Mr. Castle, as editor of the *Advertiser* for the four years from 1889 to 1893, had fearlessly opposed political corruption, knowing, as all knew, that he was at any moment fair mark for an assassin's bullet. Thinking, after 1893, that Hawaii lay safe in harbor after weathering revolutionary storms, Castle had returned to Germany for further study. On learning of the insurrection early in 1895, he had sailed at once for home with his little daughter, only to meet death in the sinking of his ship among Atlantic icebergs.

Judge Hartwell paid quiet, eloquent tribute to Henry Castle's unusual qualities of mind and achievement in Hawaii's constitutional triumph. So spoke also J. A. Magoon and Judge Perry. For Charles Carter spoke Deputy Attorney General Robertson, Minister of Foreign Affairs F. M. Hatch, likewise Queen's Counselor Paul Neumann, and S. K. Ka-ne of the Council of State. At this notable session were gathered many of Hawaii's ablest minds to record the lives of these two young colleagues and pay a last fitting tribute of public honor.

5. *Honolulu 1894–97*

On the occasion in May, 1894, of Robert Louis Stevenson's being made a corresponding member of the Hawaiian Historical Society, Dr. N. B. Emerson remarked that no full century of Hawaii's history had drawn to its affairs a tithe of the attention given to it by civilized nations during the twelve-month of 1893 to 1894. This continued to be true of immediately succeeding years, whose texture, while threaded thickly with events leading to political amalgamation with the United States, was interwoven at the same time with many a consideration of more personal moment.

When in April, 1894, Sanford Dole attained his fiftieth year, the editor of the *Hawaiian Gazette* commented on the fact that, while he had long commanded island-wide respect, it had taken the stimulus of doubts, difficulties, and dangers to bring out latent qualities of leadership, of courage and steadfastness, which he possessed. Surrounded as he had been by a band of earnest, conscientious men, he had raised the moral level of government administration, and in the hour of tribulation had been, as the best men always are, "Fed from within with all the strength he needs."

The following April President Dole still maintained his democratic objection to any official observance of his birthday. On the evening of the 23rd however, while he and his wife were quietly reading at home, they suddenly looked up in amazement to behold their front steps invaded by some seventy old-time friends, mostly Dole's schoolmates, each carrying a *hookupu* for his chief: a chicken, a few eggs tied in a cloth, carnations, roses, mangoes, grapes, figs tied in ti leaves, fans and mats, a squash, a bunch of bananas, another of coconuts and two small squealing pigs.

Pushing across the wide veranda to the parlor, each guest chanted as he crouched to lay tribute at the feet of the *alii,* some calling out, "Alo-ha, Maikai," (You are looking well,) and "Elemakule no oe," (You are getting to be an old fellow). Adepts like Lorrin Thurston kept up a quavering Hawaiian chant, while the last carried in two immense stalks of sugar cane, bent into an arch enclosing the whole *hookupu* like a rainbow. All was in great good fun of course, yet with seriousness too and an overtone of homesickness for the old Hawaii which had already passed beyond recall. Fortunately this story was related by Sereno Bishop in detail to Consul General Gorham D. Gilman in Boston.

Perhaps to prevent further surprises in 1896, a year later, after spending the forenoon quietly at home, the Doles welcomed first the Hawaiian band, then later, in "a strictly Jeffersonian manner" hosts of friends and strangers. Even this early in the year their favorite tree at the end of the house must have been hanging out its banners and showers of gold to lend glory to the shaded garden.

The summer of 1895 had been devoted by President Dole to the special legislative session of fifty days from June 12 to August 15. His message to this body explained the advisability of terminating the temporary legislative authority of the Executive and Advisory Councils by re-establishing the regular legislative function of the government. In addition, the President commended for special consideration a liberal land policy which, with amendments, became the law for over fifty years. Also, he urged government participation in the matter of submarine cable communication with North America, lacking which Hawaii must continue to remain isolated from the outer world.

Talking with a mainland friend by private letter on July 30, 1895, Mr. Dole admitted himself much pleased with the attitude of the legislators toward his comprehensive land act, favoring settlement of citizens on small farms owned and cultivated by the holders. Also, much had been gained, he felt, by the change from a one-house to a two-house legislature, a feature which might in all probability have extended the life of the monarchy by many years.

Referring in this letter to the recent severe epidemic of cholera which had installed the Board of Health as the temporary government, Mr. Dole mentioned Board President W. O. Smith and his assistants as making an enviable record, hundreds of volunteers carrying out a rigid twice-daily house-to-house inspection of the city. In more ways than one the emergency demonstrated "a fine public spirit that is the strength of the Republic, and in some measure swamped political divisions of the community, bringing many Royalists into normal relations with the Government, which may be said to have given them a new horizon. It has been a training school of faith and dependence upon the divine goodness and strength."

S. B. Dole and W. O. Smith had, since their Koloa boyhood, been so closely associated that an estimate of them by Judge Robertson, a distinguished Island contemporary, had particular point. He stated:

It is no secret that, during the uncertain and restless careers of the Provisional Government and the Republic, the man upon whom Mr. Dole principally depended to keep the government operating on an even keel was W. O. Smith. He was Dole's right hand man. He was an exceptionally active, methodical man, a prodigious worker.

It does not require a very great stretch of imagination to see an analogy between the struggles of the American national fathers which culminated in the adoption of the Constitution of 1787, and those of the leaders of Hawaii in the annexation of these islands in 1898. Both endeavored to make a monarch see the error of his ways and to realize that the course pursued could not be successfully maintained. Both drifted with many misgivings toward another form of government, attained the new position almost before they realized it, and then vigorously defended it with the use of force. The local situation was of course all in miniature. Compared with its prototype it was like looking through the large end of a telescope;

nevertheless the analogy was there. From this viewpoint it is not difficult
to see a resemblance between the characters of George Washington and
Sanford Dole, although Washington is said to have had a well deserved
reputation for punctuality.

Mr. Dole had been the leader of the Opposition in the legislature during
the middle '80's, and when the monarchy collapsed in 1893, though then
a justice of the Supreme Court, a position to which the King had appointed him to keep him out of politics, he was looked upon as the logical
man to head the new government, in much the same way that Washington
was looked up to in his time. The former was no less the father of the
Territory of Hawaii than was the latter the father of his great country.

In the same way we can see in W. O. Smith the Benjamin Franklin
of Hawaii. The philosopher, statesman, humorist, man of the world, man
of affairs, the man to whom his associates would look in an emergency to
find a ready solution for a difficult or troublesome problem.

Such a man was W. O. Smith in his prime—a good man, an able
man, a genial man, alert, forceful, dignified and of sound judgment.

Personally, the year 1897 brought for Sanford Dole happy
renewal from a distance of association with the Williams classmates of 1867. To distinguish the anniversary, the college, of
which Dole was not formally a graduate, honored itself by conferring upon him the degree of Doctor of Laws. And the college
annual released for publication in the *Boston Globe* his letter
embodying a concise review of the gradual steps toward competent representation in Hawaii's political evolution.

Not a few were the public improvements completed or initiated
under Hawaii's Republic. One of these which aroused wide-
spread public interest was the transformation of the trail from
Hilo to Kilauea Volcano into a thirty-mile paved road, a project
begun in 1889 under the dynamic interest of L. A. Thurston,
then Minister of the Interior. Progress described in his official
report for 1890 notes keen disappointment in Hilo on the premature expiration of government appropriations. At this, public-
spirited citizens of Honolulu advanced funds to continue without
interruption, trusting to be reimbursed by the next Legislature.

Before very long four-horse stages made the run daily, six
and a half hours up, five and a half down, with a long rest at
Mountain View House, Olaa. Sereno Bishop described it in *The
Friend* for September 1894 as opening up fine country to home
seekers, both for coffee up to 2,500 feet elevation and small farms
on clearings in the virgin forest from the thirteenth mile post on

mauka. At twenty dollars a ton, freight wagons with four-horse teams delivered supplies and lumber to settlers' new cottages, loading for the down trip with first-quality firewood piled ready in quantities along the roadside. The appropriation of $3,000 per mile, or a total of $90,000 would, it was confidently believed, be returned in taxes within a few years.

As well as Hilo, Honolulu could boast enlarged harbor facilities and street extensions, with a major project for changing and walling in the course of the lower Nuuanu Stream. This included cutting Vineyard Street through from the stream south to Punchbowl. Don Marin's vineyard had given the street its name, but today the only other relic of his orchard there is the great torso of his first mango tree north of the present stream. Farther south just beyond Nuuanu Street stands to this day what *kamaainas* still call the "Dole Tree," a huge monkey-pod in the middle of the street with its roots hidden in the stream below. No great hazard for horse-drawn traffic, it had been saved from slaughter by the President of the Republic in 1897, but is now being doomed by city fathers who must plan for automotive speed and congestion. One citizen, Mrs. C. B. Wood, was so grateful for the President's intervention that she called her infant son Sanford Ballard Dole Wood, a name which has accompanied him to a place of distinction in the legal department of the United States Navy.

Even more spectacular was the widening and re-grading of the Nuuanu Pali Road for 600 feet at its Honolulu approach and well over 700 feet on its sharp downward turns toward Kaneohe. Daniel Logan tells of this in that storehouse of Hawaiian lore, Thrum's *Hawaiian Annual.* The shortest route to the windward side of the island had long been a steep, winding track with its three guards, the *aumakua* of the pass, a pointed rock still bowed to by travelers, and the two towering peaks, Lanihuli to the north and Konahuanui to the south. Over the windy pass daily pack trains, with their motley conductors, brought produce to market and took city purchases back. In saddle and on foot, no inconsiderable amount of traffic wound its way across, even small wheeled vehicles however proceeding seldom, and at their peril.

Long under discussion, the new road did not begin to materialize until the Legislature of 1896 devoted $40,000 to the project. How small a fraction this, of the present-day bid of over $300,000 for half a mile construction to widen the central Pali Road! In 1897 this early appropriation permitted awarding the contract to a new firm of engineers trained at Stanford University, the late J. H. Wilson and L. M. Whitehouse; the latter a Californian, the former, destined to be many times mayor of Honolulu, was the son of C. B. Wilson, last Marshal of the Hawaiian Kingdom. By September 30, 1897, over 200 workmen, bringing the formidable project to conclusion, stood ready to handle the final and largest blast of more than a ton of dynamite to remove a dangerous rocky ledge overhanging the new route at the *pali* itself. Hundreds of residents and officials, among them Sanford Dole on horseback, rode, drove, walked or pedaled up toward the pass in time for the spectacle.

The observer of the artificial volcano might have imagined himself transported back ages unknown to Oahu's molten period. Daring hands lighted one fuse after another of the nineteen cells, and scampered for safety. Breath was held for a few seconds. Then the fated ledge belched out in smoke and dust with a muffled roar. Cell after cell exploded, none missing fire or due effect. Great windrows of forest trees inverted, mingled with boulders tons heavy, all involved in avalanches of red earth, rose and hurtled reluctantly a few yards high, then crashed and rolled down the abyss, the conglomeration piling itself an everlasting barricade across the ancient trail a thousand feet below. Yet with all the six to eight hundred tons dislodged, the scenery was scarred but a faint pin scratch by the sacrifice.

Chapter XV

ANNEXATION AND GOVERNORSHIP
1898–1903

OWING primarily to their relative geographic position political union of the Hawaiian Islands with the United States of America had been much in the thoughts of both statesmen and the man on the street for far longer even than a half-century.

1. *Annexation 1840–1898*

As early as 1840, when ships from England, France, and Russia were making frequent landfall at the Sandwich Islands, Commodore Wilkes of the United States Exploring Expedition declared that, like Oregon and California, these Islands must ultimately become a valuable part of the United States of America. Fearing filibusters from without and disturbance within, Kamehameha III authorized negotiations toward a treaty for annexation as a state of the American Union in 1854, but died before discussion with the United States could be concluded. Both Kamehameha IV and his older brother, Kamehameha V, looked rather to England and strongly opposed American influence.

Kalakaua indeed signed the ratification of the first treaty of commercial reciprocity with the United States. And in his later years became a legendary figure in the coral stone house of the McGrew family on Hotel Street, where he frequently drove in of a late afternoon for a frosted mint julep. Known as the Father of Annexation, good Dr. McGrew was not slow, even in such august company, to dwell on his vision of Hawaii's future. "Your idea is all right," the king once told him, "but wait till I am gone before you push it too far."

313

Admittedly temporary measures, both the Provisional Government and the Republic of Hawaii were based essentially on American forms of administration, and confidently anticipated political union as the next logical step.

Many, very many Americans, however, gave no acceptance to the idea, originated journalistically as early as 1845, that it was their country's "manifest destiny" to thrust its continental boundaries westward beyond the natural limits set by the Pacific Coast. But far-seeing statesmen, with expanding commerce in mind, were not slow to grasp the strategic value of the Hawaiian Islands as a coaling station and repair base both for the American Navy and her Merchant Marine.

In Hawaii itself many realized that the question, no longer one of political independence, had become divided: (1) Shall our overseas merger accept inevitable results of granting citizenship to the present overpowering numbers from Japan? (2) Shall we await absorption into Germany's or Great Britain's far-flung empire? (3) Or shall we look toward our nearest haven to place a new star among the familiar Stars and Stripes? There seemed but one solution.

In Washington, however, Minister Thurston was often so baffled by rebuffs or silence from Secretary of State Gresham that he found no little enlightenment in a weekly journal known as *Kate Field's Washington*. Miss Field was a brilliant writer and keen analyst in American politics. In his *Memoirs of the Hawaiian Revolution* Mr. Thurston stressed the significance in her accurate diagnosis of the Hawaiian angle of the situation.

As early as 1888 Miss Field had known Mr. Gresham, then a Republican leader and candidate for nomination to the presidency. Mr. Harrison's nomination so alienated Mr. Gresham that the latter turned Democrat, threw his support to the election of Grover Cleveland, and accepted from him appointment as Secretary of State. This associated him closely with former political enemies.

Mr. Cleveland, having little interest and less knowledge in matters west of the Missouri River, gladly turned over to his Secretary of State the treaty of Hawaiian annexation left by retiring President Harrison for Senate confirmation. Still at enmity with Mr. Harrison, Secretary Gresham thereupon promoted restoration of Hawaii's queen to her throne in direct opposition to annexation. Also, a sick man, he consistently took no pains to co-operate with Minister Thurston, and early in 1895 ended by asking for his recall. Thurston, having heard of this indirectly, lost no time in reporting to Honolulu, where his entire course was approved by the Executive Council. He was preparing to publish a justification of his conduct of state affairs, when news of Mr. Gresham's death rendered this impossible.

Annexation had become in fact the paramount topic of discussion in private letters and conversation, as well as through the newspapers. Not fully convinced that from the standpoint of the United States such a step was advisable, Kate Field came out to the Islands to see for herself, and to her on October 10, 1895, was granted President Dole's first interview with an American press representative. Almost from her arrival in Honolulu she and the Doles were congenial friends, and before long she became an enthusiastic advocate of annexation. After her official interview with Mr. Dole she unwittingly fulfilled part of his college forecast in her comment: "Whoever meets Mr. Dole realizes that the noblest work of God is an honest man."

Reports of the interview were eagerly read, Islanders coming to the conclusion that more than any other writer Miss Field had set the Hawaiian government in its true light before the American people. "The future of Hawaii," she wrote, "is vastly important to us, and we refuse to heed the signal." Keenly interested in every phase of life in Hawaii, she talked with officials, with the man, or woman, on the street, friendly and eager to learn. "In three things," she told a Hawaiian gathering, "no one can equal you—as horsemen, fishermen, and freemen. You must not let any nation take these from you."

In May, 1896, while on a tour through Kona with Miss Anna Paris, Miss Field was stricken with an alarming phase of a former illness. Her untimely death came a few hours after enforced return to Honolulu. She died in the home of Dr. McGrew. It was universally the loss of a personal friend.

Numerous Hawaiian subjects, who had come as young men from English, Scottish, or other European countries, naturally favored continuing the Hawaiian monarchy. J. S. Walker, of Scottish, and Paul Isenberg, Sr., of German birth, were pronounced in their Royalist sympathies.

British Minister Wodehouse also was loyal to Queen Liliuokalani, while endeavoring to show her that autocratic change in the Constitution might be going too far. Theophilus H. Davies published many letters stressing continued independence of the Islands as opposed to political union with the United States. Even Charles R. Bishop, an American born, but by marriage an *alii*, felt his adoption into the royal family so intimately that after the overthrow of the kingdom he made his home in San Francisco, where he maintained, however, the most cordial personal and social relations with educational institutions and lifelong friends such as Sanford Dole.

As active perhaps as any other ardent Royalist, the Right Reverend Alfred Willis, second English Bishop of Honolulu, was so outspoken in his printed articles that more than once he felt political arrest to be imminent. Following his repeated attacks on "missionaries" as revolutionists, the *Hawaiian Star* (symbolizing the new star of annexation) published for the Bishop's "information" the roster of the Executive and Advisory Councils which included only Dole, Smith, and Damon of American Mission descent. These three were far outnumbered by fifteen men having no Mission connection. Bishop Restarick, in his *Hawaii from the Viewpoint of a Bishop,* brings out the fact that, while from 1893 to 1898 Bishop Willis consistently prayed in public for Queen Liliuokalani the moment annexation became a fact, he gave official notice that the prayer for the President was to replace that for the Hawaiian royal family, including the invocation "God Save the State" in place of "God Save the Queen."

All of these men and their families, like the Royalists themselves, were honest political dissenters, whom one cannot but respect and admire for the courage and perseverance with which they supported their convictions.

Among Hawaiians, not a few were quick to assert that annexation would deprive them of civic rights, Senator Morgan's direct statement to the contrary notwithstanding. Another good friend and a local man, Godfrey Rhodes, assured Hawaiians that the Republic was working more for their welfare than had the late monarchy. But it was only natural that abolition of their monarchy should arouse feelings of hostility. Fearing that eventually even their flag might disappear, women began to make their own Hawaiian flags, one even hanging hers up about her high four-poster bed where she could always see it and keep it, independent of any government. Others with patient stitchery, as Hawaiian women had done in earlier crises, arranged not one only, but four newly made flags—the traditional Hawaiian number—along the four sides of immense bed quilts.

And where but among Hawaiians would such resentment have transmuted itself into song and motion? Their queen, in fact, leading them all, as she sat in her palace prison, ruling lines in a blank book to set down both words and notes. Many of her songs and hymns are still loved, especially *Ke Aloha o ka Haku,* (The Lord's Mercy) better known as the "Queen's Prayer."

Many and various were the songs composed, some for Liliu, the *alii,* on her first departure to see her good friend in Washington, Grover Cleveland, the one who would be sure to seat her once more on the throne.

One such gifted composer, Mrs. Ellen Wright Prendergast, was sitting on an afternoon of January 1893 in the lovely rose garden of her father's mansion at Kapalama. Her prized guitar lay close at hand. When guests were announced, their familiar faces proved to be the troubled ones of all but two members of the Royal Hawaiian Band on strike. "We will not follow this new government," they asserted. "We will be loyal to Liliu. We will not sign the *haole's* paper, but will be satisfied with all that is left to us, the stones, the mystic food of our native land." So they begged her to compose their song of rebellion, *Mele 'ai Pohaku* (Stone-eating Song), called also *Mele Aloha Aina* (Patriots' Song).

Long a close friend of the royal family, Ellen Prendergast found the words and music rising within her. Soon the *mele* was well known among Hawaiians. Years later, after the Royal Hawaiian Band had reassembled and again gave special afternoon concerts, it was an event when Heleluhe of the band was to sing the *Mele 'ai Pohaku.* Distance and time even then were merging bitterness with legend. The origin of this Hawaiian chant has been shared with us by the composer's daughter, Eleanor Prendergast, of the Governor's office.

Today only this song remains of the many then composed, Kawena Pukui of the Bishop Museum tells us; it is sung and danced and loved with no trace of the resentment which gave it birth sixty years ago. In fact, while Mrs. Lahilahi Webb still gave true Hawaiian welcome at the entrance to the Bishop Museum, Hawaiians from the Laie Mormon colony came once to serenade her on her birthday, and chanted every stanza of this *Mele 'ai Pohaku*. Gradually Lahilahi's eyes filled with tears, not of sadness, but of joy and sweet memories, while she recalled her life being saved by her queen at the time of King Kalakaua's lying in state, and later when she had been privileged to chant Liliu's special name song to waken the queen on her birthday.

For long years, Lahilahi Webb used to tell, she had in her heart, and often aloud, resented bitterly the overthrow of the monarchy and the annexation. But ever after the fateful bombing of Pearl Harbor in 1941 she had thanked God that the United States of America stood ready to protect little Hawaii, who must else have disappeared under overwhelming waves of destruction.

Yet even in 1897 there were Hawaiians not a few who sincerely believed that annexation was right. Two of these brave men of conviction lived in Ka-u, one a Congregational minister, the Reverend Mr. Kauhane, the other, Kawena Pukui's uncle, her mother's oldest brother. Both worked actively for annexation and, although "roundly blasted" for it by Hawaiian newspapers, stoutly maintained their belief. Nor were these by any means isolated instances.

All, of many races, had been cheered to see the Hawaiian flag continued as emblem of the Republic of Hawaii, and with equal poignancy regretted the legislative mandate of 1896 for officially supervised burning of Hawaiian postage stamps dating from the monarchy.

As potent as any other one influence toward mutual understanding was a speech given in 1897 before many Hawaiians at a mass meeting in Kawaiahao Church. The speaker was United States Senator John T. Morgan of Alabama, who was visiting Hawaii with his daughters. As chairman of the Senate Committee on Foreign Relations earlier in Cleveland's administration, Morgan's interest in Hawaii had been manifest. Now, at the mass meeting, he made a point of saying he would tell the United States Senate that Hawaii's government was as good as any in the world, and that he would gladly grasp the hands of her people as brother Americans. Furthermore, should annexation be accomplished, the Hawaiian people would not be treated as a colony, but would automatically become citizens of the great American republic.

From the earliest moment of the Hawaiian revolution the portfolio of foreign affairs had been recognized as exceedingly important. When it became necessary for President Dole to relinquish it, the very best man available had been named to it. This was F. M. Hatch whom his associate, B. L. Marx, characterized as one of the ablest of Hawaii's leaders. In 1895, Minister Hatch had been appointed to replace Thurston in Washington, and Henry S. Cooper to take the Hawaiian post as Minister of Foreign Affairs.

In October, 1896, at the height of the American presidential campaign, Minister Cooper was dispatched on a twofold mission to Washington. With him as secretary went also young Benjamin L. Marx, who has given Hawaii a lively account of their success. As a direct outcome of Honolulu's serious cholera epidemic the year before, their first mission took them to another tidewater city, Boston, where a modern sewer system was already in use. Granted every courtesy by Mayor Quincy, they were so fortunate as to find an engineer competent to make the first survey and plans for the Honolulu sewer system.

As his second mission Minister Cooper had been commissioned to get in touch with Minister Hatch as to the status of annexation. From him they ascertained that President Cleveland was still antagonistic. In November, however, Marx went on to Canton, Ohio, President-elect McKinley's home, to arrange an interview for Minister Cooper. Although this was only shortly after the election and the house was still filled with telegraph operators and newspaper men, Mr. and Mrs. McKinley were most cordial, the president-elect remarking with a smile that Marx, although twenty-six, seemed very young to be entrusted with the conduct of such an important mission. This was one of the repeated instances during Hawaii's history when a capable young lawyer stood ready to take his turn at the wheel. Minister Cooper's interview proceeded most satisfactorily, the president-elect taking a lively interest in possible annexation, and after his inauguration he proved as good as his word.

To annexationists this interview was their first sound basis for encouragement. Minister Hatch was soon joined by two special commissioners, W. A. Kinney and L. A. Thurston, who reached Washington even before the inauguration in March, 1897. A new treaty was finally negotiated on the 16th of June, and the same day forwarded to the Senate by President McKinley.

For the signing of this treaty in the formal reception room of the State Department Lorrin Thurston relates that a photograph was desired. Observing that on the wall space above the chair of Secretary of State John Sherman, the portrait of the late Secretary of State Walter Q. Gresham, would dominate the picture, a nimble second secretary, to obviate any discordant element, promptly had Gresham's portrait replaced by that of James G. Blaine.

Ratified by the Hawaiian Senate in special session, this long-awaited document was signed by President Dole September 10, 1897. Again, however, a long delay occurred in its ratification by the United States Senate.

With the Treaty of Annexation before Congress a unanimous decision was made by the government councils at Honolulu that President Dole should go east to meet President McKinley and his immediate advisors. This was Dole's first visit to the United States since 1891 when King Kalakaua had been in that country. He was accompanied by Mrs. Dole, by his secretary and staff officer, Colonel Curtis P. Iaukea, and also, since the party was proceeding in the midst of winter, by his physician, Dr. Francis R. Day. Leaving on the S.S. *Peru* January 7, 1898, they returned March 4.

San Francisco papers were full of the projected tour to national headquarters. Equally interesting, as more personal, are the memories of Maybelle Ward Walker, who with her mother went at once to call at the Occidental Hotel, which was flying the Hawaiian flag for the presidential visit. Feeling, she said, like a girl from the country, Anna Dole sought help in finding suitable gowns. So off to the well-known shop, the City of Paris, went the three ladies to select a rich black silk and set dressmakers promptly to work. When Anna demurred over handkerchiefs at two dollars and a half apiece, Annie Ward assured her that she must look and feel as fine as the President's wife should.

Back at the hotel, the ladies walked in upon the arrival of a caller, Claus Spreckels, just as he said, "You and I have not always thought alike, Mr. Dole, but that need not interfere with friendship." Whereupon, the ladies withdrew, knowing only too well that, as head of the sugar trust and interested in the growing beet sugar industry, Spreckels was a most active and influential opponent of annexation for Hawaii.

Met in Chicago by Hawaiian Minister Hatch and officers of McKinley's government, President Dole declined military escort and expressed his preference for as democratic and unpretentious procedure as possible.

In Washington, proceeding to the Arlington Hotel, placed at their disposal as guests of the nation, the Hawaiian party was accompanied by a police guard only. On the day of their arrival President McKinley's official call on President Dole was returned the same day. The one week in Washington was filled with calls from members of Congress, attentions from the federal government and visits to points of interest. These however did not include the two houses of Congress, since Mr. Dole did not consider that a proper procedure for him.

At the state dinner in honor of the nation's guests President McKinley led with Mrs. Dole's hand on his arm, Mrs. McKinley following with President Dole, Mrs. McKinley gowned in white satin with silver embroidery, the President's lady from Hawaii wearing a becoming gown of black velvet. The handsome table set with seventy-one covers, shone with orchids of great beauty, white hyacinths, and primroses, all sparkling doubly by reflection from wall mirrors wreathed in smilax and banked in white and pink roses.

President Dole's own brief recollections note little more than official facts, but Washington papers lost no item of the brilliance on this occasion, which even for the nation's capital was no everyday affair. Afterward, Mrs. Hatch delighted in describing the impression made by the Doles in official circles, Mrs. Dole dignified and most gracious, while her husband in striking good looks and courtly manner outshone members of the President's cabinet and won the admiration of everyone he met.

During the President's popular White House reception many official courtesies were extended, and many Island friends were present. One American, Dr. Mary Walker, a devotee of Queen

Liliuokalani then resident in Washington, conspicuously avoided the Doles in the receiving line. The brilliant reception tendered by Minister and Mrs. Hatch, in the elaborate parlors of the Arlington Hotel, amid palms and roses, brought out guests representing every phase of Washington's social life, particularly from the diplomatic corps, to do honor to the first President of the new republic in the Pacific Ocean.

Much as they had enjoyed the Washington sojourn, the Doles very gratefully started west by way of Buffalo, where a large dinner, for men only, complimented the Hawaiian executive. Then came a few days at Riverside, California, with the George Doles. Yet even there one reception was held, and Los Angeles claimed President Dole and his party for an elaborate welcome.

Renewed interest in annexation, aroused by this visit to Washington, had swept like a wave from California to the Atlantic Coast. One of the leading conservative journals, the *Outlook,* of New York, though never having favored the annexation project, found the interest now so intense and widespread that its editors not only requested an eight-column discussion from Lorrin A. Thurston, but themselves commented editorially in introducing his article: "It is unique in the history of the United States that a ruler should come from another nation offering to lay down his own office in order that his country may become an integral part of the nation."

Under the title, "President Dole and the Hawaiian Question," Mr. Thurston cited the definite advantages to be gained by the United States, and ably demonstrated that objections to annexation were without logical foundation. Leading up to this, however, Minister Thurston presented for thousands of Americans who would never see Sanford Dole, a word portrait of the man, so vigorous and so true that many lines in it have definite place here:

The bare statement of President Dole's position and mission indicates with precision the leading feature of his character: his unselfish and public spirited devotion to principle, regardless of personal consequences to himself.

In the prime of manhood, respected by his political opponents, loved by his supporters, the recognized head of an independent nation, he has for five years persistently advocated a policy that will reduce him to the ranks of plain citizenship, without other personal reward or benefit than will accrue to the people of Hawaii as a whole.

His disinterested devotion to what he conceives to be the public welfare is further illustrated by the fact that, although his financial resources are limited to the savings of a fair law practice, and he was holding a life position as a Judge of the Supreme Court with a salary of $6,000 per annum, he resigned this position to accept the leadership of the movement to overthrow the monarchy, with the full expectation that his official career would speedily terminate by absorption of this government into the United States.

Mr. Dole has always been a persistent opponent of the contract labor system, having held as a Judge that it was unconstitutional. His present policy is to discourage it. [In any event it] is falling rapidly into disuse.

Physically Mr. Dole is a magnificent specimen of manhood, standing six feet two inches, with a refined, intellectual expression and manner. He is of a most genial and democratic nature; fond of horseback-riding, hunting, and boating; owns a yacht, which he frequently sails himself in cruising and local yacht-racing or shark-fishing; while he takes a leading part in the literary and social life of the country.

Although he was the leader in the overthrow of the monarchy and the suppression of the insurrection of 1895, he is on personal friendly terms with the ex-Queen, Princess Kaiulani, and the leading Royalist supporters. It is literally true that he has not a personal enemy in Hawaii.

In introducing Dole's papers for the *Memoirs of the Hawaiian Revolution,* words were used by L. A. Thurston which have not yet been equaled. These were, moreover, words of the very man who, though lawyer and statesman both, was yet so radical, even impulsive, in thought and action that he instantly declined the post of leadership which he recognized Dole's disposition of steady conservatism was better suited to undertake. Thurston wrote:

In the political history of Hawaii, there are several strong men of dominating spirit; but above all others, in face, form, reputation, and character, towers Sanford Ballard Dole. He is a tall man, slow and soft-spoken, of decisive tone on occasion, but with kind brown eyes and an unfaltering gaze to friend and foe alike, which give assurance of a kindly spirit.

Without qualification—and I know whereof I speak—during the long strain from January 14, 1893, to August 12, 1898, the dominating note and unifying influence were the person and character of Sanford Ballard Dole. These were facts, recognized by all, which required neither supporting evidence nor argument. It was universally felt that a man of Dole's standing, character and disposition could not conscientiously identify himself with, or advocate, a selfish or unjust cause.

The inherent gentleness of the man, combined with his patent vigor and force when those qualities were demanded, was more potent and disarming than all the fighting men and material, and all the cold, superficial logic that could be marshaled against the revolution and the revolutionists.

In fact, to the outside world and largely to the insiders as well, Sanford Ballard Dole was the revolution. His mere participation as its leader disarmed and neutralized opposition, and brought support that could have been secured in no other way. Men such as Dole do not simply happen. They are the product of their ancestry and environment.

2. *Hawaii-Japan Negotiations 1868–1898*

As Mr. Thurston indicated, Sanford Dole had long been opposed to the contract labor system. Beginning in 1868, labor relations between Hawaii and Japan trace, even in abstract, a complicated story. Threatened economic disaster because of the American Civil War and the decline of whaling as an industry had prompted the planting of larger areas in Hawaii to sugar cane, and as early as 1865 the need for laborers was becoming acute. The first workers brought in under the Board of Immigration were Chinese, who, on the expiration of their plantation contracts, tended to branch out into such trades as shopkeeping where their success aroused resentment in the mercantile community. Efforts to secure other types of people gave little satisfaction except with the Portuguese, who proved admirable in many respects save in prohibitive cost of transportation.

Offsetting objections to the Chinese, the first group of Japanese in 1868 strengthened the belief that they would be the more suitable. So much disorder existed, however, in the hasty recruitment of this first company that for 17 years officials in Japan refused to permit further emigration. By 1871 the Treaty of Friendship and Commerce was made, allowing free access to Hawaii or Japan for the nationals of either government, without, however, any restriction as to the number of individuals involved.

In an era of growing opposition to slavery the matter of contract labor, commonly called a "coolie trade," was in disfavor with many; and the United States Congress passed a law to prohibit such a transaction by Americans in American ships. Hawaiian planters met the reproach with, as they felt, justifiable reasoning; others found the system odious, since the Masters and

Servants Act, passed in 1850 with legal basis for the shipping and control of contract laborers, savored of Southern slavery. As a matter of fact, this Hawaiian legislation was in some respects not unlike the American Seamen's Shipping Act. Japan, always sensitive to the treatment of her nationals outside her own boundaries, came also to resent implications inherent in the term "coolie."

As early as 1869 an immigration policy for the future was being actively discussed at a series of public meetings in Honolulu. Beginning to recover from a two-year depression, hopes of the sugar industry were high for ratification of a reciprocal trade treaty pending in the United States Senate. The need for laborers was urgent, especially since most of the Chinese arriving in 1865 must be replaced at the expiration of their contracts. A resolution introduced at one of these Honolulu meetings commended the contract system as "advantageous to the native laborer, and . . . quite necessary to the Asiatic immigrant."

Among speakers against the contract system appeared young Attorney Sanford Dole, who said frankly:

I oppose the system from principle, because I think it is wrong; you professedly support it as a matter of necessity and individual interest, and thus looking from different standpoints we are apt to misunderstand each other. I cannot help feeling that the chief end of this meeting, its heart and soul, is plantation profits; and that prosperity, the demands of society, the future of the Hawaiian race, only come in secondarily, if at all, on the part of the supporters of this system. Is it not so? The burden of your cry is *labor; we must have labor,* and the plan which promises that cheap, and immediate, you favor without asking any questions. . . . Tried in the balance of the 'free and equal rights' principle, the contract system is found wanting.

Agreeing with Dole were A. F. Judd, C. J. Lyons, C. C. Bennett, and J. O. Carter.

In his *The Hawaiian Kingdom, 1854-1874, Twenty Critical Years,* Dr. Ralph S. Kuykendall states: "The dual problem of labor supply and population was still unsolved at the end of the reign of Kamehameha V. In the closing months of that reign this vexing problem was again the subject of a discussion of more than ordinary significance."

Reference is here made to a series of articles in the *Pacific Commercial Advertiser* for September of 1872. In the first of these Walter Murray Gibson wrote as "Weltevreden" to discuss labor and population. Remarking advantages of Japanese over Chinese workers, he particularly stressed the need to increase Hawaii's diminishing population, and urged development of the Islands as a colony of Malaysia, rather than one of Mongolian background. He claimed the original Hawaiian migrations as stemming from Malaysia, and asserted the strengthening of this racial bond as most logical and practical.

Among other discussions in this newspaper symposium Historian Kuykendall considers "most important from every standpoint" a series of six articles by S. B. Dole. Writing at the age of 28 and under his own name, Dole characteristically viewed the problem from the angle of successful settlement of land by freeholders:

With the present rapid decadence of the population we are in a fair way of learning the very important truth that "land without people on it, is really worthless"; that the "value of land depends simply on there being somebody to collect its produce, or on the probability that there will be people." This clear proposition is universally acted upon every day the world over. The settlement of the new land of the United States is under its principle. Land associations and railroad companies know that they can afford to give away land to settlers for the sake of the rise in value thereby accruing to the adjoining lands.

Upon the premises, therefore, that if our islands are ever to be peopled to their full capacity, it must be brought about through the settlement of their lands; that homesteads, rather than field-gangs, are to be the basis of our future social and civil progress, a careful study of our land policy becomes necessary to the formation of any practical plan for effecting this result. . . .

Then followed a summary of Hawaiian lands held largely by the government and the king and as "the entailed inheritance from former administrations"; of the Crown lands, as inalienable, and usually farmed out on long-term leases; and the government holdings, alienable by law, but, in practice due to earlier usage, also under long leases. This latter condition, Dole thought, "formed perhaps the greatest obstacle to a comprehensive homestead system of settlement"; but, could such a plan be inaugurated and prospered, "the increasing demand for homesteads might be supplied by constantly expiring leaseholds."

Even during the reign of Kamahameha V this young lawyer, Dole, asserted that also a proper portion of the Royal Domain, after repeal of the Act of 1865, might be made alienable by being vested in the government to be opened to purchase by *bona fide* settlers; that nothing in such a new policy was "inconsistent with intelligent loyalty and patriotism."

Too sanguine, perhaps, these youthful opinions? Yet complete loyalty to both king and country marked his enthusiasm in believing that "this reform, entered into upon the national ground of our imperative need of a greater population, would meet with almost universal support, especially if it should be the policy of the administration; a policy which would be a most fitting sequence of the royal grant of Kamehameha III and an enlightened ratification of the principles of that far-seeing act of statesmanship."

In his final article, "Systems of Immigration and Settlement," Dole suggested that the Hawaiian government employ its own ship to bring Chinese and Japanese immigrants, who might be given the option of engaging as laborers for the plantations or taking homesteads to be worked by themselves.

Following Kings Kamehameha V and Lunalilo, came the seventeen-year reign of Kalakaua. In 1881, owing partly to the king's visit three years before in Japan, officials there sanctioned emigration of their citizens after prolonged negotiations between the empire and the Hawaiian kingdom. Difficulties in connection with the first subsequent arrivals of Japanese in 1885 had much to do with an important Immigration Convention the following year. Under this formal agreement emigrants from Japan came to Hawaii in increasing numbers, but closely supervised by the two governments.

This Convention-system of immigration came to an end in 1894. Beginning to doubt the wisdom of such extensive Japanese addition to the population as allowed by the Treaty of 1871, many again demanded a supply of workers from China and Europe.

In an effort to control the situation, the Hawaiian government enacted two laws. The first, dated March 1, 1894, required every alien entering the country to have "visible means of support which . . . may be shown by the *bona fide* possession of not less than fifty dollars in money, or a *bona fide* written contract of employment with a reliable and responsible resident of the Hawaiian Islands."

The second law, dated February 1, 1895, provided that no

person or company could bring any alien or foreigner into the country under contract to labor unless the contract had received the approval of the Hawaiian Board of Immigration. Subsequent controversies resulted from alleged violations of one or the other or both of these laws.

With grave concern, President Dole wrote December 3, 1896, to Minister Francis M. Hatch in Washington: "There is considerable activity in the bringing in of Free Immigrants [those with the required fifty dollars but without contracts, paying their own way and intending to find employment after landing in Hawaii]. The several immigration companies are working the business for profits and are prepared to run it for all it is worth. It is rather a serious business for us and we may find it necessary to try and procure a modification of our Japanese treaty on the point of the right of the Japanese to come in."

In the same week Acting Attorney General W. O. Smith voiced similar alarm to Minister Hatch: "Alone we are in a great degree helpless. We cannot prevent the tide of immigration . . . We must make a strong effort for annexation next spring."

As early as 1887 Japanese officials had protested that their countrymen had not been given the right to vote by the new reform constitution of Hawaii. In 1892 the coming of Consul-General Fujii emphasized the matter in a personal visit to John L. Stevens, United States Minister at Honolulu. That insistence on this point was prolonged is borne out by a letter in the files of diplomatic correspondence at the Archives of Hawaii. Under the date of March 23, 1893, Fujii, addressing President Dole, sharply called attention to the fact that the voting franchise, although accorded to Americans and Europeans, had been withheld from the Japanese.

States Hilary Conroy in his recent authoritative volume, *The Japanese Frontier in Hawaii, 1868–1898:*

. . . The antagonism grew day by day as expansion of Japanese interests, prosperity and numbers increased. Gradually the leaders of the Hawaiian Republic grew bolder, or more afraid, and at last the republic resorted to overt government action against them.

The overt action came in two installments. The first was a law passed in June, 1896, entitled, "An Act to Increase the Duty on Liquors, Still Wines and Other Beverages Made from Materials Other Than Grape Juice," which in effect placed an almost prohibitive duty on the importation of

Japanese *sake*. The second was the refusal of the government in the spring of 1897 to allow three successive shiploads of Japanese immigrants [a total of 1,175 individuals] to enter the country. The *sake* law, and the immigration rejection, as Japan's Foreign Minister Okuma was quick to realize, were the opening guns in a two-pronged attack on the Japanese expansion in Hawaii.

California wine-growers were vitally interested in the proposed high duty on *sake* which would be to the advantage of their own wines, and the argument they advanced for its adoption carried serious implications. Why should Hawaii benefit from the Reciprocity Treaty with the United States for her sugars, when she was herself trading with Japan against the interests of her nearest neighbor?

When the *sake* law came before the Hawaiian Legislature of 1896 it was passed by an overwhelming majority. But President Dole, never one to be swayed by popular sentiment, promptly vetoed the bill after having first advised its modification on the ground that as part of the Hawaiian community the Japanese were entitled to food and drink to which they were accustomed.

Rejection of immigrants added weight to the controversy, based though this was on the conviction of Hawaiian officials that not a few were entering illegally. Protest from Count Okuma was "swift, bitter and even threatening," going so far as to demand indemnity for such "arbitrary and capricious" action and to back up this demand by dispatching the warship *Naniwa* to Honolulu.

While long discussion ensued, a second flood-light was thrown on the Hawaiian Islands in a strong protest lodged by Japan's foreign office in Washington against the annexation of Hawaii to the United States. Reasons brought forward were possibilities of change in existing conditions in Pacific affairs and of interference with the rights of Japanese citizens in Hawaii. Salient facts on the subject of this protest, as noted by R. S. Kuykendall in 1926, were two: that between 1893 and 1897 Japan, through her defeat of China, had emerged as a world power, and also during those four years had watched the number of her citizens in Hawaii increase from 15,000 to 25,000. While this protest against annexation to the United States was finally withdrawn, Japan's demand for indemnity continued to be pressed.

Arbitration, proposed by Hawaii in connection with the immigrant rejection, and agreed to in principle by Minister Okuma, never eventuated. In order to clear up any unsettled claims before final annexation to the United States, Hawaii therefore, while admitting no wrongful act on her part, paid Japan an indemnity of $75,000 in July, 1898. This was accepted in full satisfaction of claims by the Japanese government, the sum to be apportioned among firms and individuals who through the rejections had incurred emigration losses.

In 1898, before payment of this indemnity, the *sake* law was modified by legislative action to conform with the compromise suggested by President Dole two years before. Close upon the heels of this transaction President McKinley signed the resolution which annexed Hawaii "as a part of the territory of the United States." This automatically put an end to the system of contract labor in Hawaii and, once United States tariff laws had gone into effect, closed the *sake* controversy as well.

3. *Annexation Concluded 1898*

In April of 1898 President Dole's official party started from Washington for the West. Many years later he himself recalled:

The Spanish war, on our leaving Washington, immediately became a menace on the United States horizon and on our reaching Honolulu, or about that time, blazed into full operation. As we were a neutral government the question became a very serious one in our attitude of friendship to the United States and as to our standing on the policy of annexation. We decided to break the laws of neutrality and to favor the United States, giving them a continuance of their coal pile on shore in Honolulu and the privilege of their warships remaining in our port. This led to protest, particularly from the representative here of the Spanish Government, which we ignored.

As the military operations of the United States against Spain brought about a large expedition to the Philippine Islands, Spain's possessions in the Pacific, the ships conveying military forces and army supplies found it convenient to come into Honolulu, to which we made no objection. And more than this, we entertained the military and naval forces of two fleets by giving them a kind of huge picnic entertainment in the grounds of the Capitol, seating from a thousand to fifteen hundred guests a day for about a week. The families of Honolulu sympathizing with the Republic of Hawaii volunteered in this enterprise with huge quantities of eatables, and a steam boiler was erected in the grounds for making coffee.

The arrival of the first troop ship was marked by a review before a platform erected in front of the opera house. Accompanying President and Mrs. Dole to the reviewing stand came official families, including Minister and Mrs. Henry E. Cooper with their eight-year-old daughter Alice. Turning to them, President Dole asked small Alice to stand with Mrs. Dole and himself, since they had no children of their own to bring. With her dark red hair and sparkling brown eyes she made a picture, as she watched every pair of the "Boys in Blue," saluting the President and marching past to the palace picnic ground. To this day Alice Cooper Bailey tells vividly of the significance of this occasion in her life.

The first fleet came during the heat of June when to Islanders salads seemed welcome. Young Americans of the second fleet, however, as they drew up to the wharves, lined the bulwarks of the ships shouting in unmistakable tones: "We Want Pie!"

But pie or no pie, the "boys" never forgot Honolulu. Dozens of young girls helped their fathers and mothers with the serving at the long tables. Under one of the big trees stood President and Mrs. Dole to receive the guests. One of these, of Company K in California's National Guard, was their own nephew, Alfred Rowell Dole, a volunteer in the expedition, who with others was entertained also at the home on Emma Street. After the big picnic lunch the boys delighted in taking free twelve-mile rides in the city's little tram cars, or swarming over the government buildings to write home on legislative stationery with free postage, one day leaving over seven thousand letters to be collected, franked, and posted for them.

Even more important still, these expeditions so emphasized the strategic value of the Hawaiian Islands, as an outpost of continental United States, that Congress lost little time in passing the joint resolution for political union. Signed by President McKinley July 7, it took some time to transmit the news to Honolulu. But on the morning of July 13, 1898, Sanford Dole was standing, as he often did, on the shore at his beach cottage below Diamond Head. It was a spot dearly loved, where he could get out for an early morning swim and on shore a work-out with his long Indian clubs; at low tide Hawaiians came to fish in the broad green stretches of shallow water.

Telescope in hand, Mr. Dole was this morning watching the Pacific Mail Steamship *Coptic,* as she approached from the east and slowly steamed toward the harbor. Suddenly, as if shot from a trap, a half-dozen lines of flags flew up to the masthead and caught the breeze. The ship was dressed. It meant news. It could mean annexation. Quickly the President turned and called for his horse, donned his leggings, and reached the wharf at Honolulu as the *Coptic* arrived off the mouth of the channel. National Guard officers, reading her flag signals, gave out the news. Men shouted and cheered, many crowding to shake the hand of American Minister Harold M. Sewall, who was grinning like a boy on the Fourth of July.

When the waterfront hustler for the *Advertiser* brought the first paper news ashore, Dole mounted a box to read the message aloud to the cheering throng. Uptown fire bells, factory whistles, and fire crackers were let loose, artillery from the Executive Building belching out a 100-gun salute, while the band marched down the street playing American airs. Flags waving, the wharf crowd, annexing the band, turned up Fort Street. At the Officers' Club in the palace bungalow Dr. McGrew asked the band to play the "Star-Spangled Banner" again. Professor Berger stepped out, handing his baton to the doctor, who directed the playing and afterward took three rousing cheers as Father of Annexation.

That evening a crowd of citizens lighted a huge bonfire on the floor of Lishman's quarry—now Dole Playground—at the foot of Punchbowl. But for formal celebration the Committee of One Hundred decided to await arrival of Hawaii's old friend, the U.S.S. *Philadelphia,* with Admiral Miller and the official flag.

Written at white heat, this account appeared next day, July 14, in the *Pacific Commercial Advertiser.* Its front page bore a banner headline "ANNEXATION" and under it the surprising new place line, "Honolulu H.I. U.S.A." Other front-page features displayed a portrait of the Father of Annexation, and a picture of the American flag opposite lines by the veteran newspaperman, Henry M. Whitney:

> HERE TO STAY
> And the Star-Spangled Banner
> In triumph shall wave
> O'er the isles of Hawaii
> And the homes of the brave.

Even during the reign of Kamehameha III a far-seeing advocate of political union with the United States had been Mr. S. N. Castle, business agent for the American Protestant Mission and later a founder of the firm of Castle & Cooke. Commented the *Advertiser* of August 13, 1898: Mr. Castle "freely and openly declared his opinion and placed the matter before the King in every light." As a member of the Privy Council under Kamehameha V, Castle's convictions "were always frankly expressed." At the opening of Kalakaua's reign, this defense of the annexation principle aroused bitter animosity among those evolving the theory of Hawaii for the Hawaiians. Later he joined the Annexation Club, maintaining to the day of his death in 1894 that in such a union with the United States of America lay Hawaii's only hope of survival. When the day of August 12, 1898, was finally set by the Hawaiian government as Flag Day for the formal raising of America's ensign over Hawaii, many who recalled Mr. Castle's consistent support felt a special significance in the date itself as being also the ninetieth anniversary of his birth.

The impressive, strictly official ceremony transferring Hawaii's sovereignty is described both by S. B. Dole and T. G. Thrum's *Hawaiian Annual*. Extended on the lower level by improvised platforms, the front steps of the Capitol accommodated officials and distinguished guests. The local military and police forces were assigned positions in the right and left driveways; directly in front in the main driveway stood the battalion from the U.S.S. *Philadelphia*.

Just before noon President Dole, amid cheers, took his place with the Cabinet on the *ewa* side of the platform. Next came Minister Sewall, Admiral Miller, and staff officers, Consul General Haywood, with Captains Wadleigh of the *Philadelphia* and Book of the *Mohican*. After a prayer Minister Sewall delivered to President Dole a certified copy of the Joint Resolution signed by President McKinley on the 7th of July. Relying on the treaty of political union and the cession consented to by the Republic, President Dole, with full confidence in the honor and friendship of the American people, then yielded up the sovereignty and public property of the Hawaiian Islands.

On Minister Sewall's acceptance of this transfer and a sign from Marshal Arthur Brown, the farewell salute to the Hawaiian flag of twenty-one guns boomed from the government battery at the Capitol, as also from the U.S.S. *Philadelphia* and *Mohican*. The band then played *"Hawaii Ponoi,"* a poignant service from which Director Berger had thoughtfully been relieved by President Dole. There followed a brief lull, adding new solemnity, after which the Hawaiian flag was slowly lowered from the central flagstaff of the Executive Building.

Just at the noon hour, on a signal from Admiral Miller, the band from the *Philadelphia* played the "Star-Spangled Banner," while the thirty-six-foot American flag, until then held loosely furled at the front windows by Gunner's Mate Platt of the *Philadelphia* and Boatswain's Mate Winters of the *Mohican,* was hoisted into place. Known as a No. 1 Regulation and of the largest size used in the United States Navy, this flag had been especially made at Mare Island Navy Yard and had been brought by Admiral Miller for this particular purpose. The halyards used were from the flagship *Philadelphia*. And even today this old flag, labeled by Henry E. Cooper, Minister of Foreign Affairs, remains carefully folded in its Navy pouch in the Archives of Hawaii.

Simultaneously with this official flag, smaller ensigns rose on the poles of the corner towers, and on the Judiciary Building "the identical flag which Blount hauled down there in 1893 arose again in its place." Once again the double twenty-one-gun salute burst out from shore and harbor batteries.

Few eyes were dry. For while many had longed to have the protection of the Stars and Stripes above the Capitol, still more had not found it easy to watch the Hawaiian flag come down from the main flagstaff for the last time.

Minister Sewall read a proclamation as to procedure until Congress could provide for the government of Hawaii, and spoke at length, congratulating Hawaii on this final step.

By Chief Justice Judd the oath of allegiance to the larger republic was then administered to the President and members of his Cabinet. The National Guard and police then marched to the parade ground, escorted by the *Philadelphia* battalion. And after administration of the same oath of allegiance to the government troops President Dole delivered to this first Hawaiian regiment the identical silk battle flag carried in 1893 by the landing force of sailors and Marines from the U.S.S. *Boston,* while on shore duty in Honolulu. This silk ensign was then in 1898 proudly carried at its head by the Hawaiian National Guard as it escorted the battalion from the *Philadelphia* to its landing wharf. It proved to be the last appearance of this famed Navy flag, since the four National Guard companies were than formally disbanded after having been quartered in the basement of the Capitol for nearly five years.

Although the ceremonies of August 12 did indeed transfer sovereignty of the Hawaiian Islands, the concluding process of annexation covered almost two additional years. Mr. Dole pointed out that during this interval Hawaiian consuls still functioned in different parts of the world, the Hawaiian government still collected duties on imports from the United States, and the United States still collected duties on certain imports from Hawaii as before. The Hawaiian courts remained the same and executive matters were scarcely changed, always subject, however, to the higher authority of the President of the United States. Actually, the administration of government proceeded so smoothly that few citizens were conscious of the fact that the Hawaiian government was operating within the administrative framework of two countries at the same time.

The national government interested itself in establishing additional lighthouses on Hawaiian coasts, and likewise a permanent base for armed forces near Honolulu at an elevated and beautiful mountainous region known as Leilehua, but registered by the United States as Schofield Barracks. This was in honor of General J. M. Schofield, a radical supporter of annexation, who had as early as 1873 officially examined the Hawaiian Islands; and twenty-five years later wrote Senator Morgan that he had always regarded ultimate annexation to the United States as a public necessity, adding, "No half-way measures will suffice."

The first establishment of United States forces in the Islands had been brought about in 1898 by the exigencies of the Spanish-American war. Appropriately named Camp McKinley, these temporary quarters at Kapiolani Park accommodated the troops en route to or returning from Manila. Here at Camp McKinley on Thanksgiving Day in 1898, at Mrs. Dole's suggestion, townspeople served the "Boys in Blue" a real New England dinner.

4. *An Era Closing*

The last year of the century, 1899, claimed two of the few remaining *alii* in Hawaii. At twenty-four, just on the threshold of womanhood, Princess Victoria Kaiulani died suddenly in March. And in June, after an illness of two years, followed Kapiolani, Queen Dowager, widow of the late King Kalakaua. As related by Thomas G. Thrum, both of these *alii* had been held in such special, high regard that their deaths marked the passing of an era in Hawaiian history.

By the wish of her father, Governor Cleghorn, Kaiulani was buried in the tradition of Queen Emma's obsequies fourteen years before. On Wednesday, the 8th of March, her body lay in state in her own home at Ainahau; borne thence at midnight on Friday to the Old Stone Church at Kawaiahao, the same ceremony was observed there. At both, the highest officers of the National Guard in full regalia formed her guard of honor, mounted police escorting the midnight removal. At the church eight *kahili* bearers stood guard, slowly bending their *kahilis* in stated rhythm above the gleaming golden cloak. Day and night the edifice was thronged with friends, many chanting the special songs of this beloved princess of Hawaii.

Conducted by Bishop Willis and his clergy, the Sunday afternoon service included an address by the Reverend Henry Parker, pastor of this old king's chapel. While minute guns boomed, the long journey to Nuuanu proceeded, the catafalque drawn by a company of two hundred and thirty Hawaiians who coveted this service. As special guard of honor the regal splendor of twenty-seven great *kahilis* completely surrounded the pall-bearers and the more intimate smaller *kahilis*. Within the mausoleum the Princess Kaiulani was laid to rest beside her mother, Princess Likelike.

Queen Kapiolani was equally beloved. Born at Hilo, Hawaii, in 1834 of High Chief Kuhio and his wife, Kinoiki, daughter of King Kaumualii of Kauai, Kapiolani at twenty-one married Namakeha, an uncle of Queen Emma. For his health the young couple voyaged for months by the *Morning Star* among the Gilbert Islands, but in vain, for Namakeha died in 1860. Three years later Kapiolani was quietly married to High Chief David Kalakaua, and in 1883 was crowned by him at his own coronation ceremony.

A note from Mrs. Kawena Pukui's assembling of "Hula Olapa" tells of Queen Kapiolani as so beloved a royal daughter of Kauai that she inspired many *mele* lei (songs of affection). Each of the three islands, Hawaii, Maui, and Oahu, composed such a special song for her. Kauai had two, as well as a set of three which recalled Kapiolani's talks with the women there on the king's plans for *Hooulu lahui* (increase of the race). Once when she was making a royal progress around Kauai, a dancer from each island was chosen to compete in a contest, each to interpret all of these songs. In eager excitement the people looked forward to this matching of experts, for each contestant must dance equally well to the less familiar gourd rhythm and accent of the three other islands, as to his own. So delighted was the queen with the graceful young winner that she called him Kaili Puuwai (winner of hearts), a nickname that remained with him to the end of his days.

Truly devoted was Kapiolani to her royal husband. Certain of her ladies-in-waiting, one a young girl at the time of the coronation festivities, still tell of the queen's goodness, her dignity, her regal manner in choosing fabrics displayed before her at the palace, her patience in difficulty, her generosity in founding Kapiolani Maternity Home. Often when bewildered by events such as those of 1887, the queen would send for an early schoolmate, Judge Judd, to sit quietly with her and talk things over in Hawaiian. Almost overwhelmed by the king's death in 1891, she rallied to prove her deep attachment as well as her sense of honor by assisting to liquidate his financial obligations. To obviate possible confusion at her own death, she transferred by conditional gift her large possessions on several islands to her nephews, Prince Kawananakoa and Prince Kalanianaole.

Throughout her life of sixty-four years Kapiolani showed "a grasp of affairs that well qualified her for her high station." On her death Prince David Kawananakoa made all arrangements for just such regal obsequies as those of Kaiulani three short months before. Ceremonies for the queen in some respects displayed even more of the dignity and splendor known among old-time *alii*. Draped with the royal robe in which she had been crowned, her body lay in state at Pualeilani, her residence at Waikiki, not far from Kaiulani's at Ainahau. Again the solemn ritual of a midnight march under official guards of honor bore the casket to the Old Stone Church. Impressive was the solo and chorus singing there of the successive watches of *kahili*-bearers. Many were the *kanikau,* special dirges, the *oli* or *kahea inoa* (name recitals) by the queen's own devoted retainers, an ancient tribute even then rarely heard. Again the boom of minute guns accompanied military and naval guards of honor as the stately procession took its way up the valley to the last resting place of Hawaii's *alii.*

Grief for the older queen was heartfelt, but of these two state ceremonies those for the younger, uncrowned queen of her native isles held even deeper poignancy. Stevenson's little princess, Victoria Kaiulani, born of a double race, had been reared by her Scottish father through long years in Scotland and England in the traditions of constitutional monarchy. On the accession of her aunt, Queen Liliuokalani, in 1891, this only daughter of Princess Likelike had been duly proclaimed heir apparent to the throne of Hawaii. Already, however, was the impact of great powers on the Pacific islands so unmistakable as to render impossible any continuance of the Polynesian monarchy in Hawaii, even when such had been the expressed preference of Sanford Dole as a justice of the Supreme Court.

In his message to Hawaii's first Territorial Legislature Governor Dole paid official and personal tribute to these two *alii.* Restrained yet tender, his farewell to Princess Kaiulani stands among the finest in the political annals of those changing times. He said:

The Hawaiian community of many races has been called upon to mourn the death of members of the last royal line of the Monarchy: Her late Majesty Queen Dowager Kapiolani, widow of His late Majesty King Kalakaua; and Her late Royal Highness Princess Kaiulani, daughter of Her late Royal Highness Princess Likelike and the Honorable Archibald S. Cleghorn.

Public feeling was deeply aroused by the death of Princess Kaiulani. Her beauty and charm, the romantic incidents of her short life in connection with her brilliant political prospects, as heiress-presumptive to the Hawaiian throne, and their frustration by no fault of hers, her brave acceptance of the new and difficult situation, and the tact and sincerity she displayed in her changed relations with the Government and the people, had won for her a widespread interest together with the respect and regard of the community. Coming when she had vindicated her superiority to circumstances, and had with sweetness and gentleness turned her feet to humbler paths, with the feeling that the best things in life were still hers to live for, Kaiulani's sudden death was most pathetic and at the same time most favorable to permanently tender and affectionate memories of her nobility of character.

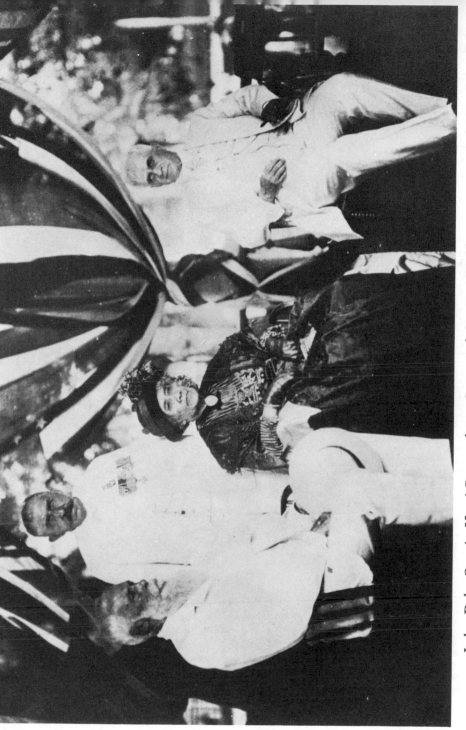

Judge Dole, Captain Henri Berger, the ex-Queen and Governor Pinkham, 1914. Berger was proud that Liliuokalani's public appearance with Dole was at his (the Kapellmeister's) request.

Punahou "boys" playing *aipuni* at the school's 75th anniversary

5. *Hawaii's First Governor 1900–1903*

Before losing the last vestige of its earlier associations in the older government across the sea, the Republic of Hawaii was confronted with one more serious hurdle, nothing less than an epidemic of bubonic plague, compounded by a disastrous conflagration in Honolulu. During December, 1899, and into the following month, seventy out of eighty cases proved fatal. Communication of the disease by means of rats was suspected, though not scientifically understood. Attempting to destroy infected houses in and near Chinatown a fire started by order of the Board of Health raged beyond control over thirty-eight acres, destroying the homes and belongings of some 6,000 Chinese, Hawaiians, and Japanese. Churches like Kawaiahao and other public buildings offered shelter, until temporary barracks two miles north of the city could be rushed to completion.

This expense, plus ultimate settlement of just fire claims for these refugees, swelled the public debt by a sum exceeding three millions of dollars. And it was not until April 30, 1900, that the Board of Health officially removed port quarantine. In the absence of the chief executive, Acting Governor Henry E. Cooper suggested in the governor's report of 1901 that Congress be asked for relief even to the extent of using for it customhouse receipts which, under the new territorial administration, were earmarked as federal revenue.

During the two-year interval between the status of republic and territory the most fundamental administrative feature was the work carried on by the Congressional Law Commission in formulating an Organic Act for the future territory. To expedite this vital service United States Senators Morgan and Cullom, and Representative Hitt, came from Washington to confer with the two local members, President Dole and Associate Justice W. F. Frear. The latter had succeeded Justice Dole in 1893 on Dole's resignation from the Supreme Bench.

This Organic Act, which became the basic law of Hawaii, was submitted to Congress late in 1898, but could not be immediately acted upon. Indeed more than one revision was required, primarily perhaps on the question of open suffrage, an American tradition for which Sanford Dole and his island colleagues felt that many residents of Hawaii were as yet unprepared. As Governor Dole later told a Boston audience: "We did not want open suffrage and did not ask for it, but we accept it and purpose to work it out. I have no criticism to make of the act of Congress. I incline to the belief that the matter will work itself out in the proper way."

By June, 1900, President McKinley had from several names selected that of S. B. Dole as first governor for the new Territory of Hawaii. And on the 14th of June a large gathering before the Hawaiian Capitol applauded their President's choice and listened with particular interest to the new Governor's characteristic inaugural address.

Who better than this devoted, experienced native son could discuss Hawaii's prospects and possible pitfalls in the new adjustments before her? No spirit of elation or satisfaction permeated this address. Rather, it was an eloquent alignment of facts, responsibilities—dangers even—coupled with more than one plea that Hawaii's citizens might measure up to the dignity of their new American heritage including the hope of statehood, and the confidence reposed in them.

And who better than this native son could sense the inevitable reaction to the powers of the open electorate as established by the Organic Act? Division of voters into Democratic and Republican camps appeared at once; likewise a third or Home Rule party began to shout Walter Murray Gibson's slogan, "Hawaii for the Hawaiians." Commented the *Gazette* earlier: "It is a great mistake to suppose that the country was rid of Walter Murray Gibson when he died. His ghost still lives and reigns and edits the *Elele,* and his estate makes up the cash deficit." Numerically superior, Hawaiian voters sent as their first delegate to Congress Robert W. Wilcox, who had headed the insurrections of 1889 and 1895.

Apparently heedless of the Governor's admonition in his message to Hawaii's first Territorial Legislature, that body proceeded to spend the 129 days of its session wrangling over such propositions as a general jail delivery, abolition of the poll tax, also of the United States quarantine laws so far as they concerned Hawaii. The most notorious measure called for repeal of the tax of three dollars on female dogs enacted by the Legislature of 1898 to improve dogs' quality and reduce the great number of inferior ones. Discussion of its repeal, however, was a crowning absurdity in 1901, the bill actually becoming law over the Governor's veto and to this day tagging the whole session as the "Lady Dog Legislature."

Serious indeed was the joint resolution addressed to the President of the United States which voted want of confidence in Hawaii's first Governor, accusing him of incompetency; likewise, finally, adjourning the session without passing the appropriation bill to meet current expenses. With his customary patient courtesy, the Governor could do no less than immediately call an extra session. Dragging on for sixty additional days, this session drained the territorial exchequer even more heavily than the regular one had done.

Thomas G. Thrum's concise annual summary pointed out that the cost of the combined sessions had far exceeded that of the most expensive previous Legislature, that of 1886 for 129 days. A ray of hope gleamed, when the Republican minority of both houses vigorously opposed repeal of compulsory vaccination, also a persistent effort to saddle the city with a fifty-year franchise in favor of the tramway company. An immature and ill-drawn measure for county government did pass, but fortunately met the Governor's pocket veto. Characteristic of the would-be leaders, said Mr. Thrum, was "egotism and senseless opposition against government measures in general and the Governor in particular." Civil rebellion, quelled in 1889 and 1895, was indeed erupting again under legal guise.

In September of 1901, on receipt of the news of President McKinley's assassination at the hand of an anarchist, Honolulu's public offices were closed, courts adjourned, flags half-masted, and the following day business was suspended. Again on Saturday the 28th all places of business closed for impressive public memorial exercises in Hawaiian and English at Kawaiahao Church. Next day all churches were crowded for special services. And at once a public subscription was started for the McKinley monument south of Thomas Square in front of the high school which has since moved to ampler quarters on King Street, with the statue to mark its administration building.

Not for an instant was Theodore Roosevelt, McKinley's successor, left in ignorance of the political storm seething in Hawaii.

Every sort of newspaper from Pacific to Atlantic sounded off in varying key and tempo of rumor and fact. Some opposed, many favored the Dole administration. With steady detachment Mr. Dole's own unpublished reminiscence later elucidated not a few new points:

Many Hawaiians felt deeply the termination of the monarchical system of the Islands. At one time in the first territorial legislature there was considerable opposition and expression of feeling against Mr. Dole who had been President.

The Government of the United States tolerated these expressions in a kindly spirit and finally gave to one of the Hawaiian legislators, whose expression had been very definite and hostile against the late President of the Republic of Hawaii, an opportunity to visit the mainland of the United States in one of the government men-of-war.

This visitor was hospitably entertained on the mainland, in Washington given an opportunity to express his opposition to the late President of the Republic of Hawaii, and was eventually brought back to the Hawaiian Islands on a government ship, without any accomplishment of his fierce and definite opposition to the late President of the Republic of Hawaii. The conduct of the American Government in this matter tended to quiet hostility of this character and similar expressions in regard to the appointments of the government in the Hawaiian Islands.

In view of the many complaints from former Royalists and from new settlers in the Hawaiian Islands—objections which were very hostile to and critical of the Territorial Governor's conduct, referring also to policies of the late President of the Republic of Hawaii—President Roosevelt requested me to come to Washington. I therefore visited the nation's capital, accompanied from California by Mr. W. N. Armstrong. In Washington I met many old acquaintances, both Democrats and Republicans, among them Hawaiian Senator George R. Carter, son of the former Hawaiian Minister H. A. P. Carter who had been favorably known in Washington during King Kalahaua's reign. Young George Carter was the brother of my staff officer, Charles L. Carter, killed in the insurrection of 1895. George had been a classmate of Theodore Roosevelt at Yale College and was considerably in the confidence of the United States Government.

The President placed in the hands of Senator Carter and myself the numerous complaints which had come from the Hawaiian Islands in regard to my administration. We spent hours examining the charges and found nothing serious or vital. They were rather political than otherwise and unattended by evidence.

At the White House I spent an evening with President Roosevelt. We discussed Hawaiian affairs freely and informally, and I suggested to him perfect freedom in dealing with my official status according to the welfare of the Hawaiian situation. No immediate official action followed this interview however, and I was glad to turn my face home again to the Islands.

A Washington dispatch of April 14, 1902, printed the following official statement from the White House as of that day:

> The President, after most careful consideration, and hearing as many men as possible, and hearing from others, has come to the conclusion that Governor Dole's course has been such as to warrant his continuance as Governor of Hawaii and entitle him to the respect and hearty support of the Administration.

With such endorsement from President Roosevelt, and entertained from coast to coast by distinguished men, the Governor of the newest United States territory expressed himself as hopeful of success in guiding Hawaii toward statehood—distant but certain. After a short visit at Riverside, California, Governor Dole told a representative of the *San Francisco Chronicle* that many Hawaiians, disappointed at the inefficiency of Home Rule leaders, were already leaning toward the "grand old party" of Lincoln and McKinley. Also that Hawaii's Delegate to Congress, having assured his followers that he was certain to have Governor Dole removed from office, had in his two years at Washington fulfilled none of his electioneering promises and would have "no walkover this fall when general elections take place."

A letter in the Archives of Hawaii attests to a change of heart on the part of many Hawaiians. This letter, postmarked Washington, D.C., is to Mrs. Dole from Mrs. Robert Wilcox, wife of the Delegate to Congress. It recalls with gratitude their kindness to Mrs. Wilcox and her children during the imprisonment of Wilcox. It tells of political moves to unseat Governor Dole, and states that Mrs. Wilcox has thrown away such petitions. She adds that, while urged from some quarters to seek the position himself, Wilcox would rather be delegate than governor, and that he desires a good, upright man in the position at Honolulu.

Certainly in June of 1902 every wharf was crowded with all sorts of men to cheer their Governor's arrival at Honolulu, all shouting again and again as the *Alameda* reached the lighthouse, and the guns of a Governor's salute boomed all the while she was making her way up the harbor.

Bearing out Governor Dole's forecast, Hawaiian elections that fall showed not only a safe, though small majority of Republicans for both Senate and House of the Legislature, but perhaps even more significant the election of Prince Jonah Kuhio Kalanianaole as Republican Delegate to Congress. And for twenty years, until his death in 1922, Kuhio continued to carry this responsibility, spending himself and his private inheritance in intelligent devotion to his native land. Many a middle-aged Hawaiian today speaks affectionately of Kuhio as a real prince, who with his gracious wife showed unbounded hospitality to strangers in Washington.

To a great extent, as indicated by George F. Nellist in his *Builders of Hawaii,* Prince Kuhio personified the history of Hawaii in its transition from monarchy to territory. Naturally an ardent Royalist, he had been tried by the military commission in 1895, charged with misprision of treason, and sentenced to a year in jail. But in later years it was his wont to regale friends, Governor Dole among them, with stories of his own participation in the revolt of 1887, as also of his token sentence to hard labor in 1895 when he was assigned to masonry repairs on the prison walls. After annexation certainly no one was more loyal to the United States than Prince Kuhio.

In addition to the delegateship, Kuhio was a consistent advocate of the Hawaiian homesteading law, serving also as a member of the Hawaiian Homes Commission. In fact, we are reminded by the bulletin of that commission for December, 1922, that on Kuhio's death the previous January his wife, Princess Elizabeth Kalanianaole, was requested by Governor Farrington to succeed her husband as a member of the Commission. In this position she proved of distinct value due to her broad knowledge of the needs of her people, coupled with her keen interest in the Prince's plans for Hawaiian welfare and ultimate rehabilitation. Not without good reason was Molokai's first homestead section called the Kalanianaole Settlement.

Feeling, amid the stress of the 1896 epidemic that another enterprising lawyer might well shoulder many of the cares multiplying in the Attorney General's office in Honolulu, President Dole had written that year an urgent invitation to a cousin in Seattle. This was Edmund Pearson Dole, son of Isaiah Dole of Skowhegan, Maine. As a law partner in Keene, New Hampshire, he had for five successive terms been elected Prosecuting Attorney. Like another cousin, the Reverend Charles F. Dole, he took an active interest—long before others—in what he called a "Supreme

Court of the World," arguing logically that such a human tribunal would remove excuse for the wholesale international butchery of war. Although not yet appointed Deputy Attorney General, when coming through California to the Islands, E. P. Dole's Ward cousins there found themselves being impressively introduced as "relatives of the General."

Identifying himself at once as an advocate of annexation, the new Deputy Attorney General wrote warmly in October 1897 to a friendly Republican Congressman, Senator Chandler. Although a private letter only, permission for its publication was granted by the writer to the Honolulu correspondent of the *Springfield Daily Republican* which apparently printed it in full. Even a few of its points smack of the true Yankee and are at the same time stimulating and vigorous:

I wish you could sail with me in Pearl Harbor in the president's little yacht, the *Bonnie Dundee*. I would not object if you could be aground with me there all night, as I was last summer, and contemplate how this harbor gives the naval power which holds it command of the great Pacific Ocean. I wish you could see how intensely American the Americans are here, how intelligent they are as a class,—the kind of stuff the G.O.P. is made of.

There is no reason why these islands should not be represented one of these days by as bright a star as there is in the American flag, with a history to be as proud of as that of New Hampshire or Massachusetts. The truth is we have it already. The spirit of 1776 has burned as bright here as ever it did at Concord or Lexington or Bunker Hill.

Our interest in annexation is the sentiment of a child for its parent. We buy American goods. We do not raise more than 10 or 12 per cent of the sugar consumed in the United States. Our coffee industry is prosperous, and rapidly growing. It would do some of the men good who are freezing their hides off on New Hampshire hill farms to come out here and keep warm the year round, and make a little money at the same time. There is no finer climate on earth than this, not a bad place for an American millionaire to have a country home in everlasting June, and at the same time enjoy the blessing, which too many millionaires do not appreciate, of living under the stars and stripes.

The natives here are a fine race. My official duties take me constantly from island to island in all parts of this little republic. You know I won't lie to you. I tell you that the Islands will make just as good an American community as can be found on Uncle Sam's farm.

We have done everything we can do. Our Senate has ratified the annexation treaty by a unanimous vote. Your distinguished colleague, Senator Morgan of Alabama, is now visiting here. When he goes back, I hope you will help him all you can, even if he is a Democrat.

From June 14, 1900, Hawaii's Admission Day as United States territory, E. P. Dole served as Attorney General until his resignation on February 1, 1903. During these two and a half years, he reported, changed conditions had given rise to innumerable questions, many of them without precedent in the law books, and necessitating his writing 341 legal opinions at the request of the Governor, the heads of departments, bureaus and other officials.

The Governor's annual report for 1903 stated that on his resignation E. P. Dole was at once deputized by his successor, the new Attorney General, Lorrin Andrews, to present the case of the *Territory of Hawaii* v. *Mankichi* before the United States Supreme Court in Washington, D.C. The resulting decision was in favor of Hawaii and went to the settlement of many vexed questions of the so-called transition period, at a great saving of expense to the Territory and the prevention of a general jail delivery of desperate characters, against some of whom the evidence had disappeared.

Had the Governor, in this official mention of the late Attorney General, not been recording the achievement of his own near relative, he might well have added that Edmund P. Dole had in his argument for the appellant before the Supreme Court of the United States presented both a close-knit summary of Hawaii's years of monarchical administration and a clear legal survey of intricate jurisdictional problems encountered by the Republic of Hawaii during its last two years.

Certainly this brilliant, eccentric cousin of Sanford Dole played no small part in the drama of Hawaii just before and after the close of the nineteenth century. And perhaps Edmund P. Dole was never more congenial than when enjoying with his Hawaiian cousin a sail in the harbor. King Kalakaua himself had taken an active interest in yachting, first as a feature of his own birthday celebrations on November 16. Especially for the Coronation Regatta the king had the *Healani* built by T. Sorenson, a fine sloop of 9 tons, which carried off the first prize.

In July of 1889 Mr. Sorenson completed the *Hawaii,* a 9-ton yacht for a number of enthusiasts like L. A. Thurston, W. O. Smith, and Luther Wilcox of Kauai, and on the 4th of July the harbor presented an animated picture of races, as T. G. Thrum tells it, races preceded by an occasional practice cruise off Hanauma Bay, noted fishing ground of Oahu chiefs in early days.

In 1892 not a little interest had been felt on the arrival of the sloop yacht *Bonnie Dundee,* a creation of Fyfe's in Scotland, built to the order of a group including S. B. Dole, Luther Wilcox, and E. O. White. Though handicapped in later years by being barred from the use of topsail or spinnaker, "our Scotch yacht" won every race she entered from 1892 to 1899. In 1896 a special day, the third Saturday of September, was by legal enactment, due to A. G. M. Robertson, set apart as Regatta Day. In September 1899 a spirited race for a challenge cup took place between T. W. Hobron's new model sloop yacht *Gladys* and the *Bonnie Dundee* skippered by President Dole. Setting a hard pace for the new *Gladys,* the *Bonnie Dundee* finally yielded for the first time both race and cup.

Among the changes wrought by annexation to the United States not the least significant was the increased growth of a colony of farmers in the high, well-watered region of Wahiawa, north of Honolulu. For years before 1898 these farmers had grown and improved export fruits, especially pineapples, first attempting canning in 1892, but finding with import duty in California that all such products proved unprofitable. After removal of this duty by annexation, these growers made repeated attempts to establish a farmers' institute, succeeding at last in 1902.

First president of this gathering was Jared G. Smith, lately arrived director of the Hawaii Experiment Station, a new division of the Federal Agricultural Bureau. Even today Mr. Smith's "Do You Remember" column in the *Advertiser* tells of looking in vain for an office and the relief of finding, when he made his first New Year's call on the Governor, that the chief executive himself took the trouble to hunt him out a vacant room in the basement of the Capitol.

Both President Smith and Secretary Thomas F. Sedgwick of the Farmers' Institute still speak of Governor Dole's active cooperation, his conviction that farming would succeed even though slow to develop, and that the political future of Hawaii depended to a great degree upon the growth of just such farming colonies in the Islands. Moreover, the Governor wrote in January of 1902 to invite the competition of every member of the Farmers' Institute in the government agricultural exhibition to be held in July; and he included in his 1903 legislative budget an item of $300 to cover cost of publication for the first annual report of the Farmers' Institute. Is it any wonder that Secretary Sedgwick claims this farming colony as forerunner of the great pineapple industry of today?

One of the seventy-two members of this institute in 1902 was, as it happened, another scion of the house of Dole, who had been impressed by his cousin Sanford's enthusiastic accounts of agricultural possibilities in Hawaii. Coming from Harvard University in 1899 and acquiring sixty acres at Wahiawa, young James D. Dole focused attention on pineapples, to improve canning processes and advertise their uses.

This was uphill work, but spectacular success attended his enterprise known as Hawaiian Pineapple Company. In fact, during a single generation this became the world's largest pineapple packer, its initial capitalization of $20,000, hard-won and a gamble, mounting to thirty millions in 1930.

James Dole married a Maui girl, Belle Dickey, a Mission Cousin of the third generation. He and his family were often visitors in the Emma Street home of his cousins, Anna and Sanford Dole, who took keen interest in his agricultural and financial progress. One winter his father and mother, the Charles Fletcher Doles of Jamaica Plain near Boston, came out not only to see their son and his family, but to renew affectionate acquaintance with the Emma Street Doles who had tarried with them on their honeymoon journey thirty years before. Asked long afterward what he considered Sanford Dole's outstanding characteristic, Jim Dole, quoting E. D. Tenney, replied with the single word: "Imperturbability."

To this day Jim Dole enjoys telling of an occasion in 1902 while Governor Dole was sojourning with his Boston cousins. Active discussion turned one evening on the fact that a long-existing law in Hawaii prohibiting importation of snakes had inadvertently been omitted from the Territorial statute books. Exercised over a report that a snake had recently invaded Hawaii as member of a traveling circus, young Jim urged the Governor to revive the old prohibition. The latter suggested that his young cousin call on James Wilson, Secretary of Agriculture at Washington.

Nothing loath, James Dole discussed Hawaiian pineapples with the Secretary, mentioning too the need for a ban on snakes. Promising to take it up at the proper office, since it would be a maritime regulation under the Secretary of the Treasury, Wilson did so and the regulation was almost immediately forthcoming. As young Dole left the Secretary's office, he was tackled by a Washington reporter avid for news. Thus pressed, Dole admitted he had discussed pineapples. This proving a dull topic to Washington ears, he enlivened it by adding that the subject of snakes had been broached. Flaring headlines next day proclaimed this relative of Hawaii's Governor, acting under his orders, as the "Saint Patrick of Hawaii," a slogan telegraphed at once to the Honolulu *Advertiser* and automatically productive of valued publicity for Dole pineapples.

Shortly after annexation Mr. W. C. Ford, of the National Archives, came from Washington, as told by Hawaii's veteran archivist, Robert C. Lydecker, for the Hawaiian Historical Society, with a view to transferring Hawaiian government documents to the nation's capital. Even though interested members of the Hawaiian Historical Society had attempted to bring order out of the chaos among state papers from the time of Minister R. C. Wyllie, these and others had not been so well preserved in later years, and were still awaiting expert attention in 132 camphor chests and disorderly heaps in corners of various government storerooms. But to send them, especially Hawaii's complicated land records, away from Honolulu was unthinkable. Mr. Ford agreed to leave them, if a fireproof building were erected for their care.

Sanford Dole, who in Washington in 1898 had with the greatest interest taken three hours to examine every nook and cranny of the Library of Congress, agreed thoroughly that Hawaii must make the move to house her own government papers and records.

The Legislature of 1903 appropriated $75,000, but later plans were made for a less elaborate structure. By 1905 this was completed and placed under a board of commissioners which included the Secretary of the Territory.

Not the least of the improvements brought by the turn of the century, as S. E. Bishop wrote his friend G. D. Gilman in Boston, was the big flourish on August 28, 1901, with which the new Honolulu Rapid Transit Company started running electric trolley busses on its first five-mile track from Wyllie Street in Nuuanu to Manoa, crossing the city on Hotel Street.

Even more spectacular was completion of the long-sought trans-pacific cable service to Hawaii. Already, as noted by W. R. Farrington in Thrum's *Hawaiian Annual* for 1902, Marconi's strange telegraph without wires was being tried out on Oahu. And today, with radio tuning in on air waves, undersea telegraphic messages no longer take first place in importance, but eighty and even fifty years ago the picture was far different. As detailed in 1911 in all its intricacies by W. D. Alexander for the Hawaiian Historical Society, the story of the Pacific Cable involved more than a generation of dreams and hopes. Of Cyrus W. Field's attempt to "girdle the globe," after laying the Atlantic Cable, even trying for co-operation from the Czar of Russia in the remote fastness of St. Petersburg; of Caesar Celso Moreno—no less—obtaining from the United States Congress in 1876 an Act to Promote Telegraphic Communication between America and Asia; of the Australian cable syndicate in 1884; of the all-British cable, forced at last to connect via Fanning's Island instead of Hawaii's Necker; of the Pacific Cable Company about 1890, its prime mover Judge A. S. Hartwell, yet its high hopes doomed finally to disappointment because government ownership was favored; and at long last the all-American cable of John W. Mackay under the Commercial Cable Company which, unlike all preceding attempts, placed no dependence on government subsidies.

Not long ago Charles E. Hogue retold in the *Advertiser* the story of that dismally rainy Sunday of December 27, 1902, when Honolulu citizens of all sorts watched near the new cable hut at Sans Souçi, Waikiki. From the harbor the cable ship, the U.S.S. *Silverton,* coaled for sea duty, steamed out into wind and tumultuous waters to lay the Molokai channel section. Delays occurred. Hours dragged by. Some onlookers turned home.

Suddenly all realized that the *Silverton* was anchoring half a mile off shore. In the late afternoon a balloon float was seen coming over her side. This was the cable-head. The steel-clad cable followed, snake-like, balloon floats at ten-yard intervals keeping it from settling to the ocean floor. Slowly it came nearer, an outrigger canoe, the *Halekulani,* bringing the guide line ashore.

An hour later it had arrived. The band struck up Captain Berger's special "Cable March." On the cable-head Mrs. A. G. Hawes, wife of Governor Dole's private secretary, placed a dedicatory lei of *maile* and *ilima*. The crowd cheered, reached out to touch the steel cable-jacket—Could it be true?—then hurried home through darkness and mud.

Half of the cable section, its balloons released, fell into place that evening. Next morning the *Silverton* again put off for the Molokai channel, into weather still too rough however to operate that day or the next. But at last it was completed on Wednesday, January 1, 1903, a New Year's gift. At 8:15 that night, Secretary of the Territory Henry E. Cooper telegraphed Hawaii's first message. With characteristic promptness President Roosevelt replied in fifteen minutes.

Professor Alexander, Hawaii's scholar, early historian and Surveyor General, found it "worthy of mention that the all-British Pacific Cable via Vancouver Island to New Zealand and Queensland was opened for business on January 1, 1903, one day ahead of the all-American Pacific Cable."

On the 2d of January all Honolulu business houses closed while in the Capitol grounds occurred "a monster mass meeting," not of protest as in earlier years, but of rejoicing that the Hawaiian Islands no longer lay isolated from the rest of the world. Six months later on the 4th of July the Hawaii end of the Pacific Cable from the Philippines via Guam and Midway was landed at the Waikiki cable hut. Clarence Mackay, president in his father's stead, was only seventy miles from the nation's capital, but, again characteristically, Theodore Roosevelt telegraphed him around the globe via Honolulu and Manila. The Pacific Cable was indeed a world event.

With other changes had come the United States District Court for the new Territory of Hawaii to provide for admiralty matters, appeals, and all other cases beyond the jurisdiction of the territorial courts. As first presiding officer of this Federal District Court President McKinley's personal choice had been Judge Morris M. Estee of Pennsylvania, long a practicing lawyer in Sacramento, California. As a man with a deep sense of civic obligation, he had already a distinguished career. In 1878 he had taken a leading part in the Constitutional Convention of California, and was at one time presiding officer of the Republican National Convention. Yet as a stranger to Hawaii, he was at first viewed with reserve. Before very long, however, both Judge and Mrs. Estee were esteemed and welcomed as members of the community.

For the same Fourth of July which completed the Pacific Cable Judge Estee called a public meeting of the Federal Court at Honolulu. Moved undoubtedly by the irregularities of Hawaii's first two legislative sessions, this experienced Federal Judge deemed it wise to call "for patriotic expression concerning the principles upon which the government of the United States had been founded and conducted." Among other addresses, Governor Dole spoke briefly and to the point, with the significant statement that "it is harder to be a good citizen in time of peace than to be a good soldier in time of war." A general conclusion, it is true, yet with its own timely and particular application, for Sanford Dole himself had given the best ten years of his life to his native land which, in that short span, had laid upon him the demands of twenty or possibly even thirty ordinary years.

On October 27, 1903, Judge Estee's death occurred. It was such a personal grief to all Hawaii that Governor Dole requested the band to remain silent at the departure of the steamer taking Mrs. Estee home to California with the ashes of her husband, who had meant so much to the Islands.

For the vacant post as presiding Judge of the Federal District Court not a few Islanders felt Governor Dole especially fitted. On the 31st of October therefore general public approval met a cable message from President Roosevelt's secretary that Governor Dole had been appointed to succeed Judge Estee, and Secretary of the Territory George R. Carter to the post of Hawaii's second Governor. Many were gratified that the new Governor was to be an Island man familiar with Island conditions.

At the annual camp fire of Hawaii's First Regiment, on November 1, 1903, Governor Dole bade farewell to the troops at the drill shed, regretting that his eleven years as commander-in-chief of the National Guard were coming to an end. In a short address he begged the men to exercise their privilege of the voting franchise in behalf of honest government. Pointing out that the present territorial form of government was but temporary as a test of citizenship, the future, he hoped, would evolve the territory into a state.

Our territory is so small, smaller than many of the cities of the United States, that we must conduct our County Government in a patriotic and intelligent manner, to prove that we will be a credit as a State.

One thing more, for I may not have another opportunity to address you officially. I want you to know that I have enjoyed my long connection with the National Guard. I have never lost confidence in it, but have always found it ready to fight and drill for the maintenance of law and order in Hawaii and for the freedom of all citizens here.

I see many Hawaiians before me tonight. It is a good sign. More and more Hawaiians are going to make up the personnel of the National Guard. It is a sign of good citizenship which will make you more and more a credit to the United States. I shall always watch your career with deep interest. And I wish you all prosperity and success.

Springing to their feet, the men of the regiment burst into three hearty cheers, and a tiger.

It was clear that Governor Dole had already declined reappointment as Hawaii's chief executive, since Judge William L. Whitney states in his "General Comments" for *The Friend* of December 1903: "It has long been known that not even the urgency of the President could persuade the Governor to accept a second term. But the vacancy caused by the death of Judge Estee seemed to offer a position well suited to the ability and learning of Governor Dole. Of his ability there can not be the slightest question: of his capacity, mental honesty and discernment, and all the other qualities that go to make a successful judge, it were waste of breath here to speak, as they are universally acknowledged."

The new appointment as Federal District Judge, however, was not accepted before Mr. Dole had talked at length with Judge Francis M. Hatch, long his close friend and very faithful and patriotic associate in government matters. Mr. Hatch advised that the change was eminently appropriate, and Mr. Dole, convinced that his services were no longer particularly required in the administration of Hawaiian affairs, tendered his resignation as Governor.

AT EASE
1903–1926

FEELINGS of both regret and relief were associated with Mr. Dole's decision to resign as Hawaii's first Governor. For he admitted frankly to a sense of pleasure in freedom once more to take up judicial duties more definitely in his professional training than administrative demands incident to the Republic and Territory. After having virtually stood at "Attention" for eleven years as Chief Executive of the Hawaiian government, transfer to the duties of the Federal Court brought a welcome shift to the Command: "At Ease."

Beginning in 1842, even before he was born, every move in the evolving American-Hawaiian association had been initiated in Hawaii. First, as a struggle against foreign encroachments, and then a need for survival against forces from within had prompted each step in "a history of continuity rather than conquest." This is a progression ably demonstrated by Governor Dole in his inaugural address of June 14, 1900.

Sanford Dole knew his Hawaii. Even on the threshold of her evolution under territorial status he had met with characteristic deliberation the question as to her ultimate admission to the Union as a state. Education, including the experience of learning not only to use, but to grasp the significance of states' rights as well as privileges—these he deemed essential. Writing on July 27, 1900, he replied to a letter from United States Senator Morgan who had taken such active interest in annexation:

I appreciate your suggestion in regard to our working for an early admission to the Union of sovereign states; this is just what interests our community and the prospect of an early attainment of that status is very popular. I feel that a period of Territorial Government will be of advan-

tage to us in an educational way and will prepare voters for the assumption
of a political responsibility which will come to them under state sovereignty.

That statehood would eventually come as a natural sequence
of annexation Judge Dole sometimes remarked in conversation.
A full quarter-century, however, after his letter of 1900 to Senator
Morgan, Mr. Dole, in an interview with Hal H. Smith for the
New York Times of May 24, 1925, was even more pronounced in
his views concerning the unwisdom of statehood for Hawaii before
a still longer time had elapsed.

At last Judge Dole was able to enjoy longer visits at Aqua-
marine, his Diamond Head beach cottage; to invite friends to
share Sunday morning breakfasts either at Waikiki or in the
old Emma Street home; and more often to work as "the small
farmer of Pauoa Valley."

The Sunday breakfasts became an institution, with guests
from next door like the young Charles Chillingworths, as well
as other local friends, and often visitors from abroad. The
long table was set for eight to twenty or more guests. The host
had perhaps himself brought in ferns and the deep blue of queen's
cloak blossoms for a high vase at the table center; at the far end
Mrs. Dole was waiting to pour out strong coffee with hot milk;
Ah Lin, cook and friend, carefully trained as Mrs. Dole's household helpers always were, had a steaming New England breakfast
ready; and at the head was the tall figure of the host himself,
prepared to carve the huge papaia before him, serving seeds also,
as a dietetic aid. At each place the guest might find words of a
hymn typed by Miss Claire Uecke of Punahou, sometimes from
lines written by Judge Dole himself. And all at the table stood
while singing this hymn to some familiar tune as grace at meat.
The experience of such a meal was patriarchal, something never
to be forgotten.

Legends and memories of course began to cluster about so
unique an event. Once Mr. Dole introduced to the other guests
a young Hackfeld clerk just from Germany, who, he said, had
relatives in the Islands and therefore counted almost as a
kamaaina.

"Oh no, Judge," came the instant disclaimer, "they all tell
me I am still a *mahine*." A ripple of smiles mystified the young
man until his host with prompt courtesy remarked, "Hawaiian

words often seem confusing, George. The word you meant to use is *malihini* [newcomer] not *mahine* or *wahine* which means woman."

The conversation at these leisurely breakfasts offered as great a feast as the groaning board described by Mrs. Jack London after she and her husband had enjoyed a special Sunday meal at the Waikiki cottage. While a warm Kona wind drove in the sea at high tide to break against the retaining wall of coral reef rock, one luscious fruit after another had been served: not only papaias, spicy Isabella grapes, avocado pears, figs, mangoes and pineapples, but the curious soursop, strangely like cotton or marshmallows drenched with lemonade and crushed strawberries. Even baked breadfruit, broken open and steaming in its soft shellful of tender meat.

"But this exotic menu was not half! Eggs appeared in variety, with crisp bacon and delicious Kona coffee—and, as if to bind us to New England tradition, brown-bread with baked pork and beans!"

At other times a dish of brown cracked wheat of the Pima Indians would appear with cream and sugar, followed by broiled *amaama* (pond mullet) with taro cakes, or creamed salt salmon and poi.

The walls of Anna and Sanford Dole's home still echo in memory to some of the best talk in Honolulu. There Henry Castle initiated the debates of the Honolulu Literary Society in 1884. There in 1896 Mabel Loomis Todd of Amherst, a recognized authority, lectured on the New England poet, Emily Dickinson. And many another project was stimulated there by the initiative of the Doles. On January 1, 1904, at the annual New Year's reception, their cousin, Mrs. Maybelle Ward Walker, was the first to pour tea from the handsome silver service presented by the mercantile community of Honolulu.

With daily sessions of the Federal District Court, Judge Dole combined addresses having a wide range of interest. In 1905 for the dedication of the Bingham memorial at Punahou he was the chief speaker, as one of the few who recalled the original Bingham cottage of thatch. In 1907 he became the first president of the American Red Cross, Hawaiian Branch. For years Dole had been an interested member of the Kilohana Art League in which his wife was active. And in 1908 he seconded wholeheartedly the beginnings of the Children's Hospital sponsored in part by his Kauai friends, Mr. and Mrs. Albert Wilcox. The same year the Outrigger Canoe Club at Waikiki commanded his enthusiastic co-operation as one of its founders and the next year as second president.

During the summer of 1910 the Sanford Doles were hosts to the David Lymans of Chicago. David, returning to the Islands for the first time in fifty years, found the grand old mountains and sky and swiftly rolling surf still unequaled in any other part of the world.

While Sanford and Anna Dole as young people had been planning their home on Emma Street, their opposite neighbors a little farther down the street had been the Cleghorn family in the storied white frame house which in 1956 is occupied by the Pacific Club. This had been built in the early years of 1870 by the Edinburgh Scot, Archibald S. Cleghorn; to it he had brought Princess Likelike as his bride; and in one of its large bedrooms their daughter, the little Princess Kaiulani, had been born in 1875. When she was a child of three her parents sold this home to James Campbell, and had moved out to the ten-acre estate, Ainahau, later a favorite haunt of Robert Louis Stevenson, now marked by the modern Princess Kaiulani Hotel.

All this early friendship, and much more, swiftly pictured itself in Sanford Dole's mind when he learned after Mr. Cleghorn's death in 1910 of his princely legacy of Ainahau to the city of Honolulu. Dole recalled too Cleghorn's enthusiastic co-operation in the earlier development of Kapiolani Park. And when Mrs. Emma Nakuina campaigned for retention of the Ainahau estate as a public park, Judge Dole was quick to support the project. When the Legislature declined, this beautiful property was divided and sold as city lots.

For the Doles, the months of 1911 filled a banner year. The 11th of February saw the laying of not one only, but actually two cornerstones for the new Y.M.C.A. building on the *mauka* corner opposite the old brick hall of 1883. The first cornerstone, in the Alakea Street wall, held records deposited twenty-eight years before; the second stone, in the Hotel Street wall, marked the new building. As first president of the Association, Judge Dole presided at both these ceremonies. And on the 23rd of February it was equally fitting that he should be chosen to unveil the statute of President McKinley at the high school bearing McKinley's name. As personal friend and associate of the martyred American President, Dole had not only been foremost in starting subscriptions for the monument in 1901, but had stayed with the project until its completion ten years later.

Among early cases in the Federal Court which Judge Dole described were those in Eminent Domain for condemnation of Fort Street land then intended for the proposed Federal Building:

The cases required half a dozen separate trials because of different titles, and involved protracted investigations as to value. The jurors, men of intelligence and public spirit, and drawn from the whole group of islands, took notes and patiently studied the intricacies of the investigations. Very just verdicts were reached, as it seemed to me. The United States Government did not see its way clear to profit by these investigations and judgments. Yet though they brought no results, they remain in the reports of the Federal Court a valuable chapter of Eminent Domain work. After some further negotiations the Federal Government decided on the block next the Court House and obtained it for the present Federal Building.

The work of the Federal Court was quite active, that in the naval department being particularly interesting, and much of the criminal work established in Hawaii being regular in this court. When my first term of six years was exhausted in 1910, the government appointed me for another term. It had been a satisfaction for me to take up the work of the Federal Court of Hawaii, but after a while this increased to such an extent that I found I could hardly carry it on alone and suggested that a second Federal Judge be appointed with me. This was favorably considered by the Attorney General in Washington and Judge A.G.M. Robertson, the appointee, assisted me with great ability until he was called to the Hawaiian Bench as Chief Justice.

In 1911 the government consented to a vacation which would give me a chance to visit Europe. On this trip I started in the spring of the year, my wife, and my niece, Dr. Emily Dole, accompanying me. Our trip, including three months in England, was very delightful and refreshing.

For many years Anna Dole had read of the wonders of the Tate and National Galleries in London, the British Museum, of Warwick Castle, Kenilworth, Windsor. More than once her husband had been forced to postpone the long journey. Now it was all like a dream come true at last. Tireless in accompanying his wife and Emily, Sanford kept a weather eye out for politics and the operation of government. Oxford seemed to him to vie with Florence as being the most architecturally beautiful town in Europe. For hours he would sit in St. James Park watching the many wild birds.

They heard Melba sing, saw Lily Langtry in *Sins of Society,* and went to hear the best non-conformist preacher in London, G. Campbell Morgan. They were invited to lunch with American Ambassador and Mrs. Whitelaw Reid, and visited Windsor Castle on the last day it was open to the public before the coronation of King George V.

In ancient style on the top of a coach Sanford rode to the Derby. As he himself wrote,

I early made the acquaintance of Lord Chief Justice Alderson, sometimes attending his court where I was accorded a seat on the Bench. On one occasion Judge Alderson invited me to a dinner of the Goldsmiths, a group in existence for eight centuries. At the end of the dinner a very interesting performance took place which reminded me of a similar formality in Hawaiian feasts thought to be of great antiquity. A shallow bowl was passed around into which the guests dipped their fingers. In the case of the Goldsmiths however the shallow dish was of solid gold, whereas the Hawaiians used an *umeke* fitted with a ridge for cleaning the fingers. On leaving, the waiter who showed me out brought me a small heavy box mounted in silver. When I reached home, Mrs. Dole said of course it was filled with gold! But we found it full of choice candy.

Invited also to lunch with the Lord Chief Justice and his sister, Judge Dole, victim of a heavy cold, was on the point of declining, but was told that that simply was not done. Both Anna and Sanford however agreed that it would be best not to attend the coronation.

While Anna and Emily went off to York and Fountains Abbey, Sanford luxuriated in going by himself to the North Sea to visit his old friend, the Reverend Alexander Mackintosh, retired from Honolulu to an ancient church at Holme-next-the-Sea. Joined by Anna and Emily next day, they all enjoyed a very homelike time, with bowling and croquet on the lawn, next day walking a mile over a real country road for a picnic at the seaside. On leaving, Sanford

was taken by Mr. Mackintosh in his dog cart by a roundabout way—over old Roman roads in good repair. It was hay-cutting time, the crops being taken off with long, oldfashioned scythes, the roadside in places brilliant with corn-flowers and poppies. Mr. Mackintosh's parish is about a mile square and his parishioners, laborers and fishermen, nicely housed in brick cottages; his church a very old one with many ancient burial stones in the grounds. The rural landscape in England is very beautiful—almost everywhere a rolling country with great diversity of landscape, no high mountains, but gently pastoral, with old buildings and castles and churches here and there.

Crossing to the continent, they all found Paris beautiful and very unlike London. For Sanford interest focused on the democratic and enthusiastic celebration in memory of destroying the monarchical prison fortress, the Bastille. Day after day festivities went on in the streets, restaurant tables being set out, almost blocking the passage. In the evening dancing to a piano or organ would stop all traffic at crossings until the dance ended, a cross section of democracy including girls and boys, young men and women, mechanics and their wives, persons in high official life— all eager to resume as soon as the next dance was called. At Versailles driving through the ancient forest, watching for deer, was equally, if not more interesting than the elegant palace of Louis XVI and Marie Antoinette.

The heat of July made especially enjoyable a drive with the William G. Irwins of Honolulu through the environs of Paris with *al fresco* lunch at an open restaurant. And always the statuary and paintings in Paris were of absorbing interest. Leaving for Brussels, the good part of a day was spent in Bruges in the beautiful old cathedral with its basement for servants of the masters and mistresses who worshiped in the main floor auditorium. But what drew Sanford's attention was the ringing of chimes every fifteen minutes from the tower of the Town Hall, and the lace makers seated along the shady side of the streets, each with her pillow and bobbins, busily at work.

Returning to Brussels in the evening through orchards and wheat fields growing high, the travelers noted Belgium's great population and prosperity. Grocers showing all kinds of produce, especially cheeses, Edam cheese rosy like fruit. On the top of rising ground stood the old Palais de Justice, wrote Sanford, "really the most interesting court house we observed in Europe. There were commodious rooms for courts and everything con-

nected with the operation of Justice. The Court House in Honolulu is built somewhat on the same plan. To get an idea of the
size of the one in Brussels, compare the supporting columns:
twelve or fifteen inches in diameter at Honolulu, as against a
diameter of about six feet in Brussels."

Up along the Rhine to Cologne, "with its immense cathedral,
I suppose the most satisfactory and beautiful church building in
all Europe"; then by river steamer to Coblenz, Mainz, Eisenach
and Dresden, for two weeks there at the famous sanitarium baths.
Here Sanford found the diet "undoubtedly beneficial to the jaded
and overfed patients who were there in large numbers. But for
me it was insufficient. I had to insist on changes, which were
allowed." In Dresden itself "of chief interest is the Gallery and
its large collection of paintings, with one room for the Sistine
Madonna alone. Men generally took off their hats before her, but
some, evidently Americans, kept theirs on their heads."

Chance meetings with Honolulu friends brought the zest of
sharing freshly these summer travels. Into the north of Italy too
they went for glimpses of those ancient cities. By invitation of
the Walter Dillinghams, they visited the beautiful villa where
Walter and Louise Dillingham had been married the year before.
And afterward, when their sister May Frear came to Emma Street
to talk over an anticipated trip to Europe, Judge Dole, standing
before a Venetian painting in his parlor, spoke especially of riding
in the gondolas of Venice, adding characteristically, "Be sure to
escape from the throng and go up one of those domestic canals
for the sheer intimate peace and beauty they give."

In London, at the entrance to the British Museum, Dole had
an unexpected encounter described in the biography of Admiral
Togo by Vice-Admiral Ogasawara. One can see the tall, plainly
dressed Mr. Dole, just leaving the building, but instantly recognizing the slight form of Admiral Togo as he entered, his uniform
glittering with gold braid and decorations for valor. Dole advanced with extended hand. Confused, the Admiral inquired of
his aide as to the identity of the stranger thus unceremoniously
accosting him. "Oh, that is former President Dole of the Provisional Government in Hawaii," was the historical cue.

Suddenly, it all came back. Honolulu—1893. The Japanese
charged with murder by Hawaiian authorities, swimming out to

his battleship, the *Naniwa,* to seek asylum in the harbor. The refusal of then Captain Togo to return the fugitive on the ground that Hawaii's Provisional Government had not been recognized by Japan; cabled orders from the more cautious imperial government, and final relinquishment of the prisoner through the Japanese consul. Also—Togo could hardly fail to recall the day in January, 1894, the first anniversary of the Provisional Government, when in Honolulu harbor Captain Togo's own ship remained silent and unadorned, with some other foreign ships, for the same diplomatic reason.

Now, in London of 1911, all in the suite of the visiting Japanese nobility had been accorded high honors, and Admiral Togo, who had received his naval education in England, was a popular hero much publicized by the London press.

As if the year 1911 were not already full, December saw Judge Dole an honor guest at the official opening of Pearl Harbor as an American naval base. The Honolulu Chamber of Commerce reported that without a single vote in opposition Congress had passed a measure in 1908 appropriating over three million dollars to dredge the harbor, straighten the approach, and construct a naval station as well as a great drydock. Work started September 1, 1909. The channel connecting the inner locks with the open sea was completed in 1911.

At nine in the morning of the 14th of December the United States armored cruiser *California,* flagship of the Pacific fleet, left Honolulu, decked out in all her bunting, the first large vessel ever to enter Pearl Harbor.

She was carrying more than 250 prominent persons, including Rear Admiral Chauncey Thomas, commander-in-chief of the Pacific fleet, and ambitious to be the first commander to make the harbor passage. On the quarterdeck of the flagship was Judge Dole; also as guest of the United States Mrs. Likiuokalani Dominis, last monarch of the Hawaiian kingdom; E. I. Spalding, president of the Chamber of Commerce; W. F. Dillingham, president of the Hawaiian Dredging Company, and the visiting Sun Fo, son of Dr. Sun Yat Sen, founder of the Chinese republic.

Following close in the wake of the *California,* was the interisland steamer *Claudine,* chartered by the Chamber of Commerce and conveying the Royal Hawaiian Band under Captain Henry Berger.

Behind the *Claudine* came the inter-island steamer *Helen* of the Hawaiian Dredging Company, and numerous launches from the warships joined the parade with whistle salutes. Gone forever the joyous days of little white private yachts sailing in and out of Pearl River without permission or inspection.

At 11:08 A.M. the *California's* bluff bow snapped a ceremonial yellow ribbon stretched across the channel between the dredge *Gaylord* and a scow. At 11:32 A.M. the cruiser tripped anchor in the harbor, opposite the long drydock then under construction.

At a signal from the ice plant that the *California* had dropped anchor, horns and factory signals began a din that lasted ten minutes.

The administration building, with all other equipment, was completed in 1915. The construction of the great drydock is a story in itself. Called often Wai Momi (Pearl River), the name of the harbor was due to great beds of pearl oysters there as early as 1817. Its usual Hawaiian name was Ke Awa lau o Pu'uloa (the Many-harbored Sea of Long Hill). Numerous small sharks were so tame and friendly, Mrs. Kawena Pukui tells us, that Hawaiians had fun mounting and riding them as cowboys ride horses. This is an actual fact, not a tall fish story, she adds. To turn these sea-mounts, one needed only to apply slight pressure just back of the eyes.

When it was proposed, says Mrs. Pukui, to build a great drydock in this Many-harbored Sea of Long Hill, old-timers shook their heads. Not with any objection to the drydock in itself, but because the location chosen was directly over the cave home of the shark chief, and the *kia'i* (guardian of the place) would resent this intrusion.

For four years the work progressed. Thrum reports that, while pumping out the completed sections of the drydock, the eight-foot layer of concrete with its piling as a flooring and the crib-work for its construction was suddenly forced up by hydrostatic pressure, wholly wrecking the work of four years in as many minutes, leaving it shattered and broken in its every part. To the Hawaiians, adds Mrs. Pukui, this was no surprise. Yet no life had been lost. When reconstruction on a revised plan was undertaken all went well and it was completed in 1919.

Early in 1912 came news to Sanford Dole of the death of his brother George on the 17th of February, in California. His closest friend. How well worth while had been those seventy years! Instinctively Sanford's memory harked back to their childhood days together, and for George's children he carefully wrote down those memories lest they be lost. That stalwart family, the Lucky Thirteen, its youngest member now twenty-two, had become very definitely an integral part of Sanford Dole's own life. Just as he himself had been as much at home in or on the water as on land, even holding his own with the Hawaiians as a shark fighter, and being recalled by his Williams College mates "chiefly as a mighty swimmer, runner, climber, walker and fighter"; so all his nieces and nephews did well in athletics, some excelling; and every one of the ten boys, except young Sanford who as a child lost the use of one eye, was outstanding at Cornell or Stanford in crew, track, football, and pole vaulting. In scholarship too their record was excellent. Well might their uncle disclaim Theodore Roosevelt's fear that American families were in danger of becoming smaller and less hardy.

Once annexation had become a fact, Sanford Dole's interest turned to a subject which he had had in mind for years, namely that possibly with government aid not poverty only but especially its causes might be gradually eliminated. To this end what was known as the Dole Plan called for unification of the thirteen local relief societies for the poor and distressed. At a meeting of representative citizens in March, 1899, Sanford Dole was made president of the Associated Charities. In 1913 he was still in office and greeted with enthusiasm the arrival of Miss Margaret Bergen, an experienced social work organizer. At the first meeting Miss Bergen spoke of a general trend toward state aid, adding weight to Mr. Dole's earlier recommendation that support be sought through legislation.

In January of 1913 Judge Dole spoke with deep interest at Punahou School when he presided at the dedication of the bronze memorial to General Samuel Chapman Armstrong. With a strong personal overtone he repeated the General's ultimate expression of gratitude: "I am most thankful for my parents, for my Hawaiian home, and for college days at Williams."

A spirit of enlargement was abroad. One of the new movements, to eliminate ugliness and to increase beauty in the city, centered in the capable hands of the women's Outdoor Circle. The members were ambitious. They hoped to do away with billboard advertising by both local and mainland firms. Sanford Dole followed the work with interest. The *Hawaiian Trustee* leaflet of May, 1953, recalls that the campaign opened with a special edition of the *Advertiser,* edited by Lorrin A. Thurston. This meant that Mr. Thurston backed the women with all the facilities at his command. A copy of that issue is now a collector's item. This was May 10, 1913. By 1927 every local firm had stopped using billboards. Also, the women later planted thousands of shrubs and trees along miles of roadways.

While the shadow of war was still far off from Hawaii, Judge and Mrs. Dole met in their home at 1534 Emma Street a group of citizens called together after Mr. Theodore Richards' stirring summons entitled "Hawaii's Golden Opportunity." This was for the relief of war orphans and widows, and is recorded in the pages of *The Friend* for October, 1914. Appointed chairman, Mr. Dole suggested local handling of funds for all nations at war, since the Red Cross was greatly overtaxed. Local British residents were raising funds for relief, also local Germans for the Red Cross. The secretary of this meeting at the Doles' recorded that within a few weeks the sum of $10,500 had been subscribed, perhaps up to that time Hawaii's greatest effort toward war relief.

Unique as an adopted son of Hawaii and created a Noble of the monarchy through his wife, the last of the Kamehameha line, Charles Reed Bishop died in San Francisco in 1915. On the 23d of June his ashes lay in state in Kawaiahao Church where the ancient *mele inoa* (name songs) of the Kamehamehas were chanted for him. And above the urn long *kahilis* waved in slow rhythm for the first time in memory of a white man connected with the Kamehameha dynasty, since the lying in state of the senior John Young, Kamehameha's trusted adviser, eighty years before. Representing royalty, Mrs. Dominis, formerly queen of the realm, took her special seat in the church, followed by the ten honorary pall-bearers, of whom Judge Dole was one. The Reverend Henry Parker gave the memorial address.

At the grounds of the Royal Mausoleum in Nuuanu the queen's automobile was the only one to enter, while the band played. This was Captain Berger's last official conducting of the band which he had led for forty years. Escorted into the tomb by the honorary pall-bearers, Mr. Bishop's urn was placed by Prince Kalanianaole on the casket of Mrs. Bernice Pauahi Bishop. After the short benediction, pall-bearers and pastor filed out of this resting place of kings, the heavy doors were closed and bolted.

One who gazed long in farewell at Mr. Bishop's flower-covered urn was young William Bishop Taylor, who later until his death in 1956 was custodian of the Royal Mausoleum. His mother, Keomailani, was of chiefish descent and therefore accompanied by two other little Hawaiian maidens as attendants when she had been sent by Mrs. Bernice Pauahi Bishop to be educated at Ascot Priory in England. On her return journey to Honolulu, Keomailani was chaperoned at Queen Emma's request by Mrs. J. S. McGrew with her small daughter Kate, now Mrs. Charles B. Cooper. To this day Mrs. Cooper tells vividly of her mother's embarrassment on needing to borrow money from a strange gentleman on the overland train to cover the unexpected expense of Keomailani's heavy English "boxes" of books and music; also of Keomailani's wedding not long after at Honolulu in the little wooden pro-cathedral of St. Andrew's; the groom was Mr. Wray Taylor, cathedral organist for many years, and small bridesmaids, Kate McGrew and Emmelita Wilder, were both very proud of their new white dresses adorned with broad red satin sashes! William Bishop Taylor, son of this marriage, was taken as an infant into Mrs. Bishop's motherly care. And well he remembered the day in 1888 when he sat on Mr. Bishop's knee during the drive in a hack out to the new Kamehameha Preparatory School to be entered among its first pupils.

Many look through the wrought iron gateway of the Royal Mausoleum today, on Nuuanu's Mauna Ala (Fragrant Mountain), but not many realize that the old mausoleum itself, erected of coral reef rock in 1864 for Kings Kamehameha II, III, IV, and V, is today no longer a burial repository. Fewer still can see that lovely and loved hillside as it was, among rocks and trees in the fragrant greenwood always fresh in breeze and shower or sunshine, its eastern slope dropping abruptly toward the roar of Kapena Falls in the Nuuanu stream. Well named had been Mauna Ala, last resting place of Hawaii's sovereigns.

And very few recall that still earlier tomb near the palace. At a meeting of the Hawaiian Historical Society in 1930 Emma

Ahuena Taylor spoke of this first tomb in the heart of Honolulu on land known as Pohukaina, belonging to High Chiefess Kekauluohi, mother of King Lunalilo. And at this same meeting in September, 1930, the Hawaiian Historical Society passed a resolution to be forwarded to Governor Judd asking that the mound of this early tomb site be surrounded by a suitable railing marked by a descriptive tablet in bronze to memorialize this historic spot. Such action was authorized by Governor Judd on October 17, 1930.

During the reign of Kamehameha IV a new tomb was begun in Nuuanu Valley. And although this more modern mausoleum at Mauna Ala was unfinished in 1863 on the death of Kamehameha IV, his body was the first to be brought to it, followed not long thereafter by that of his only child, the little Prince of Hawaii, who, dying earlier, had at first had his own small tomb very close to the royal palace. After the death of Minister Wyllie in 1865, he too rested at Mauna Ala with the king he had served and the little prince he had loved. Followed then eighteen much older caskets from the first royal tomb at Pohukaina, the south corner of the palace grounds. Richard A. Greer, in the *Advertiser* of May 8, 1955, pictures this long slow procession of drays at dead of night by full moon, and followed on foot by King Kamehameha V, and his aged father, Governor Kekuanaoa, with other chiefs and high officials.

In 1887, by the terms of Princess Bernice Pauahi Bishop's will, a new crypt for the older Kamehameha sovereigns was excavated just *mauka* of the Royal Mausoleum at Mauna Ala. On the death of the Honorable Charles R. Bishop in 1915, the placing of his urn with the others in this special crypt marked the closing of this vault forever. In 1904, just to the north, a second vault, erected by friends and relatives, had received from the original mausoleum nine remaining caskets of the Kamehamehas, as well as those of Minister R. C. Wyllie and Dr. T. C. B. Rooke, foster-father of Queen Emma. Both these newer crypts were then dedicated in solemn ceremonies under Bishop Restarick of the Episcopal Church.

In 1910 the burial of the Honorable A. S. Cleghorn was the last in the south face of the third vault, excavated by the territorial government in solid rock, now marked by a tall shaft of dark

marble. This was for the Kalakaua dynasty and is just north of
the original mausoleum. Later the empty interior of the older
temporary tomb was refinished and consecrated as a royal chapel.

At repeated urging by his vigorous younger contemporary,
Lorrin A. Thurston, Judge Dole was about 1914 preparing nine
historical papers on the Hawaiian revolution. Mr. Thurston had
in mind a historical series, including memories of his own official
connection, to be printed in the *Advertiser*. Publication of the
whole did not take place at that time. When, however, Judge
Dole first read Mr. Thurston's introduction, he wrote his instant
response which in penciled manuscript still lies in his own letter
file:

Mr. Thurston's introduction to my simple narratives, in its high praise,
took me entirely by surprise. I had not anticipated from any quarter such
favorable analysis of my part in the critical period referred to; nor do I feel
that I can accept it without recognizing the unstinted service rendered by
many regardless of its unknown dangers, and actuated by the bravest
and most unselfish devotion to the cause, men unused to exposure, spending
nights and days in the mountain forests without shelter; women who sent
their husbands to the front instead of allowing them to remain at home to
defend their families, in times when foreign representatives offered their
stations for the protection of defenseless women and children. Mr. Thurston
was himself a conspicuous leader in initiating the movement, which depended greatly on his firmness and decision and courage. Many others
could be named for like service and qualities, but I would not know where
to stop.

It was an enterprise in which our escape from serious destruction to life
and property was due, without doubt, to our ever vigilant preparedness,
excepting however, the situation at the launching of the movement, when
our organization and plans, arranged in haste, were as yet incomplete. We
certainly owed much, on this first day, to circumstances entirely out of our
control.

In 1916 occurred the death of W. E. Rowell, one of the devoted
helpers in the Revolution. Farewell services, conducted by Pastor
Henry Parker of Kawaiahao, were held on the hospitable lanai of
the Emma Street home where Anna and Sanford had so often
made Will Rowell a welcome guest. June of 1916 saw too the
seventy-fifth anniversary of Punahou School, with celebrated
mainland guests and Judge Dole presiding at its opening ceremony in Kawaiahao Church.

This same year Judge Dole's second term as Federal District Judge came to a close, although he continued on for a number of months until his successor could arrive. While retiring states Federal judges, who were seventy years old and had served ten years, received their salaries for life, that form of pension did not obtain in the case of territorial judges. The *Springfield Weekly Republican* of December 23, 1915, states that a bill for such a territorial pension had just been submitted to the United States Senate and House, "offered chiefly for the benefit of Sanford Dole, [who] saved the Hawaiian Islands from revolution and bloodshed, and more than any other man is responsible for their peaceable annexation to the United States. The Bar Association of Honolulu has sent a representative to Washington to urge favorable action for the man who was such a good friend when the government needed him.

"For many years," continued the Massachusetts paper, "the territorial Legislature of Hawaii has been voting a handsome pension to the ex-Queen, and it is claimed that, with quite as much warrant, Judge Dole should be pensioned, without regard to his judicial services. It is doubtful if Congress will pass it."

Apparently no Congressional action eventuated. Certain local firms, however, as an honorarium made up the amount of Judge Dole's official salary for the last ten years of his life. These corporations, which named him honorary advisor, were C. Brewer & Company, Castle & Cooke, Limited, and Alexander & Baldwin, Limited.

The year 1917 falling as the jubilee of Dole's year at Williams College, he and his wife once more set out on the long, delightful journey across sea and land to the Atlantic Coast. One of the classmates whom Sanford Dole particularly anticipated seeing was Dr. Hamilton Wright Mabie, for many years associate editor of the *Outlook*. But his death occurred just before the celebration. This fiftieth anniversary was the first college reunion that Sanford Dole had been able to attend. To be with nine other "boys" of the class of 1867 in beautiful Williamstown was indeed a distinction. Afterward he rejoined Anna at Castine, where summer weeks of sailing up and down the Maine coast brought him keen pleasure. At Mount Desert Island with the Charles Fletcher Doles this was continued. In the realization that they might never be seeing these friends and places again, both Anna and Sanford did indeed enjoy every moment to the full. Returning with them, to their mutual pleasure, was Clorinda (Jessamine) Low, Lizzie's daughter, who graduated that year from Smith College.

Judge Frear, who, as the President's choice for Hawaii's third governor, had closed his term of office as Chief Justice of the Supreme Court, once remarked that Judge Dole would frequently oppose people on violently controversial topics without losing their friendship. This had been particularly true in the case of the queen, for after annexation Mr. Dole always attended public receptions at her home, Washington Place, and Judge Frear knew that the kindliest feelings existed between the two who had been Hawaii's chief executives in a time of political crisis.

One who was companion to the former queen in her later years was Mrs. Lahilahi Webb, the same person whose life as a little serving-maid had been claimed and protected by the new queen in 1891 during the king's funeral ceremonies.

In 1917 Lahilahi, who slept in the queen's room, dreamed that she saw the queen's own *kahili* slowly bending low over her in the great bed. The *kahili* as symbol of the *alii* had spoken truth even in a dream. There was no question, Lahilahi knew that the queen would die, as she did that very night, the 11th of November. Mourning was sincere and wide-spread. The queen's body lay in state in the former throne room, and with wonted Hawaiian splendor was conveyed to the Royal Mausoleum.

Not many months after their return from New England Sanford Dole noticed his wife Anna was in reality saying farewell to her familiar surroundings, not in words, but with looks that bestowed a caress. Once it was at the corner of the garden against the banana trees where she had used to set up her easel. Again, walking alone between the two rows of tall royal palms leading to the entrance on Emma Street. Growing quieter, content often to sit quite still on the veranda. This lowered vitality, he wrote, brought "her gradually nearer and nearer to departure for the new land, which came in August of the year 1918." She was laid to rest in the little Mission graveyard close to Kawaiahao Church.

Sanford's mind turning more and more to the past, he set down telling recollections of old Governor Kekuanaoa and Honolulu's early Fish Market with its gala Saturday afternoon. By contrast

Harbor of Honolulu with troops drilling in Government Square

Photograph at the Emma Street home by R. J. Ba[

Sanford B. Dole on his eightieth birthday

also, childhood memories of General Meetings of the Mission in the old adobe schoolhouse still in use for Kindergarten Association offices on Mission Lane. This paper for the Hawaiian Mission Children's Society called forth a spirited reply from Titus Munson Coan, a Hilo boy, but long a resident of New York City, who had returned only in memory to the shores of his boyhood. Well he recalled, however, the day of September 3, 1852, when he and Sanford Dole joined the Mission Children's Society. "The Hawaiian Republic under your presidency," he wrote him, "I have always thought of as probably the most upright and humane government I knew of. I deplored its termination—so did President Cleveland. 'Do you think,' said Cleveland to me, 'the U.S.A. needs any more *real estate*?' But enough. May your shadow never grow less, or that noble beard any shorter."

Honors multiplied. On Judge Dole's seventy-fifth birthday in 1919 he sat by invitation as the special guest of the Bar Association at the Pacific Club. And in June of that year the eight-year-old College of Hawaii, whose founding he had followed with keen interest, conferred upon him the honorary degree of Doctor of Laws. Addressing him, President Arthur L. Dean said, in essence: "Wise administrator, eminent jurist, true friend, no man has yet measured the breadth and depth of your service to these Islands."

Published in *The Friend* of May, 1920, in compliment to the one-hundredth anniversary of the arrival of the American Protestant Mission, was Judge Dole's account of the wedding of King Kamehameha IV to Emma Kaleleonalani. With the royal standard floating from the then-white wooden spire of the old King's Chapel, this wedding was a gala event not to be missed. The year was 1856. On the fringe of the crowd, all eyes, had stood a tall lad of twelve, Sanford Dole.

Early in 1923 the death of Judge Hatch moved his friend and colleague, Sanford Dole, to give for the *Advertiser* something of his own appreciation of the tact and rare judgment shown by Hatch during revolutionary times. For many this brief reference will touch on an unfamiliar phase of the critical tension and confusion crowding those long past years:

After the Royalist uprising in 1895, certain British demands came in for damages for arrest and imprisonment of some of its subjects who were connected with the insurrection. These claims were examined by Mr. Hatch, and one, on his recommendation, was paid. He met the rest with a brief reciting their disloyal acts and quoting largely from British cases relating to similar occurrences in one of Britain's West India colonies.

The English government did not attempt to reply to Mr. Hatch's brief, but persisted in their support of the claims. Probably only annexation to the United States saved us from war with England or from their forcible collection. The claims are still unpaid.

Even in his eightieth year Sanford Dole's active mind carried the thread of his thinking which fifty years before had focused on co-operatives. In 1884 and for years thereafter his theme had been homesteading the land. Now in 1924 he was even more firmly convinced that shareholders in business enterprises would always be loyal, interested workers.

To this end he studied the marked success of mainland corporations such as Standard Oil and Sears Roebuck who for a number of years had used profit-sharing as a supplement to wages. Why could not Hawaii benefit by some such plan?

Since Mr. Dole's time more than fifty Hawaiian corporations have adopted profit-sharing plans and are demonstrating the value of the principle involved.

Interested always in old friends as well as new, Sanford lost no time in writing to congratulate a younger man taking up political responsibilities. This was Hiram Bingham III, on his election as Governor of Connecticut. This honor was the very next day resigned in favor of a vacancy suddenly occurring in the United States Senate. Recalling his Honolulu boyhood, Senator Bingham replied to tell Judge Dole of his genuine pleasure at receiving the letter of congratulation. "Ever since I was a boy," he wrote, "I have looked up to you as an ideal citizen and statesman."

On his eighty-first birthday in 1925 Sanford Dole enjoyed going out to Haleiwa at Waialua for a swim with nieces and a nephew. Dr. Emily Charlotte Dole had come to spend most of her time with him. Clara too had joined them, also Charles from his homestead on Kauai. Since their mother's death in 1916, their Uncle Sanford had hoped to move her grave as well as that of his brother George from Riverside to the little Mission cemetery at Kawaiahao. On May Day of 1925, with Clara junior, Emily, and Charles all present, this transfer was made to the old Dole plot there.

In 1925, too, Sanford Dole accepted the invitation from Central Union Church to become a member where he and Anna had so often attended. Here he was made very welcome without discussion of tenets or faiths. "Wandering in the mists of creed," as he himself once wrote, a place of worship had never seemed to him a necessity or even much of a help. Yet, never quarreling with any religious form, Sanford Dole had through the years developed an almost mystical sense of Divine purpose in the universe. Even during his Boston year this approached the Unitarianism of his cousin, Charles Fletcher Dole, yet was never perhaps so clearly defined.

The death of W. T. Brigham on January 29, 1926, at the age of eighty-five, marked the passing of the first director of Bernice Pauahi Bishop Museum. Since 1919 he had been director emeritus, but was connected with the museum for nearly forty years. For far longer than that Sanford Dole had been his devoted friend and sponsor, visiting him almost daily during his last illness.

While far from strong during his own last year, Judge Dole welcomed as a chance guest Emma Lyons Doyle, daughter of one of his earliest associates. He chatted as usual in his interesting way, she said, while the two sat quietly in the hospitable room with its books, its European art treasures, and its frieze of hand-painted flowers that had so happily passed the time for Anna. With the great golden shower tree in bloom, its sprays hung like bright drapery over the broad entrance at the top of the steps. In that familiar setting he stood at parting, gentle, kindly, as ever. No mention was made of changes already foreshadowed. But as the guest turned to go, Mr. Dole's pleasant voice said quietly, "Strange—just as we are beginning to learn something about the meaning of life, we must leave it."

Not many days after his eighty second birthday and attending the annual meeting of the Cousins' Society in April, 1926, Sanford Dole's tall, erect figure was seen for the last time on Honolulu streets. His strength had noticeably failed. His faithful Japanese helper and friend, Sabato (Shibata), would occasionally drive him in his little car up to Pauoa for a look at the thriving fruit trees. When he could no longer do even that, he lay in the upper guest room, faithfully tended by his two nieces, Clara and Emily, and by Nina Adams and Clorinda Low Lucas. On the ninth of

June he came, as had Anna, "to the departure for the new land."

By proclamation of Governor Wallace R. Farrington all public offices were closed at 12 o'clock noon, Thursday, the 10th of June and flags were placed at half-mast until sundown, Friday, June 11, 1926.

Friday was set for the state funeral. Under escort of the National Guard the urn containing Judge Dole's ashes was conveyed to the Executive Building. Before the public was admitted to the throne room the Reverend Akaiko Akana, brilliant young pastor of Kawaiahao Church, delivered a commemorative oration in the church before assembled Hawaiian societies and the public.

In the Executive Building the former throne room had been filled with exquisite flowers. At the east end on a raised platform stood the Torrey portrait of Judge Dole, a very fine one which for some time had hung, and still hangs, in the main upstairs corridor "with the other rulers of Hawaii." On either side of the portrait was a stand of colors, the American flag and the Hawaiian. Upon a *koa* table at the center of the long room, above a carpet of orchids and maiden hair fern, the *koa* casket for the urn was placed by Attorney Charles S. Dole of Kauai, after it had been received by Governor Farrington in the name of the Territory.

Under Old Guard escort to a salute of nineteen guns the urn was moved to Central Union Church at the head of Richards Street where the funeral service was conducted by the Reverend Philip Allen Swartz. The six honorary pall-bearers were W. R. Castle, W. O. Smith, Joseph Emerson, J. H. Soper, C. P. Iaukea and L. A. Thurston.

Sanford Dole's grave is with Anna's and next to that of his brother George in the small Mission burying ground southeast of Kawaiahao Church. It is marked in front of the headstone by a concrete stand and bowl of plants brought from the Emma Street home. Flowers from unknown hands are still often laid at the base of the headstone.

To those who knew him well there is still the echo of his footsteps passing up and down Emma Street, though the land of his home there now houses a community church and a school for Chinese. And his orchard in Pauoa Valley has passed by will to the family of the faithful Chinese friend who farmed it for him. And to the 355 children of the Kalihi Intermediate School, recently named the Sanford Ballard Dole Intermediate, Mr. Dole was a living person in their dramatic skit prepared for his birthday, April 23, 1956.

At a meeting of the Archives Commission in 1925 Judge Dole moved that the Governor of the Territory be asked to insert in the next legislative budget an item to cover the cost of an extension to the old Archives building. The following year Mr. Dole again expressed his conviction that such an addition was sorely needed.

During a community-wide discussion after Judge Dole's death, Bishop H. B. Restarick suggested that in place of a proposed memorial statue the Public Archives extension be named Sanford Ballard Dole Hall. This occurred at a meeting of the Hawaiian Historical Society and came in the form of a motion by Professor R. S. Kuykendall of the University of Hawaii, seconded by Judge W. F. Frear.

Still later Delegate Joseph R. Farrington concurred in the suggestion that Sanford Dole's portrait bust be cast in bronze and that this be placed in Statuary Hall in Washington. This however awaits the admission of Hawaii to the Union of Sovereign States.

The end of Sanford Dole's life was implicit in its beginning. The Islands he loved and served to the utmost were in every sense "His Hawaii."

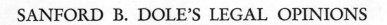

SANFORD B. DOLE'S LEGAL OPINIONS

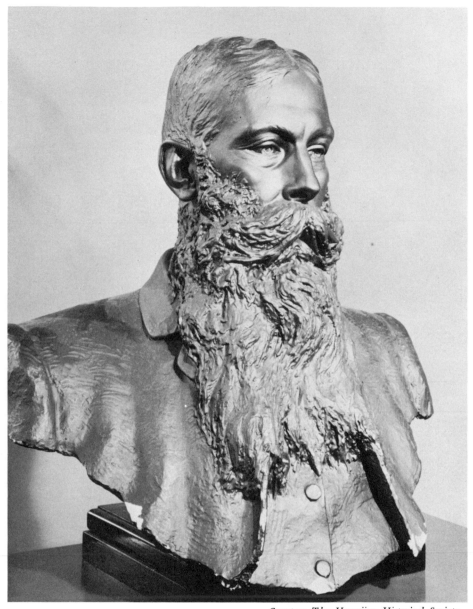

Portrait bust of Sanford B. Dole by Allen Hutchinson, noted
English sculptor

JUSTICE SANFORD B. DOLE'S LEGAL OPINIONS, 1887–1893

By Samuel B. Kemp

THE CAREER of the Honorable Sanford Ballard Dole—attorney, legislator, Justice of the Supreme Court of the Kingdom of Hawaii, President of the Republic of Hawaii, and finally, Judge of the United States Court for the District of Hawaii—spanned the most significant period in Hawaii's history.

He prepared for a judicial career by studying one year in a law office in Boston, and practicing for almost twenty years in the courts of the Kingdom of Hawaii. Back of this was his contact from birth with the Hawaiian people and his understanding of their language and psychology. Admitted to the bar in Massachusetts in 1868, he returned to Hawaii that same year to begin a long and distinguished career as a jurist and leader in the affairs of the Island people.

Shortly after his return, Hawaii was beset with a storm of political turmoil. Kamehameha V had died December 11, 1872, at the age of 42, having reigned but nine years, and with him the Kamehameha dynasty ended. During his short reign, Honolulu had developed into a modern city, with the tribulations attendant upon such growth. The late king proclaimed no successor to the throne. The Legislature met on January 8, 1873, and elected Prince William Charles Lunalilo, the highest living chief, to be king. The new king appointed strong American ministers, and negotiations were renewed with the United States for a treaty of commercial reciprocity. After ruling only a year, Lunalilo died in 1874. Again the Legislature had to elect a successor to the throne. One faction favored David Kalakaua and another the

Queen Dowager, Emma, widow of Kamehameha IV. Kalakaua, a direct descendant of two distinguished counselors of Kamehameha the Great, was elected. As soon as the election was over, a mob of supporters of Queen Emma broke in the back doors of the courthouse, and the police were unable to control them. The government was obliged to call upon marine forces from both the United States and Great Britain for aid. Kalakaua took the oath of office on February 13, 1874.

Kalakaua favored the restoration of autocratic government, and immediately sought to re-establish the ancient system of personal government by the king. In keeping with this policy, he dismissed the Cabinet in 1878 and again in 1880 without assigning any reason. Certain scandals arose and tension mounted. These events led to the formation of a citizens' committee called "The Reformers." The Reformers sponsored mass meetings of protest and demanded radical reforms. As a result, in 1887 the king was compelled to sign a revision of the Constitution, ending personal government and limiting his powers.

The preamble of the new Constitution read:

WHEREAS, the Constitution of this Kingdom heretofore in force contains many provisions subversive of civil rights and incompatible with enlightened Constitutional Government:

And WHEREAS, it has become imperative in order to restore order and tranquility and the confidence necessary to a further maintenance of the present Government that a new Constitution should be at once promulgated:

Now Therefore, I Kalakaua, King of the Hawaiian Islands, in my capacity as Sovereign of this Kingdom, and as the representative of the people hereunto by them duly authorized and empowered, do annul and abrogate the Constitution promulgated by Kamehameha the Fifth, on the 20th day of August, A.D. 1864, and do proclaim and promulgate this Constitution.

The new Constitution went into effect in 1887. In 1888, before it had come before the Supreme Court, a vacancy in the Court had been created by the death of Justice Fornander, the Fourth Associate Justice, on November 1, 1887. The name of Sanford Ballard Dole, already a power in legislative circles, came into prominence as a successor to fill the vacancy. Mr. Dole had been a member of the Legislature for two terms prior to 1888. He was identified with the Reformers, and they demanded his appointment. Kalakaua reluctantly acceded to their demands and on

December 28, 1887, appointed Mr. Dole to be Fourth Associate Justice.

By an Act of the Special Session of the Legislature approved on November 26, 1887, the Supreme Court had been reduced from five to three justices. The Act was to take effect on December 31, 1887, just three days after Justice Dole's appointment. The king expected the terms of the Third and Fourth Justices to expire on that day.

The king's opportunity to test the tenure of Justice Dole and the Third Associate Justice, Bickerton, came almost immediately. On January 3, 1888, the attorney for the Crown declined to present an indictment to the presiding Third Associate Justice on the ground that his commission had expired. Counsel for the defendant challenged the constitutionality of the statute as to incumbent judges, and Justice Bickerton reserved the question of constitutionality over to the Court *in banc*. Neither Justice Bickerton nor Justice Dole sat on the case, since they were the challenged members of the Court.

In separate opinions the three justices unanimously rejected the theory of the Crown and held that justices hold their offices during good behavior subject to removal only by impeachment. Chief Justice Judd rendered the opinion of the Court, saying:

> The office of a Justice of the Supreme Court is created by the Constitution as is also its tenure and its amenability, and this excludes all other modes, and it must follow that any legislation which infringes upon these is unconstitutional and void, and that Mr. Justice Bickerton had jurisdiction to take the plea of the defendant.[1]

The Act was held to be unconstitutional, and Justices Bickerton and Dole remained in office. But the king was not to give up his attacks on the new Constitution with only one skirmish.

Another struggle over the limitations of the king's power took place shortly after Justice Dole's appointment. Section 41 of the 1887 Constitution provided that no act of the king would have any effect unless countersigned by a cabinet member. Section 78 stated that all acts to be done by the king were to be done with the advice and consent of the Cabinet. The question arose whether

---

[1] *The King* v. *Testa,* 7 Hawaii 201 (1888).

these articles limited the king's power to veto acts of the Legislature.

The Legislature at its extraordinary session in 1887 had enacted "An Act to provide for the discharge of certain duties heretofore performed by the Governors of the different Islands." This Act required the delivery of certain records by the various governors to the sheriffs.

The certificate of the President of the Legislature appended to said Act was dated December 28, 1887. It showed that the king had vetoed the bill but that his action was not countersigned by a minister nor approved by the Cabinet.

The Governor of the Island of Maui refused to deliver to the sheriff certain records demanded pursuant to the above Act, on the ground that it was vetoed by the king and, not having been further considered by the Legislature, did not become a law.

Thus the stage was set for a contest between the king and his opponents over the question of the nature of the veto power granted to the king by Article 48 of the Constitution. The sheriff of Maui applied to the Supreme Court for a writ of mandamus to compel the Governor to obey the law.[2]

The court, in an opinion written by Chief Justice Judd, with only Justice Dole dissenting, held that Articles 41 and 78 applied only to executive acts and that the act of veto was a legislative act.

Justice Dole said in a vigorous dissenting opinion that the new Constitution—

. . . we learn from its preamble was founded by the people of the Hawaiian Islands and proclaimed by the King as their representative, for the securing of civil rights and enlightened constitutional government, and for the restoration of order, tranquility and necessary public confidence. The Constitution signifies a new departure, it abrogates the old Constitution, which it declares subversive of civil rights and enlightened constitutional government. Reading it carefully through and considering it as a whole, we find that it exhibits a definite and consistent purpose to attach responsibility to power in every case.

He concluded that the new Constitution must be interpreted with a constant reference to protection of civil rights and enlightened constitutional government. So interpreting it, he held that Article 78 required that all acts of the king, whether legisla-

---

2 *Everett* v. *Baker*, 7 Hawaii 229 (1888).

tive or executive, be done with the advice and consent of the Cabinet. It made no difference, in his opinion, whether or not a cabinet minister had to countersign the veto message. Since the veto did not have Cabinet consent, it was void. The king, being without responsibility, should not have such unchecked authority.

Justice Dole thus showed his agreement with the political views of the Reformers that the Cabinet had power under the Constitution to check every act of the king of whatever nature. Having been intimately associated with them, it was to be expected that he would share their views. He did not disappoint them.

The political turmoil resulting in the Constitution of 1887 was not quieted by the victory of the king in *Everett* v. *Baker*. The extent of the Cabinet's authority remained a subject of bitter dispute.

Finally, on August 3, 1889, the Cabinet presented to the king a statement of principles covering its power and responsibility. When the king refused to accept the statements, the Cabinet sought advice of the Supreme Court on the question: [3]

Is the authority and responsibility of the Cabinet as set forth in the statement of principles in accordance with and in pursuance of the Constitution, or not?

The opinion of the Justices of the Supreme Court,[4] joined by the same justices who constituted the majority in *Everett* v. *Baker*, showed considerable change in the Court's thinking concerning limitation of the powers of the sovereign and the authority of the Cabinet under the new Constitution.

The Court's opinion was:

. . . There can be no dual Government. There can be no authority without responsibility. The King is without responsibility. The constitution confers the responsibility of government upon the Cabinet; they, therefore, have the authority. With this in view, we are unanimously of opinion that the principles formulated by you and presented to His Majesty, above set forth, are in accordance with and in pursuance of the Constitution.

The pendulum was soon to swing back, however. In *Macfarlane* v. *Damon*[5] the plaintiff had petitioned for a writ of manda-

---

[3] Advisory opinions were then within the court's jurisdiction.
[4] *Re Authority of the Cabinet*, 7 Hawaii 783.
[5] 8 Hawaii 19 (1890).

mus to compel payment of his salary as His Majesty's Chamberlain. The Minister of Finance, Samuel M. Damon, refused payment because the appointment was not approved by the Cabinet.

Once again the Court's majority strictly construed the limitations on the powers of the king. The Court, Dole dissenting, held that the office of Chamberlain was one of personal service to the king, and that his designation of the person to perform the service was an act not requiring Cabinet approval.

The appointment was lawful and the respondent was ordered to pay the petitioner his salary.

In Justice Dole's thundering dissent he first severely chastised the king for his habitual flouting of constitutional authority, stating:

In the present reign the principle of ministerial responsibility has been gradually and steadily undermined until it finally ceased to exist under the encroachment of the Crown, and the whole executive authority became centered in the person of an irresponsible sovereign. The revolution of 1887 was a public protest against the political status, and the Constitution of that year which is now our fundamental law, was intended to remove the evil and make its return impossible.

Justice Dole then repeated the reasoning in his dissent in *Everett* v. *Baker,* and held that the Royal Chamberlain was clearly a public office, the filling of which required Cabinet approval.

As a parting shot, Justice Dole fired a broadside at the majority by repeating their recent advice to the Cabinet:

There can be no authority without responsibility. The King is without responsibility. The Constitution confers the responsibility of Government upon the Cabinet; they therefore have the authority.

Justice Dole's steadfast conviction of limited sovereign power stood firm amidst the unsure wavering of his brethren. Had the Court accepted his reasoning, much of the later trouble might have been avoided, although the spirit of unrest among the people might have made the forthcoming political upheaval unavoidable.

Justice Dole again disagreed with his colleagues in important cases involving the constitutional rights of contract laborers.

In *Hilo Sugar Co.* v. *Mioshi,* 8 Hawaii 201, the defendant contracted with the Hawaiian government to come to Hawaii and accept such employment as the said government might select for him. The Board of Immigration assigned the contract to the Hilo Sugar Company. Defendant was to be an agricultural laborer. After one year of such labor, Mioshi sought release from his employment. The company was unwilling to release him and the question of the validity of the assignment was submitted to the Court. Chief Justice Judd wrote the majority opinion upholding the validity of the assignment. Calling attention to Article 11 of the Constitution of 1852 prohibiting involuntary servitude, he said:

Our labor contract system is not slavery. . . . the principle that a person may make a binding contract to serve another for a term has remained untouched, and upon it our agricultural enterprises rest in great measure.

Justice Dole, however, strongly disagreed. He countered Chief Justice Judd's reasoning with an earlier dissenting opinion wherein Justice Judd had said:

There is no enactment of the Legislature that will compel a man to work for another or his assigns . . . these contracts are not assignable; for if a man could be passed from one to another, like a chattel, by an assignment of his contract, it reduces him at once to a chattel, and this is a form of involuntary servitude which, though for a limited period, is nevertheless, repugnant to the policy of our institutions and forbidden by Article 11 of the Constitution.[6]

Quoting the foregoing, Justice Dole tersely stated:

It would not be easy to improve on the wording of these citations in stating the prevailing legal sentiment of the civilized world on this question.

Thus he emphasized the inconsistency of the Chief Justice who now sided with the majority by praising his earlier opinion and contrasting it with his opinion in the case at bar. Declaring the liberty of all men, including aliens, to work for whom they pleased, he concluded:

How, then, can one alien dispose of such liberty? A contract waiving this right is inconsistent with this great provision of the Constitution, and is

---

[6] *Nott* v. *Kanahele*, 4 Hawaii 14 (1877).

therefore illegal and void. This is what the contract before us distinctly does.

Shortly after the decision in the Hilo Sugar Company case, another similar case arose. This was the case of *Chong Chum* v. *Kohala Sugar Company*,[7] decided February 26, 1892. It was an appeal from a decision of Justice Dole rendered while on circuit. He had overruled the demurrer of the sugar company to the bill of the laborer. The only difference from the Hilo Sugar Company case was that the contract was made direct with the company for whom the plaintiff was to labor. The terms of the employment were identical in every respect. The plaintiff, a native of China, was engaged by Kohala Sugar Company to come to Hawaii and work for $15.00 a month. The company procured for him a permit to enter and reside in the Kingdom of Hawaii. Before he left his ship, he was told that he must sign a written contract as a plantation laborer for three years at $15.00 a month and allow the company to retain $3.75 a month until $75.00 were withheld. This sum would be paid to the Board of Immigration for plaintiff's return passage to China. Plaintiff was told that unless he executed the contract he would not be allowed to land but would be sent back to China. The company representative told the poor alien that the ship was not provisioned for the return voyage and if he should have to return on her he would suffer, and perhaps die, for want of food and water. Under such persuasion he signed the contract, but under protest.

Chong Chum brought suit to declare the requirement of the permit of entry and residence to be unconstitutional and to enjoin the company from deducting from his wages. He also asked that the contract be voided and that he be paid the money which the company had already retained.

The company raised the Act of 1890 as a defense. This Act limited the term of residence of Chinese laborers in the kingdom and prohibited their working except as agricultural laborers. It authorized arrest and deportation of any laborer found in the kingdom after his permit expired. It required the employer to forward to the Board of Immigration one-fourth of the laborer's monthly wages until $75.00 were accumulated, and it authorized

---

[7] 8 Hawaii 425 (1892).

forfeiture of the $75.00 if the laborer deserted his employer or did any other type of work.

Justice Dole, sitting on the Circuit Bench, promptly overruled the demurrer, stating:

The rights of life, liberty, acquiring, possessing and protecting property, and of pursuing and obtaining safety and happiness, belong to all men within the limits of Hawaiian territory, and cannot be relinquished or the control thereof assigned to others by contract. I find, therefore, that the regulations of Chapter 67 of the Laws of 1890, above set forth, and all other provisions of the said chapter requiring the assent of the plaintiff to the terms of the said permit as a condition of landing . . . are inconsistent with his constitutional rights and did not authorize his detention on board the ship and other circumstances complained of whereby he was compelled to accept the condition of the said permit and execute the said contract.

The matter was now before the Supreme Court on appeal from Justice Dole's ruling. While the Supreme Court refrained from passing upon the constitutionality of the whole Act, it upheld the decree

on the position that the plaintiff has come to this country without the provisions as to deduction of wages, as a condition of his entry within, having been made known to him, and therefore they are not binding upon him. And if not binding upon him, he is therefore free from this obligation of the contract made under it.

The opinion of the Court, while affirming the decree of Justice Dole, disagreed with his finding that all of the provisions of Chapter 67 of the Laws of 1890 were inconsistent with the constitutional rights of the plaintiff.

. . . We are still of the opinion that it would be no infraction of the Constitution to impose conditions as to length of residence and character of the employment in which the immigrant can engage, to which he must assent before being permitted to enter this Kingdom . . .

However, the majority held that the provision requiring the withholding of a portion of wages was unconstitutional on the ground that

it would be an unwarrantable interference with the right of the individual to make him pay an arbitrary sum from his own wages to get him out of the country into which he has been invited, he having done nothing criminal meanwhile.

Justice Dole stayed with his original decision and stated briefly:

I agree with the conclusion of the Court, under the reasoning of the decision appealed from.

The foregoing case was the last involving important constitutional questions to reach the Supreme Court during the tenure of Justice Dole.

In order to appraise the impact of one's judicial service upon the political situation, the political unrest, if any, must be considered. Justice Dole came to the Court fresh from the political upheaval, which he termed "the Revolution of 1887," in which he was one of the revolutionaries.

It has been said of John Marshall, "the great Chief Justice," that he gained that title by his many politically inspired opinions construing, formulating, and strengthening the Constitution of the United States. His significance was enlarged by his ability to obtain the concurrence of his brethren on the bench.

Most of the important decisions of Justice Dole construing the Constitution were dissenting opinions and therefore without authority. Had they been majority opinions, they might have prevented the revolution. They undoubtedly helped sustain the political revolt engendered by the persistent opposition of the king to the remedial provisions of the new Constitution.

The spirit of revolt did not subside with the death of the king but carried over into the reign of Queen Liliuokalani and culminated in the overthrow of the Monarchy. The Republic was established and Justice Dole named as its first president. Thus his distinguished career as a Justice of the Supreme Court came to an end.

INDEX

Adams, Edward P., 97, 98, 99, 104, 129, 236, 269

Agassiz, Alexander, 57–58

Alexander, William D., 31, 147–48, 242–43, 351

Aliiolani Hale, 140, 142; see Judiciary Building

Allen, Elisha H. (Chief Justice), 87, 128, 141, 264

American Board of Commissioners for Foreign Missions, 5, 19, 25, 26, 50–51, 64–65, 95–96

Annexation Club, 240, 247, 259, 262

Annexation Commission, 255, 257, 258

Annexation to United States, 234, 240, 248, 249, 258, 260, 263, 267, 285, 293, 313–16, 330–35; Treaty of, 255, 260, 291, 313; signed by Dole, 320

Archives of Hawaii, 242, 349

Armstrong, Samuel C., 73, 92, 140, 160, 364

Armstrong, William Nevins, 70, 153, 156, 160, 161, 342

Ashford, Clarence W., 202, 206

Ashford, Volney V., 199, 202

Associated Charities, 364

Atkinson, Alatau T., 174, 175, 194

Austin, James W., 76, 80, 81, 87, 96, 193

Barker, Albert S., Captain (later Rear-Admiral, U.S.N.), 267, 269–70, 292, 295, 299

Barracks, Honolulu, 252, 255, 271

Bennett's Own (weekly), 93, 94

Berger, Henry, Captain, 150–51, 172, 332, 351, 365

Birds, Hawaiian, 74, 93, 148

Bishop, Artemas and Delia, 7, 12–13, 18, 21

Bishop, Bernice Pauahi (Mrs. C. R.), 54, *facing* 82, 85, 94, 98, 110, 115, 154, 183–85, 212, 213, 366–67

Bishop, Charles R., 54, 85, 98, 110, 126–27, 139, 140, 155, 200, 201, 212–13, 243, 266, 316, 365–67

Bishop Museum, 60, 212–13, 266, 300, 373

Black, J. H., 89, 96, 138

Blount, James H. (U.S. Commissioner), 258–61, 269, 276–77, 282–83

Brigham, William T., 2, 57, 59–62, 66–68, 70–71, 74, 75, 76, 85, 93, 98, 103, 144, 149, 159–60, 171, 184–85, 208, 213, 218, 223–24, 228, 230, 249, 373

Brown, Cecil, 179, 188, 201–2, 244

Cabinet and Executive Council, *facing* 210

Cables, Pacific, 299–301, 350–52; date of opening, 350

Carter, Charles L., 246, 255, 257, 302, 306–7

Carter, Henry A. P., 55, 141, 176–77

Castle, Henry N., 86, 90, 306–7, 356

Castle, William R., 55, 154, 166, 196, 246, 247, 251, 255

Cleghorn, Archibald S., 157, 178, 252, 266

Cleveland, Grover (U.S. President), 255, 258, 269, 270, 271, 273–92, 299, 371

Coinage, 174, 176–77

Committee of Safety, 1893, 247–48, 251

Committee of Thirteen, 1887, 117, 200–202

Committee of Thirteen, 1893, 246

Constitution of 1852: 88, 106–7, 112, 137, 298

Constitution of 1864: 125, 187, 223, 298

Constitution of 1887: 200–203, 206, 298, 380

Constitution (proposed), 1893: 245–47, 298

Constitution of 1894 (Republic): 294–95, 298

Constitutional Convention, 1894 (Republic): *facing* 211, 293, 295–97

Contract labor, 91, 101–2, 174–75, 323, 325

Cooper, Henry E., 240, 247, 251, 319

Co-operatives, 163–64, 372

Damon, Samuel M., 64, 99, 251, 252, 277, 303, 316

Davies, Theophilus H., 257, 263, 265

Dillingham, Benjamin F., 82, 211–12, 243

Dole, Anna P. Cate (wife), 97–98, 99, 103–4, 128–29, 130, 133, 134, 135–36, 138, 144, 147, 148, 149–50, 151–52, 162, 163, 189, 191, 192, 215, 223, 224–25, 235, 239, 241, 266, 320–22, 331, 355, 358–62; death of, 370

Dole, Charles Fletcher (cousin), 61, 69–70, 97, 104, 149, 263–64, 369

Dole, Charlotte Knapp (stepmother), 15, 16, 18, 19, 21–31, 33, 36, 37, 40, 44–45, 85, 87, 88, 96, 99, 104, 130–32

Dole, Clara Rowell (George's wife), 56, 67

Dole, Daniel (father), 4–9, 12, 13–15, 17–18, *facing* 19, 20–22, 24–25, 26, 28, 30–33, 36–37, 38, 39, 40, 44–45, 58, 60, 85, 86, 88, 96, 99, 104, 129–31, 147–48

Dole, Edmund P. (cousin), (Attorney General of Hawaii), 269, 344–45, **346**

Dole, Emily Ballard (mother), 4–10, 12, 14, 58, 60

Dole, George Hathaway (brother), 7–8, 9, 13, 14, 15, 16, 18, 20–23, 25–29, 32, 37, 41, 43, 44, 46, 49–52, 57, 67, 76, 85, 88, 99–100, 104, 127, 130, 136, 144–45, 146, 150, 177, 208, 213–14, 221–23, (1906) *facing* 306, 363, 364, 372

Dole, James D. (cousin), 348–49

Dole, Nathan (uncle), 18, 58, 61, 69

Dole, Sanford Ballard:
—birth and infancy, 12, 14, 15
—boyhood at Punahou, 15–31, 44–46
—bust of, by Allen Hutchinson, *facing* 379
—Cate, Anna P., first meeting, 97; betrothal, 98; marriage, 103–4; death of, 370
—Central Union Church, member, 373
—Chairman, European War Relief, 365
—choice of profession, 1–2
—co-editor of *Punch Bowl,* 89; an editor of *Planter's Monthly,* 166
—Constitution of 1887, working on new, 202, 203
—home, Emma Street, *facing* 115, 135, 136, 143, 355, 373, 374
—importance of free press stressed by, 171
—honors: appointment by President McKinley, 321, 340; called to Washington and endorsed by President Theodore Roosevelt,

342, 343; first Governor of Territory, 340, 353; honorary Doctor of Laws from College of Hawaii, 371; school named for, 374–75; signed Treaty of Annexation, 320; *see* other appointments under Judge, Minister, President, Supreme Court *below*

—Judge of Federal District Court, 352

—Justice of Supreme Court, 207

—Kohala, rest at, 264–65, 266–67

—Koloa, Kauai, life at, 32–49

—Law record: admitted to bar in Massachusetts, 73; law study in Boston, 67; practice in Honolulu, 80–85; *see* Judicial career, 379–88

—in Legislature, 1896, 188–93

—letter requesting raising Stars and Stripes, *facing* 178, 179

—Liliuokalani, assistance at her inauguration, 227; ruling on her right to appoint a cabinet, 234–35; *facing* 145

—Minister of Foreign Affairs, 298

—in New England, 56–75, 77

—oath of allegiance to the U.S., 334

—philosophy of life, 236

—President of Provisional Government, 251

—President of Republic of Hawaii, 298

—retirement, 369

—role in crisis of 1893, 244–63

—shouldering arms (1889), 218

—Sunday breakfasts, 355, 356

—Supreme Court, appointed to, 207; promotion in, 240; resignation, 250; judicial career, 379–88

—travels: in Europe with Mrs. Dole, 358–62; leaving Hawaii, 54; in New England, 56–57; return to Honolulu and Kawai, 75–77; returning from Washington with Mrs. Dole, *facing* 306; vacation in East, 223; at Williams College jubilee, 369

—Treaty of Annexation signed by, 320

—Unitarianism, first interest in, 68

—at Williams College, 62–66

Dominis, John O. (Governor of Oahu, husband of Liliuokalani), 146, 178, 229, 235

Dominis, Mrs. John O., *see* Liliuokalani

Emma, Queen, 62, 110, 115, 126–27, 129, 154, 183, 185–86

Epidemics, 3, 18, 24, 164, 165, 304, 309, 339

Estee, Morris M. (Federal Judge), 351–52

Ewa Church, *facing* 18

Executive Council of the Provisional Government, *facing* 210

Farmers' Institute, 347–48

Federal Court of Hawaii, 351–52, 356, 358

Field, Kate, 314–15

Fitch, George L., 171, 176

Flag, Hawaiian, 10, 44, 234, 260, 298, 300, 316–17, 318, 320, 334; of United States, 44, 234, 256, 258, 259–62, 333–34; letter from Sanford B. Dole, *facing* 178–79

Fornander, Abraham (Judge), 139, 206, 213

Frear, Walter F. (Judge and Governor), 243, 339, 370

Furneaux, Charles, 160, 162–63, 215

Gibson, Walter Murray, 101, 153, 157, 159, 165, 167, 170, 171, 172, 174, 175, 176, 180, 192, 193, 200, 203, 325, 340

Gresham, Walter Q. (U.S. Secretary of State), 261, 271, 276, 281, 282, 291, 314–15

Grove Farm, Kauai, 76, 90, 208

Grove Ranch, Maui, 90, 147, 162, 175, 197, 208, 209, 214

Gynberg Ballads, 194

Hale, Edward Everett, 67, 68, 149

Harrison, William Henry (U.S. President), 255, 278–79, 314

Hartwell, Alfred S. (Chief Justice), 71, 87, 125, 128, 181, 193, 214, 246, 249, 307

Hatch, Francis M., 207, 271, 293, 297, 303, 307, 319, 321, 322, 353, 371–72

Hawaiian Club of Boston, 68, 71, 93, 141

Hawaiian Gazette (weekly, later semi-weekly), 136, 157, 170, 175, 193, 194, 197, 199, 209, 217–18, 237, 255, 256, 262, 297

Hawaiian Historical Society, 105, 242–43, 249, 266, 297, 299, 366–67

Hawaiian League, 196, 199, 202

Hawaiian Star (daily except Sunday), 265, 316

Honolulu, 1853–1869, 3, 11, 23, 25, 78–81, 97, 143–44, 198, 210, 211, 215, 311–12, 319

Honolulu Rifles, 126, 127, 199, 202, 253

Hopkins, Mark, 2, 62, 63, 64, 65, 74

Hunnewell, James, 71, 74, 93

Iaukea, Curtis P. (Colonel), 170–71, 172

Ii, John, 89, 94–95, 137

Immigration, 91, 174, 324–30

Insurrection, 1889, 216–20

Insurrection, 1895, 301–6

Islander, The (weekly), 138, 139, 140, 141, 142, 212

Japan-Hawaii Relations, 1868–1898, 256, 324–30, 361–62

Jones, Peter Cushman, 72, 80, 81–82, 132–33, 181, 199, 200, 244, 251, 254, 295

Judd, A. Francis (Chief Justice), 74, 96, 137–38, 171, 240, 241, 295, 298, 325, 334

Judiciary Building (Aliiolani Hale, Government Building, or Court House), 140, 142, 144, 250, 255, 263

Kaiulani, Princess, *facing* 147, 159, 210, 216, 234, 249, 252, 256–57, 265, 266, 336, 338

Kalakaua, David, King, 110, 115, 117, 119, 120, 121, 125–28, 140, 141, 142, 145–46, *facing* 146, 151, 153–54, 156, 160–61, 166–70, 174, 177, 178, 183, 186–87, 196, 198, 200, 202, 207–9, 215, 216–17, 220, 227–29, 231–32, 285–86, 313, 368, 380–84, 388

Kalanianaole, Jonah Kuhio, Prince, 305, 343–44

Kalua, J. W., 179, 297, 298

Kamehameha I (Statue), 170

Kamehameha IV, wedding of, in 1856, *facing* 371

Kamehameha V, Lot, King, 45, 46, 88, 91, 101, 105, 107–9, 111, 112, 123–24, 137–38, 151

Kapiolani, Queen (wife of Kalakaua), 167, 186, 204, 216, 226, 227, 229, 336–38

Kawaiahao Church (King's Chapel), 10, *facing* 83, 92, 96, 125–26, 186, 368, 371

Kemp, Judge S. B., judicial career reviewed by, 379–88

King, James A. (Captain, member of Dole's cabinets), 183, 251, 252, 254, 299, 300, 303

Kinney, William A., 200–201, 320

Knapp, Horton and Charlotte, 4, 5, 6, 12, 13, 14, 15

Kuhio, Prince, *see* Kalanianaole, Jonah Kuhio, Prince

Labor, *see* Contract labor

Land tenure, 19, 25, 139–40, 179, 212, 242, 243, 326–27

Legislature, 1873, 109–10, 112, 118–22

Legislature, 1880, 153–54

Legislature, 1884, 177–83

Legislature, 1886, 285

Legislature, 1892, 244, 245, 286–87

Legislature, 1895, 308, 309

Legislature, 1901, 340–41

Liliuokalani, Lydia (Mrs. J. O. Dominis), 98, 165; Princess, 178, 204, 216–17, 220; Queen, *facing* 114, 227, 229, 231–36, 243–48, 251–52, 255, 271–93, 305, 306, 314–18, 321–22, 323, 362, 365, 369, 370, 388

Lottery, 175, 181, 244, 255, 286

Low, Eben, and Lizzie Napoleon, 223, 233, 235, 239, 265–67

Lunalilo, William C., King, 106, 110–25, 137–38, 141, 151

Lunalilo Home, 164

Lyons, Curtis J., 18, 88, 94, 139, 140, 298–300

McGrew, John S., M.D., 313, 332

McKinley, William (U.S. President), 233–34, 319–21, 341, 358

Mackintosh, Alexander, 178, 182, 243, 359–60

"Manifest Destiny," 314

Mann, Horace, Jr., 57, 76, 184–85

Mass meeting, 1872, 110–11, 115–16

Mass meeting, 1874, 125–26

Mass meeting, 1880, 154–56

Mass meeting, 1883, 174–75

Mass meeting, 1887, 199–203

Mass meeting, 1893, 247, 271

Mausoleums, Royal, 365–68

Mission, American, 3, 13, 26, 29, 371

Missionaries, American (in government), 316

Moreno, Celso Caesar, 154, 155, 156, 157, 161, 189, 350

Morgan, John T. (U.S. Senator), 292, 316, 318, 339, 354

Napoleon, Elizabeth (later Mrs. Eben Low), 151–52, 191, 197, 205

National Guard, 255, 259, 334–35, 352

Necker Island, 298–301

Neumann, Paul (Attorney-General), 179, 193, 305, 307

Old Royal Palace, *facing* 83

"Old Sixty-Seven" at Williams College, *facing* 50

Opium, 175, 181, 192, 198–99, 255

Organic Act, 303, 339–40

Pacific Commercial Advertiser (weekly, later daily), 96, 100–102, 105, 128, 153, 157, 170, 181, 197, 263, 325, 368

Palace (Iolani, Executive Building, or Capitol), 167–68, 198, 217–19, 255, 262–63, 374

Parker, Henry H., 86, 98, 143, 186, 296, 365, 368

Parker, Samuel (member of Queen's Cabinet), 235, 245, 281

Pearl Harbor, 141, 206, 217, 295, 362–63

Peirce, Henry A., 126, 141

Pilipo, George W., 154, 179, 182–83, 187–88

Planters' Association, 165–66

Planters' Monthly, 166

Provisional Government, 251–52, 255–56, 258–63, 274–88

Punahou School, 16, 17–18, 23, 24, 25–26, 29–31, 364

Punch Bowl (monthly), 86, 88, 89, 90, 92, 93, 94, 96, 138

Reciprocity Treaty, 141, 142, 166, 174, 206, 233–34, 299

Republic of Hawaii, 297, 316, 371

Revolution, 1893, 245–57

Rhodes, Godfrey, 179, 181–82, 316

Rice, Mr. and Mrs. William Harrison, 14, 16, 29, 30, 33, 37, 38

Rice, William Hyde, 15, 16, 20, 38, 90, 99, 146, 175, 188–89, 202

Roosevelt, Theodore (U.S. President), 342–43

Rose Ranch, Maui, 144–45

Rowell, William E., 38, 42, 43, 44, 49, 57, 62, 64, 66, 70, 74, 175, 179, 209, 219, 253, 368

Ruth Keelikolani, Princess, 109, 170, 183–84

Saturday Press (weekly), 157, 158, 171, 172, 176

Sewall, Harold M. (U.S. Minister to Hawaii), 332, 333, 334

Skerrett, J. S. (Admiral, U.S.N.), 265, 267

Smith, William O. (member of Dole's cabinet), 35, 38, 42, 90, 162, 166, 175–76, 247, 250, 251, 254, 256, 295, 296, 303–4, 306, 309–10, 316, 328

Soper, John H. (Colonel), 247, 248, 249, 250, 252, 258–59, 260

Spreckels, Claus, 157, 164–65, 167, 174, 179, 181, 192, 321

Stamps, Hawaiian, 268

Stars and Stripes, raising of the, *facing* 178, 179, 275

Statehood, 269, 355

Stevens, John L. (U.S. Minister), 247, 250, 251, 256, 261–62, 278, 280

Stevenson, Robert L., 215–16, 266, 307

Supreme Court (Hawaii), 71, 87, 89, 95, 96, 98, 99, 128, 206, 207, 234–35, 240–41, 250, 259, 306, 379–88

Tavernier, Jules, 215

Telephones, 210

Thurston, Lorrin A. (Hawaiian Minister to the United States), 105, 188, 196, 200, 201, 206, 209, 210–11, 217, 219–20, 240, 246, 247, 249, 250, 251, 255, 258, 291, 293–

94, 295–96, 314–15, 319, 322–24, 368, 374

Tramcars, 210

Treaty of Annexation, 255, 260, 291, 313; signed by S. B. Dole, 320

Trousseau, George, M.D., 127, 140, 176, 223, 266

Vacuum, a farce, 194

Walker, Maybelle Ward (cousin), 214, 224–35

Walker, Thomas Rain (British Vice-Consul), 82, 90, 135, 171, 172, 181, 216, 265

Ward, Annie Titcomb, Mrs., 71, 75

Ward, Maybelle, *see* Walker, Maybelle Ward

Water, 79, 211, 237

Waterhouse, Henry, 81, 154, 155, 157, 201, 247, 251, 295

Webb, Lahilahi, 231–32, 318, 370

Whitney, Henry M. (editor), 80, 85, 96, 100, 116, 136

Widemann, Hermann A., 89, 90, 92, 128, 235

Wilcox, Albert S., 43, 46, 48, 49, 188, 250

Wilcox, George N. (Prime Minister, "Wilcox Cabinet"), 76, 77, 90, 91, 188, 244, 295

Wilcox, Robert W. (insurrectionist, Delegate to Congress), 155–56, 157, 217–18, 220, 235, 295, 305, 340, 343

Williams College, 1–2, 62–66

Willis, Albert S. (United States Minister), 269, 270–93, 299, 305–6

Wilson, Charles B. (Marshal of Kingdom), 211, 250, 251

Wright, William B., D.D., 70, 72, 74, 104, 149, 172

Young Men's Christian Association, 82, 357